"This is a thoughtful and provocative study that rethinks the relationship between human rights and criminal law. Drawing upon sources that have escaped attention from other scholars, Adnan Sattar challenges some of the premises of today's focus on prosecution."

– William A. Schabas, Professor of International Law, Middlesex University, formerly member of the Sierra Leone Truth and Reconciliation Commission.

Criminal Punishment and Human Rights

This book examines the relationship between international human rights discourse and the justifications for criminal punishment. Using interdisciplinary discourse analysis, it exposes certain paradoxes that underpin the 'International Bill of Human Rights', academic commentaries on human rights law, and the global human rights monitoring regime in relation to the aims of punishment in domestic penal systems. It argues that human rights discourse, owing to its theoretical kinship with Kantian philosophy, embodies a paradoxical commitment to human dignity on the one hand, and retributive punishment on the other. Further, it sustains the split between criminal justice and social justice, which results in a sociologically ill-informed understanding of punishment. Human rights discourse plays a paradoxical role vis-à-vis the punitive power of the state as it seeks to counter criminalisation in some areas and backs the introduction of new criminal offences – and longer prison sentences – in others. The underlying priorities, it is argued, have been shaped by a number of historical circumstances. Drawing on archival material, the study demonstrates that the international penal discourse produced during the late nineteenth and early twentieth century laid greater emphasis on offender rehabilitation and was more attentive to the social context of crime than is the case with the modern human rights discourse.

Adnan Sattar is an independent legal and social policy consultant.

Routledge Research in Human Rights Law

Comparative Executive Clemency
The Prerogative of Mercy in the Commonwealth
Andrew Novak

Social and Economic Rights in Theory and Practice
A Critical Assessment
Helena Alviar Garcia, Karl Klare and Lucy A. Williams

Challenging Territoriality in Human Rights Law
Building Blocks for a Plural and Diverse Duty-Bearer Regime
Wouter Vandenhole

Care, Migration and Human Rights
Law and Practice
Siobhán Mullally

China's Human Rights Lawyers
Advocacy and Resistance
Eva Pils

Indigenous Peoples, Title to Territory, Rights and Resources
The Transformative Role of Free Prior and Informed Consent
Cathal M. Doyle

Civil and Political Rights in Japan
A Tribute to Sir Nigel Rodley
Edited by Saul J. Takahashi

Criminal Punishment and Human Rights
Convenient Morality
Adnan Sattar

For more information about this series, please visit:
www.routledge.com/Routledge-Research-in-Human-Rights-Law/book-series/HUMRIGHTSLAW

Criminal Punishment and Human Rights

Convenient Morality

Adnan Sattar

Routledge
Taylor & Francis Group
LONDON AND NEW YORK

First published 2019
by Routledge

2 Park Square, Milton Park, Abingdon, Oxfordshire OX14 4RN
52 Vanderbilt Avenue, New York, NY 10017

Routledge is an imprint of the Taylor & Francis Group, an informa business

First issued in paperback 2020

British Library Cataloguing-in-Publication Data
A catalogue record for this book is available from the British Library

Library of Congress Cataloging-in-Publication Data
A catalog record for this book has been requested

ISBN: 978-1-138-62579-2 (hbk)
ISBN: 978-0-367-66046-8 (pbk)

Typeset in Galliard
by Apex CoVantage, LLC

Contents

Acknowledgements

Though the seeds for this book had been sown much earlier, the bulk of research and writing was done between 2014 and 2017 as part of a doctorate in law at Middlesex University, UK. Many thanks to all those whose support saw me through more peaks and troughs than I care to remember.

To my supervisor at Middlesex, Professor William A. Schabas, for his generous help and forbearance every step of the way. It was a privilege to benefit from his knowledge and wisdom. To my second supervisor, Dr Maureen Spencer, for her guidance, friendly criticism, and many cheerful conversations. Her comments have been very helpful in improving the substance and style of this work. To the inimitable Professor Joshua Castellino, then Dean of the School of Law at Middlesex, for taking interest in my research and helping me out at a crucial stage in the process.

To my earlier teachers whom I owe a huge debt of gratitude: Professor Paul Roberts, Professor Dirk van Zyl Smit, and Professor Nigel White (University of Nottingham), and Professor Cécile Laborde (University College London).

To friends who have helped in numerous ways: Asad Jamal, Faisal Buzdar, Giulia Peccorela, Harris Khalique, Irfan Ahmed Khan, Josepha Close, Khayyam Mushir, Usman Qazi, Veronique Muscat, Zaigham Khan, Zainab Dar, and Zeeshan Noel. I can only reaffirm my commitment to the Shakespearean dictum: 'Those friends thou hast, and their adoption tried/Grapple them to thy soul with hoops of steel'.

Parts of the first three substantive chapters were published in the journal *Socialism and Democracy*.[1] Special thanks to the editor Professor Victor Wallis for his comments and advice which gave clarity to my thoughts and improved my sense of style. Finally, I would like to express my gratitude to Alison Kirk at Routledge for putting her faith in this work, to Chloe James and Emily Summers for coordinating the project, and to anonymous reviewers for their feedback.

1 Adnan Sattar, 'Neo-Retributivism in the Embrace of Human Rights' (2016) 3(3) *Socialism and Democracy*.

Table of Conventions, Treaties, and International Instruments

Covenant of the League of Nations (adopted 28 June 1919, entered into force 10 January 1920) 1 League of Nations OJ 3.

Convention to Suppress the Slave Trade and Slavery (adopted 25 September 1926, entered into force 9 March 1927) 60 LNTS 253.

Forced Labour Convention, C29, International Labour Organisation (adopted 28 June 1930, entered into force 1 May 1932) 39 UNTS 55.

Standard Minimum Rules for the Treatment of Prisoners (recommended to Governments by the Assembly of the League of Nations, September 1934) League of Nations OJ Spec. Supp. 123.

Charter of the United Nations (adopted 26 June 1945, entered into force 24 October 1945) 1 UNTS XVI.

Convention on the Prevention and Punishment of the Crime of Genocide (adopted 9 December 1948, entered into force 12 January 1951) 78 UNTS 277.

Universal Declaration of Human Rights (adopted by the General Assembly Resolution 217A (III) 10 December 1948) UN Doc A/810.

European Convention for the Protection of Human Rights and Fundamental Freedoms (adopted 1 November 1950, entered into force 3 September 1953) 213 UNTS 222.

Geneva Convention Relative to the Treatment of Prisoners of War (adopted 12 August 1949, entered into force 21 October 1950) 75 UNTS 135.

Convention concerning the Abolition of Forced Labour, C105, International Labour Organisation (adopted 25 June 1957, entered into force 17 January 1959) 320 UNTS 291.

International Convention on the Elimination of All Forms of Racial Discrimination (adopted 21 December 1965, entered into force 4 January 1969) 660 UNTS 195.

International Covenant on Civil and Political Rights (adopted 16 December 1966, entered into force 23 March 1976) 999 UNTS 171.

International Covenant on Economic, Social and Cultural Rights (adopted 16 December 1966, entered into force 23 March 1976) 993 United UNTS 3.

American Convention on Human Rights (adopted 21 November 1969, entered into force 18 July 1978) 1144 UNTS 143.

Convention on the Elimination of All Forms of Discrimination against Women (adopted 18 December 1979, entered into force 3 September 1981) 1249 UNTS 13.

African Charter on Human and Peoples' Rights ('Banjul Charter') (adopted 27 June 1981, entered into force 21 October 1986) 1520 UNTS 217.

Convention against Torture and Other Cruel, Inhuman or Degrading Treatment or Punishment (adopted 10 December 1984, entered into force 26 June 1987) 1465 UNTS 85.

Convention on the Rights of the Child (adopted 20 November 1989, entered into force 2 September 1990) 1577 UNTS 3.

Second Optional Protocol to the International Covenant on Civil and Political Rights, aiming at the Abolition of the Death Penalty (adopted 15 December 1989, entered into force 11 July 1991) 1642 UNTS 414.

Statute of the International Criminal Tribunal for Rwanda, UN Doc S/RES/955 (1994), annex.

Statute of the International Criminal Tribunal for the former Yugoslavia, UN Doc S/RES/837 (1993), annex.

Protocol to Prevent, Suppress and Punish Trafficking in Persons, Especially Women and Children, supplementing the United Nations Convention against Transnational Organized Crime (adopted 15 November 2000, entered into force 25 December 2003) 2237 UNTS 319.

European Prison Rules, Recommendation (2006) 2 of the Committee of Ministers to Member States of the Council of Europe on the European Prison Rules (adopted by the Committee of Ministers on 11 January 2006 at the 952nd meeting of the Ministers' Deputies).

ILO Declaration on Fundamental Principles and Rights at Work (adopted 18 June 1998) ILC, 86th Session, Geneva, annex revised 15 June 2010.

Rome Statute of the International Criminal Court (adopted 17 July 1998, entered into force 1 July 2002) 2187 UNTS 90.

Protocol 13 to the European Convention on Human Rights and Fundamental Freedoms on the Abolition of the Death Penalty in All Circumstances (adopted 3 May 2002, entered into force 1 July 2003) ETS 187.

Optional Protocol to the International Covenant on Economic, Social and Cultural Rights (adopted 5 March 2009, entered into force 5 May 2013) UN Doc A/RES/63/117.

European Charter of Fundamental Rights, OJ 2010/ C 83/02.

United Nations Standard Minimum Rules for the Treatment of Prisoners (the Nelson Mandela Rules) (adopted 17 December 2015) UN Doc A/RES/ 70/175.

Table of National Legislation

Cuba

Criminal Code 1930 (Bustamante, Derecho Internacional Privado, Habana, 1931, III)

India

Criminal Tribes Act 1871
The Indian Penal Code 1860 (Act No. 45 of 6 October 1860)

Italy

Penal Code (approved by Royal Decree No. 1398 of 19 October 1930)

Poland

Penal Code and the Law of Minor Offenses 1932

New Zealand

Criminal Justice Act 1985
Queensland Dangerous Prisoners (Sexual Offences) Act 2003

Russia

Criminal Code of the Russian Federation No. 63-FZ of 13 June 1996 (as amended up to Federal Law No. 120-FZ of 7 June 2017)

South Africa

Promotion of National Unity and Reconciliation Act, No. 34 of 1995

United Kingdom

Criminal Justice Act 1991
Criminal Justice Act 2003
Powers of Criminal Courts (Sentencing) Act 2000
Prevention of Terrorism Act 2005
Representation of the People Act 1983
Representation of People Act 2000
Sex Disqualification (Removal) Act 1919

Table of Cases

International Cases

European Court of Human Rights

Al-Saadoon and Mufdhi v United Kingdom (App. 61498/08) 2 March 2010
Dudgeon v UK (App. 7525/76) 22 October 1981, Series A, No. 45 (1982) 4 EHRR 149
Hirst v United Kingdom (No. 2) (App. 74025/01) 6 October 2005 [Grand Chamber] (2006) 42 EHRR 849, ECHR 2005-IX
Khamtokhu and Aksenchik v Russia (Apps. 60367/08 and 961/11) ECHR [Grand Chamber] 24 January 2017
Manoussakis and Others v Greece (App. 18748/91) ECHR [Grand Chamber] 26 September 1996
Meier v Switzerland (App. 10109/14) 9 February 2016
Modinos v Cyprus (App. 10570/89) 22 April 1993, Series A, No. 259 (1994) 16 EHRR 485 (1993)
Öcalan v. Turkey (App. 46221/99) ECHR [Grand Chamber] 12 May 2005
Reid v United Kingdom (App. 57592/08) 17 January 2017
Scopola v Italy (No. 3) (App. 126/05) 22 May 2012 [Grand Chamber] 56 EHRR 19
Stummer v Austria (App. 37452/02) ECHR [Grand Chamber] 7 July 2011
Tryer v United Kingdom (App. 5856/72) 25 April 1978, Series A, No. 26 (1979–80) 2 EHRR 1
Vinter and Others v UK (Apps. 66069/09, 130/10, and 3896/10) 9 July 2013

Human Rights Committee

A v Australia, Communication No. 560/1993 (1997) UN Doc CCPR/C/59/D/560/1993
Blessington and Elliot v Australia, Communication No. 1968/2010 (2014) UN Doc CCPR/C/112/D/1968/2010
Denis Yevdokimov and Artiom Rezanov v Russian Federation, Communication No. 1410/2005 (2005) UN Doc CCPR/C/101/D/1410/2005

De Léon Castro v Spain, Communication No. 1318/2005 (2009) UN Doc CCPR/C/95/D/1388/2005

Kaba v Canada, Communication No. 1465/2006 (2010) UN Doc CCPR/C/98/D/1465/2006

Dissanayake v Sri Lanka, Communication No. 1373/2005 (2008) UN Doc CCPR/C/93/D/1373/2005

Fardon v Australia, Communication No. 1629/2007 (2010) UN Doc CCPR/C/98/D/1629/2007

Fernando v Sri Lanka, Communication No. 1189/2003 (2005) UN Doc CCPR/C/83/D/1189/2003

Jensen v Australia, Communication No. 762/1997 (2001) UN Doc CCPR/C/71/D/726/1997

Radosevic v Germany, Communication No. (2005) UN Doc CCPR/C/84/D/1292/2004

Pustovoit v Ukraine, Communication No. 1405/2005 (2014) UN Doc CCPR/C/110/D/1405/2005

Rameka and others v New Zealand, Communication No. 1090/2002 (2003) UN Doc CCPR/C/79/D/1090/2002

Singh v New Zealand, Communication No. 791/97 (2001) UN Doc CCPR/C/72/D/791/1997

Teesdale v Trinidad and Tobago, Communication No. 677/1996 (2002) UN Doc CCPR/C/74/D/677/1996

Tillman v Australia, Communication No. 1635/2007 (2010) UN Doc CCPR/C/98/D/1635/2007

Vassilari and others v Greece, Communication No. 1570/2007 (2009) UN Doc CCPR/C/95/D/1570/2007

Yevdokimov and Rezanov v Russian Federation, Communication No. 1410/2005, UN Doc CCPR/C/101/D/1410/2005

International Court of Justice

Barcelona Traction, Light and Power Company, Limited (Belgium v Spain) Second Phase [1970] ICJ Rep 3

International Criminal Court

Prosecutor v Thomas Lubanga Dyilo, ICC-01/04–01/06–2842, Judgement pursuant to Article 74 of the Statute, Trial Chamber I, 14 March 2012

National Cases

India

Bachan Singh v State of Punjab AIR 1980 SC 898

Navtej Singh Johar v Union of India (2018) W.P. (Crl.) No.76/16 etc.

Israel

Academic Center of Law and Business v Minister of Finance (19 November 2009) HCJ 2605/05

Hungry

Decision 23/1990 (X.31) AB, Constitutional Court of Hungary

South Africa

S v Makwanyane 1995 (3) SA 391 (CC)
S v Williams 1995 (3) SA 632 (CC)

United Kingdom

Raymond v Honey [1982] AC 1 [1981] UKHL 8
R (McCann & others) v Crown Court at Manchester [2002] UKHL 39 [2003] 1 AC 787 [2002] 4 All ER 593

United States of America

Atkins v Virginia 536 US 304 (2002)
Brown v Board of Education 347 US 483 (1954)
Buck v Bell 274 US 200 (1927)
Coker v Georgia 433 US 584 (1977)
Ewing v California 538 US 11 (2003)
Furman v Georgia 408 US 238, L Ed 2d 346 (1972)
Gates v Collier 501 F.2d 1291, 5th Cir (1974)
Gideon v Wainwright 372 US 335 (1963)
Graham v Florida 130 S Ct 2011, 2030 (2010)
Gregg v Georgia 428 US 153, 49 L Ed 2d 859 (1976)
Harmelin v. Michigan, 501 US 957 (1991)
Jones v North Carolina Prisoners' Labor Union 433 US 119 (1977)
Lockyer v Andrade 538 US 63 (2003)
Miller v Alabama, 567 US 460, 132 S Ct 2455 (2012)
Roper v Simmons 543 US 551 (2005)
Trop v Dulles 356 US 86 (1958)
Wolff v McDonnell 418 US 539 (1974)

Introduction

> 'Where shall I begin, please your Majesty', he asked. 'Begin at the beginning', the King said, very gravely, 'and go on till you come to the end; then stop'.
>
> Lewis Carrol[1]

In a far-reaching critique of the legal academy, Duncan Kennedy once characterised law schools as lacking in 'theoretical ambition' or 'practical vision of what social life might be'.[2] Kennedy's criticism was directed, in part, at the preoccupation with the interpretation and application of stated legal norms which tends to be bereft of deeper theoretical and contextual debate. The doctrinal approach, or what Kennedy calls 'the trade school mentality', results in endless attention being paid to trees at 'the expense of forests'.[3] This tendency also marks human rights scholarship in relation to crime, punishment, and sentencing. The discussion seldom moves beyond the due process, the 'proportionality' of punishment to crime, and fair trial guarantees, to discuss why states categorise certain forms of conduct as crimes and why they impose punishment on individuals.[4] In relation to imprisonment, the debate within the mainstream scholarship rarely considers

1 Lewis Carrol, *Alice in Wonderland* (2nd edn, W.W. Norton 1992) 94.

2 Duncan Kennedy, 'Legal Education as Training for Hierarchy' in David Kairys (ed), *The Politics of Law: A Progressive Critique* (3rd edn, Basic Books 1998) 54–75, 54.

3 Ibid.

4 See, for example, Manfred Nowak, *U.N. Covenant on Civil and Political Rights: CCPR Commentary* (2nd edn, N.P. Engel 2005) 126–196, 233–286; Ben Emmerson, Andrew Ashworth and Alison MacDonald, *Human Rights and Criminal Justice* (Sweet & Maxwell 2007); Nigel S. Rodley and Matt Pollard, *The Treatment of Prisoners Under International Law* (3rd edn, Oxford University Press 2009); Walter Kälin and Jörg Künzli, *The Law of International Human Rights Protection* (Oxford University Press 2009) 440–465; Javaid Rehman, *International Human Rights Law* (2nd edn, Pearson 2010) 1–72, 713–920; Alastair Mowbray, *Cases, Materials, and Commentary on the European Convention on Human Rights* (3rd edn, Oxford University Press 2012) 245–487; Sangeeta Shah, 'Detention and Trial' in Daniel Moeckli, Sangeeta Shah and Sandesh Sivakumaran (eds), *International Human Rights Law* (2nd edn, Oxford University Press 2014) 259–285; Ilias Bantekas and Lutz Oette, *International Human Rights Law and Practice* (Cambridge University Press 2013) 313–365; Merris Amos, *Human Rights Law* (2nd edn, Oxford University Press 2014) 287–408.

the deeper questions as to 'who is held, why and with what consequences'.[5] The lack of focus on foundational questions also implies that analyses of international law concentrate on the enforcement of extant norms rather than exploring the ideas that do not appear in legal texts possibly because 'they were marginalised, removed or diluted during the drafting of the foundational documents'.[6]

To eschew the debate on the justifications and purposes of punishment is problematic for at least two broad reasons. In the first place, criminal punishment, by definition, involves imposition of unpleasant consequences and the exercise of coercive power over individuals. Since such treatment would generally be regarded as morally impermissible, criminal punishment stands in need of justification.[7] The power to punish cannot be taken for granted. Second, as the pre-eminent moral language and the '*doxa* of our times',[8] human rights can reasonably be expected to furnish some sort of a normative account of the institution of punishment – unless it is assumed that basic questions regarding its justification have already been resolved. To begin at the beginning, as the King advised the White Rabbit in *Alice in Wonderland*, we cannot but ask whether human rights squares with classical deontological principles of retribution and moral reprobation or utilitarian considerations of rehabilitation, incapacitation (protection of the public), and deterrence as the basis for criminal punishment. Does the doctrine of human rights offer normative and analytical tools to critique the traditional justifications? Where would social justice considerations fit into a human rights perspective on punishment?

Against the above backdrop, the central question that this study sets out to answer is: How does international human rights discourse relate to the justifications of criminal punishment? What are the causes and consequences of this relationship? The choice of the term 'discourse' is deliberate since the study is concerned not only with international human rights law, but also with scholarly works and the pronouncements of major human rights actors, namely the United Nations, Amnesty International, and Human Rights Watch. The term 'discourse' is used with an understanding gained from Michel Foucault and Edward Said

5 Susan Marks and Andrew Clapham, *International Human Rights Lexicon* (Oxford University Press 2005) 87. See also R.A. Duff, *Punishment, Communication, and Community* (Oxford University Press 2001) xi–xx.

6 Christopher NJ Roberts, *The Contentious History of the International Bill of Human Rights* (Cambridge University Press 2014) 126. On the importance of 'absences' in discourse analysis, see Linda A. Wood and Rolf O. Kroger, *Doing Discourse Analysis: Methods for Studying Action in Talk and Text* (Sage 2000) 91.

7 Ted Honderich, *Punishment: The Supposed Justifications* (2nd edn, Penguin 1984) 12; J. Ellis McTaggart, 'Hegel's Theory of Punishment' (1986) 6(4) *International Journal of Ethics* 479–480.

8 Stefan-Ludwig Hoffman, 'Genealogies of Human Rights' in Hoffman (ed), *Human Rights in the Twentieth Century* (Cambridge University Press 2011) 1–28, 1. See also Kristen Sellars, *The Rise and Rise of Human Rights* (Sutton Publishing 2002) 197; Costas Douzinas *Human Rights and Empire: The Political Philosophy of Cosmopolitanism* (Routledge-Cavendish 2007) 33; *The End of Human Rights: Critical Legal Thought at the Turn of the Century* (Hart Publishing 2000) 245–246.

that human rights language – like other specialised languages – is more than just a means of describing external reality. Rather, it promotes certain categories of thought and ways of thinking and lends structure to human experience. More on this shortly.[9]

The term 'criminal punishment' is used to signify the infliction by a state authority of pain or other consequences normally considered unpleasant, on an actual or supposed offender in response to an offence against the law.[10] Regarding the mode of punishment, the focus, of necessity, is on imprisonment, one of the most commonly applied criminal sentences from a global perspective and 'the backbone of the system of penal sanctions'.[11] Although sentences imposed by courts are a key concern, the book does not exclude invisible or add-on punishment, such as penal labour and employment restrictions on former convicts.[12] The definition excludes disciplinary measures applied in the family, schools, professional bodies, and other institutions outside the criminal law. It also omits disadvantages imposed by the state on citizens which do not relate to an offence or a breach of the law, such as taxation. We are concerned both with the 'general justifying aim' of criminal punishment and the question of the distribution of punishment.[13] In other words, we need to inquire into what values the institution of punishment fosters in society and what moral criteria determine who may be punished and how much?[14]

The methodological approach – to be elaborated shortly – is interdisciplinary and aimed at interpreting textual sources as formulated within specific historical and political contexts. Two subsidiary questions, which emanate from that methodological approach and frame the inquiry, are as follows: (i) Which normative perspectives on criminal punishment inform the discourse of international human rights, and which ones are marginalised or ignored? (ii) Which historical and political influences account for the dominant ideas on the justification of criminal punishment within the international human rights discourse?

The book takes as its reference point domestic penal law and practice and not international criminal justice per se. The reason for delimiting the scope thus is two-fold. First, since the formation of the international tribunals for the former

9 Tony Evans, 'International Human Rights Law as Power/Knowledge' (2005) 27(3) *Human Rights Quarterly* 1046, 1048.

10 Antony Flew, 'The Justification of Punishment' (1954) XXIX (III) *Philosophy* 291, 293–294; H.L.A Hart, *Punishment and Responsibility: Essays in the Philosophy of Law* (Oxford University Press 1968) 4–6; Nicola Lacey, *State Punishment: Political Principles and Community Values* (Routledge 1988) 4–12.

11 Frieder Dünkel and Dirk Van Zyl Smit, 'Conclusion' in Smit and Dünkel (eds), *Imprisonment Today and Tomorrow: International Perspectives on Prisoners' Rights and Prison Conditions* (2nd edn, Kluwer Law International 2001) 796–859, 796.

12 See Marc Mauer and Meda Chesney-Lind (eds), *Invisible Punishment: The Collateral Consequences of Mass Imprisonment* (Free Press 2002).

13 Hart (n 10) 8–13.

14 Ibid.

Yugoslavia and Rwanda in 1993 and 1994 respectively,[15] a number of scholars have examined the purposes and principles of punishment with reference to the statutory foundations and sentencing practices of the tribunals.[16] The scholarship is now expanding to cover the case law of the International Criminal Court, which was established in 2002, and reached its first verdict in March 2012.[17] There has also been considerable academic debate on the validity of amnesties for international crimes and past abuses of human rights.[18] Legal and social science scholars have commented extensively on the complexities of 'transitional justice', a new term that emerged in the 1980s, signifying 'not just any change but specifically democratic change', and was 'tied up with the rekindled human rights discourse of the previous decade'.[19] By contrast, the relationship between human rights and the justificatory foundations of punishment generally, or in the context of domestic penal law, has received much less attention. That includes the question of how human rights bodies have assessed the justification of criminal punishment in domestic jurisdictions. There has yet to be a book-length treatment of the subject.[20]

15 The Statute of the International Criminal Tribunal for the former Yugoslavia can be found in the annex to the 'Report of the Secretary-General Pursuant to Paragraph 2 of Security Resolution 808' UN SCOR, 48th Sess., 3217th mtg., UN Doc S/RES/827 (1993). For the Statute of the International Criminal Tribunal for Rwanda, see annex to Security Council Resolution 955, UN SCOR, 49th Sess., 3453d mtg., UN Doc S/RES/955 (1994).

16 See, for example, Andrew N. Keller, 'Punishment for Violation of International Criminal Law: An Analysis of Sentencing at the ICTY and ICTR' (2001–2002) 12 *International and Comparative Law Review* 53; Mark A. Drumbl, *Atrocity, Punishment, and International Law* (Cambridge University Press 2007); Barbora Hola, Alette Smuelers and Catrien Bijleveld, 'International Sentencing Facts and Figures: Sentencing Practice at the ICTY and ICTR' *Journal of International Criminal Justice* (2011) 9, 411.

17 Rome Statute of the International Criminal Court, 17 July 1998 (adopted 17 July 1998, entered into force 1 July 2002) 2187 UNTS 3. The Court's first judgment being *Prosecutor v Thomas Lubanga Dyilo*, ICC-01/04–01/06–2842, Judgment pursuant to Art 74 of the Statute, Trial Chamber I, 14 March 2012. On the emerging jurisprudence, see Annika Jones, 'Insights into an Emerging Relationship: Use of Human Rights Jurisprudence at the International Criminal Court' (2016) 16(4) *Human Rights Law Review* 701; Colin J. Flynn, *Sentencing at the International Criminal Court: A Practice in Search of a Rationale* (PhD thesis, University of Leicester 2017).

18 See, for example, Jessica Gavron, 'Amnesties in the Light of Developments in International Law and the Establishment of the International Criminal Court' (2002) 51 *International and Comparative Law Quarterly* 91; Louise Mallinder, *Amnesty, Human Rights and Political Transitions: Bridging the Peace and Justice Divide* (Hart Publishing 2008); Ben Chigara, *Amnesty in International Law: The Legality Under International Law of National Amnesty Laws* (Longman 2002).

19 Kim Christian Priemel, *The Betrayal: The Nuremberg Trials and German Divergence* (Oxford University Press 2016) 6–7. See also Robert Cryer, *Prosecuting International Crimes: Selectivity and the International Criminal Law Regime* (Oxford University Press 2005); Priscilla B. Hayner, *Unspeakable Truths: Transitional Justice and the Challenge of Truth Commissions* (Taylor & Francis 2010).

20 For chapters in edited volumes which deal with the application of international human rights standards to domestic penal law, see Leena Kurki, 'International Standards for Sentencing and Punishment' in Michael Tonry and Richard S. Frase (eds), *Sentencing and Sanctions*

Second, it seems that commentaries on international criminal law written from a human rights perspective are underpinned by certain premises about the relationship between punishment and human rights, which vary depending upon a particular scholar's outlook and their sense of justice. For example, in one of the earlier contributions on the subject, William Schabas pointed out that the Nuremburg and Tokyo Tribunals – set up in the aftermath of World War II – had left few sentencing guidelines.[21] He built a case for a greater focus on 'rehabilitation' as a punishment objective, arguing that the newly established tribunals, in light of their potential influence on judges around the world, should aim to provide 'a model of enlightened justice', never losing 'sight of rehabilitation, conscious of its relationship to the social imperative of reconciliation in a war-torn country'.[22] Dirk Van Zyl Smit analysed the judgments of the Yugoslavia tribunal to find the application of 'rehabilitation' in the tribunal's case law as being devoid of content and subsumed under general statements of penal objectives.[23] Subsequently, Ralph Henham arrived at the same conclusion, identifying the overriding emphasis on retribution and deterrence as a problematic feature in international criminal sentencing.[24]

Other writers, whilst recognising the relevance of human rights norms, have leant in favour of deterrence as the preferred aim of punishment and sentencing in international tribunals.[25] Yet others have contended that 'utilitarian aspirations associated with international criminal prosecutions should be abandoned as sentencing rationales because they distort the individual perpetrator's culpability'.[26] Given these divergent positions, the present book could make a small indirect contribution to the scholarship on international criminal justice through a broad examination of the normative structure of international human rights in relation to the idea of punishment.

Seen broadly, the question of penological justifications within the project of international criminal justice has already received very nuanced and sophisticated

in Western Countries (Oxford University Press 2001) 331–378; Marks and Clapham (n 5) 71–90; Eammon Carrabine, 'Punishment, Rights and Justice' in Lydia Morris (ed), *Rights: Sociological Perspectives* (Routledge 2006) *191–208; Dirk van Zyl Smit, 'Punishment and Human Rights' in Jonathan Simon and Richard Sparks (eds), The Sage Handbook of Punishment and Society* (Sage 2013).

21 William A. Schabas, 'Sentencing by International Tribunals: A Human Rights Approach' (1997) 7 *Duke Journal of Comparative and International Law* 461.

22 Ibid 503, 516.

23 Dirk van Zyl Smit, 'Punishment and Human Rights in International Criminal Justice' (2002) 2(1) *Human Rights Law Review* 10.

24 Ralph Henham, *Punishment and Process in International Criminal Trials* (Ashgate 2005) 21; Ralph Henham 'Developing Contextualized Rationales for Sentencing in International Criminal Trials' (2007) 5 *International Criminal Justice* 757.

25 Mikro Bagaric and John Morss, 'International Sentencing Law: In Search of a Justification and a Coherent Framework' (2006) 6 *International Criminal Law Review* 191.

26 Shahram Dana, 'The Limits of Judicial Idealism: Should the International Criminal Court Engage with Consequentialist Aspirations?' (2014) 3(1) *Penn State Journal of Law & International Affairs* 30, 112.

treatment at the hands of the American scholar Mark Drumbl. In *Atrocity, Punishment, and International Law*, Drumbl has established how retributivism and expressivism (communication of moral outrage), and, to a lesser extent, deterrence, constitute the preferred justifications of punishment for international criminal law institutions, squeezing out other legitimate penal goals, including peace, reconciliation, and rehabilitation.[27] Drumbl demonstrates the fraught nature of the traditional liberal criminal law when transposed on to international criminal justice. Inchoate as it is, the sentencing philosophy adopted by international tribunals and special courts runs into severe difficulties in operationalising each of the predominant punishment rationales. The legitimacy of retribution is undercut by prosecutorial selectivity, plea bargaining, and the impossible task of creating proportionality between the severity of sanction and mass atrocities.[28] Expressivism – a variant of retributivism – offered by international bodies as a possible way out of the inevitable charge of vengefulness, is tainted by selective narration of historical truths.[29] Similarly, the uncertainty of prosecution and punishment in the aftermath of armed conflicts erodes the legitimacy of deterrence as a penological justification. Further, deterrence theory rests on the unrealistic assumption of perpetrators behaving rationally amid cataclysmic events. Drawing on anthropology of armed conflicts, Drumbl concludes that punishment is unlikely to deter those who participate in massacres as a sense of commitment to a larger cause, or those who see it as a survival strategy when surrounded by mass violence.[30]

I do not have much to add to this clear-eyed analysis except for a couple of points. One, some of the moral quandaries exposed by Drumbl in the context of accountability for mass atrocities also crop up in ordinary penal law. Moral expressivism in traditional criminal sentencing, for example, has to contend with a truncated version of the story of crime if it is to address condemnation to the individual offender rather than to the society and its failings. Likewise, deterrence in domestic laws hinges conveniently on the assumption of rational behaviour. It is one thing for judges and academic lawyers to assume that punishment dissuades individuals from offending or re-offending. It is quite another thing to back it up with empirical data. Two, the present book will reinforce Drumbl's call for fresh thinking by explaining the limits of human rights in furnishing a fine-grained account of penological aims and, particularly, in sustaining the retributive model of justice. The latter point has been articulated by Karen Engle, Samuel Moyn, and Vasuki Neisah in a recent volume tracing the trajectory of 'anti-impunity' and 'the criminal turn in human rights'.[31] But once again, these contributions are set in contexts involving

27 Drumbl (n 16) 61–63.
28 Ibid 150–169.
29 Ibid 173–180.
30 Ibid 171–173. cf. Kathryn Sikkink, *The Justice Cascade: How Human Rights Prosecutions Are Changing World Politics* (W.W. Norton and Company 2011) 231, 258.
31 Karen Engle, 'A Genealogy of the Criminal Turn in Human Rights' in Engle, Zinaida Miller and DM Davis (eds), *Anti-Impunity and the Human Rights Agenda* (Cambridge University Press 2016) 15–67, 15.

large-scale human rights abuses and regime change. The contributors illustrate in varied ways how the human rights movement is implicated in narrowing our perspectives with its insistence on combating 'impunity' in a certain way (retributive justice rather than reconciliation)[32] and for certain types of social harms (war crimes and mass atrocities but not the ravages of the global economic order).[33]

This book complements the critical accounts outlined above but with a difference in emphasis. In probing human rights discourse, I will primarily be referencing domestic penal law and practices rather than transitional justice. The diagnostic part will certainly address the engendering circumstances of that discourse. But, unlike most other works on the topic, it will also grapple with the theoretical moorings of the reigning orthodoxy.

Theoretical and methodological approach

This research locates itself within the tradition of critical legal studies, which draws on diverse theoretical insights from Marxism, feminism, and post-modernism.[34] Central to critical legal approaches is a sceptical attitude towards Anglo-American black-letter approach to understanding law, and a commitment to making explicit the biases behind seemingly neutral legal rules, institutions, and practices.[35] Questioning the basic assumption of liberal jurisprudence that law is an autonomous and self-contained realm, critical scholarship seeks to incorporate broader social science perspectives into legal analysis. As well as advancing an understanding of law in context, social science knowledge has been deployed successfully by radical lawyers in courts, as illustrated memorably by the US Supreme Court's 1954 decision in *Brown v Board of Education*, declaring racial segregation in public schools as unconstitutional.[36]

This study follows, in particular, theoretical signposts offered by the Italian theorist Antonio Gramsci, who has been credited with 'revitalising the moral vision of Marxism'.[37] Much before the advent of post-modernist critiques, it was Gram-

32 Samuel Moyn, 'Anti-Impunity as Deflection of Argument' in Engle, Miller and Davis (n 31) 68–94.

33 Vasuki Neisah, 'Doing History with Impunity' in Engle, Miller and Davis (n 31) 95–122.

34 See Roberto Unger 'The Critical Legal Studies Movement' (1983) 96 *Harvard Law Review* 561; Peter Fitzpatrick and Alan Hunt, 'Introduction' in Fitzpatrick and Hunt (eds), *Critical Legal Studies* (Blackwell 1987); Mark Tushnet, 'Critical Legal Studies: A Political History' (1991) 100 *Yale Law Journal* 1515; Alan Hunt, 'Getting Marx and Foucault into Bed Together' (2004) 31(4) *Journal of Law and Society* 592.

35 See, for example, Gerry J. Simpson and Hillary Charlesworth, 'Objecting to Objectivity: The Radical Challenge to Legal Liberalism' in Rosemary Hunter, Richard Ingleby and Richard Johnstone (eds), *Thinking About Law: Perspectives on the History, Philosophy and Sociology of Law* (Allen & Unwin 1995) 86–132.

36 *Brown v Board of Education* 347 US 483 (1954). See also Rachel F. Moran, 'What Counts as Knowledge? A Reflection on Race, Social Science and the Law' (2002) 44(3/4) *Law & Society Review* 515.

37 Victor J. Seidler, *The Moral Limits of Modernity: Love, Inequality and Oppression* (Palgrave Macmillan, Basingstoke 1991) 3.

sci who alerted us to the diffuse nature of power in society, captured by his notion of 'hegemony'. Fundamentally different from the common understanding of the term as domination through force, hegemony, on Gramscian theory, implies a combination of coercion and consent as distinct from domination, which he equates with coercive force.[38] Law is central to a state's hegemonic project as it combines coercion and consent or persuasion.[39] On the one hand, it lends 'authoritative legitimations to the norms and projects through which the state seeks to govern civil society', and on the other, it 'provides a facilitative framework for private transactions' as well as guarantees of fundamental rights and the rule of law, sometimes to the explicit disadvantage of the rulers themselves.[40]

Gramsci stressed the educational role of law 'whereby the standards and ways of thought embodied in it penetrate civil society and become a part of common sense'.[41] 'Common sense' refers to the conceptions of the world one has. It is ambiguous and often contradictory. It contains elements of truth as well as misrepresentation. In the field of criminal punishment, a lot of ambiguity that pervades 'common sense' is probably reflective of a 'hegemonic' discourse that combines 'retribution' and 'rehabilitation' as sentencing aims, or punitive practices, which penalise 'street crimes' but go soft on harmful corporate practices such as ecological destruction.[42] In terms of praxis, the task for critical scholars is to produce a criticism of the 'common sense', and enable people to develop it into a positive, coherent outlook, or what Gramsci called 'good sense' as part of establishing a 'counter-hegemony'.[43]

The study makes use of critical discourse analysis, a qualitative research method that originated in linguistics, but is now employed in a variety of disciplines to examine social and cultural practices. With this methodology, the emphasis is on understanding of discourse in relation to social problems and structural variables such as race, gender, and class. As a specialised language, a discourse constructs objects and subjects. Medical discourse, for example, 'constitutes a variety of objects (e.g. particular diseases)', and 'it also constitutes people as doctors and patients'.[44] To illustrate, mental illness on Michel Foucault's account, is not a trans-historical and trans-cultural objective fact. Rather, it was

> constituted by all that was said, in all statements that named it, divided it up, described it, explained it, traced its development, indicated its various

38 Antonio Gramsci, *Selections from the Prison Notebooks* (Lawrence and Wishart 1971) 57–58.

39 Ibid 195.

40 Gramsci (n 38) 182. See also Alan Hunt, 'Rights and Social Movements: Counter-Hegemonic Strategies' (1990) 17(3) *Journal of Law and Society* 309, 316.

41 Ibid 197. For a commentary on the Gramscian notion of 'common sense', see Maureen Cain, 'Gramsci, the State and the Place of Law' in David Sugarman (ed), *Legality, Ideology and the State* (Academic Press 1983) 95–117.

42 cf Celia Wells, *Corporations and Criminal Responsibility* (2nd edn, Oxford University Press 2001) 13–39.

43 Roger Simon, *Gramsci's Political Thought* (Lawrence and Wishart 1982) 25–26.

44 Wood and Kroger (n 6) 21.

> correlations, judged it, and possibly gave it speech by articulating in its names, discourses that were to be taken as its own.[45]

Similarly, in *Discipline and Punish* Foucault analysed how the 'delinquent' subject was produced and disciplined in early nineteenth-century France.[46] Edward Said applied Foucault's notion of a discourse to demonstrate how the European culture 'managed and produced . . . the Orient politically, sociologically, militarily, ideologically, scientifically, and imaginatively during the post-Enlightenment period'.[47]

In much the same way, human rights discourse does not serve merely as a neutral descriptive medium. Rather, it constructs or legitimises existing categories, such as 'crime' and 'punishment'. It confers subjectivities on human beings as 'rights-bearers' and 'victims' or 'perpetrators', often subsuming complex situations, contexts, and identities, which defy rendering in simplistic terms.[48] David Kennedy, a key figure in critical human rights scholarship, sounds a note of caution when he speaks of 'human rights language' as encouraging us to 'think of evil as a social machine, a theater of roles, in which people are "victims", "violators", and "bystanders"'.[49] In producing such schemes of classification and truth, the discourse operates as a self-policing regime; it encourages certain kinds of statements or texts and discourages the ones which violate its norms.[50]

Discourse and practice stand in a dialectical relationship. A mode of representing and making sense of say, domestic violence, supports certain ways of responding to it, for example, incarceration instead of community service or some other non-custodial or non-penal measure.[51] The dominant and abiding practices, in turn, legitimate particular ways of making sense of, articulating, and representing social reality. As an apparatus of assembling knowledge, and as a tool of classification and representation, human rights is bound up with power, in the sense that it wields moral, cultural, and political authority and legitimates exercise of

45 Michel Foucault, *Archaeology of Knowledge* (A.M. Sheriden Smith tr, Routledge 1989) 32. See also, Foucault, *Power/Knowledge* (Harvester 1980) 115; Stuart Hall, 'Foucault: Power, Knowledge and Discourse' in Margaret Wetherell and others (eds), *Discourse Theory and Practice: A Reader* (Sage 2001) 72–81.

46 Michel Foucault, *Discipline and Punish: The Birth of the Prison* (Penguin 1977) 100.

47 Edward Said, *Orientalism* (Vintage 1978) 3.

48 See Richard A. Wilson, 'Representing Human Rights Violations: Social Contexts and Subjectivities' in Wilson (ed), *Human Rights, Culture & Context: Anthropological Perspectives* (Pluto Press 1997) 134–160; Costas Douzinas, 'The End of Human Rights' (n 8) 11.

49 David Kennedy, *The Dark Sides of Virtue: Reassessing International Humanitarianism* (Princeton University Press 2004) 14. See also Makau Mutua, 'Savages, Victims and Saviours: The Metaphor of Human Rights' (2001) 42(1) *Harvard International Law Journal* 201; *Human Rights: A Political and Cultural Critique* (University of Pennsylvania Press 2002) 10–38.

50 Michel Foucault, 'Politics and the Study of Discourse' in Graham Burchell, Colin Gordon and Peter Miller (eds), *The Foucault Effects: Studies in Governmentality: With Two Lectures and an Interview with Michel Foucault* (Harvester Wheatsheaf 1991) 53–72, 60.

51 Hall (n 45) 73–81, 76.

authority in its name.[52] In other words, we are concerned with 'power in discourse' as well as 'power over discourse'.[53] In Gramscian terms, human rights discourse – as embodied in international human rights instruments, jurisprudence of international courts and treaty monitoring bodies, academic commentaries, and human rights reporting by major international NGOs – lends itself to be seen as a hegemonic project in that it confers a moral respectability to a regime which espouses its norms. Admittedly, that discourse is not a unified whole. Even as we remain alert to points of intersection and divergence dotting the discourse, it is also instructive to note that not all voices are heard and not every actor has the same authority. There are, within the discourse of human rights, 'authorities of delimitation'.[54] These authorities enjoy the power to produce knowledge and determine the authoritative meanings of events and concepts. Knowledge in this sense is constitutive of power and also constitutes power. Within the context of the present research, a relatively small NGO, such as the Howard League for Penal Reform, may advance a different understanding of punishment than the one espoused by Amnesty International. However, with its authoritative position, it is the latter whose knowledge and interpretations are likely to wield influence at a larger scale.

What distinguishes critical discourse analysis most significantly from typical textual analysis in legal scholarship is that on this method speech or writing is seen from 'the point of view of the beliefs and values they embody'.[55] Instead of taking text at face value, we analyse it 'on the basis of the practices and rules that produced [it] and the methodological organisation of thought underlying [this text]'.[56] Such critical scrutiny necessitates an examination of how a discourse emerges within certain 'institutional sites' and under particular social and political circumstances.[57] Ideas and concepts that are today accepted uncritically as universal truths or 'common sense' are often a product of deep historical contestation. The temporal element of the study thus draws on 'genealogy', the historical method formulated by Nietzsche and Foucault to problematise contemporary beliefs and practices, or to write a 'history of the past in terms of the present'.[58] The analysis is aimed at understanding how notions such as 'punishment', 'proportionality', 'commensurate deserts', 'rehabilitation', or 'prisoners'

52 Richard A. Wilson, 'Introduction' in Wilson (ed), *Human Rights, Culture and Context: Anthropological Perspectives* (Pluto Press 1997) 1–27, 23; Conor Gearty, *On Fantasy Island: Britain, Europe and Human Rights* (Oxford University Press 2016) 56–57.
53 John E. Richardson, *Analysing Newspapers: An Approach from Critical Discourse Analysis* (Palgrave Macmillan 2006) 26.
54 Foucault, 'Archaeology of Knowledge' (n 45) 46.
55 Bonny Ibhawoh, *Imperialism and Human Rights: Colonial Discourses of Rights and Liberties in African History* (State University of New York Press 2007) 9.
56 Ibid.
57 Foucault, 'Discipline and Punish' (n 46) 56–57.
58 Ibid 30–31. For an overview of the genealogical method, see David Garland, 'What Is a "history of the present"? On Foucault's Genealogies and Their Critical Preconditions' (2014) 16(4) *Punishment & Society* 365.

rights' emerged historically, and how they were adopted, justified, legalised, or worked upon within the human rights regime (understood as 'the totality of standards, procedures, and institutions in the field of human rights').[59] In mapping what Foucault calls 'the surfaces of emergence', the study explores the intersection between international human rights discourse on the one hand, and international penal discourse on the other, as it evolved on international fora in the late nineteenth and early twentieth century before the advent of the modern human rights movement.[60]

Structure and outline

The chapters which follow sit at the intersection of the theory and history of both criminal punishment and human rights. Chapter 1 questions commonly held assumptions about the concepts of 'crime' and 'punishment' and offers a reappraisal of classical penal theory as conducted between retributivist and utilitarian schools. As well as probing the divergent justifications of criminal punishment embodied in Immanuel Kant and G.W.F. Hegel's retributivism on the one hand, and utilitarian ideas formulated by Cesare Beccaria and Jeremy Bentham on the other, the chapter attempts to point out certain common assumptions about human nature that lay at the heart of Enlightenment thinking and animated both strands of classical penal theory. The chapter offers some preliminary clues to understanding how and why Kantian and Hegelian philosophy underpins the predominant conception of criminal punishment in human rights orthodoxy.

The second substantive chapter charts the discredited history of positivist criminology as rooted in the changing intellectual and social landscape of the nineteenth century, and as a reaction to metaphysical speculations of Enlightenment thinkers, particularly their belief in individual autonomy and free will. The chapter tracks the influence of positivist thinking on international penal discourse, especially with reference to the International Prison Commission, formed in 1872, and renamed International Penal and Penitentiary Commission in 1935. Examining the proceedings of the quinquennial congresses convened by the Commission till its functions were rather unceremoniously taken over by the United Nations in 1950, the chapter draws attention to some notably progressive ideas that marked the contemporaneous penal thinking, such as social rehabilitation and 'aftercare' of prisoners. The association of positivist criminology and the Penitentiary Commission with Nazism and fascism, the chapter argues, has resulted in a repudiation of the less sinister side of the movement's legacy in the form of the development of individualised sentencing, parole, and probation, and the tradition of empirical inquiries into the causes of crime. The implications are assessed in terms of the normative orientation of the contemporary human rights discourse vis-à-vis penological justifications.

59 Gred Oberleitner, *Global Human Rights Institutions: Between Remedy and Ritual* (Polity 2007) 6.
60 Foucault, 'Archaeology of Knowledge' (n 45) 45–46.

Chapter 3 turns to the revival of retributivism and the intellectual eclipse of the positivist school in the 1970s against the backdrop of the crisis of the modern welfare state and the presumed failure of the 'rehabilitative ideal'. Although the era registered the birth of the modern human rights movement, the chapter suggests that scholars charting the history of contemporary retributivism on the one hand, and those documenting the evolution of human rights on the other, seem to talk past each other. It is argued that the political and intellectual developments of that period – supplemented by the revival of the 'Nuremburg spirit' in the 1990s – have had an abiding influence on human rights thinking in relation to the justifications of punishment. Drawing insights from moral philosophy, criminology, and history and sociology of punishment, the chapter brings some seminal texts of the period, such as Foucault's *Discipline and Punish* and Andrew von Hirsch's *Doing Justice*, under scrutiny.[61] The analysis also probes some key concepts that human rights canon shares with modern retributivism or the 'just-deserts' movement, such as the principle of proportionality, and the idea of criminal justice and social justice as separate and distinct domains. It is suggested that to be morally tenable, modern retributivism depends, in large part, on the suspension of empirical evidence on how a criminal sentence is experienced by people in concrete social circumstances.

The next three chapters are framed as a response to the teleological version of history, which narrates the story of human rights as an inexorable march of humanity from barbarism to civilisation. Despite the publication of several powerfully argued revisionist histories in recent years, the standard account of human rights history as it pertains to the idea of punishment, has yet to receive scholarly attention.[62] The textbook narrative of the evolution of human rights, it is suggested, is marked by some unexplained temporal leaps and an uncritical celebration of the legacy of the Enlightenment. Chapter 4 turns to the links between slavery and the institution of prison, tracing the long history of the exclusion of penal labour from the prohibition of forced and compulsory labour under international law. It is argued that the permissibility of compulsory penal labour is indicative of the paradoxical nature of human rights, its loyalty divided between human emancipation on the one hand, and acceptable forms of repression on the other. The chapter also underlines the relevance of the League of Nations experience in understanding the contemporary human rights regime. The past may be another country, but it has some unexpected connections with the present.

61 Andrew von Hirsch, *Doing Justice: The Choice of Punishments. Report of the Committee for the Study of Incarceration* (Hill and Wang 1976).

62 See, for example, Tony Evans, *US Hegemony, and the Project of Universal Human Rights* (Palgrave Macmillan 1996); Roger Normand and Sarah Zaidi, *Human Rights at the UN: The Political History of Universal Justice* (Indiana University Press 2008); Samuel Moyn, *The Last Utopia: Human Rights in History* (Harvard University Press 2010); *Human Rights and the Uses of History* (Verso 2014); Christopher N.J Roberts, *The Contentious History of the International Bill of Human Rights* (Cambridge University Press 2015).

Chapter 5 mines some unexplored archival materials to chart the history of an international campaign by the Howard League for Penal Reform, in collaboration with the International Penitentiary Commission, to push an 'International Charter on Prisoners' through the League of Nations Assembly. The fact that the idea of a specific international convention on prisoners' rights receded into a distant background in the post-World War II human rights project is posited as a counterexample to the tale of progressive humanisation in the penal field. Further, the chapter elaborates how the Howard League's intellectual moorings in the Quaker and Christian socialist ideas on the one hand, and positivist criminology on the other, resulted in a far greater appreciation of the interconnections between criminal justice and social justice than is the case with the modern human rights discourse.

Chapter 6 casts fresh light on the drafting of the 'International Bill of Human Rights' in the aftermath of the Second World War. It problematises the idea of two distinct and separate categories of human rights – namely, civil and political rights on the one hand, and economic, social, and cultural rights on the other – inasmuch as the dichotomy mirrors the split between criminal justice and social justice. Charting the ideological and political influences under which the United Nations came to bifurcate what had originally been proposed as a single covenant, the chapter discusses the implications of that decision on how the idea of punishment is framed and understood today.

Chapter 7 turns the spotlight onto some specific provisions within the foundational human rights documents, particularly Article 10, para 3 of the International Covenant on Civil and Political Rights (ICCPR), which posits the 'reformation and social rehabilitation' of prisoners as the 'essential' aim of the penitentiary system.[63] The *travaux préparatoires* are analysed to elaborate how a stronger earlier version of the provision got watered down with implications on the way international bodies would subsequently interpret the purposes of punishment. The analysis further draws on a cross-section of contemporary human rights discourse, including the Universal Periodic Review[64]; the case law, the General Comments, and the Concluding Observations of the Human Rights Committee (the body mandated to monitor the implementation of the ICCPR); the Concluding Observations of the Committee on Economic, Social and Cultural Rights; selected case law of the European Court of Human Rights; and the pronouncements of Amnesty International and Human Rights Watch in relation to the justifications and purposes of punishment.

63 International Covenant on Civil and Political Rights (adopted 16 December 1966, entered into force 23 March 1976) 999 UNTS 171.

64 The Universal Periodic Review is a mechanism created in 2006 as part of the newly constituted Human Rights Council to periodically review the human rights records of all 193 members of the United Nations. For an overview and initial assessments, see Hilary Charlesworth and Emma Larking (eds), *Human Rights and the Universal Periodic Review: Rituals and Ritualism* (Cambridge University Press 2014).

Without discounting a great deal of good that 'human rights' has done in terms of reducing the suffering of those who encounter criminal justice, the conclusion to the book brings into focus certain silences, tensions, and paradoxes that are historically inscribed into human rights discourse and have a bearing on contemporary penal trajectories in terms of how, why, and what states can justifiably punish.

Before we proceed, a word on what this book does not cover. The analysis to follow is more diagnostic than prescriptive; it lays the groundwork for comprehending the limits and potential of human rights and the liberal criminal law in countering penal excesses. Developing the contours of an alternative model is a separate task, best left for another day. Second, the book is not intended to be a comprehensive account of the theory and history of either human rights or penal law. Rather, it simply re-historicises human rights from the vantage point of penal aims, taking into account the underlying ideological currents. And third, although the book draws on examples from various jurisdictions, it does not offer an exhaustive coverage of a country-context or a regional human rights system. There would, of course, be merit in detailed inquiries into specific jurisdictions, but such an undertaking is beyond the scope of this book.

1 The crime of punishment

Reassessing classical penal theory

> [It] is not a pretty thing when you look into it too much. What redeems it is the idea only. An idea at the back of it: not a sentimental pretence but an idea; and an unselfish belief in the idea – something you can set up, and bow down to, and offer a sacrifice to.
>
> Joseph Conrad[1]

On 15 March 2006, the United Nations General Assembly voted to replace the Commission on Human Rights with the Human Rights Council. Originally the primary site for the drafting of an 'International Bill of Human Rights', and an ideological battleground between the West and the erstwhile communist bloc, the Commission had increasingly faced criticism for failing to fulfil 'challenges of human rights protection'.[2] In a 2005 report on UN Reform, Secretary-General Kofi Annan noted with concern 'the declining credibility and professionalism' within the Commission.[3] The Secretary-General further observed that states had 'sought membership of the Commission not to strengthen human rights but to protect themselves against criticism or to criticize others'.[4]

The General Assembly Resolution, which 'sealed the fate of the Commission on Human Rights', also created the Universal Periodic Review (UPR), 'a cooperative mechanism, based on interactive dialogue', to periodically review the record of all 193 members of the UN in relation to their obligations under international human rights and humanitarian law.[5] Scholars have recently begun to shine light on the institutional architecture of the Human Rights Council as well as

1 Joseph Conrad, *The Heart of Darkness* (Penguin Classics 2007) 7.
2 Bertrand G. Ramacharan, *The UN Human Rights Council* (Routledge 2011) 20.
3 United Nations General Assembly (UNGA), *In Larger Freedom: Towards Development, Security and Human Rights for All: Report of the Secretary-General* (21 March 2005) UN Doc A/59/2005, para 182.
4 Ibid para 182.
5 UNGA Res 60/251 (15 March 2006) UN Doc A/RES/60/251, para 5 (e). See also Rhona Smith, '"To see Themselves as Others see Them": The Five Permanent Members of the Security Council and the Human Rights Council's Universal Periodic Review' (2013) 1(35) *Human Rights Quarterly* 1, 8.

procedural and substantive dimensions of the UPR.[6] Opinions remain divided on whether the mechanism forges a new trail in human rights monitoring or simply renovates an old model of self-reporting that goes right back to the League of Nations Mandates System. In line with the broader studies of the human rights regime, the emerging scholarship on the UPR does not examine it through the lens of penal policy and penological justifications.

A summary of the UPR process is provided in Chapter 7 where we will delve deeper into its proceedings. At this stage, it would suffice to note that the documentation accumulated under the mechanism holds some vital clues as to the underlying tendencies within international human rights discourse regarding the aims and purposes of punishment. To illustrate, one of the largest sets of recommendations put forward during the UPR second cycle concerned the criminalisation and punishment of human rights violations, particularly those involving sexual, gender, or identity-based violence and discrimination.[7] By contrast, recommendations that speak to restorative approaches to justice are so few that they can be counted on the fingers of a hand. When it comes to decriminalisation, the emphasis remains on countering repressive laws that affect political expression and sexual freedoms or result in identity-based discrimination and violence. There are several examples from the UPR where member countries received recommendations to make greater use of non-custodial penalties to ease overcrowding and improve the conditions of detention. However, in the absence of an underlying commitment to prison abolitionism, social justice or restorative forms of justice, prison expansion could just as well be mooted as a solution to overcrowding. That perception is borne out by some recommendations, such as the United States suggesting that Benin 'reduce overcrowding by building more prisons or reducing the length of pre-trial detention'.[8] Similarly, whilst there are frequent calls within the UPR documents for countries under review to abolish the death penalty and corporal punishment, the issue of prisoners' reintegration into society receives hardly any attention – a silence which reverberates in almost the entire corpus of human rights scholarship.[9]

6 See, for example, Hilary Charlesworth and Emma Larking (eds), *Human Rights and the Universal Periodic Review: Rituals and Ritualism* (Cambridge University Press 2014); Rosa Freedman, *The United Nations Human Rights Council: An Early Assessment* (Routledge 2013); 'The United Nations Human Rights Council: More of the same?' (2013) 31 (2) *Wisconsin International Law Journal* 208.

7 The first cycle of the UPR ran from April 2008 to October 2011. The second cycle began in May 2012 and ended in May 2017. The third cycle commenced in April 2017 and will conclude in the winter of 2021.

8 Human Rights Council, *Report of the Working Group on the Universal Periodic Review: Benin*. Twenty-second session, 11 December 2012, A/HRC/22/9 (Recommendation 108.39).

9 See, for example, Ben Emmerson, Andrew Ashworth and Alison MacDonald, *Human Rights and Criminal Justice* (Sweet & Maxwell 2007); Nigel S. Rodley and Matt Pollard, *The Treatment of Prisoners Under International Law* (3rd edn, Oxford University Press 2009); Walter Kälin and Jörg Künzli, *The Law of International Human Rights Protection* (Oxford University Press 2009); Javaid Rehman, *International Human Rights Law* (2nd edn, Pearson 2010).

This study is strategically aimed at historicising the present and problematising what looks natural and timeless, namely the idea of punishment within the discourse of human rights.[10] The genealogical strands of that discourse can be traced back to the Enlightenment thinkers who shared certain assumptions about the individual as a free rational agent and 'a vision of a consensual society' inaugurated by the social contract theory.[11] Also underlying their theories is a common revulsion against religious dogma, 'superstition and fanaticism', and the arbitrary use of power.[12] Beyond this, the positions of classical liberal thinkers on moral principles, including penological justifications, differed widely, resulting in certain deep-rooted ambiguities in human rights discourse as we know it today. The orthodox scholarship on human rights, as we shall see, reproduces the best and the worst in classical penal theory. On the one hand, it reiterates the liberal principles of legality, the prohibition of cruel and inhuman punishment, and proportionality of punishment to crime. On the other hand, being conceptually parasitic on liberal Enlightenment thought, it sustains the notion of individual responsibility at the expense of wider social justice considerations. Retributive justice, in particular, has an abiding appeal for human rights advocates on account of strong theoretical affinities between the human rights doctrine and classical retributivist philosophy. The notion of 'impunity' which animates modern human rights discourse is modelled on Kantian and Hegelian logic, respectively as an absolute moral obligation and the right of the victim. An attempt will be made in this chapter to demonstrate that a number of classical 'common sense' ideas about criminal punishment, offered without any sort of critical analysis in the human rights canon, do not necessarily stand up to theoretical and evidentiary scrutiny.

Thinking about crime and punishment

The late Norwegian criminologist and sociologist Nils Christie once famously stated in an interview that 'crime does not exist'.[13] This claim would make little sense from the orthodox legal and human rights perspective in which 'crime' is typically taken as a given.[14] With his characteristically provocative assertion, Christie called attention to the fact that crime had no ontological reality: a whole

10 For methodological insights, see Jen Bartelson, *A Genealogy of Sovereignty* (Cambridge University Press 1995) 7–8, 73–78; Ruti Teitel, 'Human Rights Genealogy' (1997–1998) 67 *Fordham Law Review* 301.

11 Alan Norrie, *Crime, Reason and History: A Critical Introduction to Criminal Law* (3rd edn, Cambridge University Press 2014) 53; Dan Edelstein, 'Enlightenment Rights Talk' (2014) 86(3) *Journal of Modern History* 530.

12 Peter Gay, 'The Enlightenment in the History of Political Theory' (1954) 69 *Political Science Quarterly* 374, 389.

13 Cited in Ezzat A. Farrah, *Criminology: Past, Present and Future* (Palgrave Macmillan 1997) 30.

14 See, for example, Sangeeta Shah, 'Detention and Trial' in Daniel Moeckli, Sangeeta Shah and Sandesh Sivakumaran (eds), *International Human Rights Law* (2nd edn, Oxford University Press 2014) 259–285; Merris Amos, *Human Rights Law* (2nd edn, Oxford University Press 2014) 287–408.

range of quite disparate actions – from petty thefts and street brawls to rape and murder – got lumped under the sweeping category of crime.[15] It is the decision to stick the label 'crime' on certain acts and to channel them through the criminal justice system – instead of some other policy measure – which is being called into question here. As Margaret Wilson (from whose 1931 classic I have borrowed the title of this chapter) exhorted her readers: 'We must remember that crime, as distinguished from wrong-doing, is a fact manufactured entirely by law'.[16]

The British social historian E.P. Thompson traced the origins of the infamous Black Act of 1723 – which designated various transgressions against private property as capital crimes – as situated within the 'long decline in the effectiveness of old methods of class control and discipline'.[17] The statute, Thompson argued, was a product of the transition in the eighteenth-century capitalist development toward 'an increasing impersonality in the mediation of class relations'.[18] The Indian scholar Anand Yang brings a similar perspective to bear on penal policy in colonial India with reference to the official decision of designating traditional agrarian practices such as cattle grazing in common fields as crimes.[19] What kind of actions get categorised as offences against the state, then, depends on the context and the shifting political and cultural forces.[20] Nils Christie, in another enduring contribution to sociology of punishment, also illustrated how social conflicts are appropriated by institutional actors once categorised as crimes, turning them into a property of lawyers and other professionals, rather than issues to be owned up, managed, and resolved by ordinary individuals and communities.[21]

From this sceptical perspective, all prisoners are essentially political prisoners in the sense that the decision to incarcerate them is always the result of a political choice to penalise certain forms of behaviour and not others.[22] Suspending the conventional understanding of crime, one may ask why some extremely destructive and harmful practices, including ecological damage wreaked by powerful oil companies, are typically subject to civil penalties, whereas petty theft is dealt with

15 Louk Hulsman, 'Critical Criminology and the Concept of Crime' in H. Bianchi and others (eds), *Abolitionism: Towards a Non-Repressive Approach to Crime. Proceedings of the Second International Conference on Prison Abolition, Amsterdam, 1985* (Free University Press 1986) 25–40, 33.

16 Margaret Wilson, *The Crime of Punishment* (Jonathon Cape 1931) 39. See also David Nelken, 'Critical Criminal Law' (1987) 14 *Journal of Law and Society* 105.

17 E.P. Thompson, *Whigs and Hunters: The Origins of the Black Act* (Pantheon Books 1975) 205–206.

18 Ibid.

19 Anand A. Yang, 'The Agrarian Origins of Crime: A Study of Riots in Saran District, India, 1886–1920' (1979) 13(2) *Journal of Social History* 289.

20 Collin Summers, 'Criminology Through the Looking Glass' in Anthony Amatrudo and Regina Rauxloh (eds), *Law in Popular Belief: Myth and Reality* (Manchester University Press 2017) 15–29, 18.

21 Nils Christie, 'Conflicts as Property' (1977) 17(1) *British Journal of Criminology* 1.

22 Joan Smith and William Fried, *The Uses of American Prison* (Lexington Books 1974) 140. See also Lauren Gazzola, 'Political Captivity' in Lori Gruen (ed), *The Ethics of Captivity* (Oxford University Press 2014) 113–132.

under the criminal law?[23] Likewise, labour safety has historically been administered under civil procedures. As was the case in Victorian Britain, destructive activities of business appear even today less closely policed and less strictly criminalised than 'crimes of the working classes'.[24] The state continues to deploy its punitive power selectively. Similarly, the project of international criminal justice, revived at the end of the Cold War, focuses on individual responsibility for violence and atrocities. In the process, it abstracts individual actions from the broader context of social conflicts and overlooks other less visible forms of violence, such as inequality and poverty generated by 'the economic liberalisation policies' of the international financial institutions, namely the World Bank and the International Monetary Fund.[25]

There are some forms of conduct, traditionally criminalised in many parts of the world, which have successfully been challenged from a human rights perspective. For example, the Supreme Court of India, in a judgment delivered on 6 September 2018, decriminalised same-sex relationship.[26] In doing so, it followed into the footsteps of the ECtHR, the UN Human Rights Committee, besides constitutional courts in other jurisdictions, including Canada, South Africa, and the US. At issue was Section 377 of the Indian Penal Code – another relic of British colonialism – which laid down the penalty of life imprisonment or a sentence of up to ten years in prison for 'carnal intercourse against the order of nature'.[27] Although convictions were rare, the threat of criminal prosecution was used frequently to harass and exploit the members of the LGBTI (lesbian, gays, bi-sexual, transsexual, and inter-sex) community. Drawing a curtain on the past, the court held Section 377 to be repugnant to the right to equality, non-discrimination, freedom of expression, and dignity and privacy laid down in the Constitution of India, and corresponding provisions in international human rights instruments. The Strasbourg Court, which is known to have led the way in decriminalising gay sex,[28] has also held criminalisation of the unauthorised use of a place of worship by a religious group as a disproportionate measure incompatible with freedom of religion.[29] Promising as these judgments are, calls for decriminalisation within international human rights discourse are generally indexed to civil and political rights, reflecting the primacy of these rights and the ascendance of identity

23 See Dawn L Roth and David O Friedrichs, *Crimes of Globalization* (Routledge 2015).

24 David Garland, *Punishment and Welfare* (Gower Publishing 1985) 37. See also Barbara Hudson, 'Punishing the Poor: Dilemmas of Justice and Difference' in William C. Heffernan and John Kleinig (eds), *From Social Justice to Criminal Justice: Poverty and the Administration of the Criminal Law* (Oxford University Press 2000) 189–216.

25 Tor Krever, 'Ending Impunity? Eliding Political Economy in International Criminal Law?' in Ugo Mattei and Joh D. Haskell (eds), *Research Handbook on Political Economy and Law* (Edward Elgar 2015) 298–314, 308.

26 *Navtej Singh Johar v Union of India* (2018) W.P.(Crl.) No.76/16 etc, paras 158–204.

27 The Indian Penal Code 1860 (Act No. 45 of October 6, 1860).

28 *Dudgeon v UK* (App. 7525/76) 22 October 1981, Series A, No 45 (1982) 4 EHRR 149.

29 *Manoussakis and Others v Greece* (App 18748/91) ECHR [Grand Chamber] 26 September 1996.

politics since the 1970s. It will also become apparent in due course that 'human rights' also has an 'offensive role', where it serves to trigger and expand the application of the criminal law in certain areas.[30]

Nonetheless, human rights law sets some important limits on how the state may punish. It provides guidelines on the acceptable forms of punishment and the way punishment is imposed and executed through three key norms. These include the principle of legality, the prohibition of certain forms of punishment described variously as cruel and unusual or inhuman and degrading, and the principle of proportionality of punishment to crime.[31] The idea of punishment is typically framed in human rights and legal scholarship around these norms. Let us briefly examine each in turn.

Legality

The principle of legality is believed to have acquired the status of a customary norm in international law.[32] The underlying idea that no crime or punishment can exist without a legal ground is captured in the Latin phrases, *nullum crimen sine lege* (no crime without law) and *nulla poena sine lege* (no punishment without law). The norm was prefigured in Article 4 of the French Declaration of the Rights of Man and Citizen of 1789, which provided that 'the limits of liberty can only be determined by law'. In its modern formulation, legality translates into specific due process guarantees concerning precise definitions of penalties and the prohibition on retrospective punishment.[33] The principle represents a tremendous advance, for example, on the British colonial practices in Burma, where, as George Orwell put it in the most autobiographical of his novels, an officer could simply send an errant servant to the jail with a note saying, 'Please give the bearer fifteen lashes'.[34] E.P. Thompson, in the work quoted earlier, parted ways with the orthodox Marxist interpretation of legality and procedural justice merely as an instrument of class oppression.[35] To Thompson, the idea of 'the rule of law' was a cultural achievement of universal significance, 'an unqualified human good', in that it had some restraining effect on the ruling class.[36] But, as Thompson recognised, 'in a context of gross class inequalities, the equity of the law must always be in some part sham'.[37] In constraining the arbitrary exercise of penal power,

30 Francoise Tulkens and Michel Van de Kerchove, 'Criminal Law and Human Rights: A Paradoxical Relationship' in Sophie Bady-Gendrot and others (eds), *The Routledge Handbook of European Criminology* (Routledge 2014) 91–108, 94.
31 Dirk van Zyl Smit, 'Punishment and Human Rights' in Jonathan Simon and Richard Sparks (eds), *The Sage Handbook of Punishment and Society* (Sage 2013) 395–415, 395.
32 See Kenneth S. Gallant, *The Principle of Legality in International and Comparative Criminal Law* (Cambridge University Press 2009).
33 Smit, 'Punishment and Human Rights' (n 31) 395–415, 403.
34 George Orwell, *Burmese Days* (Penguin 2009) 27.
35 Thompson (n 17) 261.
36 Ibid 266.
37 Ibid.

the principle of legality embodies the protective role of human rights. However, it leaves the deeper issues of substantive equality and social justice untouched.

Prohibition of torture and cruel, inhuman, and degrading punishment

The prohibition forms part of the Third Common Article of the Geneva Conventions[38] and features, in varying formulations, in a number of international and regional human rights documents.[39] It has evolved as a human rights norm to restrict the state's power to punish in at least two ways. First, it forbids certain forms of punishment; second, it prescribes conditions for the implementation of punishment, which human rights principles do not 'outlaw summarily'.[40] International and domestic courts have interpreted the norm to hold corporal punishment as an inherently unacceptable form of punishment. In one of its earlier judgments, *Tryer v United Kingdom*, the ECtHR found corporal punishment involving birching of a boy on the Isle of Man to be degrading punishment within the meaning of Article 3 of the European Convention on Human Rights.[41] Taking its lead from *Tryer*, the Constitutional Court of South Africa similarly outlawed judicial corporal punishment as contradictory to Section 10 (right to dignity) and Section 11, sub-section 2 (prohibition of cruel, inhuman, or degrading treatment or punishment) of South Africa's interim constitution.[42] As regards the implementation of punishment, international human rights bodies, including the ECtHR,[43] and the Human Rights Committee (the body mandated to monitor the implementation of the International Covenant on Civil and Political Rights)[44] have found prison conditions to constitute inhuman or degrading treatment in large numbers of cases.

38 Common Article 3 applies to non-international armed conflicts, and outlaws cruel treatment and torture and humiliating and degrading treatment of non-combatants and 'those placed hors de combat by sickness, wounds, detention, or any other cause' (art 3, para 1).

39 Art 5, Universal Declaration of Human Rights (adopted by the General Assembly Resolution 217A (III) 10 December 1948) UN Doc A/810; art 7, International Covenant on Civil and Political Rights (adopted 16 December 1966, entered into force 23 March 1976) 999 UNTS 171; art 3, the European Convention on Fundamental Rights and Freedoms (adopted 1 November 1950, entered into force 3 September 1953) 213 UNTS 222; art 5, African Charter on Human and Peoples' Rights ('Banjul Charter') (adopted 27 June 1981, entered into force 21 October 1986) 1520 UNTS 217; art 5 (2), American Convention on Human Rights (adopted 21 November 1969, entered into force 18 July 1978) 1144 UNTS 143.

40 Smit, 'Punishment and Human Rights' (n 31) 395, 388–406. See also Dirk van Zyl Smit and Andrew Ashworth, 'Disproportionate Sentences as Human Rights Violations' (2004) 67 *Modern Law Review* 541.

41 *Tryer v United Kingdom* (App. 5856/72) 25 April 1978, Series A, No 26 (1979–80) 2 EHRR 1.

42 *S v Williams and Others* [1995] 3 SA 632.

43 Alastair Mowbray, *The Development of Positive Obligations Under the European Convention on Human Rights by the European Court of Human Rights* (Hart Publishing 2004) 48–59; William Schabas, *The European Convention on Human Rights: A Commentary* (Oxford University Press 2015) 173–174.

44 Sarah Joseph and Melissa Castan, *The International Covenant on Civil and Political Rights: Cases, Materials, and Commentary* (3rd edn, Oxford University Press 2013) 280–328.

The prohibition of corporal punishment as a form of cruel and inhuman punishment enjoys wide consensus within the international human rights regime. Paradoxically though, the same cannot be said of long prison terms or life imprisonment. As anthropologist Talal Asad has argued, the legal prohibition of torture and ill-treatment represents a historically and culturally contingent way of conceptualising human suffering.[45] International human rights law prohibits the imposition of life sentences 'without the possibility of release' for children but not adults.[46] The European Court missed another opportunity to declare life sentences as incompatible with the Article 3 prohibition of cruel and inhuman punishment in the case of *Khamtokhu v Russia* decided by the Grand Chamber on 24 January 2017.[47] Nonetheless, ECtHR's current position on the subject – that to comply with Article 3 a life sentence has to be reducible de facto and de jure – is ahead of the UN human rights regime, which remains ambiguous when it comes to imposing whole-life sentences on adults.[48] The prohibition of cruel and inhuman punishment has also been applied successfully to invalidate the death penalty in some jurisdictions, such as Hungary[49] and South Africa.[50] It has also been the normative linchpin of the global campaign to end capital punishment. The advances made in the abolition, and in limiting the scope of the death penalty globally, represent a great achievement of the modern human rights movement.[51] However, in some jurisdictions, courts have tolerated the death penalty as an acceptable limitation on the right to life, balancing the severity of that form of punishment with its retributive, deterrent, and preventive functions.

Proportionality of punishment to crime

Whilst stopping short of total abolition, the United States Supreme Court has held the death sentence for rape to be 'grossly disproportionate and excessive punishment' and hence forbidden by the Eighth Amendment prohibition of 'cruel and unusual punishment'.[52] It has also found the death sentence to be 'disproportionate' when imposed on the mentally impaired[53] and those who were

45 Talal Asad, 'On Torture, or Cruel, Inhuman and Degrading Treatment' in Richard A. Wilson (ed), *Human Rights, Culture & Context: Anthropological Perspectives* (Pluto Press 1997) 111–133.

46 Art 37 (a) Convention on the Rights of the Child (adopted 20 November 1989, entered into force 2 September 1990) 1577 UNTS 3.

47 *Khamtokhu and Aksenchik v Russia* (Apps. 60367/08 and 961/11) ECHR [Grand Chamber] 24 January 2017. See also Öcalan v. Turkey (application no. 46221/99) ECHR [Grand Chamber] 12 May 2005.

48 More will be said on this in Chapter 7.

49 Decision 23/1990 (X.31) AB, Constitutional Court of Hungary at p 4.

50 *S v Makwanyane* 1995 (3) SA 391 (1995) 16.

51 Roger Hood and Carolyn Hoyle, *Death Penalty: A Worldwide Perspective* (5th edn, Oxford University Press 2015) 16–17.

52 *Coker v Georgia* 433 US 584 (1977) 592.

53 *Atkins v Virginia* 536 US 304 (2002).

minors at the time of the crime.[54] However, the court has held a mandatory life sentence without parole imposed on adults for possession of drugs not disproportionate within the terms of the Eighth Amendment.[55] The proportionality principle in the sense of imposing limits on the mode of punishment is articulated most clearly in Article 49(3) of the European Charter of Fundamental Rights: 'The severity of penalties must not be disproportionate to the criminal offence'.[56] No equivalent provision is to be found in the European Convention or international human rights treaties. As will be shown in due course, the defensive dimension of proportionality is undercut by prevailing cultural and political attitudes towards punishment. Further, the principle is employed in international human rights law more frequently to legitimise tougher punishment rather than as a limiting principle. Human rights bodies and major NGOs, such as Amnesty International and Human Rights Watch, invoke the principle to censure lenient penalties for certain crimes, such as torture, political persecution, domestic violence, and harassment based on gender, ethnic identity, or sexual orientation. The roots of this phenomenon lie in both the engendering circumstances of the contemporary human rights discourse and the relationship between the doctrine of human rights and classical justifications of punishment.

Although there are some overlaps, 'proportionality of punishment to crime' – which is going to be our primary concern in this book – is not to be confused with the broader notion of 'proportionality' as a principle of constitutional and human rights law. Courts around the world routinely invoke the principle to determine whether an interference with a right is justified. Barring a small set of absolute rights (prohibition of torture and slavery, and the guarantee of a fair trial, for example), international human rights treaties recognise permissible limits on the exercise of rights. The ICCPR, for example, permits restrictions on the right to freedom of movement (Article 12) and the freedom of expression (Article 19) to 'protect national security, public order (ordre public), public health or morals or the rights and freedoms of others'. The European Convention too sets out limitations on rights contained in Articles 8–11. Similar restrictions are to be found in domestic Bills of Rights, either as provisos to specific substantive rights, or in the form of a general limitation clause as is the case with the Canadian Charter of Rights and Freedoms,[57] and the Constitution of South Africa.[58]

Whenever a government defends restrictions on fundamental rights, domestic courts and human rights bodies engage in a balancing exercise, often referred to as the 'proportionality test'. In the ECtHR jurisprudence, this takes the form of a three-stage assessment to determine whether there has been a violation of a convention right. At the outset, the court will inquire whether the impugned

54 *Roper v Simmons* 543 US 551 (2005).
55 *Harmelin v Michigan* 501 U.S. 957 (1991).
56 European Charter of Fundamental Rights, OJ 2010/ C 83/02.
57 Canadian Charter of Rights and Freedoms, Constitution Act 1982. s 1.
58 The Constitution of the Republic of South Africa 1996 (as adopted on 8 May 1996 and amended on 11 October 1996 by the Constitutional Assembly) s 33, ss 1 and 2.

measure is prescribed by law (the legality requirement). The second stage involves an assessment of whether the measure pursues a legitimate aim, including limits prescribed in the Convention and other goals, such as promotion of democracy and pluralism. It is rare for the court to find a problem at this stage as it tends to give the states a wide 'margin of appreciation'.[59] For example, in *Hirst v UK (No. 2)*, where the Grand Chamber found a blanket ban on prisoners' voting rights as contradictory to Article 1 of Protocol 1 to the Convention, it did not challenge the government's contention that the ban 'pursued the intertwined legitimate aims of preventing crime and punishing offenders and enhancing civic responsibility and respect for the rule of law'.[60] It is at the third stage that the Strasbourg court undertakes a balancing exercise, inquiring whether the impugned measure is 'necessary in a democratic society' and proportionate to the 'legitimate aim' pursued. Thus, in *Hirst*, the Grand Chamber found the automatic blanket ban on all convicted prisoners as a disproportionate measure that fell outside the margin of appreciation.[61] As is often the case with the application of proportionality, the court sidestepped some vexing questions in *Hirst*, for example, how disenfranchisement could contribute to civic responsibility or how it squared off with the long-standing principle of liberal penal law that offenders are sent to the prison as a punishment and not for punishment.[62] That proportionality assessment does not always lead to anti-majoritarian judgments is borne out by the court's subsequent case law on prisoners' voting rights. In 2012, the Grand Chamber held that Italy's legislation, imposing a voting ban on those convicted of specific offences against the state, and those serving sentences longer than five years, was not a disproportionate measure.[63]

Human rights and classical retributivism

'If you believe in universal human rights, you are probably not a utilitarian', according to Harvard philosopher Michael Sandel.[64] The underlying idea is that in according primacy to utility or maximisation of general welfare, utilitarianism fails to sufficiently recognise individual autonomy. Taken at face value, Sandel's assertion could lead one to doubt the commitment of domestic and international courts to human rights. For one, neither the Human Rights Committee nor the ECtHR has challenged states for structuring their sentencing regimes around

59 Pieter van Dijk and others, *Theory and Practice of the European Convention on Human Rights* (4th edn, Intersentia 2006) 339–340. See also Marie-Bénédicte Dembour, *Who Believes in Human Rights? Reflections on the European Convention* (Cambridge University Press 2006) 68–113.

60 *Hirst v United Kingdom* (No 2) (App. 74025/01) 6 October 2005 [Grand Chamber] (2006) 42 EHRR 849, ECHR 2005-IX, para 50.

61 Ibid para 82.

62 Stavros Tsakyrakis, 'Proportionality: An Assault on Human Rights?' (2009) 7(3) *International Journal of Constitutional Law* 466, 486.

63 *Scopola v Italy* (No. 3) (App 126/05) 22 May 2012 [Grand Chamber] 56 EHRR 19.

64 Michael Sandel, *Justice: What's the Right Thing to Do?* (Penguin 2009) 103.

a hybrid of goals, with utilitarian aims of deterrence and public protection featuring alongside retribution, or the idea of punishment as deserved harm for freely chosen individual actions rather than as a means to a social good. Some contemporary philosophers and constitutional theorists have taken issue with proportionality tests, or the balancing of human rights with competing interests, precisely on the grounds at which Sandel hints. To Gugliolmo Verirame, rights 'generally limitable through proportionality are a category error'.[65] Such rights, he argues, should either be downgraded to ordinary statutory rights, or ringfenced as absolute and well-defined constitutional or human rights instead of being subject to 'the Damocles' sword of proportionality'.[66]

Despite the pervasiveness of utilitarian reasoning in constitutional jurisprudence, the idea of human rights as categorical claims is deeply embedded within 'human rights orthodoxy'.[67] The intellectual roots of this perspective can be traced back to John Locke's defence of natural rights in his *Two Treatises of Government* and, more readily, to Immanuel Kant's anti-utilitarian deontological morality. Common to Locke (1632–1704) and Kant (1724–1804) is a commitment to the social contract tradition albeit with a fundamental disagreement with Thomas Hobbes' claim that people give up their natural rights when they leave the state of nature to enter civil society.[68] Both Locke and Kant posited a small set of rights conceived negatively as limits on the power of the state. To Locke, man's natural duty to self-preservation entailed the right to 'Lives, Liberties and Estate', which he combined under the category of 'Property'.[69] Locke's influence on the eighteenth-century Enlightenment texts, particularly in the opening words of the US Declaration of Independence of 1776 ('Life, Liberty and the pursuit of Happiness'), is well recognised within human rights scholarship.[70] What is less fully appreciated is how Lockean ideas legitimised appropriation of land and possessive individualism in liberal political theory.[71]

The great contribution of Kant to human rights thinking was that he secularised natural rights, replacing the divine plan of natural-law theory with the

65 Gugliolmo Verirame, 'Rescuing Human Rights from Proportionality' in Rowan Cruft, S Matthew Liao and Massimo Renzo (eds), *Philosophical Foundations of Human Rights* (Oxford University Press 2015) 341–357, 353–354.

66 Ibid 356. An interesting debate on the topic can be found in the International Journal of Constitutional Law. See Tsakyrakis (n 62); Madhav Khosla, 'Proportionality: An Assault on Human Rights? A Reply (2010) 8(2) *International Journal of Constitutional Law* 298; Stavros Tsakyrakis, 'Proportionality: An Assault on Human Rights? A Rejoinder to Madhav Khosla' (2010) 8(2) *International Journal of Constitutional Law* 307; Matthias Klatt and Moritz Meister, 'Proportionality – A Benefit to Human Rights? Remarks on the I.CON Controversy' (2012) 10(3) *International Journal of Constitutional Law* 689.

67 Dembour (n 59) 87.

68 Nickel James W. 'Are Human Rights Utopian?' (1982) 2(3) *Philosophy and Public Affairs* 246, 253–254.

69 Cited in C.B Machpherson, 'Natural Rights in Hobbes and Locke' in Machpherson (ed), *Political Theory and the Rights of Man* (Palgrave Macmillan 1967) 198.

70 See, for example, Ed Bates 'History' in Moeckli, Shah, and Sivakumaran (n 14) 15–33, 18.

71 Machpherson (n 69) 197–262.

faculty of reason. Whilst the idea of natural or inalienable rights still has rhetorical currency within human rights discourse, it is on Kant's giant shoulders that 'the modern theory of human rights largely rests'.[72] To steer clear of trade-offs involved in utilitarian reasoning, most contemporary theories of human rights fall back on Kant's duty-based or deontological justifications of morality.[73] Robert Nozick, a leading figure in modern liberal theory (about whom we shall have more to say in Chapter 3), explicitly drew on Kantian philosophy in describing rights as 'side constraints' or limits on consequentialist pursuits, including general welfare.[74] To Ronald Dworkin, rights were best 'understood as trumps' over political decisions purporting to advance collective goals.[75]

Central to Kantian morality is the concept of the categorical imperative, which, in one of its formulations requires that individuals ought never to be used as merely a means to an end. In Kant's own words, 'Act in such a way that you treat humanity, whether in your own person or in the person of another, always at the same time as an end and never simply as a means'.[76] This formulation is bound up with the Kantian notion of autonomy. It is an individual's capacity to reason or his freedom as a moral agent which warrants respecting him as an end in himself. Positing 'freedom' as the first of the three 'pure rational principles of external human right' a state is bound to honour, Kant roundly denounced the idea of a '*paternal government*', which seeks to impose some conception of welfare or happiness on the subjects.[77] Everyone, he argues, ought to be free to seek happiness in 'his own way . . . so long as he does not infringe upon the freedom of others'.[78] The second right in Kant's scheme is that of '*equality before the law*', which, in line with the Enlightenment spirit, struck at the heart of legal privileges enjoyed by the nobility. However, Kant had no problem accepting wider social and economic inequalities as being compatible with formal-legal equality.[79] The third principle right, on Kant's account, is that of 'independence' of citizens to participate in political affairs as 'co-legislator[s]'. Hobbled

72 Michael Rosen, *Dignity: Its History and Meaning* (Harvard University Press 2012) 19. See also Jack Mahoney, *The Challenge of Human Rights: Origin, Development and Significance* (Blackwell Publishing 2007) 33–36. Jerome J. Shestack, 'The Philosophic Foundations of Human Rights' (1998) 20 *Human Rights Quarterly* 201, 216.

73 See, for example, Jeremy Waldron, *Liberal Rights: Collected Papers 1981–1991* (Cambridge University Press 1993) 209; Andrew Ashworth and Mike Redmayne, *The Criminal Process* (4th edn, Oxford University Press 2010) 46–47.

74 Robert Nozick, *Anarchy, State and Utopia* (Basic Books Inc. 1974) 30.

75 Ronald Dworkin, 'Rights as Trumps' in Jeremy Waldron (ed), *Theories of Rights* (Oxford University Press 1984) 153–167, 153.

76 Immanuel Kant, *The Metaphysical Elements of Justice: Part I of the Metaphysics of Morals* (John Ladd tr, Bobbs-Merril Co. Inc. 1965) 102.

77 Immanuel Kant, 'On the Common Saying: "This May be True in Theory but it Does Not Apply in Practice"' in Hans Reiss (ed), *Kant: Political Writings Political Writings* (H.B. Nisbet tr, Cambridge University Press 1991) 61–92, 74.

78 Ibid.

79 Ibid 75–76.

once again by the political context he was writing in, Kant restricted this right to propertied men.[80]

Kant's theory is both a priori in the sense of transcending any practical experience and non-instrumental in so far as it requires that a moral principle be derived from its generalisability from the standpoint of an autonomous individual and not with reference to potential outcomes.[81] Attractive as it may seem, positing autonomy as the primary justification for human rights is not without problems. It is precisely this autonomy-based conception that has historically been pressed into service to deny rights to children, the mentally disabled, those suffering from dementia, and others deemed lacking in the capacity to reason.[82] To some, the very idea of autonomy is fraught with difficulties. The philosopher Simon Blackburn, for example, has observed that so much of our 'desires, choices and actions are all partly caused by factors outside our control [that] true autonomy can easily seem to be a myth'.[83] Privileging autonomy over other values also mirrors at the individual level what was once the colonial theory of progress. The native was categorised as childish and hence lacking in maturity, and in need of paternal tutelage by the colonial masters. The denial of rights in the colonies was premised on the assumption that the native lacked the autonomy the white man possessed.[84] A similar racially oriented hostility underpinned 'the Nazi execution of the mentally retarded and mentally ill'.[85]

Challenges to autonomy-based theories of human rights, however, need not collapse into post-modernist nihilism where the quest for moral foundations is itself sometimes dismissed as unfeasible.[86] One could, for example, draw on Bryan Turner's illuminating account of human rights as 'juridical expressions of social solidarity, whose foundations rest in the common experience of vulnerability and precariousness'.[87] On this theory – somewhat reminiscent of Kierkegaard's assertion that 'fear and annihilation live next door to every man' – human beings are 'ontologically vulnerable and insecure, and their natural environment

80 Ibid 77.

81 See Immanuel Kant, *Foundations of the Metaphysics of Morals* (Lewis White Beck tr, Bobbs-Merrill Co. Inc., New York 1959) 62–63.

82 Massino Renzo, 'Human Needs, Human Rights' in Cruft, Liao and Renzo (n 65) 570–587.

83 Simon Blackburn, *The Oxford Dictionary of Philosophy* (Oxford University Press 2005) 30. See also Kent Greenfield, *The Myth of Choice: Personal Responsibility in a World of Limits* (Biteback Publishing 2011).

84 Bhikhu Parekh, 'Finding a Proper Place for Human Rights' in Kate E. Tunstall (ed), *Displacement, Asylum, Migration: The Oxford Amnesty Lectures 2004* (Oxford University Press 2006) 17–43, 22.

85 Jeffrie G. Murphy, *Punishment and the Moral Emotions: Essays in Law, Morality and Religion* (Oxford University Press 2012) 260.

86 See, for example, Richard Rorty, 'Human Rights, Rationality and Sentimentality' in Stephen Shute and Susan Hurley (eds), *On Human Rights: The Oxford Amnesty Lectures, 1993* (Basic Books, New York 1993) 111–134. cf. John Tasioulas, 'On the Foundations of Human Rights' in Cruft, Liao and Renzo (n 65) 45–70.

87 Bryan S. Turner, *Vulnerability and Human Rights* (Pennsylvania State University Press 2006) 26.

doubtful'.[88] The human insecurity requires a strong state to protect us. Paradoxically, strong states can also be a source of abuse and exploitation.[89] It is our natural and institutional vulnerability, and precariousness inherent in being human, that provides justification for human rights. Conor Gearty speaks to the same point in the context of 'English exceptionalism over Europe' when he posits that the basic 'human rights insight is that none of us has a guaranteed space among the fortunate, that the border between affluence and misfortune is more porous than we assume'.[90]

One of the biggest paradoxes in Kant's moral philosophy gets manifested in his views on punishment. His unflinching defence of a particularly strong version of retributivism makes for a sharp contrast with the emancipatory possibilities of his notion of human dignity. Entwined with the categorical imperative, punishment on Kantian theory is based on an inherent duty to punish a wrongdoer regardless of any other good or potential consequences. In Kant, we find a modern articulation of *lex talionis*, the principle of an eye for an eye, a tooth for a tooth. In *The Metaphysical Elements of Justice*, Kant makes it clear that it is 'only the Law of retribution' that can determine appropriate penalties for specific crimes.[91] The following quotation by Louis B. John from an article on the protection of individual rights in international law, reproduced uncritically in a major textbook,[92] provides an illustration of the attraction of *lex talionis* for some contemporary human rights advocates:

> The oldest method of protecting the rights of individuals was self-help, not only by the victim, but also by his family, his clan, his nation, and ultimately his sovereign or state. The Bible documents numerous applications of the old adage 'an eye for an eye, a tooth for a tooth,' or, more often, a life for a life.[93]

It has been argued that the *lex talionis* of the Old Testament is not meant to be taken literally. According to Morris Fish, the Mosaic code departed significantly from the Code of Hammurabi by ruling out the punishment of an innocent person for the culpable actions of another.[94] The *lex talionis* in the Rabbinic and Christian tradition, Fish argues, operated as a restraint on excessive retaliation

88 Cited in Linda Sanford, *Strong at the Broken Places: Overcoming the Trauma of Childhood Abuse* (Virago Press 1991) 15.

89 See Edward Royce, *Classical Social Theory and Modern Society: Marx, Durkheim, Weber* (Rowman & Littlefield 2015) 167–201.

90 Conor Gearty, *On Fantasy Island: Britain, Europe, and Human Rights* (Oxford University Press 2016) 7.

91 Kant, 'The Metaphysical Elements of Justice' (n 76) 101.

92 Dinah Shelton, *Regional Protection of Human Rights* (Oxford University Press 2008) 1.

93 Louis B. John, 'The New International Law: Protection of the Rights of Individuals Rather than States' (1982) 32 *American University Law Review* 1.

94 Morris J. Fish, 'An Eye for an Eye: Proportionality as a Moral Principle of Punishment' (2008) 28(1) *Oxford Journal of Legal* Studies 57, 59.

rather than a justification of cruelty. However, Kant's writings on the subject drive one to take a less charitable view of the principle. As he put it in a famous passage laying out an absolute injunction to punish every murderer with death:

> Even if a civil society were to dissolve itself by common agreement of all its members (for example, if the people inhabiting an island decided to separate and disperse themselves around the world), the last murderer remaining in prison must first be executed, so that everyone will dully receive what his actions are worth and so that the bloodguilt thereof will not be fixed on the people because they failed to insist on carrying out the punishment; for if they fail to do so, they may be regarded as accomplices in this public violation.[95]

Here, Kant is taking the categorical imperative to its logical end by arguing that in failing to execute the last murderer the society would be remiss in treating her as an end in herself. That the execution would be of no use to a society about to dissolve itself is irrelevant.[96] Punishment is purely retrospective. Reference to any instrumental value or societal good is unacceptable on Kantian ethics. Kant also provided intellectual foundations for the contemporary anti-impunity movement by insisting that 'the sovereign should on no account exercise [the right of pardon]', except when he himself 'has been done an injury'.[97] Mitigating or remitting the criminal's punishment would otherwise, in Kant's view, amount to a great injustice.

It is obvious that Kantian theory is a double-edged sword. On the one hand, it rules out punishing the innocent for the sake of preventing future crimes or punishing the guilty excessively for that purpose. On the other hand, it also undermines the potentially liberating, or at least less-repressive, idea of rehabilitating offenders. It is not hard to imagine the situations where elevating punishment to the level of an absolute duty could generate more complex moral problems than it solves. Would it be morally acceptable for a state, for example, to divert resources on punishing criminals when the same resources could be spent on providing food to people dying of starvation?[98] The Kantian theory of punishment is 'built on tension', as Jeffrie Murphy has reminded us, contrasting the respect for human dignity with 'smugness and self-righteousness' associated with Kant's conviction that punishment is an absolute moral obligation.[99] To Nietzsche, who saw retributive justice as masking revenge or a vicarious desire to inflict suffering,

95 Kant, 'The Metaphysical Elements of Justice' (n 76) 140.

96 Barbara A. Hudson, *Understanding Justice: An Introduction to Ideas, Perspectives and Controversies in Modern Penal Theory* (Open University Press 1996) 51.

97 Kant, 'The Metaphysics of Morals' in Reiss (n 77) 131–175, 160.

98 Nicola Lacey, *State Punishment: Political Principles and Community Values* (Routledge 1988) 15.

99 Jeffrie G. *Murphy, Retribution, Justice and Therapy* (D. Reidel Publishing Company 1979) 90.

the categorical imperative gave off 'a whiff of cruelty'.[100] Elsewhere, he famously counselled: 'Whoever fights with monsters should take care that in the process he does not become a monster'.[101]

To be fair, the idea of punishment fitting the crime on a literal interpretation of *lex talionis* can be a source of considerable discomfort to contemporary liberal philosophers and human rights advocates. A strict application of the principle would make room for punishments too absurd and gruesome for modern sensibilities. As Hugo Bedau asks in his critique of the retributivist model of punishment: 'Should we punish a rapist by raping him? His wife or daughter?'[102] To avoid such potentially unpalatable implications of *lex talionis*, modern retributivists have argued that torture as punishment ought to be avoided due to 'desert-independent moral demands of humanity'.[103] Frequently, these demands are articulated in the language of human rights. In an illuminating discussion of what he calls 'humanitarian limits' on punishment, Nigel Walker (a noted critic of retributivism) correctly suggests that the language of rights allows 'humanitarians' to claim that 'some forms or degrees of severity' of punishment are so 'cruel, inhuman or degrading' that no one ought to be subjected to them regardless of the dictates of desert or utility for that matter.[104] However, there are limits to this norm, which the orthodox scholarship has little to say about. For instance, as suggested earlier, it is not clear why corporal punishment falls foul of the prohibition of cruel and inhuman punishment, whereas long prison sentences remain acceptable. Equally problematic is the assumption underlying retributivism, both in its classical version and contemporary accounts, that proportionate sentences would entail equal effects on differently situated individuals. In reality, a term of prison – even when it can be demonstrated to be proportionate to the seriousness of an offence – will lead to qualitatively dissimilar experiences of suffering for individuals guilty of the same offence depending on their familial background, psychological makeup, and social circumstances. These and other conundrums, which we will explore in Chapter 3, underlie modern retributivism, such as the censure-based desert theory offered by Andrew von Hirsch and Andrew Ashworth, even as they renounce the 'talionic version of retributivism'.[105]

Its intuitive appeal notwithstanding, the idea that we need to get even with the criminals is not above questioning. Nor is it tenable to equate justice with punishment. In Plato's *Republic*, narrated in the form of a dialogue between Socrates

100 Friedrich Nietzsche, *On the Genealogy of Morals* (Douglas Smith tr, Oxford University Press 1996) 47.

101 Friedrich Nietzsche, *Beyond Good and Evil* (Walter Kaufman tr, Vintage 1989) 89. See also, Friedrich Nietzsche, *Thus Spoke Zarathustra* (R. J. Hollingdale tr, Penguin 1961) 128.

102 Hugo Adam Bedau, 'Retribution and the Theory of Punishment' 1978 LXXV(11) *Journal of Philosophy* 601, 611.

103 Ibid 613.

104 Nigel Walker, *Why Punish? Theories of Punishment Reassessed* (Oxford University Press 1991) 133.

105 Andrew von Hirsch and Andrew Ashworth, *Proportionate Sentencing: Exploring the Principles* (Oxford University Press 2005) 76.

and Polemarchus, we are told that the equation of justice with punishment or the infliction of harm even on 'one's enemy if he is evil' is plainly self contradictory.[106] What is easier to endorse is the descriptive assertion that most of us feel moral outrage when confronted with some kinds of harmful behaviour. Such outrage in the face of cruelty and violence is completely understandable. Very often, it signifies self-respect or empathy for the victims. Conversely, a willingness to forgive too easily may manifest a lack of self-respect and disregard for one's own worth or that of others harmed by wrongful actions. In a disordered world that we inhabit, feelings of anger and resentment are also necessary for self-protection.[107] However, as we learn from Nietzsche, retributive judgments could just as well be motivated by 'hatred, envy, resentment, rancour . . . revenge'.[108] Nevertheless, the crucial point is that having retributive feelings – no matter how justified – is one thing, acting on those feelings and shaping state institutions around those feelings is quite another.[109]

It is important at this stage to take on board another classical version of retributivism, which also resonates in modern penal theory.[110] Whereas Kant defended punishment in terms of the dictates of moral obligations, his compatriot, Hegel (1770–1831), formulated his account of retributivism around the concept of rights whilst retaining the centrality of autonomy to moral philosophy. Despite some apparent differences, Hegel's philosophy was, to quote Bertrand Russell, 'the culmination of the movement in German idealism that started from Kant'.[111] In *Elements of the Philosophy of Right*, Hegel proceeded to provide justifications for retributive punishment by first differentiating crime from civil wrongs and deception (fraud), two other forms of wrongdoing on his account.[112] Crime, as distinct from the other two categories, is a coercive act by a free and rational agent representing a three-fold negation. Not only does a crime violate the rights of the victim, argued Hegel, but also of the criminal himself. Further, in committing the crime, the criminal, as a free and rational agent, violates the very concept of rights itself.[113] Hegel specifically took issue with Cesare Beccaria's opposition to capital punishment on the 'grounds that it could not be presumed that the social contract included the consent of individuals to allow themselves to be killed'. Hegel's position is that the state is required to enforce the rationality underpinning 'the individual's volition'.[114] It is through punishment that the state honours the criminal as a rational being. The justification for punishment is

106 Plato, *The Republic* (Desmond Lee tr, 2nd edn, Penguin 2003) 8–15.
107 Geoffrey Scarre, *After Evil: Responding to Wrongdoing* (Ashgate 2004) 17–18.
108 Nietzsche, 'Beyond Good and Evil' (n 101) 54.
109 Walker (n 104) 139.
110 See Herbert Morris, 'Persons and Punishment' (1968) 52 *Monist* 475.
111 Bertrand Russell, *History of Western Philosophy* (Routledge 2004) 650.
112 GWF Hegel, *Elements of the Philosophy of Right* (H.B. Nisbet tr, Cambridge University Press 1991) 116.
113 Ibid 124–127.
114 Ibid 126–127.

to be derived from the criminal's own act, and not 'with a view to deterring or reforming him'.[115]

To address the rather counter-intuitive nature of the argument that the criminal violates his own rights in committing the crime, Jane Johnson has pointed out that what is at stake here is the whole 'recognitive' basis of society. By refusing to acknowledge the rights of the victim, the criminal disrupts the 'recognitive relations' that determine him as a rights-bearing subject. In committing the crime then, Johnson interprets Hegel to be arguing, the criminal wills punishment as her right by negating the reciprocal nature of rights in society. It is through retribution that the law 'restores and thereby actualizes itself as valid through the cancellation of crime'.[116] As critics have pointed out, the notion of annulment of crime is not convincing. To quote D.J.B. Hawkins:

> If you could bring the murdered person back to life by executing the murderer, you could truly be said to negate the evil act, and if you can reform the criminal, you can truly be said to negate his evil will. But how the infliction of a punishment which neither reverses the evil act nor necessarily reforms the evil will, can be said to negate the wrong done is surely beyond . . . comprehension.[117]

Jane Johnson steps in to rescue Hegel by suggesting that the annulment of crime by punishment is not referring to 'the actual existence of the criminal act but rather annulling the broader implications and meaning of crime for the victim, criminal and (the concept of right)'.[118] If the violation of a right is allowed to stand, she goes on to observe, 'then rights are not real – they have no purchase or meaning'.[119] However, the idea that punishment somehow re-establishes or rehabilitates rights begs the question: Why could restitution combined with efforts at rehabilitating the criminal not do the same job? Nor is punishment necessarily the appropriate means of treating the criminal as a rational agent who has 'chosen' to commit a criminal act. Would it not be more in keeping with the concern for the moral agency of the offenders that the state gave them a chance to make amends for the harm done?[120] Further, it is not obvious why the recognition of the victim's rights must always be expressed in the form of punishing the criminal. This justification of punishment on Hegelian theory is predicated on a specific model

115 Hegel (n 112) 127.

116 Jane Johnson, 'Hegel on Punishment: A More Sophisticated Retributivism' in Mark D. White (ed), *Retributivism: Essays on Theory and Policy* (Oxford University Press 2011) 146–168. See also Hegel (n 112) 127–130.

117 DJB Hawkins, 'Retribution' in Stanley E Grupp (ed), *Theories of Punishment* (Indiana University Press 1972) 13–18, 16.

118 Johnson (n 116) 154.

119 Ibid.

120 Vincenzo Ruggiero, *Penal Abolitionism* (Oxford University Press 2010) 63; Allegra M. McLeod, 'Prison Abolition and Grounded Justice' (2015) 62 *UCLA Law Review* 1156, 1237.

of victims' behaviour and implicitly rejects wider possibilities of human understanding and human sympathy. In a sense, the insistence on punishment as the sole response to crime can be seen as imposing limits on the victims' rights. As Roger Pilon puts it, 'The criminal act, no less than the tort act, creates a right in the victim, though a much more extensive right than is the case with torts'.[121] To have rights, he correctly points out, is to have options: 'We may choose to exercise our rights or we may choose not to'.[122] The Hegelian model of retributive justice deprives the victim of the choice to opt for forgiveness or restitution should they so desire.

Another aspect of Hegel's theory of punishment which has received little attention in literature is the full implication of this notion of 'recognition of rights'. Surely, just as the criminal negates rights on multiple fronts by committing a criminal act, so does the state by violating certain rights, which potentially leads an individual into committing a crime in the first place. The recognitive and reciprocal basis of rights, it can be argued, falls apart where the state fails to provide basic rights to subsistence and physical security to all. But this view requires a more expansive understanding of rights than the concept of traditional liberties and political rights presumed by classical liberal thinkers, including Kant and Hegel.

Punishment in the utilitarian tradition: Beccaria and Bentham

Kant and Hegel with their robust retributivism represent one strand of classical liberal theory as it impinges on criminal punishment. The eighteenth century, after all, not only gave us Kant and Hegel, and their 'relentless retributive theory', it also produced Cesare Beccaria (1738–1794), 'whose thought, though influenced by utilitarianism, shows no tendency to minimize the dignity and majesty of the law'.[123] Beccaria's *Dei delitti et delle pene* (*On Crimes and Punishment*), published in 1764, was, to quote Leon Radzinowicz, 'the manifesto of the liberal approach to criminal law, its rallying cry and its plan of campaign'.[124] The treatise is also regarded widely as the founding text of classical criminology. This perception has been challenged by David Garland on the grounds that Beccaria's work 'is essentially the application of legal jurisprudence to . . . crime and punishment' and is not informed by the 'human sciences of the nineteenth century', which would form the basis of the 'criminological enterprise' as we know

121 Roger Pilon, 'Criminal Remedies: Restitution, Punishment, or Both?' (1978) 88(4) *Ethics* 348, 356.
122 Ibid.
123 WC De Pauley, 'Beccaria and Punishment' (1925) 35(4) *International Journal of Ethics* 404, 406.
124 Leon Radzinowicz, *Ideology and Crime: A Study of Crime in Social and Historical Context* (Heinemann Educational Books 1966) 9.

it today.[125] Garland, however, has no problem granting that Beccaria (and Jeremy Bentham) are 'a part of criminology's genealogy' as they left a mark on some of the subject's central aims and characteristics.[126]

Beccaria shared with Kant a deep admiration of Enlightenment thinkers, particularly Montesquieu. But unlike Kant, he had little time for metaphysical speculations. A product of his times, Beccaria's thought is infused with a commitment to social contract and a belief in science and progress. Also underlying his critique of prevalent legal and penal practices are concerns about the arbitrary use of judicial power, uncertainty in law, its inequitable application based on individual status, and excessive penalties. Beccaria's treatise, *On Crimes and Punishment*, is set largely within utilitarian ethics.[127] The purpose of punishment, Beccaria stated in no uncertain terms, 'is not to inflict torment and pain on a sentient being, nor to undo the crime that has already been committed'.[128] 'Punishments, and the method of inflicting them', he argued, 'must be chosen according to the amount needed to make an impression more useful and more lasting on the minds of men, and less to torment the body of the offender'.[129] The justification for punishment, then, is not based on desert or annulment of a wrong. Invoking Montesquieu, Beccaria ruled out as unjustified 'every punishment that does not derive from absolute necessity'.[130] That necessity is determined by the dual goal of prevention and deterrence. The key to prevention – a far more desirable aim than punishment, on Beccaria's account – was to have laws that were clear and simple, with the strength of the nation 'focused on defending them'.[131] As regards deterrence, Beccaria's formula appealed more to the certainty of a well-moderated punishment rather than severe punishment that is accompanied by the hope of impunity.

A belief in the certainty of punishment as a deterrent also underpinned Beccaria's disapproval of the concept of executive pardon. As he put it, 'Let the laws . . . be unrelenting in particular case but let the legislator be milder, charitable, and humane'.[132] In the chapter, 'The Proportion between Crime and Punishment', Beccaria remarked, 'Not only is it in the common interest that crimes are not committed, but when they are, the evil brought on society should be the

125 Garland, 'Punishment and Welfare' (n 24) 14–15. See also Lawrence W. Sherman, 'The Use and Usefulness of Criminology, 1751–2005: Enlightened Justice and Its Failures' (2005) 600 *Annals of the American Academy of Political and Social Science* 115, 120.

126 David Garland, 'Of Crimes and Criminals: The Development of Criminology in Britain' in Mike Maguire and Rod Morgan (eds), *Oxford Handbook of Criminology* (3rd edn, Oxford University Press 2002) 7–50, 19.

127 There is at least one point in his account, however, where he arguably incorporated a retributive justification of punishment into his utilitarian model, as will be discussed shortly.

128 Cesare Beccaria, *On Crimes and Punishment* (G.R. Newman and P. Marongiu tr, 5th edn, Transaction Publishers 2009) 33.

129 Ibid.

130 Ibid 11.

131 Ibid 107.

132 Ibid 119.

least possible'. This assertion provides little guidance on the actual quantum and the mode of punishment. Beccaria attempted to address the problem by suggesting that punishment must 'correspond both to the amount of harm done to society, and the degree of temptation faced by the offender'.[133] The reference to the amount of harm done could plausibly be read as importing retributive logic into what is broadly a utilitarian account. However, as James Q. Whitman has reasoned, Beccaria was probably more concerned about the arbitrary power exercised by judges in a highly stratified society whereby they could vary the penalty for a particular crime based on the social status of the offender rather than the gravity of the offence.[134] The argument makes sense when read together with Beccaria's vigorous attack on judicial discretion elsewhere in the treatise and his insistence that nothing be left to the whims of judges. Utilitarian reasoning dominates Beccaria's attempts to sketch a proportionality principle of sorts hedged in by a strong injunction against exemplary punishments. 'Punishment', he noted, 'obtains sufficient effect when its severity just exceeds the benefit the offender receives from the crime . . . any additional punishment is superfluous and therefore a tyranny'.[135]

Beccaria was modest enough to recognise that it was impossible to construct a scale of punishments corresponding to 'the infinite and hardly observable complexities of human action'.[136] Thus, his suggestion was that 'it would be sufficient for a wise legislator to identify the principle points of corresponding punishments from the highest to the lowest'.[137] The notion of graded penalties on Beccaria's account, to be fleshed out later by the leading light of utilitarianism, Jeremy Bentham, is meant largely to avoid giving out perverse incentives to criminals. If penalties for minor offences were as harsh as major ones, then the potential offenders might as well commit more serious crimes.[138]

The validity of this principle, however, rests on the assumption that the subjects of law are rational, calculating agents, carefully weighing costs and benefits before committing a crime. That may be true for some potential offenders and in relation to certain crimes, but for many offenders, such as those born into street crime, acting in conformity with the demands of the sub-culture could be a bigger constraint on the choices they make, compared to avoidance of 'pain' associated with punishment.[139] The case is particularly weak as far as individual deterrence goes considering high recidivism rates in many countries. In England and Wales, for example, 46 per cent of adults are reconvicted within one year of release.[140]

133 Ibid 19.
134 James Q. Whitman, *Harsh Justice: Criminal Punishment and the Widening Divide Between America and Europe* (Oxford University Press 2003) 49.
135 Beccaria, (n 128) 69.
136 Ibid 20.
137 Ibid.
138 Jeremy Bentham, *An Introduction to the Principles of Morals and Legislation* (Oxford University Press 1996) 165.
139 Donald Black, *The Behavior of Law* (Academic Press 1976) 79.
140 Prison Reform Trust, Prison, *The Facts: Bromley Briefings* (Summer 2014).

Further, imprisonment as the predominant mode of criminal punishment in the modern world has a self-fulfilling aspect in that it has historically helped create 'a class of hardened criminals' instead of deterring them from future crimes.[141] Thus, there is considerable force in the argument that deterrence does not work for those who actually need it. And the ones it 'works' for do not need it in the first place – avoidance of crime on their part being related to factors other than the fear of punishment, such as adherence to dominant social norms and expectations.[142] The idea of deterrence as a punishment rationale passed over uncritically in human rights scholarship is therefore difficult to sustain on utilitarian grounds, let alone normative concerns about individuals being used as a means to an end.[143]

Be that as it may, contrary to general anxieties about utilitarian theory on the grounds that it might approve of punishing the innocent or punishing the guilty excessively, Beccaria's thought compares favourably against Kantian theory. The latter, as we have seen, was unconcerned about the severity or harshness of punishment if it accorded with the law of retribution.[144] Beccaria, and later Bentham, both stood against severity of punishment in excess to what was necessary for utilitarian purposes. Some philosophers have shown subsequently that it is plausible to build a case against punishing the innocent within the bounds of utilitarianism. Since the practice of imposing exemplary penalties is likely to evoke feelings of revulsion in most people and generate a general climate of fear, the practice would be untenable on the over-arching utilitarian goal of happiness for the greatest numbers.[145] Further, it may be argued that just as some retributivists circumscribe the demands of retributivism within the desert-independent prohibition of cruel and inhuman punishment, so can a utilitarian appeal to non-utilitarian values as a defence against gruesome punishment.

The immediate and long-term influence of Beccaria's thought in purging penal codes across Europe of a range of draconian aspects – uncertainty of laws, arbitrary exercise of power, excessive and severe penalties – is well documented.[146] The imprint of his thought, alongside that of other Enlightenment thinkers, can be noticed in in the French Declaration of the Rights of Man (1789).[147] It is

141 Patricia O'Brien, 'Crime and Punishment as Historical Problem' (1978) 11(4) *Journal of Social History* 508, 509.

142 See McLeod (n 120).

143 Thomas Mathiessen, *Prison on Trial* (Sage, London 1990) 48–78.

144 Walker (n 104) 53.

145 William Lyons, 'Deterrent Theory and Punishment of the Innocent' (1974) 4(4) *Ethics* 346–348.

146 See for example, Radzinowicz (n 124) 9, 14–28; Elio Monachesi, 'Cesare Beccaria' in Hermann Mannheim (ed), *Pioneers in Criminology* (Stevens & Sons Ltd. 1960) 36–49.

147 See, in particular, Art 5 of the French Declaration of the Rights of Man, which provides that 'the law can only prohibit such actions as are hurtful to society'; Art 6, guaranteeing equal penalties for all without social distinctions; Art 7, embodying the principle of legality; and Art 8, requiring that 'the law shall provide such punishments only as are strictly and obviously necessary'.

misleading, however, to classify Beccaria's thought as entirely progressive. His general insistence on the mildness of punishment and his repudiation of judicial torture[148] sit uneasily with an endorsement of corporal punishment for crimes 'committed against the person' as distinct from those against property, for which he favoured imprisonment.[149] Likewise, Beccaria's famous rejection of the death penalty is accompanied by a preference for the punishment of slavery, which he thought a superior deterrent than capital punishment for the most serious offences.[150] The move is somewhat similar to the tendency among some contemporary abolitionists of proposing life without parole as an alternative to the death penalty. Finally, as already suggested, Beccaria's commitment to social contract and a belief in the socially abstracted, rational individual prevented him from fully recognising the relevance of social conditions to criminality and criminal responsibility.[151] As was the case with Kant and Hegel, Beccaria operated with what sociologist Norbert Elias dubbed the long-standing notion of *homo philosophicus* in European thought, i.e. the idea of the individual as a 'closed personality' who is inwardly quite self-sufficient and separate from all other people.[152] The emphasis on the 'moral self-responsibility of the individual' can plausibly be interpreted as having echoes of the Judeo-Christian belief in individual soul.[153] The *homo philosophicus* of classical epistemology and moral theory lives on in secular ideals of modern liberalism, including the discourse of human rights.

In Jeremy Bentham (1748–1832), who called Beccaria the 'first evangelist of reason', we find a more full-blown and unflustered application of the utilitarian philosophy to the idea of punishment. Much as he admired Beccaria, Bentham with his commitment to legal positivism, took issue with his predecessor for invoking natural rights, liberty, or property in abstract.[154] As long as these concepts lacked a foundation in positive law, and could not be shown to contribute to utility, they were to be avoided altogether. Bentham parted company with the *philosophes* with his famous rebuke of natural rights. Rights, he had little hesitation in declaring, 'were the child of law; from real law come real rights; but from imaginary laws, from law of nature, come imaginary rights. . . . Natural rights is simple nonsense; natural and imprescriptible rights, rhetorical nonsense, nonsense upon stilts'.[155]

Modern notions of deterrence, both individual and general, can be traced back to Bentham. As regards the former, he approved of instilling fear of punishment

148 Beccaria (n 128) 41–42.
149 Ibid 53.
150 Ibid 69–70.
151 Radzinowicz (n 124) 12; Stephen Jones, *Criminology* (3rd edn, Oxford University Press 2006) 111.
152 Norbert Elias, *The Civilizing Process* (6th edn, Blackwell 2000) 470.
153 Richard Tarnas, *The Passion of the Western Mind: Understanding the Ideas That Have Shaped Our World View* (Pimlico 1991) 321.
154 Jeremy Bentham, *The Theory of Legislation* (Forgotten Books 2012) 67.
155 Jeremy Bentham, 'Anarchical Fallacies' in John Bowring (ed), *The Works of Jeremy Bentham*, vol. 2 (W. Tait 1843) 523.

and 'reforming' offenders to eliminate the desire of offending. With his belief in individuals as pleasure-maximising and pain-avoiding creatures, Bentham also accepted the validity of punishment as an example to a would-be offender of 'what he himself will have to suffer, if is guilty of the same offense'.[156] There is, however, no room in Bentham's penal philosophy for retributive justice à la Kant and Hegel, which he saw as 'base and repugnant to all generous sentiments . . . an act of wrath or vengeance against a guilty or unfortunate individual who has given way to mischievous inclinations'.[157] Bentham saw nothing particularly meritorious in the idea of punishment itself; he made room for it only for a 'greater good', as 'an indispensable sacrifice to the common safety'.[158] However, in a manifestation of the dark side of utilitarian thinking, Bentham went on to propose the confinement of not only criminals but also paupers and the insane.[159] Karl Marx, in a jocular mood, once branded Bentham 'a genius of bourgeoisie stupidity' who 'strutted about in so self-satisfied a way'.[160]

Marx and punishment

In the early 1850s, as he wrestled with poverty and agonised over the illness of his daughter Jenney – who would die in the spring of 1853 – fearing that *Capital*, 'will not even pay for the cigars I smoked writing it', Karl Marx earned his paltry income by contributing pieces for the *New York Daily Tribune*.[161] One of the 500 articles Marx wrote during that period takes apart classical justifications for punishment, both utilitarian and deontological, through the prism of capital punishment. His critique goes to the very foundations of the death penalty unlike relatively surface objections based on the prohibition of cruel punishment. His idea clearly was not to sanitise the death penalty but to dispense with it altogether. Paradoxically, he also employs the language of rights in a far more insurrectionist manner than typical human rights accounts:

> Punishment in general has been defended as a means either of ameliorating or of intimidating. Now what right have you to punish me for the amelioration or intimidation of others? And besides there is history – there is such a thing as statistics – which prove with the most complete evidence that since

156 Cited in Hudson, 'Understanding Justice' (n 96) 19.

157 Jeremy Bentham, 'Principles of Penal Law' in John Bowring (ed), *The Works of Jeremy Bentham* (volume 1, W. Tait 1843) 396.

158 Ibid.

159 Bentham, 'An Introduction to the Principles of Morals' (n 138) 174.

160 Cited in Gilbert Geis, 'Jeremy Bentham' in Mannheim (n 146) 36–50, 36.

161 Mark G. Spencer, 'Introduction' in Karl Marx, *Capital* (Wordsworth Editions 2013) xi–xxii, xx. Some would point out that Marx had his friend Engel's largesse to rely on. But probably, as historian Aijaz Ahmad has noted, Marx would have stayed away from journalism, had he 'not needed the money so very desperately'. See Aijaz Ahmad, *In Theory: Classes, Nations, Literatures* (Verso 1992) 231.

> Cain the world has been neither intimidated nor ameliorated by punishment. Quite the contrary.[162]

By questioning the validity of deterrent punishment on the basis of rights, Marx is best seen as employing the technique of interrogating liberalism on its own ground, challenging its stated assumptions and promises. There is a more radical critique of liberal theory and jurisprudence in Marx's works where he calls into question egoism, alienation, and the separation of political emancipation from human emancipation inherent in the very concept of rights and the rule of law.[163] The said article uses both strategies. In the passage cited above, he is launching a rather modest critique by simply pointing out the polarity between the rhetoric and the reality of rights, between the ideal and the actual state. How could a state – any state – with its formal commitment to human rights, ever justify using a criminal to deter others?

The second prong of this modest criticism demands that the proponents of deterrence furnish empirical support for their claim that deterrence works. The assumptions, intuitions, and deductive reasoning of classical thinkers would not do. Not for Marx. As noted earlier, deterrence in penal theory and practice is a worn-out hypothesis that passes off as a justification for punishment. Its abiding popularity does not make it justifiable on deontological grounds. Further, its validity as a rationale for the penalty of incarceration is suspect even on instrumental grounds considering high recidivism rates in many countries.[164] In what may be read, at first blush, as an approval of classical retributivism,[165] Marx goes on to state in the same article that 'from the point of view of abstract right, there is only one theory of punishment which recognises human dignity in the abstract'.[166] That theory, says Marx, is that of Kant 'especially in the more rigid' Hegelian formula, according to which, 'punishment is the right of the criminal'.[167]

Marx's reference to the abstract nature of rights, seen with his general critique of German idealism, suggests that he considered the theory of retributive punishment to be formally correct in the sense of its validity for 'some possible world'

162 Karl Marx, *Dispatches for the New York Tribune: Selected Journalism of Karl Marx* (Penguin 2007) 119–122, 121.

163 See, for example, Marx's 1843 essay, 'On the Jewish Question' in Karl Marx, *Early Writings* (Greger Benton tr, Penguin 1992) 211–241. See also *Allen E. Buchanan, Marx and Justice: The Radical Critique of Liberalism* (Rowman & Littlefield 1984) 158–159. For the alternating techniques of testing law on its own ground, and challenging its underlying assumptions, see Ngaire Naffine, *Law & the Sexes: Explorations in Feminist Jurisprudence* (Allen & Unwin 1992).

164 Deryck Beyleveld, 'Deterrence Research and Deterrence Policies' in Andrew von Hirsch and Andrew Ashworth (eds), *Principled Sentencing. Readings on Theory and Policy* (2nd edn, Hart Publishing) 66–85.

165 Rodney G. Peffer, *Marxism, Morality and Social Justice* (Princeton University Press, Princeton 1990) 121.

166 Marx (n 162) 121.

167 Ibid.

but 'materially incorrect' as being inapplicable to the world we live in.[168] Marx makes his position on retributive philosophy clear in the article where he refers to the imaginary individual as the subject of the criminal law:

> Is it not a delusion to substitute for the individual with his real motives, with multifarious social circumstances pressing upon him, the abstraction of 'free-will' – one among the many qualities of man for man himself! This theory, considering punishment as the result of the criminal's own will, is only a metaphysical expression for the old *jus talionis*. . . . Now, what a state of society is that, which knows of no better instrument for its own defense than the hangman, and which proclaims through the "leading journal of the world" its own brutality as eternal law.[169]

Thus, what began as a relatively modest 'rights-based' critique, focusing on capital punishment, moves on to challenge the very foundations of the institution of punishment and the notion of the abstract, atomised legal subject it operates with. The break with classical penal theory – both utilitarian and deontological – is complete with Marx striking at one of its sacred foundations, namely the notion of free will. The disavowal of this abstract idea would later form a central plank of the positivist school in criminology albeit with some rather sinister policy implications as we shall see in the next chapter. But let us remember that psychological work with offenders over the years has demonstrated how criminality often stems from troubled childhood histories, mental disorders, and the experience of confinement in institutions, including the institutions designed to prevent crime. As Craig Haney has quipped,

> With apologies to the Free Will Baptists, . . . Modern psychological theory now finally recognises the extent to which the roots of evil – at least as evil is thought to be manifested in criminal behaviour – are formed in more than simply the morally blameworthy free choices of equally autonomous individuals.[170]

Advances in neuroscience have raised similar doubts about how human agency and moral responsibility are conceptualised in penal theory and criminal law.[171]

In making a plea for altering the social system that 'breeds these crimes instead of glorifying the hangman who executes a lot of criminals to make room only for

168 Jeffrie G. Murphy, 'Marxism and Retribution' (1973) 2(3) *Philosophy & Public Affairs* 217, 232.

169 Marx (n 162) 122.

170 Craig Haney, 'The Contextual Revolution in Psychology and the Question of Prison Effect' in Alison Liebling and Shadd Maruna (eds), *The Effects of Imprisonment* (Willan Publishing 2005) 66–93, 87.

171 See Sam Harris, *The Moral Landscape: How Science Can Determine Human Values* (Black Swan 2010) 135–147.

the supply of new ones', Marx takes issue with another basic tenet of classical liberal faith, i.e. the split between criminal justice and social justice.[172] This compartmentalised vision of justice is mirrored within the corpus of international human rights law in the separation of civil and political rights from economic, social, and cultural rights. This fragmentation impinges deeply on the way criminal punishment is framed and understood today.

The point of underscoring the shortcomings in the classical belief in individual moral responsibility is not to recommend an absolute rejection of 'free will' or letting wrong-doers off the hook. Rather, it is arguing for a more holistic view of human behaviour, which locates individual responsibility on a continuum that includes free choice as well as a range of individual and social factors that have a bearing on the choices we make.[173] The policy implication of such a conception of human behaviour would be a greater focus on preventive rather than punitive measures, and a stronger appreciation of various forms of deprivation in assessing culpability.

Finally, it would be a mistake to read the Marxist critique of punishment as a wholesale repudiation of the liberal Enlightenment values. His objective was not simply to reject liberalism but to move beyond it.[174] Marx had enough of a sense of history to appreciate the advance that the Enlightenment represented over the *ancien régime*. However, he was also perceptive enough to see through the ambiguities in the classical liberal thought and to notice that the changes it brought often involved 'mixed blessings'.[175] We owe to the philosophy of the Enlightenment not only the principles of rationality and legality in law, but also elements of irrationality and contradiction.[176] Orthodox legal scholarship celebrates the former but fails to acknowledge the latter.

Crucial as it is, the philosophical debate on the lines suggested above can still limit our understanding of penological purposes in the absence of a proper social and historical perspective.[177] The structure and scope of penal measures, after all, differ widely in temporal and spatial terms. Incarceration rates do not necessarily correspond to the incidence of crime in a society.[178] Sentencing practices and prison regimes can be particularly harsh in certain contexts and time periods despite the stability of the underlying justifications and theories of punishment. Similarly, even where legal norms can be demonstrated to be applied 'fairly' and 'impartially', we nonetheless notice certain groups bearing the brunt of penal

172 cf. Wojciech Sadurski, 'Social Justice and Legal Justice' (1984) 3 *Law and Philosophy* 329.

173 Adrian Raine, *The Psychopathology of Crime: Criminal Behavior as a Clinical Disorder* (Academic Press 1993) 309–312; Michael Dow Burkhead, *The Search for the Causes of Crime* (McFarland & Company 2006) 21–27.

174 Bob Fine, *Democracy and the Rule of Law; Liberal Ideals and Marxist Critiques* (Pluto Press 1984) 205.

175 Roy Porter, *The Enlightenment* (2nd edn, Palgrave Macmillan 2001) 61.

176 Norrie (n 11) 9–38.

177 RA Duff and David Garland, 'Introduction: Thinking About Punishment' in Duff and Garland (eds), *A Reader on Punishment* (Oxford University Press 1994) 43, 21–35.

178 Nils Christie, *Crime Control as Industry* (Routledge 1983) 53–54.

measures far more than other groups. In fact, socially deprived groups have consistently been at the receiving end of the punitive arm of the law from the era of public hangings and transportation to present-day incarceration.[179]

Against this backdrop, orthodox human rights scholarship suffers from a dual deficit: a lack of critical engagement with penal theory on the one hand, and the absence of broader social science perspectives and an empirical grounding for penological justifications on the other hand.[180] This may simply be a result of the division of intellectual labour within academia. Nonetheless, it obscures our vision and limits our comprehension of the nature and effects of punishment. There is also a rather important latent relationship between normative theorising and empirical evidence: almost all philosophical theories of punishment operate with certain empirical presuppositions about human nature, individual behaviour, and society.[181] Punishment, we would do well to remember, is not simply a moral puzzle. It is a socially and historically contingent reality. The subsequent chapters will thus widen the debate, taking into account broader historical and social science perspectives.

179 See Robert Hughes, *The Fatal Shore* (Collins Harvill 1987) 71–74; Farley Grubb, 'Penal Slavery' in Seymour Drescher and Stanley L. Engerman (eds), *A Historical Guide to World Slavery* (Oxford University Press 1998) 312–314; Hanns von Hofer, 'Punishment and Crime in Scandinavia, 1750–2008' in Michael Tonry and Tapio Lappi-Seppälä (eds), *Crime and Justice in Scandinavia: Crime and Justice – A Review of Research* (Volume 40, University of Chicago Press 2011) 33–108, 93–94; *Jessica Jacobson, Catherine Herd and Helen Fair, Prison: Evidence of Its Use and Overuse from Around the World* (Institute for Criminal Policy Research 2017) 1–2.

180 See, for example, Rhona KM Smith, *Textbook on International Human Rights* (5th edn, Oxford University Press 2011); Rehman (n 9); Moeckli, Shah and Sivakumaran (n 14).

181 Duff and Garland (n 177) 1–43, 28.

2 The gods that failed

Positivist criminology and the legacy of the international penal and penitentiary commission

'Who controls the past', ran the Party slogan, 'controls the future: who controls the present, controls the past'.

George Orwell[1]

As we have seen, whilst classical thinkers differed in the justifications they advanced for punishment, they were united in espousing the image of the human as an atomised, rational, and self-calculating being. Despite its general opposition to religious dogma, Enlightenment thought somehow preserved the Judeo-Christian ideal of absolute individual responsibility almost as a theological necessity connected with divine retribution for choices human beings made. Further, there was little attention paid in classical accounts to the causes or the context of crime. It resulted, as Raymond Saleilles put it, 'in a view of the criminal act as an abstraction . . . a sort of algebraic quantity independent of the personality of the offender'.[2] The positivist school broke fresh ground by turning to the factors which presumably shaped 'deviant' behaviour and by challenging the assumptions about individual responsibility that underpinned classical thinking.

From around the last quarter of the nineteenth century up until the 1950s and 1960s, the ideas of positivist criminology had gained a firm foothold in penal discourse and practice. Predicated on the positivist belief in the possibility of furnishing scientific solutions to social problems, the penal discourse during that period laid great emphasis on the prevention of crime and rehabilitation of offenders as against the focus on retribution in Kantian and Hegelian theory. The justificatory foundations of punishment through the heydays of positivist criminology were anchored within utilitarian philosophy. Many penal reformers dismissed retribution altogether as unnecessary in the 'scientific project' of preventing crime and treating criminals. To some, the period was decidedly 'the "age of reform" in which calls for progress were not only made but answered'.[3] The

1 George Orwell, *Nineteen Eighty-Four* (Penguin 2003) 38.
2 Raymond Saleilles, *The Individualization of Punishment* (Little Brown and Company 1911) 18.
3 Francis T. Cullen, Rehabilitation: Beyond Nothing Works in Michael Tonry (ed), *Crime and Justice in America, 1975–2025. Crime and Justice: A Review of Research* (Volume 42,

impact of the positivist ideas was also reflected in the establishment of a number of international bodies to facilitate collaboration on penal matters, most notably the International Penal and Penitentiary Commission.[4] But the positivist creed had its darks side, manifested most chillingly in the Nazi experimentation with eugenics and the cynical exploitation of social Darwinism and Lombroso's idea of 'atavistic type' or 'born criminal' during Hitler's Third Reich.[5]

The resurgence of what is variously described as retributivism, 'just deserts', or, more euphemistically, the 'justice model' seems to have been a consequence of the presumed failure of the 'rehabilitative ideal', and perceived inconsistences in sentencing practice due to wide discretion given to judges and probation officers as part of indeterminate sentencing schemes.[6] However, changes in penal theory and practice rarely occur in a social and political vacuum. The revival of retributivist ideas and the growing disapproval of positivist criminology during the 1970s were bound up with a more general distrust in the 'overreach' of the welfare state. There are, of course, no neat dividing lines or sequential compartments which penal ideas fit into. The dominance of positivist ideas through the first half of the twentieth century did not herald the demise of retribution in penal policy and practice. Nor did the revival of retributivism entail a complete rejection of rehabilitation or other forward-looking criteria in criminal sentencing and penal administration. The accent, in both theory and practice, nonetheless shifted decidedly on retribution, proportionality of punishment to crime, and fixed sentencing.[7] This vision of justice, as shall be explained later, gels in rather well with the discourse of human rights and constitutes a hegemonic legal and moral project of our age. This chapter is concerned primarily with the historical legacy of positivist criminology and some pioneering attempts at international collaboration on penal matters. An attempt will be made to demonstrate that some progressive ideas put forward by penal reformers during the nineteenth and early twentieth century have been overshadowed by the association of positivist criminology with Social Darwinism and fascism. The central concern is that in dismissing those reformist ideas in favour of classical penology, modern human rights discourse may actually have lost the baby with the bathwater.

University of Chicago Press 2013) 299–376, 312. See also Francis T. Cullen and Karen E. Gilbert, *Reaffirming Rehabilitation* (Anderson Publishing 1982) 7.

4 Leon Radzinowicz, *Ideology and Crime* (Columbia University Press 1966) 57.

5 Nicole Rafter, 'Criminology's Darkest Hour: Biocriminology in Nazi Germany' (2008) 41(2) *The Australian and New Zealand Journal of Criminology* 287.

6 Gardner, Martin, 'The Renaissance of Retribution: An Examination of "Doing Justice"' (1976) *Wisconsin Law Review* 781.

7 See Michael Tonry, 'Punishment and Human Dignity: Sentencing Principles for Twenty-First Century America' in Tonry (ed), *Crime and Justice: A Review of Research* (Volume 47, University of Chicago Press 2018) 119–158, 127–129; David Garland, *The Culture of Control: Crime and Social Order in Contemporary Society* (Oxford University Press 2001) 9.

The age of optimism

To understand the legacy of positivist criminology, it is essential to place it within the context of several advances in knowledge occurring in mid-nineteenth-century Europe against the backdrop of a rapidly industrialising and urbanising society. With the publication of *On the Origin of Species* in 1850, Charles Darwin revolutionised biology and paved the way for a fundamentally new worldview, throwing religious beliefs about the status of man into doubt. Darwin's findings, as Sigmund Freud put it, was one of the two major blows which science dealt to 'the naïve self-love of men', the other being the discovery that the earth was not the centre of the universe.[8] In time, the theory of evolution and natural selection would go on to influence fields well beyond biology.

Darwin's theory of evolution came as a natural ally to 'positivist philosophy', a term coined by the French thinker Auguste Comte in the 1830s, as part of his laws of three stages of knowledge. The pursuit of knowledge in any field, Comte held, began with theological speculation followed by the transitional phase of metaphysical theorising. Knowledge is perfected only in the third and the final stage, or what Comte called the positivist or scientific era. He described 'the fundamental character of the positive philosophy' as consideration of all 'phenomena as subject to invariable natural laws'.[9] It would be 'the exact discovery of these laws and their reduction to the least possible number' that would constitute the goal of all positivist effort.[10] Comte sought to apply 'the system of observational sciences' – namely, astronomy, physics, chemistry, and physiology to the study of social phenomena for which he chose the term 'social physics'.[11] Subsequently, the English philosopher Herbert Spencer laid the foundations of sociological positivism in the 1850s, requiring explanations of social phenomena to be grounded in empirical evidence. Spencer was also a precursor of what is now pejoratively remembered as Social Darwinism, a school of thought which espoused the image of society as a struggle between competing individuals akin to the process of natural selection.[12]

The positivist spirit, inaugurated by Comte, found its practical application in the work of the French lawyer André-Michel Guerry (1802–1866) and the Belgian mathematician Adolphe Quetelet (1796–1874), who began analysing crime rates and their relationship with sex, education, and other variables under the

8 Cited in Roger Smith, *The Fontana History of Human Sciences* (Fontana Press 1997) 701.

9 Auguste Comte, *Introduction to Positive Philosophy* (Frederick Ferret tr, Bobbs-Merril Company 1970) 8.

10 Ibid. See also Lewis A. Coser, *Masters of Sociological Thought: Ideas in Historical and Social Context* (2nd edn, Harcourt Brace Jovanovich Inc.) 3–41.

11 Comte (n 9) 13, 56–57.

12 Mike Hawkins, *Social Darwinism in European and American Thought, 1860–1945: Nature as Model and Nature as Threat* (Cambridge University Press 1997) 82; Coser (n 10) 89–127.

quaintly named field of moral statistics.[13] Karl Marx, in his critique of the deterrent value of capital punishment, discussed in the previous chapter, took note of Quetelet's work as 'excellent and learned'.[14] Marx's enthusiasm strikes a jarring chord today in light of the later critiques of 'moral statistics' as amateurish.[15] It does, however, make sense by the standards of the times he lived in. At the height of the industrial revolution in Victorian England, Friedrich Engels, Marx's longtime companion, recorded empirical observations of Manchester factory workers published as *The Conditions of the Working Classes of England* in 1845.[16] With the concept of dialectical materialism, Marx and Engels turned Hegel over its head, insisting that ideas were a product of material conditions. 'My dialectic method is not only different from the Hegelian, but is its direct opposite', as Marx put it in the preface to the second edition of *Capital Volume 1*. With Hegel, 'the Idea' was an independent subject, the moving force of history. To Marx, by contrast, 'the ideal is nothing else than the material world reflected by the human mind and translated into forms of thought'.[17]

The emergence of positivist philosophy and sociology during the nineteenth century was matched by several advances in medicine and psychiatry, which, in due course, would provide the basis for humanitarian penal reform as well as a far more sinister project of racial hygiene and eugenics.[18] By the turn of the nineteenth century, among the 'scientifically inclined modern thinkers, idealist metaphysics could not command widespread philosophical acceptance', as Richard Tarnas remarks in his elegantly written history of Western thought.[19] Instead, it was materialism and positivism that captured the spirit of the times. It was in the midst of these new intellectual currents, and the changing social landscape of the late nineteenth century, that the historically tainted ideas of positivist criminology took shape.

13 Michael Dow Burkhead, *The Search for the Causes of Crime* (McFarland & Company 2006) 171. See also Eric Hobsbawm, *The Age of Revolution: 1789–1848* (Abacus 1962) 344.

14 Karl Marx, *Dispatches for the New York Tribune: Selected Journalism of Karl Marx* (Penguin 2007) 122.

15 On the crude methods of interpretation employed by 'moral statisticians', see David Garland, 'Criminal and His Science: A Critical Account of the Formation of Criminology at the End of the Nineteenth Century' (1985) 25(2) *The British Journal of Criminology* 109, 113.

16 Friedrich Engels, *The Conditions of the Working Classes of England* (Penguin 2009).

17 Karl Marx, *Capital* (Wordsworth Editions 2013) 15.

18 The term 'eugenics' was coined by Charles Darwin's half-cousin, the self-styled geneticist and explorer Francis Galton. He defined 'eugenics' as 'study of the Agencies under social control, that improve or impair the racial qualities of future generations either physically or mentally'. See Francis Galton, 'Eugenics, its Definition, Scope, and Aims' (1904) 10(1) *The American Journal of Sociology* 1. See also Clare Anderson, *Legible Bodies: Race, Criminality and Colonialism in South Asia* (Berg 2004) 181; Siddhartha Mukherjee, *The Gene: An Intimate History* (Allen Lane 2016) 64–77.

19 Richard Tarnas, *The Passion of the Western Mind: Understanding the Ideas That Have Shaped Our World View* (Pimlico 1991) 352.

Enter positivist criminology

In what is considered to be the opening salvo in positivist criminology, the Italian physician Cesare Lombroso put forward the idea of the 'born criminal' associated with 'savage races'. These criminals, on his account, exhibited 'numerous specific characteristics that are almost always atavistic', such as 'low cranial capacity, retreating forehead, highly developed frontal sinuses', and so on.[20] The classification scheme contained other categories. These included 'criminaloids', who, while separate from the 'born criminal', had become 'habitual criminals, thanks to a long sojourn in prison'; the 'criminal insane', an exaggerated type of the born criminal; 'criminals by passion', who did not exhibit the jarring physical characteristics of the born criminal; and finally, the 'occasional criminals . . . who do not seek the occasion for the crime but are almost drawn into it'.[21] Crime, under Lombroso's 'science', or what he called 'criminal anthropology', was to be seen as sickness. Lombroso dismissed offhand the classical retributive idea of punishment. Instead, he was concerned with the 'criminal and his victim more than the crime' and the 'welfare of society more than the punishment'.[22] That led him to propose indeterminate sentencing schemes to be set in consultation with expert criminal anthropologists.

Borrowing both Lombroso's idea of inherent criminality, and the concepts of eugenics or racial hygiene developed elsewhere under the influence of Social Darwinism, the Nazis would go on to justify the extermination of not only persistent law-breakers, but also Jews and Gypsies, in what has aptly been called 'criminology's darkest hour'.[23] The irony seldom recounted is that Lombroso himself was Jewish. Also, whilst the influence of Lombrosian ideas on the treatment of social outsiders under the Third Reich is quite evident, the employment of eugenics in the service of racism can actually be traced back to Imperial Germany toward the end of the nineteenth century. Colonial officers in Rwanda had used 'ethnographic manuals' to create new racial identities of Hutu and Tutsi, sowing the seeds of one of history's most gruesome genocidal massacres that took place in 1994.[24]

Likewise, the British authorities in India adopted the notion of hereditary criminality by designating entire castes and tribes as born criminals through a series of Criminal Tribes Acts starting in 1871.[25] The use of sterilisation as a

20 Cesare Lombroso, *Crime: Its Causes and Remedies* (William Heinemann 1911) 365.
21 Ibid 373–375.
22 Ibid 385.
23 Rafter (n 5) 287. See also Roger Griffin, *Modernism and Fascism: The Sense of Beginning Under Mussolini and Hitler* (Palgrave Macmillan 2007) 310–335. On the Nazi legal system under the Third Reich, see Ingo Muller, *Hitler's Justice: The Courts of the Third Reich* (Deborah Lucas Schneider tr, I.B. Tauris & Co Ltd. 1991).
24 Richard J. Evans, *The Third Reich in History and Memory* (Little Brown and Company 2015) 11, 59–86.
25 Anderson (n 18) 6; Michael Mann, 'Torchbearers Upon the Path of Progress: Britain's Ideology of a Moral and Material Progress in India. An Introductory Essay' in Herald Fischer-Tine and Michael Mann (eds), *Colonialism as Civilizing Mission: Cultural Ideology in British India* (Wimbledon Publishing 2004) 1–26, 10.

method of 'treating' incorrigible criminals and 'defectives' – for which the Third Reich achieved historical notoriety – had actually begun in the United States with Indiana introducing a compulsory sterilisation law in 1907.[26] In 1927, as the rhetoric of eugenics seeped into political and penal discourse, the US Supreme Court ruled that compulsory sterilisation of the 'feeble-minded' did not violate the equal protection and due process clauses of the Fourteenth Amendment.[27] Hitler, it has been argued, was an admirer of the British Empire, and that his National Socialist government relied on American sterilisation laws in formulating the 1933 'Law for the Prevention of Genetically Diseased Offspring'. At the Nuremburg trial, Nazi doctors cited American precedents in their defence.[28]

It has been said in Lombroso's defence that he was a well-meaning reformer who changed his views over time, eventually accepting the validity of social determinants of criminality. His ideas influenced the work of his son-in-law Enrico Ferri (1856–1929). Trained as a lawyer, Ferri dismissed the Lombrosian notion of measuring the heads of criminals. However, he was unreservedly in favour of using the inductive method to study crime. Inspired by socialism early in his career, Ferri expanded the scope of positivist inquiry from genetic and neurobiological to social causes of crime, including age, sex, education, climate, migration, and urbanisation.[29] Repudiating classical penal systems as 'bankrupt', Ferri considered 'volitional liberty' or free choice an illusion.[30] As a corollary, retributive punishment had no place in Ferri's account. The positivist belief in dispositional and situational influences as causes of crime led Ferri and his successors to support individualised and indeterminate sentencing schemes. In time, the idea of penal individualisation, or what they called *'le principe de l'individualisation'* in French, took ground in penal policy across European countries, with the Italian Penal Code of 1930 (Article 54), the Polish Penal Code and the Law of Minor Offences of 1932 (Article 64), and the Swiss Penal Code of 1937 (Article 69) containing relevant provisions. The influence could be seen as far afield as Cuba where the Criminal Code of 1930 'embodied many of Enrico Ferri's ideas'.[31] Referring to the 'necessity of taking into consideration, in all the stages of criminal justice, the personality of the offender', Leon Radzinowicz observed with

26 Alexandra Stern, *Eugenic Nation: Faults and Frontiers of Better Breeding in Modern America* (University of California Press 2005) 99. See also Mukherjee (n 18) 78–85.

27 Delivering the majority opinion in the case which concerned Virginia's sterilisation statute, Justice Oliver Wendell Holmes, Jr. infamously stated: 'It is better for all the world if, instead of waiting to execute degenerate offspring for crime or to let them starve for their imbecility, society can prevent those who are manifestly unfit from continuing their kind'. *Buck v Bell* 274 US 200 (1927) 207.

28 Harry Bruinius, *Better for All the World: The Secret History of Forced Sterilization and America's Quest for Racial Purity* (Vintage Books 2007) 17.

29 Thorsten Sellin, 'Enrico Ferri (1856–1929)' in Herman Mannheim (ed), *Pioneers in Criminology* (Stevens & Sons Limited 1960) 277–300, 283. See also Margery Fry, *Arms of the Law* (Victor Gollancz Ltd. 1951) 63.

30 Enrico Ferri, *Criminal Sociology* (Unwin 1895) 202.

31 Leon Radzinowicz, *Adventures in Criminology* (Routledge 1999) 377, 388.

satisfaction in the year 1942, 'Today in the penal legislation of every country this principle is not only adopted but also defined in almost identical terms'.[32]

The idea of foregrounding personality characteristics in sentencing surely had a downside. For one, it legitimised preventive and indefinite detention even where an individual had committed no crime but supposedly posed a threat to the society. On the other hand, it signified a shift away from retributive punishment and towards offender rehabilitation – at least in theory, if not always in practice. In some other respects too, Ferri's ideas represented an advance of sorts on old practices. He demanded, for example, that prisons must change from 'places of torture and slavery, into establishments of physical and moral treatment similar to hospitals, special clinics, and insane asylums'.[33] Applying to the penal system the principle of reparation as a private and civil obligation, he proposed that prisoners work in the industries where they receive 'full compensation, but deducting their board, clothing, and lodging, and repaying in full or in part their victims for the harm done them'.[34] Ferri is also credited, along with his contemporary and compatriot, Raffaele Garofalo (1851–1934), with popularising the term 'social defence'. Implicit in the idea is a utilitarian focus on the prevention of crime and the protection of society in contrast to the deontological view of punishment as an independent moral imperative.

In 1948, the newly established United Nations set up a Section of Social Defence built into the Division of Social Activities (later to become part of the Department of Social Affairs) with Leon Radzinowicz as its first chief.[35] Subsequently, the term 'social defence' lost currency within the official United Nations discourse. The UN Social Defence Research Institute (UNSRDI), established in 1969, was renamed the UN Interregional Crime and Justice Research Institute (UNICRI) in 1989, symbolising the retributivist turn in penal thinking and repudiation of positivist criminology.[36] The notion of social defence (with its underlying rejection of retribution) was one that Radzinowicz had himself grown uncomfortable with over time. His anxiety about the term when he was called upon by the UN to head the social defence programme, made for a sharp contrast with his enthusiasm for the positivist project until a few years earlier.[37] As he had written in in the 1942 article, which I previously referred to:

> The knowledge of crime and of criminals which we have accumulated shows that the fight against crime must not be left to the emotional reaction of the

32 Leon Radzinowicz, 'International Collaboration in Criminal Science' (1941–1942) 4 *University of Toronto Law Journal* 307, 311.

33 Ferri (n 30) 518.

34 Ibid 518–520.

35 Radzinowicz, 'Adventures in Criminology' (n 31) 380–387. Radzinowicz held the position for less than a year. He was replaced by Belgium's Adolph Delierneux in 1949. See Adolph Delierneux, 'The United Nations in the Field of Prevention of Crime and Treatment of Offenders' (1949) *United Nations Year Book* 248.

36 The institute was renamed on 24 May 1989 via Resolution No. 1989/56, ECOSOC.

37 Radzinowicz, 'Adventures in Criminology' (n 31) 383. See also Manuel Lopez-Rey, 'United Nations Social Defence Policy and the Problem of Crime' in Roger Hood (ed), *Crime,*

> individual or of the group, but must be conducted on a scientifically planned and executed campaign of social defence.[38]

Whilst Ferri ended up putting his faith in Mussolini's fascism, some thinkers, most notably the Dutch sociologist William Bonger, worked more consistently within the Marxist tradition, relating crime to capitalist political economy.[39] In retrospect, the links drawn between criminality and class by Bonger would appear to be overly deterministic, characteristic of what some historians have called 'vulgar Marxism'.[40] Nevertheless, his work prefigured some of the basic ideas of conflict and radical and Marxist theories of crime by restoring the centrality of social environment as a causal factor in place of individual pathology. A similar sociological focus could be seen in the work of Raffaele Garofalo, a student of Lombroso's, who also stimulated 'the continental jurist' to consider alternatives to imprisonment by 'laying stress on the right of the injured party to compensation'.[41] At the turn of the century, these ideas were taken up by some eminent European jurists, for example, the German Professor Franz von Liszt, who stressed the relevance of the social conditions to crime and recidivism, rejecting the retributivist notion of punishment for the sake of punishment.[42]

It is common these days to dismiss the founders of positivist criminology as cranks.[43] The distaste evoked by the idea of inherent criminality and racial stereotyping as they prefigured in Lombroso and their appropriation by the Nazi Germany is quite understandable. Some peripheral voices are heard from time to time, however, arguing that the ideas put forward by Lombroso and his disciples made sense within 'the specific historical context in which they were first articulated', as a reaction to the naiveté of classical penology and a 'new language of social representation' in an era of social unrest.[44] Renowned neuroscientist and criminologist Adrian Raine has made a bold attempt to rehabilitate Lombroso by arguing that violent crime has biological roots. Whilst distancing

---

Criminology and Public Policy: Essays in Honour of Sir Leon Radzinowicz (Heinmann 1974) 489–508.

38 Leon Radzinowicz, 'International Collaboration in Criminal Science' (n 32) 334.

39 William A. Bonger, *Criminality and Economic Conditions* (Little, Brown, and Company 1916).

40 See Donald Sasson, *One Hundred Years of Socialism* (3rd edn, I.B. Tauris 2014) 5–6.

41 Evelyn Ruggles-Brise, *Prison Reform at Home Abroad* (Palgrave Macmillan 1925) 76; Francis A. Allen, 'Raffaelle Garofalo' in Herman Mannheim (ed), *Pioneers in Criminology* (Stevens & Sons Limited 1960) 254–276.

42 Richard F. Wetzell, 'The Medicalization of Criminal Law Reform in Imperial Germany' in Norbert Finzsch and Robert Jutte (eds), *Institutions of Confinement: Hospitals, Asylums, and Prisons in Western Europe and North America, 1500–1950* (Cambridge University Press 1996) 275–283.

43 For a case against broad-brush dismissal of positivist criminology, see David Garland, 'Criminal and His Science. A Critical Account of the Formation of Criminology at the End of the Nineteenth Century' (1985) 25(2) *The British Journal of Criminology* 109.

44 Daniel Pick, *Faces of Degeneration: A European Disorder, c. 1848 – c. 1918* (Cambridge University Press 1989) 110.

himself from 'racial stereotyping', Raine believes that Lombroso 'was on the path toward sublime truth'.[45] Perhaps, Raine is being too charitable. But the crucial point is that positivist criminology did not just provide intellectual ammunition to fascist regimes for their genocidal designs. As Leon Radzinowicz conceded in his appraisal of what he called the 'deterministic position', the 'provocative assertions' of positivists 'stirred up similar enquiries in different parts of the world' and provided the impetus for resources of sciences to be mobilised for understanding offenders.[46] Marvin Wolfgang complements this sentiment as he credits Lombroso for having played an important role in 'shifting focus from metaphysical, legal and juristic abstraction as a basis for penology to a scientific study of the criminal and the conditions under which he commits crime'.[47]

Through much of the first half of the twentieth century, positivist ideas, in conjunction with Keynesian economics, also informed what has been termed the era of 'penal welfarism', marked by the development of probation, parole, and rehabilitative measures in the prison.[48] It would be facile to overlook the repressive tendencies inherent within the positivist creed. However, to dismiss that tradition altogether is to play right into the hands of modern retributivists. Once neurobiological, psychological, and situational influences are ignored, it becomes that much easier to anchor sentencing practices and prison regimes in retributive justice by pronouncing that the individual offender is always the one to blame. We need not revert to Lombrosian racial stereotyping or any deterministic version of Marxism to appreciate individual and situational factors that contribute to criminality or harmful behaviour. For one, even as biological explanations of crime have fallen into disrepute, contemporary evidence demonstrates how mental illnesses and social circumstances draw – and often trap – individuals into crime. In Britain, for example, 'mental disorders of every variety (psychosis, neurosis, addictions, learning disabilities and personality disorders) are present [in prisons] at vastly elevated levels relative to the surrounding community'.[49] According to one estimate, 70 per cent of the prisoners in England and Wales

45 Adrian Raine, *The Anatomy of Violence: The Biological Roots of Crime* (Allen Lane 2013) 13. On the decline of biological-oriented studies in criminology, see John P. Wright and others, 'Lombroso's Legacy: The Miseducation of Criminologists' (2008) 19(3) *Journal of Criminal Justice Education* 325.

46 Radzinowicz, 'Ideology and Crime' (n 4) 56–57. See also Leon Radzinowicz, 'Lombroso and His Place in Modern Criminology' (1936) V(1) *The Sociological Review* xxviii; Wetzell (n 42) 275–283, 278.

47 Marvin E. Wolfgang, 'Cesare Lombroso' in Herman Mannheim (ed), *Pioneers in Criminology* (Stevens & Sons Limited 1960) 168–227, 222.

48 Garland, 'The Culture of Control' (n 7) 34–40.

49 Ian Cumming and Simon Wilson, 'Mentally Ill Prisoners and Mental Health Issues in Prison' in Simon Wilson and Ian Cumming (eds), *Psychiatry in Prisons: A Comprehensive Handbook* (Jessica Kingsley Publishers 2010) 40–51, 41. See also Jill Peay, 'Mental Health, Mental Disabilities, and Crime' in Alison Liebling, Shadd Maruna and Lesley McAra (eds), *The Oxford Handbook of Criminology* (6th edn, Oxford University Press 2017) 639–662.

'will have a substance misuse problem on entering prisons'.[50] Similarly, evidence has been put forward for a high incidence of cognitive dysfunction in 'criminals'.[51] Studies have also revealed links between learning disability and juvenile and adult offending.[52] In addition to psychological causes, familial and social factors can also explain criminal behaviour. It has been shown, for example, that having a criminal parent increases the likelihood of children growing up to pursue a criminal career. Likewise, physical and sexual abuse in childhood can lead to criminal and violent behaviour later in life.[53]

The American psychologist Philip Zimbardo – who himself grew up in poverty in the Bronx – ran a mock prison experiment at Stanford University in 1971. In an absorbing account published in 2007, Zimbardo recounted how the simulated prison environment turned healthy and intelligent students into sadistic 'guards' and 'pathological' prisoners within a week.[54] Drawing broader conclusions from the Stanford Prison Experiment, and a vast collection of other psychological studies, Zimbardo provided a stimulating account of how social situations can drive 'good people' into committing horrible atrocities.[55]

None of this is to suggest that criminals lack control over their behaviour and ought to be absolved of all responsibility. Rather, the point is to locate human behaviour along a spectrum between moral responsibility and free choice on the one end, and psychological, social, and biological or genetic influences on the other end. Just as Lombroso committed the mistake of leaning toward the deterministic neurobiological explanations, retributivists get conveniently stuck at the other end represented by free will and rational choice. In reality, much of socially harmful behaviour falls somewhere in between.[56] Trying to understand such behaviour is not to condone or justify it. This point remains unappreciated within orthodox legal scholarship.

The forgotten legacy of the international penal and penitentiary commission

The nineteenth century, especially its second half, was marked by an efflorescence of international organisations dealing with criminological, legal, and penal

50 John Podmore, 'The Current Structure of Prison Service' in Wilson and Cumming (n 49) 16–23, 21.

51 Adrian Raine, *The Psychopathology of Crime: Criminal Behavior as a Clinical Disorder* (Academic Press 1993) 12, 103–127.

52 Ibid 241.

53 Cathy S. Widom, 'Does Violence Beget Violence? A Critical Examination of the Literature' (1989) 106(1) *Psychological Bulletin* 3. See also Joyce A. Arditti, *Parental Incarceration and the Family: Psychological and Social Effects of Imprisonment on Children, Parents, and Caregivers* (New York University Press 2012) 56.

54 Philip Zimbardo, *The Lucifer Effect: How Good People Turn Evil* (Rider 2007) 195–228.

55 Ibid 258–379.

56 Burkhead (n 13) 27. See also Jeffery Blustein, *The Moral Demands of Memory* (Cambridge University Press 2008) 93.

matters. Many of them bore an imprint of the self-confident optimism of the time. International Association of Criminal Anthropology, set up in 1885, carried forward the tradition of the Italian positivist school. The International Association of Criminal Law, known in German as *Internationale Kriminalistische Vereinigung* (IKV), was founded in 1889, with Franz Ritter von Liszt as one of its founders. The association brought together leading lawyers and jurists from across Europe. Despite some internal resistance, the association could not escape the influence of positivist criminology as well as Marxist ideas, or 'social liberalism', as Leon Radzinowizc dubbed it.[57] The most relevant body for our purposes is the International Penal and Penitentiary Commission (hereinafter referred to as the 'Penitentiary Commission'). Initially called the International Prison Commission, the organisation came about as a result of a remarkably progressive cross-Atlantic collaboration. It continued to operate until 1950 when its functions were rather unceremoniously taken over by the United Nations.

Given the unprecedented scope of the initiative – both in terms of the number of countries represented and the breadth of issues tackled – it is surprising that there is so little scholarship on the topic. As far as I am aware, not a single book has been published in English dealing exclusively with the work of the Penitentiary Commission. Scholarly works on the history of penal policy in an international and comparative perspective have dealt with the legacy of the Commission rather tangentially.[58] In a volume published in 1925, Evelyn Ruggles-Brise presented a summary of eight international prison congresses held under the aegis of the Commission between 1872 and 1910 at five-yearly intervals.[59] Journal articles on the topic are few and far between, mostly dating back to the 1940s and 1950s.[60] Human rights literature, in particular, is silent on the legacy of the Penitentiary Commission. History, as we shall see, has not been kind to the Commission on account of its association with positivist criminology and an unfounded

57 Leon Radzinowicz, *The Roots of the International Association of Criminal Law and Their Significance: A Tribute and a Re-Assessment on the Centenary of the IKV* (Eigenverlag Max-Plank-Institut 1991).

58 See for example, Roger S. Clark, *The United Nations Crime Prevention, and Criminal Justice Program: Formulations of Standards and Efforts at Their Implementation* (University of Pennsylvania Press 1994) 11, 19, 50. W.J. Forsythe, *Penal Discipline, Reformatory Projects and the English Prison Commission 1895–1939* (University of Exeter Press 1990) 234–235; Clive Emsley, *Crime, Police and Penal Policy: European Experiences 1750–1940* (Oxford University Press 2004) 266.

59 Ruggles-Brise (n 41).

60 See, for example, 'Current Notes: International Penal and Penitentiary Commission' (1934) 25(3) *Journal of Criminal Law and Criminology* 481; Radzinowicz, 'International Collaboration in Criminal Science' (n 32) 307; Sanford Bates, 'International Penal and Penitentiary Commission' (1946) *Proceedings of the Annual Congress of Correction of the American Prison Association* 243; 'One World in Penology' 1948 38(6) *Journal of Criminal Law and Criminology* 565; Negley K Teeters, 'The International Penal and Penitentiary Congress 1910 and the Indeterminate Sentence' (1949) 39(5) *Journal of Criminal Law and Criminology* 618; Paul Cornil, 'International Standards for the Treatment of Offenders' (1968) 26(3) *International Review of Criminal Policy* 3.

allegation of 'Nazification' during the 1930s. To get a rounded understanding, it is necessary to put the organisation into a proper historical context.

The international exchange of ideas on penal matters can be traced back at least to the late eighteenth century. John Howard, the legendary British prison reformer, famously toured Holland, Germany, Italy, Spain, France, and Turkey, before writing his classic comparative account of the state of prisons, first published in 1777.[61] Howard, of course, was a deeply religious man. It was the cellular system as practiced in Silentium, Clement XII's prison of San Michele in the Vatican, with its strict discipline and monastic silence, which impressed upon his mind most.[62] In an early example of the transfer of penal ideas across the Atlantic, the Quakers in Philadelphia, inspired by Howard's account, introduced segregation of male and female prisoners, isolating them into separate cells. Later in 1823, the Auburn State Prison in New York introduced a monotonous regime of total separation at night and co-operative work in silence during the day.[63] In London, Pentonville Prison, built in 1842, was a paradigmatic penitentiary with its stress on silence, solitude, and discipline. Nonetheless, it represented an advance on the privately run and disease-infested prisons of the eighteenth century, described so vividly by Charles Dickens in his novels.[64]

To Michel Foucault, the prison, right from its inception, was more than a mere 'deprivation of liberty'. 'It was from the outset', he argued, entrusted with the task of the technical 'transformation of individuals'.[65] Foucault's account, however, suffers from a problematic generalising tendency where the public spectacle of punishment – represented by the horrific quartering of Damiens the regicide – is juxtaposed with a fundamentally transformed, albeit no less insidious, disciplinary regime of the nineteenth-century penitentiary system.[66] There is a lot more to be said about Foucault's thesis, as we shall see in the next chapter. Suffice it to note here that the idea of reforming individuals – which itself evolved in stages – never totally replaced the subjection of prisoners to brute physical power, both as a means of discipline and extraction of unpaid labour.

According to Harry Barnes and Negley Teeters, 'Early penitentiary houses were supposed to reform, but the active machinery of reformation was lacking'.[67]

61 John Howard, *The State of the Prisons* (J. M. Dent & Sons Ltd. 1929). See also Max Grunhut, *Penal Reform: A Comparative Study* (Clarendon Press 1948) 468.

62 Martin Southwood, *John Howard: Prison Reformer: An Account of His Life and Travels* (Independent Press 1958) 40–41; Michael Ignatieff, *A Just Measure of Pain: Penitentiary in the Industrial Revolution 1750–1850* (Columbia University Press) 53.

63 Roger Matthews, *Doing Time: An Introduction to the Sociology of Imprisonment* (2nd edn, Palgrave Macmillan) 16.

64 Paul Schlicke, *The Oxford Companion to Charles Dickens* (Oxford University Press 2011) 473–475. See also Henry Mayhew and John Binny, *The Criminal Prison of London and Scenes of Prison Life* (Charles Griffin and Company 1862) 111–172.

65 Michel Foucault, *Discipline and Punish: The Birth of the Prison* (Penguin 1977) 233.

66 Ibid 3–31.

67 Harry Elmer Barnes and Negley K Teeters, *New Horizons in Criminology: The American Crime Problem* (Prentice-Hall 1943) 547.

The religious ideas of the early prison reformers, in time, gave way to what Max Weber – in a broader context – called the Protestant ethic, which chimed in with secular concerns and the functional requirements of capitalism.[68] As worked out by Luther and Calvin during the Reformation, salvation was to be attained not in fatalistic monasticism but through sobriety, hard work, discipline, and efficiency in a worldly vocation.[69] Whereas the earlier penitentiary was characterised by the idea of penance through silent contemplation, later-day reformatories, most notably the Elmira Reformatory built in New York in 1876, were influenced by the emerging ideas in the field of criminology and the Protestant-capitalist spirit of the times.[70] At the turn of the century, population mobility, rapid industrialisation, urbanisation, and the large impersonal structures of capitalism sparked deep anxieties among professional bourgeoisie about the perceived menace of crime, alcoholism, beggary, idleness, and vagrancy. Christian charity, liberal humanitarianism, the Protestant ethic, and the new social sciences coalesced into the intellectual landscape within which the Penitentiary Commission evolved.

Most sources trace the origins of international collaboration on penal matters to America, specifically to a meeting of the National Prison Association held in 1870 at Cincinnati on the initiative of Enoch Cobb Wines (1806–1879), the secretary of the Prison Association in New York.[71] Leon Radzinowicz, in his memoirs, cited an 1869 paper by Count Vladimir Alexandrowitsc Sollhub, director of the Moscow House of Correction and Industry and president of the Commission for Penal Reform in Russia. The paper proposed 'an international reunion of specialists . . . who under the patronage of their respective governments should be charged with the duty of giving penitentiary science its definitive principles'.[72] It was this idea, Radzinowicz noted, which led Wines to propose an international gathering, first at the Cincinnati meeting and then to the US Congress. Within America, the Cincinnati Congress itself would be remembered as the 'beginning of a renaissance in penal philosophy'.[73] The Declaration of Principles adopted at Cincinnati represented, in many ways, a reaction against old ideas of punishment and an endorsement of offender rehabilitation, indeterminate sentencing, probation, and preventive measures in place of punitive ones. Within the prison system, the Cincinnati Declaration called for an end to degrading punishment and its replacement by a classification system (on the model introduced by Sir Walter Crafton in Ireland) which would reward good behaviour and honour prisoners'

68 Max Weber, *The Protestant Ethic and the Spirit of Capitalism* (Allen & Unwin 1930). See also Frank Parkin, *Max Weber* (Routledge 1982) 40–70.
69 Tarnas (n 19) 243–246.
70 Alexander W. Psciotta, 'Scientific Reform: The "New Penology" at Elmira' (1983) 29 *Crime and Delinquency* 620.
71 Barnes and Teeters, (n 67) 551–553; Ruggles-Brise, (n 41) 18–34; Radzinowicz, 'The Roots of the International Association' (n 57) 19.
72 Radzinowicz, 'Adventures in Criminology' (n 31) 359–360.
73 Barnes and Teeters (n 67) 551.

self-respect.[74] The Declaration had a significant influence on the expansion of the penitentiary and indeterminate sentencing although they did little in the way of preventing racial injustices embedded in the penal system.[75]

Lobbying by Wines led both houses of the US Congress to pass a joint resolution indicating the desirability of an international meeting on prison questions in London. In the run up to the proposed event, Wines travelled through Europe, seeking support for the idea.[76] The first International Prison Congress (also referred to as International Penitentiary Congress in some documents) was held in London in 1872, bringing together in the hall of the Middle Temple delegates from twenty-three countries. Apart from the United States and European nations, Japan, Chile, Brazil, and Australia participated. Also represented were India and Hong Kong, though it is vital to note that neither at the inaugural London Congress, nor at the congresses held subsequently, did the matters of penal policy in Asia and Africa came up for discussion. The willingness for self-reflection amongst Western penal reformers rarely extended to embrace their colonial outposts. That began to change partially in the 1920s and 1930s when the Howard League for Penal Reform drew the attention of the League of Nations and the British government to the situation of prisoners in colonies and mandated territories.[77]

Nonetheless, the 1872 London Congress did showcase the urge among both religious and secular-minded penal reformers to 'improve the treatment of offenders'.[78] The agenda reaffirmed the tone set by the Cincinnati Declaration. In his opening address, the Earl of Carnarvon stated that though it was

> The duty of the State to punish and punish sternly, there yet remains a certain proportion of the criminal class as to whom some more improvement is not utterly hopeless, and upon whom Christian charity may exercise its most beneficial influence.[79]

74 Esther Heffernan, 'Irish (or Crofton) System' in Mary Bosworth (ed), *Encyclopedia of Prisons and Correctional Facilities* (Volume 1, Sage 1995) 482–485.

75 Edgaro Rotman, *Beyond Punishment: A New View on the Rehabilitation of Criminal Offenders* (Greenwood Press 1990) 40–41.

76 E.C. Wines, *International Congress on the Prevention and Repression of Crime, Including Penal and Reformatory Treatment: Preliminary Report of the Commissioner Appointed by the President to Represent the United States in the Congress in Compliance with a Joint Resolution of March 7, 1871.* (Washington 1872) 5–6; Radzinowicz, 'International Collaboration in Criminal Science' (n 32) 319.

77 Howard League for Penal Reform, *Annual Report (1929–30)* 12; Gordon Rose, *The Struggle for Penal Reform: The Howard League and Its Predecessors* (Stevens & Sons 1961) 314.

78 Thorsten Sellin, 'Preface' in *Twelfth International Penal and Penitentiary Congress, The Hague 14–19 August 1950. Proceeding Volume II. The Record of the Meetings* (IPPC 1951) xi–xvi, xii.

79 Edwin Pears (ed), *Prisons and Reformatories at Home and Abroad Being the Transactions of the International Penitentiary Congress Held in London July 3–13, 1872* (Longmans Green and Co. 1872) 368. See also, Howard Association, 'The Prison Congress of London, July 1872' (1872).

Whilst the need for reforming offenders drew large agreement at the congress, there were differences on what exactly constituted the correct means of reformation. British prison governors, most of whom came from a military background, argued that 'deterrence should continue to be the primary object of prison discipline, and reformation a mere secondary accompaniment'.[80] Bearing in mind what was to become of the penal system in Germany a few decades later, it is ironic that one of the German delegates would write a letter to *The Times* a month after the London Congress, condemning the English practice of using treadmill and flogging to discipline prisoners.[81] In what was evidently a progressive trend those days, delegates from Continental Europe and America also opposed corporal punishment as a means of prison discipline and extracting labour. There were some 'advocates of the lash' who 'almost exclusively' happened to be the English members of the Congress.[82] But the general resolution adopted by the congress steered clear of such a regimen. It stated instead that the 'moral regeneration of the prisoner should be the primary aim of prison discipline'.[83] The recommendations gave a seal of approval to 'progressive classification of prisoners', and called for an end to 'disciplinary punishments that inflict unnecessary pain, or humiliation'.[84] In what would be the guiding principle of the ideology of rehabilitation for decades to come, the recommendations proposed work, education, and religion as the three 'great forces on which prison administrators should rely'.[85]

The International Prison Commission was formed at the end of the 1872 Congress with a mandate to organise quinquennial international conferences, collect relevant statistics, and support penal reform. A permanent International Commission was established in Berne, Switzerland. The Commission's programme gradually expanded to cover legislative and preventive issues reflected in the new name, the International Penal and Penitentiary Commission.[86] The congresses were subsequently held in Stockholm (1878), Rome (1885), St. Petersburg (1890), Paris (1895); Brussels (1900), Budapest (1905), and Washington (1910). The next congress scheduled to be held in London in 1915 was cancelled due to the outbreak of World War I. When the next congress was eventually held in London in 1925, it drew, besides other luminaries, Enrico Ferri.[87] Subsequently, congresses were held in Prague (1930), Berlin (1935), and finally The Hague (1950), a few months before the Penitentiary Commission got assimilated into the United Nations.

80 Ibid 5.
81 Herk Eugene D' Alinge, cited in Howard Association (n 79) 10.
82 Ibid 8.
83 Sellin, 'Preface' (n 78) xiii.
84 Ibid.
85 Ibid xvi. See Howard Association (n 79) 16; Wines, 'International Congress on the Prevention and Repression of Crime' (n 76) 1–6.
86 Grunhut (n 61) 469.
87 Bates, 'One World in Penology' (n 60) 567.

The Berlin Congress will be discussed in some detail shortly as the major part of the criticism about the Commission's role has centred on that event. First, a word about the Commission's contributions over 75 years of existence. As Evelyn Ruggles-Brise recognised in 1925, the congresses held under the aegis of the Penitentiary Commission had come to represent an 'international movement for the treatment of crime'.[88] The direction which the movement took had a strong influence on indeterminate sentencing, conditional conviction, and the reformatory system, particularly in relation to juvenile offenders through the first quarter of the century. During the period 1929–1939, the Penitentiary Commission collaborated with the League of Nations whilst continuing its independent status and agenda.[89] The ground for such engagement had been prepared by the Howard League for Penal Reform in the mid-1920s, due in large part, to the initiative of its then secretary, Margery Fry.[90] In 1929, the Howard League published a memorandum recommending that the question of prison reform be put on the agenda of the League of Nations and a code on prisons be adopted. A sub-committee of the Penitentiary Commission drew up the text of 'Standard Minimum Rules for the Treatment of Prisoners', which was published in the 'Bulletin of the International Penitentiary Commission' in 1929 and presented at the 1930 Penitentiary Congress in Prague. The Rules came up before the Fifth Committee of the League of Nations, mandated to deal with humanitarian and penal matters, which distributed it to the 'Council and the Members of the League'.[91] The Rules were adopted by the Assembly of the League of Nations on 26 September 1934, as will be shown in Chapter 5.[92]

To Sanford Bates, one of the most influential American penal reformers of the twentieth century, the 'Standard Minimum Rules' were the single most important contribution made by any organisation in the field of international collaboration on penal matters.[93] The 'Standard Minimum Rules for the Treatment of Prisoners' adopted by the First United Nations Congress on the Prevention of Crime and the Treatment of Offenders in 1955, were, in fact, an updated version of the document originally drafted by the Penitentiary Commission.[94] The Rules were revised further with additional provisions on medical care, documentation

88 Ruggles-Brise (n 41) 9.

89 Leon Radzinowicz, 'International Collaboration in Criminal Science' (n 32) 326–332.

90 Howard League for Penal Reform, 'International Co-operation in Penal Matters' (1930); Radzinowicz, (n 32) 376; Rose (n 80) 314–317.

91 League of Nations, 'Improvements in Penal Administration: Standard Minimum Rules for the Treatment of Prisoners Drawn up the International Prison Commission', League of Nations Doc C.620.M.241. 1930. IV.

92 League of Nations OJ, Spec. Supp. 123 (1934). See also Paul Cornil, 'International Standards for the Treatment of Offenders' (1968) 26(3) *International Review of Criminal Policy* 3.

93 Bates, 'One World in Penology' (n 60) 565. For a first-hand account of his experiences as a prison administrator and reformer, see Sanford Bates, *Prisons and Beyond* (Palgrave Macmillan 1937).

94 Adopted by the First United Nations Congress on the Prevention of Crime and the Treatment of Offenders, held at Geneva in 30 August 1955, and approved by the Economic and Social Council by its resolutions 663 C (XXIV) of 31 July 1957 and 2076 (LXII) of 13 May 1977.

of detention, prevention of torture, and so on, and adopted by the UN General Assembly in 2015 as the 'Nelson Mandela Rules'.[95] Human rights and international law scholarship has yet to recognise the intellectual pedigree and ideological genesis of the document.[96]

In addition to organising international congresses, the Penitentiary Commission also initiated comparative studies in penal law, which, together with the congress proceedings and a regular bulletin, provided a wealth of knowledge on a range of subjects. The practice was initiated in the run up to the first International Prison Congress in London (1872), where participating governments had been invited to submit reports on the prisons and prison administration of their respective countries.[97] In a question that would reverberate some 70 years later in the drafting of the 'International Bill of Human Rights', the governments were asked, '(Is) the reformation of the prisoners made the primary aim in the prisons of your country?'[98]

The breadth of the subjects covered, and the quantum of material produced in the reports commissioned subsequently, is impressive. For example, four volumes prepared for the eighth International Prison Congress in Washington in 1910 spanned over 1500 pages, covering the subjects of prison reform and criminal law, penal and reformatory institutions, preventive treatment of neglected children, and preventive agencies and methods.[99] Each five-yearly congress itself was divided into four sections, namely 'Penal Legislation', 'Penal Administration', 'Prevention', and 'Children and Youth Issues'. Questions for discussion under each section were decided in advance and discussed in committees during the congress with the assembly voting on resolutions at the end of the debate around each question. Even as participants were official delegates, invariably they happened to be leading criminologists, academic lawyers, prison administrators, and philanthropists. Among the recurrent legislative questions was recidivism as an aggravative factor in sentencing; criminal responsibility of the mentally disabled; the penalty of transportation; and crucially, alternatives to imprisonment, particularly for minor crimes. Overall, much more space was given to administrative and preventive issues compared to legislative ones. Under 'Penal Administration',

95 United Nations Standard Minimum Rules for the Treatment of Prisoners (the Nelson Mandela Rules) (adopted 17 December 2015) UN Doc A/RES/70/175.

96 See, for example, Nigel S. Rodley and Matt Pollard, *The Treatment of Prisoners Under International Law* (3rd edn, Oxford University Press 2009) 383; Javaid Rehman, *International Human Rights Law* (2nd edn, Pearson 2010) 25, 98. cf. Roger S. Clark, *A United Nations High Commissioner for Human Rights* (Martinus Nijhoff 1972) 11–12, 98.

97 Reports were submitted by Austria, Belgium, Denmark, France, Germany, Italy, the Netherlands, Norway, Russia, Sweden, Switzerland, United States, and the United Kingdom. See Pears (n 83) 5–353.

98 EC Wines, *Report on the International Penitentiary Congress of London, Held July 3–13, 1872* (Government Printing Office 1873) 14, 7–126.

99 Charles Richmond Henderson, *Correction and Prevention: Four Volumes Prepared for the Eighth International Prison Congress* (Russell Sage Foundation, Charities Publication Committee 1910).

the congresses repeatedly engaged with the merits and de-merits of the cellular system versus the reformatory system based on co-operative work; the best means of enforcing prison discipline; moral and technical education as a means of reformation; and the aims of prison labour. 'Prevention' – also referred to as 'social defence' in conference proceedings – bore an imprint of positivist ideas, utilitarian philosophy as well as the emerging Protestant-bourgeois ethic. There was thus plenty of arguing on the connection between alcoholism and vagrancy and repeated offences, effective probationary measures, employment opportunities, and so on.

The debate on castration and sterilisation as preventive measures, which reached its crescendo at the Berlin Congress in 1935, had begun to surface as early as 1910 during the congress in Washington.[100] Judged by today's norms, the proceedings manifested insensitivity toward children, women, and the mentally ill. Thus, one cannot ignore references to 'criminal lunatics' (Paris Congress 1895), 'female depravity' (Budapest Congress 1905), and 'feeble-minded children' (Washington Congress 1910). Similarly, many of the ideas geared toward offender rehabilitation and crime prevention seemed to have a class-bias with strong concerns about the criminal tendencies of the unemployed youth and 'vagabonds'. At the same time, most views expressed up until the 1935 Berlin Congress were firmly against retributive penalties, custodial sentences for minor crimes, corporal punishment as a means of prison discipline, and solitary confinement. It is fair to say that the Penitentiary Commission was a trend-setter for some penal norms that are taken for granted today, such as the segregation of children and adults in prisons. On some issues, the contents of the debates compare favourably against the contemporary human rights discourse. To illustrate, one of the questions discussed at the Washington Congress in 1910 was: 'How is it possible, while paying attention to the correction of the offender, to lighten the heavy economic burden falling upon families owing to the imprisonment of those upon whom they are dependent?'[101] As will be shown in Chapter 7, the present-day discourse of human rights filters out the suffering of the families of offenders since it focuses on the formal equality of abstract individuals as embodied in the principle of proportionate sentencing.

Within the scant academic literature on the legacy of the Penitentiary Commission, most extensive comments are to be found in the writings of Leon Radzinowicz. However, it has to be said, with due respect, that Radzinowicz's views on the Penitentiary Commission are marked by ambiguity and some self-contradiction. In the first relevant piece he wrote as a young scholar in 1942, Radzinowicz noted the great merits of international collaboration represented by organisations such as the Penitentiary Commission. The resolutions adopted at the conferences, in his view, 'had a great influence on the shaping of penal legislation throughout the world'.[102] Radzinowicz also saw great merit in bringing together theorists and

100 Ruggles-Brise (n 41) 153.
101 Ibid 197–200.
102 Radzinowicz, 'International Collaboration in Criminal Science' (n 32) 322.

practitioners as a means of managing criminal justice on 'scientific lines'.[103] He was concerned though, in that early evaluation, about the need 'for advancing beyond the boundaries of the traditional doctrine of national sovereignty' and the absence of an organisation with 'adequate prestige and adequate power'.[104] This assertion rings true in the sense that the Penitentiary Commission never had a formal status as a standard-setting body in international law. But it contradicts Radzinowicz's own acknowledgement of the impact of Commission's resolutions on domestic legislation.

In a 1991 publication, Radzinowicz credited the Penitentiary Commission for initiating 'the modern stage of international collaboration in criminal matters'.[105] Having achieved the remarkable feat of reading and reflecting upon the proceedings of all the congresses held, he could conclude that 'the end-product of the IPPC (the Penitentiary Commission) is in scope, thoroughness, and volume superior' to the contribution made by other international associations.[106] Whilst expressing dissatisfaction with the treatment given to the question of the death penalty, Radzinowicz put it down to the highly controversial and political nature of the issue during the period the Penitentiary Commission was in existence. Further, referring to the Washington Congress of 1910 – where delegates were invited to present country reports on the death penalty – he acknowledged that the Commission 'mounted an impressive collection of material on the state of capital legislation in several countries, a collection which even today has its value'.[107] This grateful acknowledgement would be contradicted by Radzinowicz's assertion in his professional memoirs published in 1999. The reports on the death penalty presented at the Washington Congress, he noted then, had amounted merely to 'a matter of conveying straightforward information'.[108] Although it is true that there had been no extensive debate on the topic at the 1910 Washington Congress, delegates had shared important national statistics on the use of the death penalty. The representatives of Italy and Norway declared that the abolition in their countries had had no appreciable effect on crime.[109] Were it not for the discrediting of the Penitentiary Commission in the post-World War II era, scholars could perhaps look back at the 1910 Washington Congress in a different light – possibly as one of the earliest international attempts at questioning the legitimacy of capital punishment.

The rest of the narrative dealing with the Penitentiary Commission in Radzinowicz's memoirs is marked by self-contradiction. Reflecting on the contents of the congresses, he rates them as superior to 'any Proceedings of any congresses in the field of history, social or political sciences or comparative law' and that

103 Ibid.
104 Ibid 327.
105 Radzinowicz, 'The Roots of the International Association' (n 57) 26.
106 Ibid 21.
107 Ibid 27.
108 Radzinowicz, 'Adventures in Criminology' (n 31) 367.
109 Ruggles-Brise, (n 41) 187–192.

even though the prevailing tone was 'cautious, restricted, conservative', it did not favour the status quo.[110] This idea is turned over its head a few pages into the chapter, where he suggests that 'the commission never took the initiative to inquire into any important sector of criminal justice where there was evidence that remedies were called for'.[111] In what has become a standard line of attack on the Commission, Radzinowicz also referred to the 'continued acceptance of fascist governments . . . as permanent members' and the imposition of 'Nazi criminological and penal doctrine' on the Berlin Congress convened in 1935.[112] In a subsequent assessment, albeit a brief one, another scholar alleged that the Commission had fallen prey to 'Nazification'.[113] That charge rests on a partial reading of the 1935 congress proceedings, at best. The criticism hinges on how the German hosts lectured the delegates on the virtues of National Socialism. It does not tell the other half of the story, which concerns the stance taken by the veterans of the Penitentiary Commission who were present at the Berlin Congress.[114] More on this shortly.

Some accounts dealing with the evolution of the United Nations Crime Prevention and Criminal Justice Programme tangentially mention the takeover of the activities of the Penitentiary Commission pursuant to a General Assembly Resolution in 1950.[115] They do so without discussing the context and reasons for the move.[116] This apolitical approach, where conflict and disagreement are written out of history, is quite common in human rights historiography. An official publication summarising the engagement of the United Nations with crime prevention reiterates the charge of Nazification. It links the 'downfall' of the Penitentiary Commission in the wake of World War II with the floundering of the League of Nations.[117] The latter point does not stand to reason. This is because the Penitentiary Commission's affiliation with the League had always been

110 Radzinowicz, 'Adventures in Criminology' (n 31) 363.

111 Ibid 367.

112 Ibid 368.

113 Paul Knepper, *International Crime in the 20th Century: The League of Nations Era 1919–1939* (Palgrave Macmillan 2011) 82–85.

114 cf. WJ Forsythe, *Penal Discipline, Reformatory Projects and the English Prison Commission 1895–1939* (University of Exeter Press 1990) 234–235; Clive Emsley, *Crime, Police and Penal Policy: European Experiences 1750–1940* (Oxford University Press 2004) 266.

115 UNGA, 'Transfer of Functions of the International Penal and Penitentiary Commission', Res. 415 (v), 5th Sess., Supp. (No. 20) at 37. UN Doc A/1775 (1950).

116 See for example, Herman Woltring, 'The Evolution of United Nations Policy Approaches to Crime Prevention and Criminal Justice: From the Committee on Crime Prevention and Control to the Commission on Crime Prevention and Criminal Justice' in M Cherif Bassiouni (ed), *The Contributions of Specialized Institutes and Non-Governmental Organizations to the United Nations Criminal Justice Program: In Honor of Adolfo Beria di Argentine* (Martinus Nijhoff Publishers 1995) 65–82, 65; Roger S. Clark, *The United Nations Crime Prevention and Criminal Justice Program: Formulation of Standards and Efforts at Their Implementation* (University of Pennsylvania Press 1994) 11, 19.

117 United Nations, *The United Nations and Crime Prevention* (UN 1996) 5.

tenuous and rather loosely structured. About the creeping influence of the Nazis, the document mounts a series of allegations:

> When the United Nations was formed after the close of the war, it was decided that the control and prevention of crime would be included in its brief. The Organization declined, however, to accept affiliation with the IPPC, and for understandable reasons. Seventy-five years of valuable work and collection of research materials were tarnished by the Commission's 1935 conference, held in Berlin and dominated by adherents of the Nazi Government in power in Germany. During the war years a substantial part of funding for the IPPC came from the Axis powers, and the Commission all too frequently served as a publicist for theories on the racial and biological roots of crime and draconian measures for its control.[118]

The UN did not cite a single document to back its claim. In asserting that the newly formed organisation refused to affiliate with the Penitentiary Commission for 'understandable reasons', the document seems to imply that the 1935 Berlin Congress had somehow entailed an approval of Nazi policies. Yet, as we will see, many delegates from outside Germany had taken a brave stand against some of the ideas put forward by their German counterparts. Further, meeting for the first time after the end of the war, the executive committee of the Penitentiary Commission had condemned Nazi atrocities and lent unconditional support to the prosecution of the Nazi officials.[119] Sure enough, the leadership of the Commission was averse to the idea of a merger with the UN. But that had more to do with a desire to retain an independent status rather than any ideological sympathies with Nazism.

When the executive committee met in April 1946, Edward Cass, General Secretary of the American Prison Association, sitting in for Sanford Bates, informed other members about the discussions taking place at the temporary Social Commission of the newly formed United Nations about 'collaboration' with the pre-existing international organisations, including the Penitentiary Commission.[120] Three distinct possibilities existed for such collaboration: a) the Commission could be made part of a larger specialised agency under Articles 57 and 63 of the Charter of the United Nations; b) it could be dissolved and its functions transferred to the UN Economic and Social Commission; and c) it could retain its independent status whilst collaborating with the United Nations. Cass went on to state that the 'third alternative namely, that of maintaining the Commission in its present form and of developing collaboration, has a great many advocates

118 Ibid.

119 *Minutes of the Meeting of the Executive Committee of the International Penal and Penitentiary Commission. Berne, April 1946* (Staempfli & CIE., Berne 1946) 23.

120 'Current Notes, Relations to Be Developed Between the International Penal and Penitentiary Commission and the United Nations Organization (U. N. O.)' (1946) 37(3) *Journal of Criminal Law and Criminology* 242.

among the American penal experts'.[121] In the event, it was the last option that drew the support of the executive committee, including then President of the Commission Alexander Paterson.[122] The following resolution was adopted as the basis for future negotiations:

> The Executive Committee of the International Penal and Penitentiary Commission, meeting for the first time after the war of 1939 to 1945, expresses the wish that, in the sphere of the prevention and treatment of delinquency and crime, close co-operation shall be established between the Economic and Social Council of U.N.O and the International Penal and Penitentiary Commission, provided always that the [Commission] shall retain its complete independence as an organisation.[123]

In addition to condemning the Nazi atrocities, the meeting also addressed the issue of the payment of fees by member states. Under organisational rules, each member state was required to make annual contributions at the rate of 170 francs per million inhabitants. The executive committee decided not to ask Germany for the payment of its dues but considered whether to consider the 'special situation' of Franco's Spain, which had left the country in arrears. By the end of 1947, however, Spain had withdrawn its membership of the Penitentiary Commission, thus removing the last vestige of its 'association' with Axis powers.[124] Interestingly, Manuel Lopez-Rey, chief of the UN Social Defence Section from 1952 to 1960, once suggested that Washington had become disillusioned with the Penitentiary Commission because 'it was financially too dependent on United States contribution' despite its predominantly European character.[125] The charge levelled by the UN (in the document cited above) that the Penitentiary Commission was receiving the bulk of its funding from Axis powers stands in contradiction to this view. The veracity of this allegation is also suspect, because, as we have seen, the members were obligated to make financial contributions based on their population. The United States, being more populous than any of the Axis powers, would logically have put in greater contributions.

In the negotiations that followed, members of the Penitentiary Commission made their co-operation or affiliation conditional on the holding of a quinquennial congress; continued participation of the present delegates in future congresses; the retaining of the commission's permanent office in Berne and its financial assets; the continuation of the practice of employing personnel with 'professional, technical, or scientific experience in penal and penitentiary matters'; and a guarantee that

121 *Minutes of the Meeting of the Executive Committee of the International Penal and Penitentiary Commission. Berne, April 1946* (Staempfli & CIE., Berne 1946) 18.

122 Alexander Paterson was Commissioner for Prisons in England and Wales from 1922 until 1946.

123 *Minutes of the Meeting of the Executive Committee of the International Penal and Penitentiary Commission. Berne, April 1946* (Staempfli & CIE., Berne 1946) 20.

124 Bates, 'One World in Penology' (n 60) 570.

125 Lopez-Rey (n 37) 489–508, 490.

all delegates continue to 'have complete freedom to express their opinion on any matter before the organisation'.[126] As late as October 1947, then President of the Penitentiary Commission Sanford Bates saw no reason why the organisation he represented and the United Nations could not exist side by side.[127] This was not to be, however. The General Assembly authorised the Secretary General of the United Nations to take over the functions of the Commission on 1 December 1950.[128]

The Berlin Congress: setting the record straight

Turning to the 1935 Berlin Congress, there is no doubt that the German government had done everything in its power to justify Nazi penal policy, and to dispel the 'prejudiced' coverage of National Socialism in the foreign press, as Minister of Justice of the Reich Franz Gurtner put it in his opening address. Gurtner justified replacing the principle of legality with a new vision of criminal law, whereby 'a wrong is possible in Germany in future even when no law threatens it with punishment'.[129] Informed by a uniform 'view of life dominating the whole nation', Gurtner went on to note smugly, the judge will 'obtain a secure feeling of right and wrong'.[130] Far from affirming the ideas of positivist criminology, Minister Gurtner actually attacked psychological and sociological explanations of crime as this, in his opinion, resulted in a tendency to excuse the criminal act. The task of criminal law, on Gurtner's account, would be to express 'the moral responsibility of the offender to the community'.[131] The fascination of other German delegates with retributivism as distinct from the prevention and rehabilitation-oriented agenda of the Penitentiary Commission would become evident in the plenary discussions to follow.

When, as president of the session, Sanford Bates opened the discussion on prison administration on the morning of 20 August 1935, the question put up for discussion was:

> Are the methods applied in the execution of penalties with a view to educating and reforming criminals (intensive humanisation, favours granted, considerable relaxation of coercion in the execution of penalties by degrees) calculated to bring about the effects aimed at and are these tendencies generally advisable?

126 Bates, 'One World in Penology' (n 60) 570.

127 Ibid.

128 'Transfer of Functions of the International Penal and Penitentiary Commission' UNGA, Res. 415 (v), 5th Sess., Supp. (No. 20) at 37, UN Doc A/1775 (1950). The Commission's funds were transferred to the International Penal and Penitentiary Foundation (IPPF). Registered in Switzerland in July 1951, and awarded a consultative status with the UN Economic and Social Council, the IPPF would be relegated to an obscure existence.

129 Bureau of the International Penal and Penitentiary Commission, *Proceedings of the XITH International Penal and Penitentiary Congress Held in Berlin. August 1935* (Staemfli & Cie. Printers 1937) 10.

130 Ibid 10–11.

131 Ibid 21.

M. Muller, the rapporteur general, shared his synthesis of 11 reports submitted on the above question.[132] In response to speeches made by the European and American delegates, stressing the importance of education in prisons and other opportunities for rehabilitation, Paul Herr of Germany insisted that the 'interests of the community only should prevail and not those of a small group of criminals'.[133] The criminals must be shown, Herr insisted, 'by a severe treatment . . . that they have done wrong and that they have to take account of the interests of the community and of the people who defend themselves against criminality'.[134] Similarly, Novelli Giovani from the Italian Ministry of Justice put in a brief for retributivist ideology by stating 're-education should by no means suppress the idea of retribution, otherwise the penalty in its proper sense would no more exist'.[135] Touching on a theme that reverberates in the present-day neoliberal law and order rhetoric, Paul Herr spoke in favour of the principle of 'less eligibility'.[136] The life inside prison, Herr took the view, should be more severe in conditions of economic recession so that the criminal is not inclined 'to find a shelter in the prison against the general economic misery'.[137] In an evident jibe at the reformatory movement in the United States, another German delegate Edgar Schmidt said it was 'not right to give the prisoners privileges, for instance cinematographic representations, concerts, practice of sports and similar distractions which the free population is not able to get for themselves'.[138]

History owes an unacknowledged debt of gratitude to several delegates, who, far outnumbered by the Germans, pressed on with the case for a reformatory regime. Amid a swelling chorus of German voices, all arguing for strict prison discipline and retributive penalties, Lord Polwarth, former chairman of the Scottish Prison Commission, spoke his mind bluntly: 'We have no right to keep a man in prison and send him out again without having given him every chance to better himself. We consequently have no right to release him with a sick body or mind'.[139] A compromise resolution was proposed providing that the interests of the community be given priority in the criminal law; that 'the execution of penalties must not be confined to the imposition of punishment but must also provide for the education and betterment of the prisoners'; and that the methods applied for the education of offenders remain 'within reason, without exaggeration and with due regard to the individuality of the prisoners'.[140]

132 Bureau of the International Penal and Penitentiary Commission, *Proceedings of the XITH International Penal and Penitentiary Congress* (n 133) 168.
133 Ibid 181–182, 187.
134 Ibid 187.
135 Ibid 196.
136 See Rotman (n 75) 112.
137 Bureau of the International Penal and Penitentiary Commission, *Proceedings of the XITH International Penal and Penitentiary Congress* (n 133) 188.
138 Ibid 191.
139 Ibid 200.
140 Ibid 227.

When M. Delierneux of Belgium sought an amendment to strengthen the part dealing with offender rehabilitation and removing the word 'punishment' altogether, he invited a retort from M.E Schafer of Germany who said that, 'A wrong idea would be provoked if the resolution would only speak of education and amendment, without mentioning at all the fact that the penalty must nevertheless remain a punishment'.[141] When Delierneux's amendment was put to vote it led to a bizarre result, reflecting the disproportionate numbers of German delegates. By the numbers of voting members, 47 were in favour and 137 against. However, of the countries represented at the session, ten voted in favour of the amendment and nine against.[142] The president's announcement that the amendment had been rejected led to a noisy protest by foreign delegates. Some delegates led by Edward Cass of the United States suggested that the resolution be dropped altogether and taken up afresh at the next congress.

The Germans would have none of it since the 'Congress Regulations' provided that the votes would be taken by roll call. In an extraordinary move at this stage, Sanford Bates stated that since the delegates could not agree on the appropriate voting method, he would use his discretion. In his opinion 'the vote by countries must be decisive and conforming'.[143] This ruling, he suggested, was necessary to preserve the right of the small nations to have a say in the matter. Infuriated by the announcement, a German delegate said the decision did not 'belong to the President's competence and did not seem to be justified'.[144] It was decided eventually that the president would bring the result of the vote as it had taken place – by roll call and as well by countries – to the knowledge of the Bureau of the Congress and leave the decision to it. It is a cruel irony that instead of being remembered as the demonstration of courage by a small group of committed individuals, the Berlin Congress was construed as an example of capitulation to the Nazis. The United Nations' claim that 'seventy-five years of valuable work and collection of research materials were tarnished by the Commission's 1935 conference' amounts to a most unfortunate distortion of history.[145]

The question of sterilisation as a penal measure came up at the Berlin Congress in the section on prevention of crime. The discussion centred on reports from a number of countries. The German rapporteur described the 'results of sterilisation and castration' as practiced in his country and recommended that 'eugenic sterilisation . . . be employed by all States as a means of preventing transmission of hereditary taints'.[146] The Italian rapporteur expressed approval of the laws for eugenic sterilisation with the consent of those concerned but was

141 Ibid 229.
142 Ibid 232.
143 Ibid 233.
144 Ibid.
145 United Nations *(n 121)* 5.
146 Bureau of the International Penal and Penitentiary Commission, *Proceedings of the XITH International Penal and Penitentiary Congress* (n 133) 297.

opposed to compulsory sterilisation. Pal Popenoe, a biologist from California, whole-heartedly supported the sterilisation of 'certain weak-minded or mental offenders incapable of producing healthy offspring or of bringing up children in favourable moral conditions'.[147] By contrast, the French rapporteur claimed that the limited knowledge on heredity that was available did not justify the practice of sterilisation on eugenic grounds, 'even with the consent of those concerned'.[148] The Netherlands, Belgium, and Hungary set out certain religious objections to sterilisation.[149] It was these notes of caution which led the unanimously adopted resolution in favour of sterilisation as a preventive measure against 'disordered sexual inclination' to also include a caveat. The 'compulsory castration and sterilisation', according to the resolution, should be 'undertaken with the greatest precaution only, and in proper proceedings which provide for a thorough investigation of the case by a committee of jurists and medical men'.[150]

Even this qualified approval of sterilisation cannot be justified if we are to take the bodily integrity of human beings seriously. What can be said in defence of the Penitentiary Commission though is that it is unfair to judge it solely on the standards of our time, and to overlook its progressive stance on a range of other issues. By the early twentieth century the eugenics movement had attracted such celebrities as H.G. Wells, W.B. Yeats, Aldous Huxley, and T.S. Eliot with their anxieties about the inferior breeds, invalids, and philistine masses.[151] Yet, it would be facile to use this as a reason to renounce 'Sailing to Byzantium', 'Brave New World' or 'The Waste Land'.

The venue for the eleventh Penitentiary Congress had been decided before Hitler came to power. As the policies of the Third Reich began to be known outside Germany, some opposed the holding of the congress in Berlin. In Britain, the Howard League took this position whereas Alexander Paterson – Her Majesty's Commissioner of Prisons from 1922 to 1947 – was in favour of participation. Paterson persisted in his belief that reason would prevail at the congress.[152] Those censuring the Penitentiary Commission for holding the Congress in Berlin in 1935, should, at least, recount the fact that Britain, the United States, France, and several other Western nations went on to participate in the 1936 Berlin Olympics. The British Prime Minister David Lloyd George was overwhelmed by the 'economic miracle' produced by Hitler when he visited Germany in 1936.

147 Ibid 295.
148 Ibid 295–296.
149 Ibid 302.
150 Ibid 340–342.
151 John Carey, *Intellectuals and the Masses: Pride and Prejudice Among the Literary Intelligentsia, 1880–1939.* (Faber and Faber 1992) 13. See also Donald Childs, *Modernism and Eugenics: Woolf, Eliot, Yeats and the Culture of Degeneration* (Cambridge University Press 2001).
152 Howard League for Penal Reform, *Annual Report (1934–5)* 10; Enid Huws Jones, *Margery Fry: The Essential Amateur* (Oxford University Press) 181.

Upon his return to England, he described 'Hitler as a born leader of men, trusted by the old, idolized by the young, who had lifted his country from the depths'.[153] If those running the affairs of the Penitentiary Commission had failed to anticipate the full extent of the horrors that lay in store, they were hardly alone in lacking the requisite foresight.

153 Cited in A.N. Wilson, *Hitler: A Short Biography* (Harper Press 2012) 10.

3 Retributivism in the age of human rights

Everything that we see is a shadow cast by that which we do not see.
Martin Luther King Jr.[1]

The decade of the 1970s represents a crucial turning point in the history of modern criminal justice and penology. Significantly, that period also marks the ascendance of human rights as a pre-eminent moral language of our times.[2] In terms of penological and criminal justice context, the 1970s saw growing disenchantment, especially in the United States, with the long-standing tradition of positivist criminology. The project of 'offender rehabilitation' and 'indeterminate sentencing' came under attack from both the political right and the left.[3] Conservatives denounced 'penal welfarism' for failing to take victims' rights seriously, for being soft on crime, and for being unnecessarily lenient toward the offenders. For those on the left, primary concerns were racism and the abuse of authority by prison administrators and wardens acting in the name of rehabilitation. Some memorable films of the era, such as Stanley Kubrick's *A Clockwork Orange*, and Ken Kesey's *One Flew Over the Cuckoo's Nest*, spoke to these anxieties as they captured the twisted sense of paternalism that characterised some correctional institutions.

The '70s was also a period when philosophers began to assess social problems in the language of rights.[4] Some of the major theoretical accounts of human rights emerged during that period.[5] At the same time, a number of thinkers revived Kantian and Hegelian ideas to propose an essentially retributive vision of justice and with it the image of the human as 'a metaphysical or calculating, self-interested

1 Martin Luther King Jr., *The Measure of a Man* (Fortress Press 1988) 40.
2 Samuel Moyn, *The Last Utopia: Human Rights in History* (Harvard University Press 2010).
3 Charles H Logan and Gerald G. Gaes, 'Meta-Analysis and the Rehabilitation of Punishment' (1993) 10 *Justice Quarterly* 245, 246.
4 Rolf Sartorius, 'Utilitarianism, Rights and Duties to Self' (1985) 22(3) *American Philosophical Quarterly* 241.
5 See, for example, Robert Nozick, *Anarchy, State and Utopia* (Basic Books Inc. 1974); Ronald Dworkin, *Taking Rights Seriously* (Harvard University Press 1978).

being conceived of in an asocial way'.[6] Without discounting regional variations, it would hardly be an exaggeration to claim that ours is an era marked by the intellectual hegemony of both retributivism and human rights. There is a significant body of literature tracing the revival of retributivism and the punitive turn in penal policy roughly since the closing years of the 1960s through mid-1980s, or what we could call, taking a cue from Eric Hobsbawm, the 'long seventies'.[7] In recent years, scholars have enriched the debate by addressing the expansion of the state's punitive power in regions outside Western Europe and North America.[8]

What seems missing in the expanding scholarship on the subject is an analysis of the theoretical affinity between neo-retributivist or neoclassical perspectives on penal policy and the discourse of human rights. Some of the most brilliant critics of retributivism and the expanding reach of the criminal justice dragnet manage to skirt around this relationship. Where scholars have looked at the twin phenomena of 'anti-impunity' and human rights movement, the focus has been transitional justice and international criminal law.[9] There is a parallel story which has received much less attention – namely, the relationship between the resurgence of retributivism in domestic penal policies and the rise of human rights as the principal moral language of our times.

It is no quaint coincidence, this chapter will argue, that almost the entire corpus of human rights scholarship is virtually silent on the idea of offender rehabilitation and alternatives to prison-based retributive justice. Contemporary human rights scholars do not seem to have much interest in either the context of crime or the collateral consequences of punishment, for example, in terms of the effects of incarceration on a prisoner's children.[10] Human rights discourse, as embodied

6 Alan Norrie, *Crime, Reason and History: A Critical Introduction to Criminal Law* (3rd edn, Cambridge University Press 2014) 31. See also Thomas Andrew Green, *Freedom and Criminal Responsibility in American Legal Thought* (Cambridge University Press 2014) 18, 284–343.

7 Hobsbawm famously characterised the period 1789 to 1914 as the 'long 19th century'.

8 See, for example, Markus-Michael Müller, 'The Rise of the Penal State in Latin America' (2012) 15(1) *Contemporary Justice Review* 57; Ramiro Avila Santamaria, 'Citizen Insecurity and Human Rights: Toward the Deconstruction of the Security Discourse and a New Criminal Law' in Cesar Rodriguez-Garavito (ed), *Law and Society in Latin America: A New Map* (Routledge 2015) 251–278.

9 Some of the most thoughtful contributions in this area are to be found in Karen Engle, Zinaida Miller and DM Davis (eds), *Anti-Impunity and the Human Rights Agenda* (Cambridge University Press 2016).

10 See, for example, Ben Emmerson, Andrew Ashworth and Alison MacDonald, *Human Rights and Criminal Justice* (Sweet & Maxwell 2007); Nigel S. Rodley and Matt Pollard, *The Treatment of Prisoners Under International Law* (3rd edn, Oxford University Press 2009); Alastair Mowbray, *Cases, Materials, and Commentary on the European Convention on Human Rights* (3rd edn, Oxford University Press 2012) 245–487; Sangeeta Shah, 'Detention and Trial' in Daniel Moeckli, Sangeeta Shah and Sandesh Sivakumaran (eds), *International Human Rights Law* (2nd edn, Oxford University Press 2014) 259–285; Ilias Bantekas and Lutz Oette, *International Human Rights Law and Practice* (Cambridge University Press 2013) 313–365; Merris Amos, *Human Rights Law* (2nd edn, Oxford University Press 2014) 287–408. For a more philosophically oriented perspective, which, nevertheless, uncritically adopts the metaphor of proportionate punishment, see James W. Nickel, 'Personal Deserts and

in academic commentaries and textbooks, it shall be my contention, signifies an implicit approval of the central tenets of modern retributivism, i.e. individual criminal responsibility, retribution, and proportionality as the basis of sentencing, and the fragmentation of criminal justice and social justice. Once you endorse these basic premises, the ground rules and terms of reference are already set. All involved begin to play the game of criminal justice on 'the home ground of conservative law-and-order politicians', and then, 'the genteel visions of retribution', as John Braithwaite and Phillip Petit have cautioned, 'count for naught'.[11]

Contrary to what contemporary proponents of retributivism would have us believe, it is not possible to exculpate retributivist ideas altogether in analysing the punitive turn in penal policy and practice. At the very least, modern retributivism must contend with the fact that proportionality-based punishment is mediated by broader contextual factors, and that it gets implicated in sociologically ill-informed responses to crime.

The life and death of the rehabilitative ideal

Michel Foucault's *Discipline and Punish*, published in 1971, left a deep impression on an entire generation of criminologists, and historians and sociologists interested in penal institutions.[12] Foucault's complex and multi-layered text supplied intellectual ammunition to the campaigners for prisoners' rights as well as those who were already growing dissatisfied with the 'rehabilitative ideal'.[13] A few were candid enough to admit that reading the 'dense volume' they had no idea 'what Foucault was saying most of the time'.[14] Sure enough, whilst postmodernist thought may have its virtues, clarity of expression is not one of them.

It is a merit of *Discipline and Punish* that it provides a much-needed corrective to the idealistic tradition of Whig historiography in which the story of penal practice was narrated as comprising incremental progress, a steady march away from cruelty toward more humane ways of dealing with convicts.[15] The stated intentions and professed ideals of reformers were taken at face value. The translation of theory into practice was viewed as a straightforward process.[16] Following

Human Rights' in Rowan Cruft, S. Matthew Liao and Massimo Renzo (eds), *Philosophical Foundations of Human Rights* (Oxford University Press 2015) 153–165, 160.

11 John Braithwaite and Philip Petit, *Not Just Deserts: A Republican Theory of Criminal Justice* (Clarendon Press 1998) 15–16.

12 Michael Foucault, *Discipline and Punish: The Birth of the Prison* (Penguin 1977) 100; John Pratt, 'This is not a Prison': Foucault, the Panopticon and the Pentonville' (1993) 2 *Social & Legal Studies* 373.

13 Francis T. Cullen, 'Rehabilitation: Beyond Nothing Works' in Michael Tonry (ed), *Crime and Justice in America, 1975–2025: Crime and Justice: A Review of Research* (Volume 42, The University of Chicago Press 2013) 299–376, 299.

14 Ibid 316.

15 See, for example, Evelyn *Ruggles-Brise, The English Prison System* (Palgrave Macmillan 1921).

16 For a critique of Whig historiography, see Lucia Zedner, *Women, Crime and Custody in Victorian England* (Calrendon Press 1991) 93; Stanley Cohen, *Visions of Social Control: Crime Punishment and Classification* (Polity Press 1985) 15–16.

Rusche and Krikhiemer, Foucault exhorts his readers early on in the text to shed all illusion that the prison is simply a means of reducing crime.[17] Whilst denying a 'strict correlation' between a mode of punishment and a given system of production (slavery in slave economy, corporal punishment in feudalism, forced labour in mercantile economy, and corrective detention under free-market industrial economy) that animates Rusche and Krikhiemer's avowedly Marxist account, Foucault problematises the proposition that the role of the eighteenth-century prison was humanitarian in contrast to previous forms of punishment as torture and public humiliation. The underlying aim, Foucault argues, was not to punish less, but to punish better – more economically and effectively. By imposing a strict routine, surveillance, and a labour regime, which, Foucault suggests, was never meant to be profitable or productive, the modern prison sought to create docile bodies and to transform 'the violent, agitated, unreflective convict into a part that plays its role with perfect regularity'.[18]

In place of the negative conception of 'sovereign power' that inhered in earlier forms of spectacular punishments, the prison represented power in the positive and productive sense of training and disciplining the body. Far from being an expression of reformers' humanism, the prison, to Foucault, represents a penalty *par excellence*, an instrument 'that could be made general throughout the entire social body, capable of coding all its behavior and consequently of reducing the whole diffuse domain of illegalities'.[19] The 'corrective function' of imprisonment, on Foucault's account, is not a later-day invention; rather the prison 'from the beginning of the nineteenth century, covered both the deprivation of liberty and the technical transformation of individuals'.[20] Reiterating this point in a 1975 interview, he said that the prison was, 'from the beginning . . . meant to be an instrument comparable with – and no less perfect than – the school, the barracks, or the hospital, acting with precision upon individual subjects'.[21]

Foucault's thesis alerts us to the unstated and covert functions of criminal punishment, and potentially sinister implications of seemingly benign projects, such as social rehabilitation of offenders. Alongside Erving Goffman's 1961 classic on 'total institutions', *Discipline and Punish* is an abiding reminder of the tiny intricacies of life inside the prison and the immense power that it wields over an inmate.[22] Through unobstructed access to the body of the prisoner, the prison becomes the site of the production of knowledges – criminology, medicine, and psychiatry – which constitute power and facilitate the exercise of power. By implication, *Discipline and Punish* nudges us to critically reflect on the limitations of

17 Georg *Rusche* and Otto *Kirchheimer, Punishment and Social Structure* (Columbia University Press 1939); Foucault (n 12) 24.

18 Foucault (n 12) 242.

19 Ibid 93, 231.

20 Foucault (n 12) 233.

21 Michel Foucault 'Prison Talk' in C Gordon (ed), *Power/Knowledge: Selected Interviews and Other Writings, 1972–1977* (Pantheon Books 1980) 37–54, 40–41.

22 Erving Goffman, *Asylums: Essays on the Social Situation of Mental Patients and Other Inmates* (Penguin 1961).

emancipatory discourses, including the discourse of human rights, in articulating abuses that work in subtle and elusive ways. And finally, even as it has echoes of materialist history, Foucault's thesis shows how social institutions – in this case the prison – could potentially generate a logic of their own, not always reducible to political economy.[23]

That said, as a historical account, the book suffers from certain flaws. Critics have charged Foucault with 'cavalier treatment of evidence' in claiming that the eighteenth-century penal system represented a break from earlier modes of punishment, that too in a somewhat uniform manner.[24] To Lucia Zedner, the operation of penal policy remained 'multi-faceted' and 'contradictory' well into the nineteenth century, barring a few 'model penitentiaries'.[25] The regime described in *Discipline and Punish* corresponded less to the actually existing prisons than Foucault's idealised account of Jeremy Bentham's Panopticon, the architectural device meant to ensure constant surveillance of inmates.[26] Along the same lines, David Garland and John Pratt have respectively argued, in the context of Victorian Britain and New Zealand, that there had been no sudden and complete transformation from punishments on the body to the corrective regime as suggested by Foucault.[27] Pratt draws attention to the official endorsement and application throughout the eighteenth century of the Victorian principle of 'less eligibility' meant to warn law-breakers that they would have to endure worse conditions than those prevailing for the worst-off in society.[28] The ideology of reformation itself evolved significantly over time from an early belief in penance through monastic silence to the Protestant ethic of industriousness to the late nineteenth- and early twentieth-century psychiatric interventions. Further, even during the heydays of positivist criminology, the idea that the prison was, above all, a means to punish and deter would-be offenders never vanished. Not only was there a gulf between rhetoric and reality, the reforming intentions that Foucault ascribes to nineteenth-century European penology were far from uniform or unequivocal.[29]

In relation to the link between prison labour and the reformation of offenders, Foucault appears to have read down the underlying objective of reminding the prisoner of the consequences of law-breaking and getting them to contribute

23 Cohen (n 16) 27. For a wider discussion of this aspect of Foucault's work, see Stevens Best and Douglas Kellner, *Postmodern Theory: Critical Interrogations* (Palgrave Macmillan 1991) 48.

24 Zedner (n 16) 97. See also David J. Rothman. *The Discovery of the Asylum: Social Order and Disorder in the New Republic* (2nd edn, Little Brown and Company 1990) xv.

25 Ibid.

26 Ibid 95; The idea of the Panopticon was originally conceived by Bentham's brother Brigadier-General Samuel Bentham. See Christopher Hibbert, *The Roots of Evil: A Social History of Punishment* (Sutton Publishing 2003) 151; Michael Ignatieff, *A Just Measure of Pain: The Penitentiary in the Industrial Revolution 1750–1850* (Palgrave Macmillan 1978) 77–78. On Bentham's failed bid to use the Panopticon as a model for England's first penitentiary, see Giles Playfair, *The Punitive Obsession: An Unvarnished History of the English Prison System* (Gollancz 1971) 26–29.

27 Pratt (n 12) 373; David Garland, *Punishment and Welfare* (Gower 1985).

28 Pratt (n 12) 375.

29 David J. Rothman, *Conscience and Convenience: The Asylum and Its Alternatives in Progressive America* (2nd edn, Aldine de Gruyter 2002) 10.

towards their board and lodging rather than transforming their souls.[30] The nineteenth-century European prison heralded a shift away from the disorder and chaos of earlier penal institutions. It did not, however, signify a radical break from the past on the lines suggested by Foucault. Toward the end of the nineteenth century, the renewed focus on rehabilitation increasingly led to the replacement of the treadmill with more productive forms of prison labour. But the practice, historically tied up with slavery, has yet to be freed from its punitive dimensions.[31]

Patricia O' Brien has made an attempt to rethink one of the main themes of *Discipline and Punish*, i.e. surveillance as guided by assumptions other than the rehabilitation of prisoners. Surveillance in the nineteenth-century French penal system, on her account, was predicated on the belief that the prison failed to rehabilitate the criminal and the criminal posed a continued threat to the society. O' Brien's work points up a major gap in Foucault's thesis – namely, a failure to account for the treatment of prisoners post-release. The exclusionary (rather than the rehabilitative) intent of the criminal penalty meant that the prisoner carried a stigma upon release and 'had limited choices in readjusting to civil society'.[32] As is the case today in many countries, statistics from the nineteenth century France suggested that 'post-institutionalization treatment' for many meant a 'return to a life of crime'.[33] O'Brien's analysis brings to mind Jean Valjean's desperate cry for help in Victor Hugo's *Les Miserables* as he is released having served 19 years in the galleys for stealing a loaf of bread:

> I was liberated four days ago, and am on my way to Pontarlier, which is my destination. I have been walking for four days since I left Toulon. I have travelled a dozen leagues today on foot. This evening, when I arrived in these parts, I went to an inn, and they turned me out, because of my yellow passport, which I had shown at the town-hall. . . . No one would take me. I went to the prison; the jailer would not admit me. I went into a dog's kennel; the dog bit me and chased me off, as though he had been a man. . . . Yonder, in the square, I meant to sleep on a stone bench. A good woman pointed out your house to me, and said to me, 'Knock there!' I have knocked. What is this place? Do you keep an inn? I have money – savings. One hundred and nine francs fifteen sous, which I earned in the galleys by my labour, in the course of nineteen years. I will pay. What is that to me? I have money. I am very weary; twelve leagues on foot; I am very hungry. Are you willing that I should remain?[34]

30 Ibid 381–382.

31 Helena Henrikson and Ralph Krech, 'International Perspectives' in Dirk van Zyl Smit (ed), *Prison Labour: Salvation or Slavery?* (Ashgate 1999) 297–312.

32 Patricia O' Brien, *The Promise of Punishment: Prisons in Nineteenth-Century France* (Princeton University Press 1982) 256.

33 Ibid.

34 Victor Hugo, *Les Miserables* (Volume I & II, Isabel FH Hapgood tr, First World Library 2007) 103.

To be fair, Foucault never attempted to generalise his thesis beyond modern Europe. Nonetheless, assessing the validity of his arguments in the context of the colonial prison is helpful in teasing out the paradoxes of modernity and imperial hypocrisies – legacies which continue to cast their shadow on the prison and other social institutions in the post-colonial world.[35] Looking at the history of imprisonment in Vietnam (Indochina) during the period 1862–1940, Peter Zinoman has marshalled evidence of the absence of 'modernist impulse' among colonial officers in charge of penal policy and prison administration. At a time when new disciplinary techniques were spreading in Europe and the United States, the prison system in French Indochina resembled the 'brutality and squalor of the eighteenth-century Bastille'.[36] Zinoman argues that the 'essentially racist orientation' of the imperialist project and an emerging conviction in '19th century French criminology that some lawbreakers were innately incorrigible' prevented the deployment of new disciplinary techniques in Indochina.[37]

The cynical use of prison labour in the name of rehabilitation was also brought dramatically into focus by the British policy of forcing Mau Mau insurgents in Kenya to work in detention during the 1950s. When 11 men were clubbed to death by guards in Hola prison camp in March 1959 for refusing to dig irrigation ditches, the Colonial Secretary Alan Lennox-Boyd defended the policy in the House of Commons: 'Experience has shown, time after time, that unless hard-core detainees can be got to start working their rehabilitation is impossible. Once they have started working, there is psychological breakthrough and astonishing results are achieved'. The speech drew a pithy retort from Sydney Silverman MP: 'Who told the Right Honourable Gentleman that? Stalin?'[38] The lack of any meaningful emphasis on prisoners' reform is also borne out by archival research into the colonial prison in British India. According to David Arnold, throughout the nineteenth century, despite some avowed recognition of the need to rehabilitate the prisoners, the colonial prison served as a site of repression and labour exploitation. Drawing on examples of frequent riots over poor diet and violations of religious edicts on caste-based segregation, Arnold has also demonstrated, contra Foucault, that prisoners were anything but an inert collection of bodies to be rendered docile by disciplinary techniques.[39]

The reinterpretation of Foucault's work helps restore the vivid complexity of the modern prison in a global perspective. It also illuminates the extant practice of punishment and rehabilitation in several ways. The assault on the 'rehabilitative

35 Gyan Prakash, 'Introduction: After Colonialism' in Prakash (ed), *After Colonialism: Imperial Histories and Postcolonial Displacements* (Princeton University Press 1994) 1–20.

36 Peter Zinoman, *The Colonial Bastille: A History of Imprisonment in Vietnam,* 1862–1940 (University of California Press 2001) 7.

37 Ibid 17.

38 Hansard, *Commons*, Vol 607, 16.6, 59, Col. 207; cited in Kirsten Sellars, *The Rise and Rise of Human Rights* (Sutton Publishing 2002) 87.

39 David Arnold, 'The Colonial Prison: Power, Knowledge and Penology in Nineteenth-Century India' in Arnold and David Hardman (eds), *Subaltern Studies VIII: Essays in Honour of Ranjit Guha* (Oxford University Press 1994) 148–187, 179.

ideal' in the long seventies, including blunt pronouncements of 'Nothing Works',[40] could be seen as targeting a phantom inasmuch as rehabilitation and individualised treatment had never been the exclusive goal of penal policy or prison administration.[41] To be sure, the ideas inspired by Christian charity, Calvinism, and positivist criminology made significant inroads into penal thinking during what is known as the 'progressive era' in the United States, spanning the final decades of the nineteenth century up until the third quarter of the twentieth century.[42] Model penitentiaries, such as the Elmira reformatory, had set some remarkable examples of treating inmates with compassion and respect, listening to their concerns, and providing them purposive activity.[43] However, few jurisdictions ever implemented the reform agenda to any degree of comprehensiveness.[44] As John Pratt has remarked, the disciplinary model that features so strongly in Foucault's work 'has a fairly limited role within modern penal institutions' given limited resources and political constraints, which keep governments from developing such projects to their full potential'.[45] According to Thom Brooks, 'Most countries lack a clear national strategy' and 'rehabilitation is rarely made a priority'.[46]

The rehabilitative ideal is further hobbled by the competing penological rationales of retribution and deterrence, not to mention the unstated penal goals of scapegoating, stigmatising, and marking the convicts out from law-abiding citizens. With majority of offenders drawn from lower strata of society, and in the absence of broader structural changes, even the most well-intentioned rehabilitation programmes cannot avoid the following question: What is it exactly that the offenders are being rehabilitated to?[47] To some, the idea of rehabilitation within the institution of prison contains a fundamental contradiction. As Ahmed Uthmani, the late founder of Penal Reform International, who spent nearly ten years in Tunisian jails noted in his memoirs:

> On the one hand, [the prison] creates dependence: you eat, sleep, piss, and wash at set times, in a life devoid of any responsibility. This removal of responsibility, this infantilisation, runs counter to any idea of rehabilitation

40 The slogan used by the American press to sum up Martinson's study. See Robert Martinson, 'What Works? – Questions and Answers About Prison Reform' (1974) 35 *The Public Interest* 22. See also, Charles H Logan and Gerald G Gaes, 'Meta-Analysis and the Rehabilitation of Punishment' (1993) 10 *Justice Quarterly* 245.

41 Joe Sim, *Punishment and Prison: Power and the Carceral State* (Sage 2009) 5–6.

42 Rothman, 'Conscience and Convenience' (n 29) 43.

43 William G. Hinkle and William J. Hartley, *The Decisive Decade in the History of the Elmira Reformatory* 1867–1877 (Edwin Mellen Press 2012).

44 Francis T Cullen and Karen E Gilbert, *Reaffirming Rehabilitation* (Anderson Publishing 1982) 81. See also, Sim (n 41) 6.

45 Pratt (n 12) 389.

46 Thom Brooks, *Punishment* (Routledge 2012) 59.

47 Pat Carlen, 'Against Rehabilitation; For Reparative Justice' in Kerry Carrington and others (eds), *Crime, Justice, and Social Democracy* (Palgrave Macmillan 2013) 89–104. 91. On this point, see also Barbara Hudson, *Justice through Punishment: A Critique of the "Justice" Model of Corrections* (Palgrave Macmillan 1987) 176.

> or social reintegration; in prison, you don't decide anything save what is forbidden: the only surviving freedom resides in transgression.[48]

Despite these conceptual tensions, one cannot help but sympathise with Donald Cressey's observation that without the 'humanizing influence' of the rehabilitative ideal, 'the history of corrections in America' – and elsewhere in the Western world – 'would be even bleaker than is now the case'.[49] Francis T. Cullen, an indefatigable chronicler and born-again advocate of offender rehabilitation, had himself been a great sceptic of the state's capacity to improve offenders' lives early in the 1970s. As the condemnation of rehabilitation and indeterminate sentencing reached its crescendo toward the end of the decade, Cullen had a change of heart:

> When rehabilitation is eliminated as the guiding correctional theory, will the alternative paradigm and its accompanying policies be better? Until this point, I had lacked the reflexivity to question the received wisdom about rehabilitation. But once the question was posed, the answer seemed stunningly obvious – No. Why would a system that overtly intends to inflict pain on offenders be preferable to one that at least pretends to try to improve their lives?[50]

In evaluating offender rehabilitation, one should be wary of over-generalisation as a variety of programmes go under the title. Pat Carlen has helpfully drawn attention to what she calls five dimensions of rehabilitation discourse. These involve: a) the formal-legal dimension concerned with the removal of stigma via expunging criminal records; b) psychiatric initiatives and behaviour modification programmes; c) social welfare approaches that seek to address gaps in education, employment skills, and housing; d) psycho-social approaches that combine individualised psychiatric approaches with social welfare interventions; and e) socio-political interventions that seek to rehabilitate offenders within the community through non-custodial sentences and community support.[51] Despite her misgivings about the idea of rehabilitation generally, Carlen could report some empirical evidence, as of 2013, indicating that a number of people desist from re-offending where in-depth support is provided along multiple dimensions and where offenders' own efforts are supported and appreciated through re-entry

48 Ahmed Othmani and Sophie Bessis, *Beyond Prison: The Fight to Reform Prison Systems around the World* (Marguerite Garling tr, Berghan 2008) 16. For another first-hand account, see John Bryant and others, 'Life Behind Bars' in Lori Gruen (ed), *The Ethics of Captivity* (Oxford University Press 2014) 102–112. See also Craig Haney, 'Foreword' in David Jones (ed), *Humane Prisons* (Radcliff Publishing 2006) vi–x; David Gordon Scott, *Ghosts Beyond Our Realm: A Neo-Abolitionist Analysis of Prisoner Human Rights and Prison Officer Occupational Culture* (PhD thesis, University of Central Lancashire 2006) 13–21, 276.

49 Donald R. Cressey, 'Foreword' in Cullen and Gilbert (n 44) xxix.

50 Cullen (n 13) 299–376, 303. See also John Braithwaite, *Crime, Shame and Reintegration* (Cambridge University Press 1989) 116.

51 Carlen (n 47) 93.

ceremonies and friendship circles.[52] Scholars have also identified the fallacy of the 'null hypothesis thesis', arguing that the absence of enough evidence to establish statistically significant outcomes of a rehabilitation programme does not necessarily mean that the programme has no impact or it does not work.[53]

Historically, the most commonly stated aim of rehabilitation programmes has been a reduction in recidivism, and through it, a net reduction in crime. An exclusive focus on this objective is somewhat limiting in that it may result in evaluators losing sight of other potentially positive outcomes. Rehabilitation programmes, for example, may contribute to better readjustment to personal and family life, attitudinal changes, educational achievement, and so on. Using recidivism rates as the evaluation criterion brings its own methodological problems as well; 'recidivism' gets employed to refer to a range of offender behaviour from arrests to reconviction to parole violation.[54] That problem was recognised by Robert Martinson in his 1974 'meta-study' even as he concluded that 'with few and isolated exceptions, the rehabilitative efforts that have been reported so far have had no appreciable effect on recidivism'.[55] Alongside the 'just deserts theory' – to be discussed shortly – Martinson's article became a rallying cry for the campaign against the rehabilitative ideal and for sentencing reforms in the United States. In substance, all Martinson had established was that 'there are no sure ways of reducing recidivism for offenders as a whole and that in this particular sense our available methods do no "work"'.[56] Martinson would subsequently withdraw his original conclusion. Based on fresh evidence, he was to argue in 1979 that 'no treatment program now used in criminal justice is inherently either substantially helpful or harmful'.[57] The critical fact, on the revised account, seemed to be 'the conditions under which the program is delivered'.[58] The finding, Martinson suggested, held true for a wide range of correction programmes as well as for parole supervision. But the tide had already turned against the rehabilitative ideal.

In England and Wales, a 1969 government White Paper, which stated the primary purpose of the prison service as 'to hold those committed to custody and to provide conditions for their detention which are currently acceptable to society', was interpreted, in retrospect, as having relegated Prison Rule 1 (the training and treatment of convicted prisoners to assist them to lead a good life)

52 Ibid 94.

53 David Weisburd, Cynthia M Lum and Sue-Ming Yang, 'When Can We Conclude That Treatments or Programs Don't Work?' (2003) 31(32) *Annals of the American Academy of Political and Social Science* 587.

54 Martinson, 'What Works?' (n 40) 24.

55 Ibid 24.

56 Ted Palmer, 'Martinson Revisited' (1975) 12 *Journal of Research in Crime and Delinquency* 133, 149. For a critique of Martinson's thesis and a historical account of its influence, see Garland, 'The Culture of Control' (n 7) 60–70.

57 Robert Martinson, 'New Findings, New Views: A Note of Caution Regarding Sentencing Reform' (1979) 7(2) *Hofstra Law Review* 243, 254.

58 Ibid.

to a secondary status.[59] In time, the retributive principle that criminal sentencing be based primarily on the seriousness of the offence (proportionality) rather than consequentialist goals, would be articulated in the famous 1990 White Paper, 'Crime, Justice and Protecting the Public', and the Criminal Justice Act 1991 and the Powers of Criminal Courts (Sentencing) Act 2000.[60] From the 1970s on, as Nicola Lacey and Hannah Pickard have noted, 'the retributive tradition, repackaged as the "just deserts movement" or the "justice model", had begun to capture the imagination of both policy makers and penal philosophers in the USA, the United Kingdom and many other countries'.[61]

The revival of retributivism and penal populism

John Kleinig observed in a 2011 essay that a review of philosophical literature of the first half of the twentieth century had left him with an impression that 'an earlier generation and its forebears had already consigned the notion of desert, along with its punitive expression, retribution, to the dustbin of history'.[62] Although academic discourse did not always translate into concrete practice, consequentialist theories held sway for a hundred years or so, providing a blueprint for a range of policy measures including indeterminate sentencing, probation, parole, and therapeutic interventions in prisons across the Western world. The welfarist approaches of dealing with crime also left their mark on the United Nations through the organisation's formative years.[63] That began to change considerably during the long seventies, when, according to Kleinig, 'desert underwent something of an academic revival, as liberal theorists sought to disentangle it from its emotivist associations and to articulate its connections with important dimensions of justice'.[64]

Returning to classical Enlightenment approaches, philosophers in the seventies justified punishment in terms of a backward-looking Kantian moral imperative couched in the language of 'just deserts'. The quantum of punishment was to be determined through a fixed sentencing scheme on the basis of 'proportionality' to the seriousness of an offence rather than any attempt to reform offenders.

59 Roy D. King and Kathleen McDermott, 'British Prisons: The Ever-Deepening Crisis' (1989) 29 *British Journal of Criminology* 107, 108.

60 For an overview, see Tim Newburn, '"Tough on Crime": Penal Policy in England and Wales' (2007) 36(1) *Crime and Justice* 425.

61 Nicola Lacey and Hanna Pickard, 'The Chimera of Proportionality: Institutionalising Limits on Punishment in Contemporary Social and Political Systems' (2015) 78(2) *Modern Law Review* 216, 225.

62 John Kleinig, 'What Does Wrongdoing Deserve?' in Michael Tonry (ed), *Retributivism Has a Past? Has It a Future?* (Oxford University Press 2011) 46–62, 47.

63 'United Nations Activities in the Field of Social Defence' (1968) 26 *International Review of Criminal Policy* 101; Manuel Lopez-Rey, 'The Quinquennial United Nations Congresses on the Prevention of Crime and the Treatment of Offenders' (1978) 34 *International Review of Criminal Policy* 3.

64 Ibid 47. See also Gardner (n 6).

With echoes of Hegel clearly discernible, some appealed to reprobation or the expressive function of punishment as providing the basis for criminal punishment and sentencing.[65] The extent to which modern retributivists delivered a philosophically convincing account of punishment is a topic we shall take up shortly. The question that concerns us primarily at this stage is how and in what context did the modern retributivist or proportionality theory emerge? What facilitated its rise and with what consequences?

One of the most remarkable features of the post-World War II West had been a wide consensus on welfare policy and a minimum social democratic programme. Under the tutelage of Keynesian economics, governments in the United States and Western Europe oversaw exponential state-led economic growth, expansion of public-sector education and health services, and full employment in what was dubbed by some as *les trentes glorieuses*.[66] As the economic boom began to falter in the 1970s in the wake of the global oil crisis, the 'nanny' state was attacked for inefficiency, wastefulness, and for sapping the moral fibre of the nation. What followed, as Stuart Hall recalled in the context of Britain, was 'the proposal to curb state intervention, cut state bureaucracy and public expenditure, reduce welfare, restore state-run enterprise to the private economy . . . restrict the power of the unions, and restore competitive individualism'.[67] In their assault on the 'welfare consensus', the New Right drew on the largely forgotten argument by economist Fredric von Hayek that freedom and collectivism were incompatible and social democracy was a contradiction in terms.[68] Margaret Thatcher eventually gave a very crude expression to this viewpoint when she proclaimed, 'There is no such thing as society'.[69]

Translated into policy agendas in the form of privatisation and economic deregulation, insecure labour arrangements, and public-spending cuts, the neoliberal worldview was rolled out globally during the 1980s by the International Monetary Fund (IMF) and the World Bank through Structural Adjustment Programmes.[70] Ostensibly designed as a remedy for the 'Third World Debt Crisis', the structural adjustment programmes also heralded an era of interventions in the Third World institutions, 'most notably legal and regulatory institutions,

65 See Joel Feinberg, *Doing & Deserving: Essays in the Theory of Responsibility* (Princeton University Press 1970) 95–118.

66 Donald Sasson, *One Hundred Years of Socialism: The West European Left in the Twentieth Century* (I.B. Tauris 2010) 145; Mark Mazower, *Dark Continent: Europe's Twentieth Century* (Allen Lane 1998) 359.

67 Stuart Hall, 'The State in Question' in Gregor McLennan, David Held and Stuart Hall (eds), *The Idea of the Modern State* (Open University Press 1984) 1–28, 13. See also Selina Todd, *The People: The Rise and Fall of the Working Class* (John Murray 2014) 299–315. A contemporaneous perspective on the 1970s economic crisis can be found in C.B. Macpherson, *The Life and Times of Liberal Democracy* (Oxford University Press 1977) 106.

68 Fredric Hayek, *The Road to Serfdom* (George Routledge & Sons Ltd. 1944) 67, 84.

69 Interview with Douglas Keay, *Woman's Own*, 31 October 1987.

70 Raewyn Connell and Nour Dados, 'Where in the World Does Neo – Liberalism Come from? The Market Agenda in Southern Perspective' (2014) 43(2) *Theory and Society* 117, 119.

including the rule of law'.[71] Ironically, the real structural issues, such as massive inequalities in wealth and status that characterised societies in the global South, remained untouched by the managerial solutions packaged as 'structural adjustment'. To date, the IMF and the World Bank have escaped accountability for causing 'legendary devastation' to a number of Asian, African, and Latin American societies.[72] The rise of the international criminal justice project in the 1990s would conveniently side step the crimes wreaked by global financial institutions, focusing instead on individual criminal responsibility within the context of more readily recognisable forms of violence.[73]

The 'long seventies' was also a period when human rights came into bloom, spreading out from the hallways of the United Nations and into the space of social activism. To Samuel Moyn, human rights emerged as 'the last utopia' because other visions – anti-colonialism, nationalism, socialism – had 'imploded'.[74] The emerging discourse, on Moyn's account, was focused heavily on civil and political rights and was marked by a strong anti-communist streak.[75] In Europe, it was during the mid-'70s that the Strasbourg Court began developing 'a substantial body of case law which brought the convention text to life' and revealed its contemporary relevance.[76] The Inter-American Court of Human Rights was established in 1978 although it came of age only towards the late 1980s and early 1990s, devising innovative means of monitoring criminal investigations in member countries and recommending specific remedies for human rights violations, including a duty to prosecute and punish offenders.[77] It was during the long seventies that feminist, sexuality, and identity movements rose to prominence, articulating their demands in the language of human rights.[78] These movements were instrumental in exposing the relations of domination within family and community that had earlier been subsumed under the broad categories of class and nation. At the same time, as social historian Selina Todd has reminded us,

71 Sundhya Pahuja, *Decolonising International Law: Development, Economic Growth and the Politics of Universality* (Cambridge University Press 2011) 192.

72 Ruth Gordon and Sylvester Jon, 'Deconstructing Development' (2004) 22 *Wisconsin International Law Journal* 1, 43.

73 Tor Krever, 'Ending Impunity? Eliding Political Economy in International Criminal Law?' in Ugo Mattei and John D. Haskell (eds), *Research Handbook on Political Economy and Law* (Edward Elgar Publishing 2015) 298–314. See also Vasuki Neisah, 'Doing History with Impunity' in Karen Engle, Zinaida Miller and DM Davis (eds.) *Anti-Impunity and the Human Rights Agenda* (Cambridge University Press 2016) 95–122.

74 Moyn (n 2) 16.

75 Ibid 17.

76 Ed Bates, *The Evolution of the European Convention on Human Rights: From Its Inception to the Creation of a Permanent Court of Human Rights* (Oxford University Press 2010) 24.

77 Alexandra Heuneeus, 'International Criminal Law by Other Means: The Quasi-Criminal Jurisdiction of Human Rights Courts' (2013) 107 *American Journal of International Law* 1.

78 Wendy W. Williams, 'The Equality Crisis: Some Reflections on Culture, Courts, and Feminism' in Linda Nicholson (ed), *The Second Wave: A Reader in Feminist Theory* (Routledge 1997) 71–91, 71; Andy Beckett, *When the Lights Went Out: Britain in the Seventies* (Faber and Faber 2009) 209–233.

the economic and political power enjoyed by the working class since the Second World War began to decline with the resurgence of neo-liberal economics and government surveillance and policing of trade union activities.[79]

Writing in 1974, Robert Nozick, the central figure in what has been dubbed the 'neo-classical moment' in the evolution of rights in liberal theory, advocated a minimal state whilst constructing a case for rights as side-constraint.[80] Rights, on Nozick's account, were justified on the basis of the Kantian categorical imperative and conceived of in negative Lockean terms as individual freedom to be left alone:[81]

> A minimal state, limited to the narrow functions of protection against force, theft, fraud, enforcement of contracts, and so on, is justified; that any more extensive state will violate persons' rights not to be forced to do certain things, and is unjustified; and that the minimal state is inspiring as well as right.[82]

It is not difficult to see that the idea of the minimal state gelled in well with the assault on the rehabilitative ideal, which was itself predicated on state assistance and intervention. The de-legitimisation of the welfare state and that of offender rehabilitation went hand in hand. The liberal conception of rights and freedoms put forward by Nozick is also of a piece with the retributivist conception of the individual as an isolated, autonomous entity responsible for her own failings. Nozick, in fact, articulated the connections between neo-retributivism and the New Right worldview more generally by furnishing a widely quoted 'non-teleological' account of retributive punishment. Punishment, Nozick reasoned, was meant to give effect to the 'correct values' which the wrongdoer had become disconnected from.[83] In the process, Nozick drew a rather spurious distinction between retribution and revenge, which we shall confront in a while.

In the United States, the attack on individualised sentencing and the rehabilitative ideal came on the heels of what some historians have called a dual social and economic crisis of capitalism in the late '60s.[84] Against the backdrop of the Vietnam debacle and anti-war agitation, Conservatives stoked fears of a breakdown in law and order and the spread of drugs in the American society. Starting with Richard Nixon's so-called war on drugs and climaxing with Ronald Reagan's belligerent brand of neo-liberalism, the criminal justice system underwent major transformations manifested in the expansion of the 'prison-industrial complex', soaring imprisonment rates, and an array of punitive legislative measures, including

79 Todd (n 67) 299–315.
80 Ian Shapiro, *The Evolution of Rights in Liberal Theory* (Cambridge University Press 1986) 151–203.
81 Nozick, 'Anarchy, State and Utopia' (n 5) 10, 26–53.
82 Ibid ix.
83 Robert Nozick, *Philosophical Explanations* (Belknap, Harvard 1981) 375–377.
84 Christian Parenti, *Lockdown America: Police and Prisons in the Age of Crisis* (2nd edn, Verso 2008) xii.

mandatory-minimum penalties and three-strikes-and-you-are-out laws.[85] Writing in the broader European context, Mark Mazower saw the decades of the '70s and '80s as the era when there was a remarkable boom in prison populations even in some countries which had traditionally been known for moderate criminal justice systems. Mazower highlighted the case of the Netherlands, where, between 1979 and 1993, the number of prisoners per 100,000 of population more than doubled from 23 to 52.[86] Crucially, the rise in people being sent to prison in the Netherlands – as elsewhere in Europe – did not correspond to an increase in crime rates, suggesting that there were other factors to blame for the incarceration boom.[87]

Sociologists and criminologists have offered several explanations for this punitive turn. In a seminal contribution, David Garland located the changes in the criminal justice system in America and Britain in the conditions of late modernity.[88] On this account, the third quarter of the twentieth century was characterised by a specific set of 'social, economic and cultural relations' in the Western world that brought with it a 'cluster of risks, insecurities and control problems'. Key transformations that took place in this era, according to Garland, included a shift toward more capital-intensive technology and restructuring of labour markets; changes in family structure and family norms; greater mobility and migration; and mushrooming of electronic mass media.[89] High crime rates, increased insecurity, and the collapse of faith in welfarism in late modernity constituted 'a crime complex', where 'crime issues were politicized and regularly represented in emotive terms'. Policy reactions, in turn, took the form of impulsive initiatives such as tougher penalties, or adaptive measures, including privatisation of the criminal justice system.[90]

The category of 'late modern society' has its limits in explaining changes in criminal justice given varied policy responses to crime and insecurity within the industrialised world. We need to consider other explanatory accounts to avoid generalisation. For instance, in describing Italy as a non-punitive society, David Nelken has called attention to the role of judges and prosecutors in 'defining the crime problem', and a relative lack of focus on victims who are expected to forgive in line with the country's Catholic spirit.[91] Within the context of the juvenile justice system in Italy, Nelken describes how the long, drawn-out, multistage trial

85 See Tara Herivel and Paul Wrights (eds), *Prison Profiteers: Who Makes Money from Mass Incarceration* (The New Press, New York 2007); Parenti (n 84) 10, 48; Tod R Clear and Natasha A Frost, *The Punishment Imperative: The Rise and Failure of Mass Incarceration in America* (New York University Press 2014) 71–112.

86 Mazower (n 66) 349.

87 Frieder Dünkel and Dirk Van Zyl, 'Conclusion' in Smit and Dünkel (eds), *Imprisonment Today and Tomorrow: International Perspectives on Prisoners' Rights and Prison Conditions* (2nd edn, Kluwer Law International 2001) 796–859, 808.

88 Garland, 'The Culture of Control' (n 7).

89 Ibid 77–89.

90 Ibid 163–165.

91 David Nelken, 'When Is a Society Non-Punitive? The Italian Case' in John Pratt and others (eds.), *The New Punitiveness: Trends, Theories and Perspectives* (Willian Publishing Devon 2005) 225.

process enables judges to make use of several ordinances to confer a 'judicial pardon', impose a pre-trial probation, or arrive at some other lenient decision. This leniency, Nelken argues, is facilitated by the less serious nature of youth crime, corporatist, 'group-based' and family loyalties, and lower levels of competitiveness in Italian society.[92]

To Nicola Lacey, it is 'the specific institutional features of different kinds of political economy' which account for differences between countries in terms of levels of punitiveness and exposure to penal populism, i.e. convergence between criminal justice systems and penal policy on the one hand, and the real or perceived demands of the public on the other. Institutional arrangements determine if countries can avoid the 'prisoners' dilemma' (the title of her eminently readable book), in which sanity demands that policy makers maintain a moderate penal system, but 'lack of communication and coordination' and an effort to outdo the political opponent leads them to opt for tough-on-crime policies.[93] On Lacey's thesis, 'coordinated market economies' are less vulnerable to penal excess due to longer-term employment and investment structures, the system of proportional representation, greater bargaining power of smaller left-leaning parties, moderating influence of coalition politics, and greater deference to expert opinion in policy formulation. By contrast, the United States – and to a lesser extent Britain – with flexible labour markets, a first-past-the-poll electoral system, and a tradition of single-party majoritarian rule, have witnessed politicisation of criminal justice and harsher penal policies compared to continental Europe.

Exponents of just deserts theory insist that the growth in prison populations and severity in sentencing cannot be attributed to retributive proportionality and fixed sentencing schemes. In one of the earlier complaints against criticism of the 'justice model' as promoting harsher penalties, Andrew von Hirsch, for example, accused Barbara Hudson of '*post hoc ergo propter fallacy*' (the assumption that because B follows A in time, A causes B).[94] To von Hirsch, penal severity in California (one example used by Hudson) was the consequence not of determinate sentencing but conservative law-and-order rhetoric, pre-existing trends towards excessive use of imprisonment, and continued discretionary powers enjoyed by judges within the terms of the new statute.[95] More recently, Andrew Ashworth, another leading architect of the justice movement, has reiterated this argument in response to an essay by Nicola Lacey and Hannah Pickard, which we shall take up separately later.

Ashworth has attempted to explain the failure of 'desert theory and proportionality' to prevent sentencing severity through the 1990s and 2000s in England and Wales with reference to certain extraneous factors. These include judges privileging deterrence over retribution in sentencing decisions, introduction of

92 Ibid 227, 230.

93 Nicola Lacey, *The Prisoners' Dilemma: Political Economy and Punishment in Contemporary Democracies* (Cambridge University Press 2008) 118.

94 Andrew von Hirsch, *Censure and Sanctions* (Clarendon Press 1993) 91. cf. Hudson, 'Justice Through Punishment' (n 47) 65–68.

95 Ibid 91–94.

mandatory-minimum penalties for recidivists in 1997, and indeterminate sentences for public protection (IPPs) in 2003.[96] Ashworth goes on to cite the example of the Nordic countries, particularly Finland and Sweden, 'where the prominence of desert theory and proportionality has gone hand in hand with penal moderation'.[97] Elsewhere, in Ashworth's view, 'the proportionality theory did not fail to produce a penal moderation, because it was not implemented as intended'.[98] However, this line of argument is itself open to the charge of *post hoc ergo propter fallacy*. Just because Finland and Sweden evaded a punitive turn following the enactment of determinate-sentencing statutes does not establish that the latter was the cause of penal moderation. Although these countries did institutionalise just deserts philosophy in penal codes in the 1970s, the roots of 'Scandinavian exceptionalism' are much deeper and linked with 'highly egalitarian cultural values and social structures of these societies'.[99] In the criminal justice system, this ethos is reflected in generally mild statutory sentencing provisions, an emphasis on non-custodial penalties and suspended sentences, and a humane prison system. The moderation in penal and prison polices in Scandinavia, relative to the Anglo-American world, did not begin with the revival of retributivism. Rather, it goes back at least to the immediate post-World War II period.[100] It is also owing to this well-entrenched culture that the proportionality principle is applied in the Scandinavian penal law primarily as imposing the upper limit on punishment rather than enhancing its quantum to fit the crime. Normal sentences that are imposed are usually far lower than legislated maximum penalties.[101]

Ashworth is quite right in stating that law and order rhetoric and statutory measures justified in consequentialist terms (public protection and deterrence) had a major role in the ratcheting-up of punishment in England and Wales in recent times. But the tacit assumption that retributivism and populist punitiveness are mutually exclusive categories does not hold. The basic intuition that inheres in retributivist thinking that the offender ought to receive pain and condemnation as a moral desert ties in rather well with the tough-on-crime ethos. As the former British Prime Minister David Cameron said in a speech laying down the blueprint of a 'tough but intelligent' criminal justice policy:

> Committing a crime is always a choice. That's why the primary, proper response to crime is not explanations or excuses, it is punishment – proportionate, meaningful punishment. And when a crime is serious enough, the only thinkable

96 Andrew Ashworth, 'Prisons, Proportionality and Recent Penal History' (2017) 80(3) *Modern Law Review* 473, 479, 487.

97 Ibid 480.

98 Ibid 486.

99 John Pratt, 'Scandinavian Exceptionalism in an Era of Penal Excess: Part I: The Nature and Roots of Scandinavian Exceptionalism' (2007) 48 *British Journal of Criminology* 119, 120.

100 Ibid.

101 Ville Hinkkanen and Tapio Lappi-Seppälä, 'Sentencing Theory, Policy, and Research' in Michael Tonry and Tapio Lappi-Seppälä (eds), *Crime and Justice in Scandinavia: Crime and Justice – A Review of Research* (Volume 40, University of Chicago Press 2011) 349–404, 356.

> punishment is a long prison sentence. This is what victims – and society – deserve. Victims need to know the criminal will be held to account and dealt with. And the 'society' bit really matters: retribution is not a dirty word, it is important to society that revulsion we all feel against crime is properly recognised.[102]

As the above passage illustrates, retributivist justification for punishment furnishes yet another reason for politicians to deflect attention from broader social justice issues and to present themselves as siding with victims of crime. It might also be pointed out here that when the British government introduced the Representation of the People Act 2000, it justified barring all convicted prisoners who remained in prison from exercising the right to vote in retributivist terms, as a means of conferring an 'additional punishment'.[103] Further, as we shall see in Chapter 7, the notion of proportionate or commensurate sentencing has carried over into international human rights law not as a restraint on penal excess (as modern retributivists might have expected); rather, it serves quite distinctly as a device to back longer prison sentences, typically for crimes involving violations of civil and political rights.

Historians documenting the rise of punitiveness since the long seventies and those tracing the genealogy of modern human rights are somewhat like 'ships passing in the night', each unaware of the presence of the other, to borrow an expression used by Philip Alston in a different context.[104] There has not been much dialogue between the two sets of scholarship. Sure enough, the emerging human rights movement imparted moral and legal resources for the protection of vulnerable groups, including prisoners. Crucially, however, there was nothing in the emerging human rights discourse – including in the theoretical work produced by scholars such as Robert Nozick – that could pose a fundamental challenge to the ideology of retributive justice or the institution of prison. Rather, in some very important ways, retributivism and human rights shared the same logic and grammar. There was a strong convergence of views on the nature of the human as free and autonomous being exclusively responsible and accountable for his or her actions. The social context of criminality was barely relevant

102 'Transcript of the Prime Minister's Speech to the Centre for Social Justice'. Available at: www.gov.uk/government/speeches/crime-and-justice-speech.

103 Representation of People Act 2000, s 2. Besides other amendments in the electoral process, the Act made changes to section 3 of the Representation of People Act 1983 to enable remand prisoners to vote but not those in detention. See the examination of the UK government's position in the majority judgment in the challenge before the European Court, in which the Grand Chamber decided by a narrow majority of 5–4 that the blanket disenfranchisement of prisoners violated Article 3 of Protocol 1 to the European Convention. *Hirst v United Kingdom* (No 2) (App. 74025/01) 6 October 2005 [Grand Chamber] (2006) 42 EHRR 849, ECHR 2005-IX, para 74.

104 Philip Alston, 'Ships Passing in the Night: The Current Status of Human Rights and Development Debate Seen Through the Lens of the Millennium Development Goals' (2005) 27(3) *Human Rights Quarterly* 755.

to the prevailing theories of punishment – a blind spot that went unaddressed in human rights scholarship. Both modern retributivism and human rights canon operated with a split between criminal justice and social justice. Both sprang from the same intellectual soil of Enlightenment philosophy represented by Kant and Hegel. Those who did challenge the ideology of retributivism head-on came from entirely different intellectual traditions of prison abolitionism, critical theory, Marxist criminology, and restorative justice.[105]

That said, there seems to be a lack of reflexivity among non-retributivist scholars regarding the theoretical affinity between retributivism and human rights. There are certain limitations inherent in the discourse of human rights in terms of posing a challenge to 'new punitiveness', which have received little attention in critical scholarship. Let us unpack this claim with reference to a couple of contemporary critiques of the penal dragnet.

In a journal contribution that builds on her arguments presented in *The Prisoner's Dilemma*, Nicola Lacey, with co-author Hannah Pickard, exposes the false promise of the proportionality principle.[106] The 'just-deserts' or 'justice' movement, on this account, was, at least in part, built on the well-meaning premise that determinate and proportionate sentencing schemes would 'foster robust limits on State's power to punish'.[107] In reality, the scale of punishment has increased considerably over the past three or four decades in 'liberal market countries such as England and Wales, Scotland, Australia, New Zealand and – most spectacularly – the United States'.[108] By contrast, the Nordic countries have, by and large, resisted the punitive turn owing to distinct institutional arrangements of political economy that prioritise co-operative behaviour, consensus, long-term relationships, and reconciliation among citizens, or what Lacey and Pickard have called, a high 'Associational Value'.[109] In sum, it is not appeals to proportionality but particular social arrangements that have enabled certain countries to maintain relatively moderate criminal justice systems.

The principle of proportionality of punishment to crime is a modern re-working of *lex talionis*, which provides no independent substantive criteria on how to punish and how much to punish. Answers to these questions remain open 'to the sway of convention, political decision, or expediency'.[110] The fittingness of a penalty for

105 See, for example, Vincenzo Ruggiero, *Penal Abolitionism* (Oxford University Press 2010); *Nils Christie, Limits to Pain: The Role of Punishment in Penal Policy* (Wipf & Stock 2007); Thomas Mathiesen, *Prison on Trial* (3rd edn, Waterside Press 2006); John Braithwaite and Philip Petit, *Not Just Deserts: A Republican Theory of Criminal Justice* (Clarendon Press 1998); Barbara A Hudson, *Penal Policy and Social Justice* (University of Toronto Press 1993).

106 Lacey and Pickard (n 61) 216. As mentioned in Chapter 1, the principle of proportionality carries a broader meaning within human rights law where it functions as a doctrinal tool for assessing the validity of state-imposed limitations and restrictions on rights. The present discussion is concerned primarily with the other dimension of proportionality, namely the proportionality of punishment to crime.

107 Ibid 225.

108 Ibid 227.

109 Ibid 236.

110 Ibid 235.

a particular offence varies substantially across jurisdictions and over time. What Lacey and Pickard do not address though is that the proportionality principle, in our times, is nested within human rights law. International and national courts routinely invoke proportionality to assess the legitimacy or constitutionality of certain types of statutory penalties (life imprisonment, the death penalty, voting ban on prisoners, etc.) against the protected scope of fundamental rights. Less frequently, human rights bodies also examine whether a specific sentence imposed by a domestic court is proportionate to the gravity of the offence committed. Mainstream human rights scholars invariably adopt a deferential stance toward the principle when discussing criminal punishment. It is a notion that we inherit in a taken-for-granted way in our human rights culture. The limitations of the principle of proportionality in restricting the state's punitive power then are, *inter alia*, the limitations of the human rights doctrine. Also missing in Lacey and Pickard's otherwise illuminating thesis is any engagement with the collateral consequences of criminal penalties for the offenders and their families, which further weaken the substantive import of proportionality as a limit on punitiveness.[111]

Coming from a penal abolitionist perspective, criminologist Deborah Drake has attempted to show the futility of the prison system in the pursuit of safety and security. Based partly on an ethnographic study in Britain's maximum security prisons, Drake's work brings into focus the symbolic functions of the prison as an aid to law-and-order politics, exclusionary political rhetoric, and rapidly intensifying security ideologies.[112] Politicians tap into the prison as political capital by constructing prisoners as the dangerous Other, the enemy within, 'undeserving of human rights'.[113] Any benign pretentions to the effect that the prison could create law-abiding citizens, on Drake's account, is defeated by the focus on punishment and a neglect of the 'social or structural factors and barriers . . . that lead people to the prison in the first place'.[114] A central claim Drake makes is that 'the moral underpinnings' and the rhetoric of rationality attached to the criminal justice system deflect attention from the failures of the system to deliver either justice or security.[115] Crucially, Drake does not appear to contemplate the fact that the better part of what she calls the moral underpinnings of the system is supplied in our times by the ideology of human rights. The notion of legality, the principle of proportionality, and the prohibition of ill-treatment of prisoners, for example, are anchored to the ideology of human rights. Without wishing to tarnish the positive contribution of these norms in reducing the suffering of convicts, we need to underscore the limitations of their emancipatory potential.

111 Andrew Ashworth, in his response to the Lacey and Pickard article discussed earlier, lets the matter rest with a single sentence: 'The consequentialist effect [of a proportionate sentence] on partners and children should be taken into account'. The remainder of the essay is given over to justifying the proportionality ideal. See Ashworth (n 96) 484; Lacey and Pickard (n 61).
112 Deborah H. Drake, *Prisons, Punishment and the Pursuit of Security* (Palgrave Macmillan 2012).
113 Ibid 108.
114 Ibid.
115 Ibid 134.

The prison, after all, is taken for granted not only in crime control agendas, as Drake correctly points out, but also in the discourse of human rights. I have not come across a single academic commentary on human rights which questions the moral validity of the prison per se.

Drake's conclusion that the way out of the punitive dragnet is to stop moralising and judging the behaviour of others is perhaps the weakest part in the thesis. In identifying the hypocrisies of the criminal justice system, Drake herself repeatedly makes moral statements. Curiously enough, in advocating possible ways of 'ending punishment', Drake cites the example of the South African Truth and Reconciliation Commission, an initiative that was itself informed by a deep sense of morality.[116] It is a telling indicator of the hegemony of the 'justice movement', and the ideology of human rights, that morality in our times gets equated with punishment and retributive justice. Alternative ways of dealing with crime are categorised as pragmatic at best, and moral sell-outs at worst.[117]

Just deserts and the expressive function of punishment: a critique

In 1976, the 'Committee for the Study of Incarceration' published its report, *Doing Justice*, setting out a case for a 'desert-based' system of punishment. Following its publication, several states in the US introduced sentencing guidelines, foreshadowing the adoption of similar schemes in England and Wales, Scotland, Denmark, Sweden, Finland, Australia, and New Zealand.[118] It was, as the author of the report Andrew von Hirsch would later note, 'the first systematic exposition of desert theory in penological literature'.[119] Even as the report eschewed the term 'retribution', it was, at its heart, a repackaged version of Kantian theory that made room for deterrence as an additional general justification for punishment. It constituted a clarion call for a return to Enlightenment ideas. With desert and deterrence being the predominant justifications for punishment and sentencing rationales in the contemporary world, the report acquires added genealogical significance.[120]

116 Drake (n 112) 172. cf. William Schabas, *Unimaginable Atrocities* (Oxford University Press 2012) 168.

117 This type of dichotomous thinking is quite common in the area of transitional justice. See, for example, Andreas O' Shea, *Amnesty for Crime in International Law and Practice* (Kluwer Law International 2004); Tristan Garcia, 'Amnesties and the Rome Statute – A Legitimate Bar to Prosecution?' (2006) 13 *Australian International Law Journal* 187.

118 On the historical influence of *'Doing Justice'* on policy and practice, see Hudson, 'Justice Through Punishment' (n 47) 48; *Garland, 'The Culture of Control' (n 7)* 59–60; Andrew Von Hirsh, 'Penal Theories' in Michael Tonry (ed), *The Handbook of Crime and Punishment* (Oxford University Press 1998) 659–82, 666; Hinkkanen and Lappi-Seppälä (n 101) 352; Norrie, (n 6) 344–345; Susan Easton and Christine Piper, *Sentencing and Punishment: The Quest for Justice* (4th edn, Oxford University Press 2016) 59.

119 von Hirsch, 'Censure and Sanctions' (n 94) 89.

120 Andrew von Hirsch, *Doing Justice: The Choice of Punishments. Report of the Committee for the Study of Incarceration* (Hill and Wang 1976) 54, 61–62, 130. On von Hirsch's account, those who violate others' rights deserve to be punished on Kantian grounds but given that

The introduction to the report sets a gloomy tone upfront by admitting that 'the quality of heady optimism and confidence of reformers in the past, and their belief that they could solve the problem of crime and eradicate the presence of deviancy, will not be found in this document'.[121] In many ways, this frank admission sums up the tenor of the mainstream human rights scholarship as well. One struggles in vain to find a reference in contemporary human rights texts and commentaries to criminological and other social science investigations into crime. Before moving on to Kantian justifications, von Hirsch refers to the intuitive, 'common sense' appeal of the idea that a wrongdoer ought to be punished because she 'deserves' it. Punishment, on this seductively simple account, is a priori a self-evident good. As von Hirsch put it, 'Ask the person on the street why a wrongdoer should be punished, and he is likely to say that he "deserves" it'.[122] Why should we add more misery to an already miserable world or supplement a pre-existing evil (crime) with another one (punishment) may not be universally self-evident, however.[123]

Doing Justice harkens back to the empirical blindness of classical penal theory by generating its conclusions from an ahistorical and acontextual standpoint. Little attention is paid to how public perceptions and intuitive associations come about in the first place. Do people know of alternative ways of dealing with crime? How informed are they about the prevalence of mental disorders and a history of unemployment among convicts? Summarising research into public opinion in the context of the Australian state of New South Wales, David Brown, for instance, has shown that 'punitive attitudes to sentencing and punishment become less punitive the more extensive the information provided about the circumstances of the offence and the background to the offender'.[124] Leaving aside the question as to whether public opinion should be a yardstick for sentencing policies, empirical research conducted in America suggests that people, when made aware of alternative ways of doing justice, express greater acceptability of indeterminate sentencing and restorative justice, especially where non-violent offenders are involved.[125] Likewise, Jeremy Travis draws on periodic Gallup surveys between 1989 and 2000 to claim that when given policy choices, the American public

punishment involves imposition of suffering, 'deterrence' may serve as a countervailing justification for punishment. However, he is sceptical of deterrence as a sentencing aim, given that judges do not have sufficient evidence to determine the deterrent effect of a particular sentence.

121 Willard Gaylin and David J. Rothman, 'Introduction' in von Hirsch, 'Doing Justice' (n 121) I –xIi xxxiv.

122 Ibid 45.

123 Gardner (n 6) 785.

124 David Brown, 'Continuity, Rupture or Just More of the "Volatile" and "Contradictory"? Glimpses of New South Wales' Penal Practice Behind and Through the Discursive' in Pratt and others (n 91) 27–46, 40.

125 Francis T Cullen, Bonnie S Fischer and Brandon K Applegate, 'Public Opinion About Punishment and Corrections' (2000) 27 *Crime and Justice* 1.

favours prevention of crime through 'education and jobs' as against reactive law enforcement through 'more prisons, police and judges'.[126]

To return to von Hirsch's account, the 'common sense' notion of punishment as deserved suffering is supplemented with philosophical justifications based on 'commensurate desert' and 'moral reprobation'. The starting point is the Kantian idea of 'fair dealing among free individuals'. Punishment, we are told, restores equilibrium by 'imposing a counterbalancing disadvantage on the violator'.[127] That this view is predicated on a consensual view of society as an assemblage of free and equal individuals is quite obvious. Anticipating criticism on the grounds of the inherently contradictory nature of 'just deserts in an unjust society', von Hirsch devotes a few pages to the question of social justice almost as an afterthought.[128] Reasonably enough, he interprets Marx's critique of punishment as based on a disapproval of utilitarian justifications.[129] Understating the irony of Marx's comments in his famous essay on the death penalty, von Hirsch claims that 'desert is essential' in Marx's view to 'the case for punishing'. Whilst von Hirsch recognises the point that punishment is not defensible in a fundamentally unjust social system, he finds it difficult to embrace 'the logic of that position' as 'it leads to opposing the existing institutions of punishment'.[130] But there are more modest implications of the Marxist critique than the one von Hirsch ascribes to it.

In his seminal work, *The Idea of Justice*, Amartya Sen reminds us of the Sanskrit literature on jurisprudence which made a distinction between *niti* (procedural justice) and *naya* (substantive or 'realized justice').[131] Legal theorists in ancient India warned against what they called *matsyana*, i.e. '"justice in the world of fish", where a big fish can freely devour a small fish'. Preventing 'the justice of fish' is itself an essential part of the pursuit of justice.[132] Sen takes issue with Roman Emperor Ferdinand I's famous edict, 'Let justice be done, though the world perish', as a very severe form of *niti*. The same could be said of the kind of robust Kantian retributivism that von Hirsch set out to revive with its indifference to the consequences of punishment and a focus on procedural fairness (*niti*) rather than fair outcomes (*naya*). A substantive or 'realization focused perspective', Sen forcefully argues, requires that we prevent 'manifest injustice in the world, rather than seeking the perfectly just'.[133]

126 Jeremy Travis, 'Invisible Punishment: An Instrument of Social Exclusion' in Marc Mauer and Meda Chesney-Lind (eds), *Invisible Punishment: The Collateral Consequences of Mass Imprisonment* (Free Press 2002) 15–36, 28.

127 von Hirsch, 'Doing Justice' (n 120) 47.

128 Ibid 143–149. cf. David L. Bazelon, 'The Morality of the Criminal Law' (1975–76) 49 *Southern California Law Review* 385. See also Stephen J Morse, 'The Twilight of Welfare Criminology: A Reply to Judge Bazelon' (1975–1976) 49 *Southern California Law Review* 1247.

129 von Hirsch, 'Doing Justice' (n 120) 144; Karl Marx, *Dispatches for the New York Tribune: Selected Journalism of Karl Marx* (Penguin 2007) 119–122.

130 Ibid 145.

131 Amartya Sen, *The Idea of Justice* (Penguin 2010) 20.

132 Ibid 20.

133 Ibid 21.

One possibility, then, is to readjust the focus of criminal justice by aiming its punitive arm toward the crimes of the mighty and the powerful rather than ordinary, everyday crime. Sensitivity to the disadvantaged backgrounds that many offenders come from would also warrant greater reliance on non-custodial rather than custodial sentences and a renewed focus on offender rehabilitation. That is a notion which finds only a marginal place in the theory worked out by von Hirsch.[134] Another dimension of the criminal justice-social justice interface, which von Hirsh is rather quick to dismiss, is the question of social deprivation as a criminal defence. Somewhat reminiscent of novelist Anatole France's observation that the law in its majestic quality 'forbids the wealthy as well as the poor from sleeping under bridges, begging in the streets, and from stealing bread',[135] under von Hirsch's 'commensurate-deserts principle, an impoverished defendant would be punished no more severely than an affluent individual convicted of an equally serious crime'.[136] Whilst acknowledging the co-relation between crime and social deprivation, von Hirsch does not think that 'this is an issue that judges can be expected to deal with fairly'.[137] The issue then, it would appear, is more of convenience rather than principle. The best that a sentencing scheme can hope to achieve, we are told, is to not aggravate the disadvantage that the poor already suffer pre-conviction. That is to be achieved through procedural guarantees of fair trial and a determinate sentencing scheme. To be convincing, this argument, typical of deontological theory, rests on the suspension of empirical perspective. How is it possible, one may ask, that two differently situated individuals will experience the same length of imprisonment in the same manner?[138] Will a poor and a rich person be in the same situation coping with the stigma of punishment as they try to reintegrate into society?

Note also that the other general justification for punishment that von Hirsch endorses – namely, the 'reprobative' function of punishment – may actually be seen as adding to the disadvantages that some offenders already suffer up to the time of conviction.[139] In modern times, the most prominent advocate of the expressive function of punishment, or punishment as reprobation, is Joel Feinberg, whose work von Hirsch draws on.[140] By implication, the reprobation thesis also serves to dilute the relevance of rehabilitation even further. Over and above

134 According to von Hirsch, 'Even if rehabilitation works, basing the sentence on the offender's need for treatment falls afoul of the commensurate principles'. Rehabilitation, he believed, 'should be distinguished from helping an offender with his own problems', which 'ought to be offered on a voluntary basis'. von Hirsch, 'Doing Justice' (n 120) 127–128.

135 Anatole France, *The Red Lily* (IndyPublish.com 2002) 62.

136 von Hirsch, 'Doing Justice' (n 120) 147.

137 Ibid 146.

138 See Nigel Walker, 'Desert: Some Doubts' in Andrew von Hirsch and Andrew Ashworth (eds), *Principled Sentencing: Readings on Theory and Policy* (2nd edn, Hart Publishing 1998) 156–160, 156.

139 von Hirsch, 'Doing Justice' (n 120) 48–49.

140 Joel Feinberg, *Doing & Deserving: Essays in the Theory of Responsibility* (Princeton University Press 1970) 95–118.

'hard treatment', punishment on this account is symbolically significant as an expression of society's 'attitudes of resentment and indignation, and of judgments of disapproval and reprobation'.[141] That is an important point and cannot be brushed aside lightly. Feelings of anger and indignation that many of us feel, especially in the face of violent crime against weaker sections of the society, are an important moral resource. The problem with the reprobative theory, however, is that it does not account for possible attitudinal variations within and across societies and over different time periods. As discussed earlier with reference to Nicola Lacey and Hannah Pickard's critique of the moderating influence of the proportionality principle, feelings of anger and resentment toward criminals do not exist above the flux of history; rather, they are enmeshed with prevailing institutional arrangements and political ideologies. The free-market ethos legitimises such attitudes by scapegoating individuals for society's ills. This is much less the case in societies where there is a high premium put on social solidarity and reconciliation. Members of the public may also feel empathy and compassion for at least some disadvantaged offenders. This perspective, however, gets edged to the margins in the theories based on the reprobative function of punishment. As was the case with Hegel and Kant, Feinberg and von Hirsch operate with a particular understanding of human nature, rejecting wider possibilities of human sympathy and capacity to communicate across painful memories and profound differences.

Further, if the purpose of punishment is to express indignation, why bother with attempts at helping the offender escape a life of crime? On the theory put forward by Feinberg – and cited approvingly by von Hirsch – it is not adequate for the state merely to express censure or disapproval of wrongdoing. Rather, it is 'unpleasant treatment' in the form of incarceration that appropriately serves the expressive function, as Feinberg clarifies in an attempt to draw a line between punishment and a 'mere penalty'.[142] Since the theory is essentially deontological, whether the expression of reprobation through penal hard treatment leads to offenders mending their ways or turning into hardened criminals is irrelevant. Further, if punishment, by definition, involves hard treatment and reprobation, why seek to improve prison conditions? One major paradox that marks the discourse of human rights is its simultaneous commitment to retributive punishment and prisoners' rights. It is hardly surprising that improving the conditions of incarceration has proven a hard nut to crack. More importantly, the reprobative theory of punishment does not say at what point the expression of indignation ought to cease: as soon as a prison sentence has been served out? Even if a 'criminal record' is formally expunged, does the element of 'indignation' built into the conviction not send out a signal to the society that the released offender is an untrustworthy outsider?[143] There is a vast amount of evidence to

141 Ibid 98.

142 Feinberg (n 140) 95–118, 99.

143 For an analysis in relation to the British disclosure rules and the jurisprudence of the ECtHR, see Elena Larrauri Pijoan, 'Criminal Record Disclosure and the Right to Privacy' (2015) 10 *The Criminal Law Review* 723.

demonstrate that ex-offenders run up against massive difficulties in finding jobs and participating in civic life, suggesting that the 'expressive function' of punishment carries over into life outside the prison.[144]

It must be said in favour of Feinberg though that he is forthright in stating that the expression of the attitudes of 'contempt', 'indignation', 'vengeance', and 'condemnation' is a defining feature and justificatory basis of punishment.[145] That contrasts with Robert Nozick's famous attempt at making a distinction between 'retributive punishment' and revenge. Nozick's views chime with reprobation theory in that he sees punishment as a means of reconnecting 'the wrongdoer' to 'correct values' – values he has become disconnected from. Whether the supposed 're-connection to correct values' has any deterrent effect is not relevant to what Nozick calls a 'non-teleological view' of 'retributive punishment'.[146]

Nozick lists several features of retributive punishment, which, he suggests, distinguish it from revenge. 'Retribution', we are told, 'is done for a wrong, while revenge may be done for an injury or harm or slight and need not be for a wrong'. Nozick goes on to suggest that retribution, unlike revenge, 'sets an internal limit to the amount of the punishment'. A further supposedly distinguishing feature is that 'revenge is personal . . . whereas the agent of retribution need have no special or personal tie to the victim of the wrong for which he exacts retribution'. More controversially, Nozick argues that 'revenge involves a particular emotional tone, pleasure in the suffering of another, while retribution either need involve no emotional tone, or involves another one, namely pleasure at justice being done'.[147] Finally, we are told that the 'imposer of retribution' is committed to some general principles or justifications for punishment, which is not necessarily the case with a 'revenger'.[148] The entire account rests on untenable anthropological assumptions.

Leo Zaibert and Nigel Walker have both taken apart each of the so-called contrasts between retribution and revenge and demonstrated them to be exaggerations at best.[149] Zaibert, for example, has pointed out, using a hypothetical case, that it would be incorrect to assume that revenge does not have any internal limits. Even in the modern folklore of Hollywood Westerns, where revenge is portrayed sympathetically and celebrated as justice, for a hero to deploy a weapon of mass destruction to avenge the burning of his painstakingly built ranch would be recognised more as comedy than revenge.[150] Some traditional societies, after all, were known to have codes specifying limits on the legitimacy of revenge and restrictions on indiscriminate destruction, or targeting of the old, women, and

144 See, for example, Becky Pettit, *Invisible Men: Mass Incarceration and the Myth of Black Progress* (Russell Sage Foundation 2012) 39.

145 Feinberg (n 140) 98, 116.

146 Nozick, 'Philosophical Explanations' (n 83) 77, 374–375.

147 Ibid 367.

148 Ibid 366–370.

149 Leo Zaibert, *'Punishment and Revenge' (2006) 25 Law and Philosophy* 81; Nigel Walker, *'Nozick's Revenge' (1995) 70(274) Philosophy* 581.

150 Ibid 97–98.

children.[151] It is even harder to accept Nozick's claim that retributive punishment is somehow cool and detached, lacking in emotional tone that characterises revenge. The calls for 'justice' by tabloids and some human rights organisations, for example, are every bit infused with the emotional tone of 'getting back' at the criminals, blurring the distinction between punishment and revenge.

In reviewing literature prior to the resurgence of retributivism in the seventies, von Hirsch had noted with dismay that 'penologists were preoccupied' with theories of rehabilitation, incapacitation or deterrence and the best means of 'promoting public safety'. 'Seldom was the word "justice" even mentioned in the literature of sentencing and corrections', he complained.[152] In a major reversal of fortunes, the word 'rehabilitation' is seldom mentioned nowadays in the mainstream literature on punishment and human rights.[153] 'Justice' is the buzzword, and it is not always easy to distinguish it from revenge.

The myth of proportionality

There is no reason to doubt that von Hirsch had put forward his 'commensurate-deserts' theory as a corrective to long indeterminate sentences. He and many others who followed in his footsteps deserve merit for bringing the detriments of judicial discretion into sharper focus. What we are questioning is the substance of their arguments and not the underlying motivations. The punitive turn in the United States and elsewhere has shown that determinate sentencing and the allocation of penalties based on proportionality, or 'commensurate deserts' (Andrew von Hirsch's preferred expression), does not necessarily lead to shorter sentences.[154] The parsimony in the use of incarceration that von Hirsch had hoped for has not been realised either. Since we have already discussed the issue at some length, there is no point labouring it further. But there is another dimension to the proportionality principle, which has not received much attention. In what follows, I will argue that the idea of proportionality is far less determinate than it is thought to be. Further, it is blind to the full extent of the suffering that attends a custodial sentence. Typical of Kantian ethics, the principle of proportionality rests on the image of the offender as an abstract, autonomous being detached from the concrete context of personal and social relationships.[155] As a disembodied idea, it fails to capture the human drama and the anguish of real people behind criminal punishment. It is important to recognise this weakness since otherwise

151 See, for example, Francis Jennings, *The Invasion of America: Indians, Colonialism, and the Cant of Conquest* (W.W. Norton 1975) 152–153.

152 von Hirsch, 'Doing Justice' (n 120) 5.

153 See, for example, Emmerson, Ashworth and MacDonald (n 10); Kälin and Künzli (n 10) Shah (n 10) 259–285; Bantekas and Oette (n 10) 313–365; Amos (n 10) 287–408.

154 von Hirsch, 'Doing Justice' *(n 120) 64–94. See also Andrew von Hirsh, 'Penal Theories' in Michael Tonry (ed), The Handbook of Crime and Punishment* (Oxford University Press 1998) 659–682.

155 For a broader critique of Kantian ethics on these lines, see Victor J. Seidler, *The Moral Limits of Modernity: Love, Inequality and Oppression* (Palgrave Macmillan 1991).

we slip into assuming that retributive justice and proportionality is all we have as the endpoint of history.

The brief critique presented here addresses something other than the socially contingent nature of any exercise in determining relative seriousness of offences (ordinal proportionality) or specific penalties for various offences (cardinal proportionality).[156] Let us also leave aside the issue as to whether it is the seriousness of the actual harm done or motive for the performance of the harmful act that should govern the scale of cardinal proportionality.[157] The point I wish to stress is that a custodial sentence can only be thought of as proportionate in a very loose and indeterminate manner. We cannot let the case rest with the 'intuitively appealing' assertion that 'only grave wrongs merit severe penalties; minor misdeeds deserve lenient punishments'.[158] The principle of proportionality as it is proclaimed in theory and as it is experienced are distinct matters. The privations of incarceration are never experienced uniformly by all convicts nor are they restricted to the convicts alone. Just as a criminal act often affects not only the individual victim but his or her family as well, so too the experience of imprisonment engulfs the prisoner's dependants and loved ones. Further, the suffering that attaches to a term in prison does not cease magically at the point when a convict steps out of the prison gates. The insidious effects of incarceration, including the social stigma it carries, follow an ex-offender around like a shadow. In calling a custodial sentence 'proportionate', we thus trade in half-truths and self-delusion. It is quite another matter that the principle of proportionality even in its restrictive import (as imposing upper limits on criminal penalties or prohibiting grossly disproportionate sentences) has been rendered ineffective in some jurisdictions under the influence of conservative ideology. Examples would include failed legal challenges to California's 'three strikes' laws which provide a sentence of 25 years to life for a third felony even if it involves a minor or non-violent offence.[159]

There is a fast-growing body of literature emerging mostly from the United States that deals with the collateral consequences of punishment. I have struggled in vain to find a single reference to this literature in human rights scholarship. Some scholars tend to use the term 'collateral consequences' or 'invisible punishments' to include administrative and legal measures piled up on top of a custodial sentence: restrictions on voting rights, eviction from public housing, and the requirements of criminal record disclosure.[160] At this stage, we are more interested in exploring the other set of 'collateral consequences' – namely, the impact of imprisonment on offenders' children and partners. Even though it is only recently that sociologists have begun to map out the collateral consequences, the realisation of this reality is not entirely new. Sanford Bates, a towering figure in

156 Nigel Walker, 'Desert: Some Doubts' in Andrew von Hirsch and Andrew Ashworth (eds), *Principled Sentencing: Readings on Theory and Policy* (2nd edn, Hart Publishing 1998) 156–160.

157 John Kleinig, *Punishment and Desert* (Martinus Nijhoff 1973) 127–128.

158 von Hirsch, 'Doing Justice' (n 120) 66.

159 *Ewing v California* 538 US 11 (2003); *Lockyer v Andrade* 538 US 63 (2003).

160 Travis (n 126) 15–36.

the International Penitentiary Commission and director of the US Federal Bureau of Prison, whom we encountered in the previous chapter, had this to say in a 1937 publication:

> The prisoner's life is ordered for him. His meals, though simple, come regularly. No landlord presses for his rent. . . . But the wife and children have to carry on the battle – and many times it is a losing battle – deprived of their source of income, obliged to scrimp and economize in every way, and, worst of all, forced to face the taunts or shrugs of their neighbours.[161]

As part of a broader study that looks at the disproportionate impact of 'mass incarceration' on America's black population and how the exclusion of inmates and former inmates from official survey data creates an illusion of 'black progress', Becky Petit sheds light on the unseen casualties of penal expansion, focusing in particular on children. Petit's claim that 'incapacitation by the criminal justice system not only shapes the lives of adult inmates but has potentially long-term effects on their children' is of crucial importance in unmasking the conceptual holes in the doctrine of proportionality.[162] She provides empirical support for the argument that not only children suffer as a result of reduced economic capacity and family instability that result from parental incarceration, they also run a greater risk of developing emotional and behavioural problems.[163] Other scholars have classified collateral consequences on children as comprising 'strain', 'socialization', and 'stigmatization' to refer respectively to economic deprivation, absence of parental role modelling, and the shame and stigma that the children of prisoners have to live with.[164] Research focusing on maternal incarceration has revealed particularly profound impact on children's lives that accentuates pre-existing disadvantages. Evidence has been put forward to link maternal incarceration with 'school failure, antisocial and delinquent behaviour, and higher rates of inter-generational incarceration'.[165] To Holly Foster and John Fagan, 'Americans rarely think of prison inmates – black or white, men or women – as parents'.[166] We will have occasion to demonstrate that this view of prisoners as abstracted from their contingent circumstances, including parenthood, is not confined to the American public. The tendency runs deep within the legal academy and the discourse of human rights.

161 Sanford Bates, *Prisons and Beyond* (Palgrave Macmillan 1937) 233.
162 Pettit (n 144) 83.
163 Ibid 84.
164 John Hagan and Ronit Dinovitzer, 'Collateral Consequences of Imprisonment for Children, Communities, and Prisoners' in Michael Tonry and Joan Petersilla (eds), *Crime and Justice: A Review of Research, Vol. 26 (Prisons)* (University of Chicago Press 1999) 121–162, 123.
165 Joyce A. Arditti, *Parental Incarceration and the Family: Psychological and Social Effects of Imprisonment on Children, Parents and Caregivers* (New York University Press 2012) 59.
166 Holly Foster and John Hagan, 'The Mass Incarceration of Parents in America: Issues of Race/Ethnicity, Collateral Damage to Children, and Prisoner Re-Entry' (2009) 623 *Annals of the American Academy of Political and Social Science* 179, 180.

It should be clear in the light of the previous discussion that retributivist theory, including the principle of proportionality, is directly implicated in our failure to notice the collateral consequences. The theory, after all, is avowedly non-consequentialist. It espouses the fragmentation of criminal justice and social justice and operates with the image of the legal subject as an abstract moral agent. The demonisation of offenders as part of the law-and-order politics and moral panics generated by the media makes it even more difficult for us to give attention to the collateral consequences of incarceration.

To be fair, we must recognise also that confinement of a violent or abusive partner may sometime benefit a family. In a fascinating ethnographic study that combines participant observation in the waiting area of San Quentin State prison in California with in-depth interviews of women whose partners were behind the bars, Megan Comfort attempts to provide a corrective to the body of scholarship that views 'correctional system as a monolithically negative force in the lives of inmates and their families'.[167] Describing women's complex interactions with the institution of prison and prison guards as 'secondary prisonisation', Comfort argues that partners' incarceration allows some women to escape domestic violence and 'to reframe and manage troubled relationships'. But, fundamentally, these women rarely express their experiences in black and white terms.[168] As Comfort clarifies, a woman with a drug-abusing husband behind bars 'might keenly miss his companionship but find herself more financially secure during his incarceration'.[169] The enabling role of the prison, such as it is, emerges only against the context of a failure of other state institutions – income support, healthcare, psychological counselling, childcare benefits – to intervene positively in women's lives.[170] Summing up her findings, Comfort agrees that any short-term benefits women may extract out of their partners' incarceration do not override the 'much more obvious and amply demonstrated destructive effects of forced separation and confinement on families'.[171]

In ignoring the failings of other social institutions and the destructive effects of incarceration, the criminal law diverges from what Amartya Sen has called *naya*, i.e. substantive or 'realized justice'. Does international human rights law fare any better? How attuned is it to conceptual fault lines running through the notion of just deserts and proportionality? Might it supply a more rounded and fine-grained account of the requirements of justice? These questions will be addressed more fully in the subsequent chapters. Needless to say, we have already found ourselves wrestling with the shadow side of human rights. As the opening line of one of Walt Whitman's poems goes: 'Something startles me where I thought I was safest'.[172]

167 Megan Comfort, *Doing Time Together: Love and Family in the Shadow of the Prison* (University of Chicago Press 2008) 2, 9.
168 Ibid 12, 17.
169 Ibid 17.
170 Ibid 185–198.
171 Ibid 196.
172 Walt Whitman, 'This Compost' in *The Complete Poems* (Penguin 2005) 390.

4 Punishment and the origins of international human rights law

An uncensored account

They build a prison and call it progress.

George Orwell[1]

The history of human rights has traditionally been told as a moral success story, involving an inexorable march of humanity from savagery to civilisation. Writing in the tradition of Whig historiography, conventional historians typically recognise the debt owed to the seventeenth and eighteenth-century Enlightenment ideas as they take note of the US Declaration of Independence (1776), the US Bill of Rights (1791, and the French Declaration of the Rights of the Man and the Citizen (1789) as forerunners of the international corpus of human rights. This form of historiography itself carries an imprint of that foremost of Enlightenment thinkers, Immanuel Kant, who saw humanity as 'engaged in progressive improvement in relation to the moral end of its existence'.[2]

Typically, as Jan Herman Burges pointed out in his widely quoted critique, the standard story of human rights makes a big unexplained jump from the classical rights declarations 'to the San Francisco Conference of 1945 where the promotion of human rights was included among the purposes of the United Nations'.[3] In what might well be a meaningful attempt to widen the legitimacy for the concept, some scholars have concentrated efforts on excavating 'ancient roots' of human rights. Such accounts invariably fall into reductionism though, conflating human rights with morality and justice. In the process, they edit the

1 George Orwell, *The Burmese Days* (Penguin 2001) 41.

2 Immanuel Kant, 'On the Common Saying: "This May Be True in Theory but It Does Not Apply in Practice"' in Hans Reiss (ed), *Kant: Political Writings Political Writings* (H.B. Nisbet tr, Cambridge University Press 1991) 61–92, 88. See also William A. Galston, *Kant and the Problem of History* (University of Chicago Press 1975).

3 Jan Herman Burges, 'The Road to San Francisco: The Revival of the Human Rights Idea in the Twentieth Century' (1992) 14 *Human Rights Quarterly* 447, 448. See also Miia Halme-Tuomisaari and Pamela Slotte, 'Revisiting the Origins of Human Rights: An Introduction' in Slotte and Halme-Tumisaari (eds), *Revisiting the Origins of Human Rights* (Cambridge University Press 2015) 1–36, 5–6.

multiplicity of ethical languages out of global history.[4] To question the 'tale of imagined antiquity', however, is not to deny the universal applicability of human rights today.[5] Rather, it is merely underscoring the fallacy involved in reading human rights retroactively into every past movement for individual reform and social change.

Be that as it may, human rights historiography is now being reinvigorated. Over the past couple of decades, a number of revisionist historians have been at work challenging what the editors of a collection of essays have called 'the textbook narrative', defined as 'the unilinear, forward-looking tale of progress and inevitable triumph of human rights'.[6] With varying degrees of sophistication, the revisionist historians have helped recover the complexity that underlies the emergence and expansion of the international human rights regime. Although they differ in their interpretations, the revisionists are united in their repudiation of the teleological belief in the inevitability of moral progress. They also see politics as central to the development of human rights norms. As Seth Mohney sums up his overview of the new revisionist histories, 'Human rights are cast in a political oven and evolve through the influence of diverse, and on occasion, unlikely forces'.[7]

Significantly, despite the expansion of new critical histories, the standard account of the human rights norms pertaining to the idea of punishment has yet to come under scrutiny. The standard story told repeatedly in international law and human rights textbooks is uncritical and triumphalist, often marked by unexplained temporal leaps. The story is typically anchored to two pivotal moments: the eighteenth-century rights documents and the Nazi atrocities during World War II, both of which comprise the cognitive lens through which the history of human rights is filtered. The standard account focuses on the current prohibitions of inhuman punishment and ill-treatment, the principles of legality and proportionality, the right to a fair trial and due process, and a catalogue of substantive standards for the treatment of prisoners as having deep roots in the Enlightenment thought.[8] The widespread revulsion at Nazi atrocities is described as the moment of awakening as to the abiding relevance of these universal norms of justice. There is a great deal of truth in these claims. Contrary to what Samuel

4 See Micheline R. Ishay, *The History of Human Rights: From Ancient Times to the Globalization Era* (University of California Press 2008); Paul Gordon Lauren, *The Evolution of International Human Rights: Visions Seen* (University of Pennsylvania Press 1998). cf. Elaine Pagels, 'Human Rights: Legitimizing a Recent Concept' (1979) 442 *Annals of the American Academy of Political and Social Science* 58; Roger Normand and Sarah Zaidi, *Human Rights at the UN: The Political History of Universal Justice* (Indiana University Press 2008) 11–12.

5 Halme-Tuomisaari and Slotte (n 3) 5.

6 Ibid 1.

7 Seth Mohney, 'The Great Power Origins of Human Rights' (2013–2014) 35 *Michigan Journal of International Law* 827, 860.

8 See, for example, Dirk van Zyl Smit, *'Regulation of Prison Conditions' (2010) 39(1) Crime and Justice* 503, 507.

Moyn has suggested in his seminal revisionist contribution,[9] the Enlightenment thought and the experience of the Holocaust have both left a deep impression on international human rights law albeit not entirely to the exclusion of other forms of political consciousness and ideological beliefs.[10]

There are other reasons why the standard story is unsatisfactory from the perspective of criminal punishment and justice. These include, first and foremost, an uncritical valorisation of penal ideas embedded in the Enlightenment thought; second, the celebration of the Universal Declaration of Human Rights as the 'big bang' moment with earlier legal developments and reform efforts during the nineteenth and the early twentieth century dismissed as irrelevant or insignificant[11]; and finally, a failure to recount the prevalence of penal servitude and convict labour outside the context of Nazi Germany and Stalinist Russia. Addressing the above problems might help illuminate certain inherited paradoxes and constraints within international human rights discourse. For example, after its formal abolition, slavery in the European colonies was widely replaced by various forms of forced labour, including convict labour, which endured up to the closing days of colonial rule.[12] In the United States, the convict leasing system, described by some as 'worse than slavery', was in operation from 1865 to 1928 as a functional alternative to plantation, and its legacies can still be found today in the country's prison-industrial complex. It is a sad reflection on the state of human rights canon that this otherwise well-documented historical reality has simply dropped out of the 'textbook narrative'. What accounts for this omission and what are its implications for the position of human rights law vis-à-vis penal labour?

The story that emerges out of this historical survey does not bear out the faith in the inevitable and steady triumph of virtue over evil, empathy over indifference. There are continuities as well as changes, remarkable achievements as well as significant setbacks. The 'arc of moral universe', contrary to the enticingly optimistic view that Martin Luther King Jr. once took of it, does not necessarily bend toward justice.[13]

9 Samuel Moyn, *The Last Utopia: Human Rights in History* (Harvard University Press 2010) 44–83; *Human Rights and the Uses of History* (Verso 2014) 69–97. cf. David Little, *Essays on Religion and Human Rights: Ground to Stand on* (Cambridge University Press 2015) 57–80.

10 Louis Henkin, 'International Human Rights and Rights in the United States' in Theodor Meron (ed), *Human Rights in International Law: Legal and Policy Issues* (Clarendon Press 1984) 25–67, 29; Johannes Morsink, 'The Philosophy of Universal Declaration' (1984) 6 *Human Rights Quarterly* 309; *The Universal Declaration of Human Rights: Origins, Intent, Drafting* (University of Pennsylvania Press 1999) 43–51; 'World War Two and the Universal Declaration' (1993) 15 *Human Rights Quarterly* 357; Kerri Woods, *Human Rights* (Palgrave Macmillan 2014) 32–37.

11 Halme-Tuomisaari and Slotte (n 3) 5.

12 See, for example, Suzanne Miers, *Slavery in the Twentieth Century: The Evolution of a Global Problem* (Altamira Press 2003) 48; Stacey Hynd, '. . . a Weapon of Immense Value'? Convict Labour in British Colonial Africa, c. 1550–1950s' in Christian Giuseppe De Vito and Alex Lichtenstein (eds), *Global Convict Labour* (Brill 2015) 253.

13 Martin Luther King Jr., *A Testament of Hope: Essential Writings of Martin Luther King* (James Washington ed, Harper & Row 1986) 141.

Slavery's long shadow and the dark side of enlightenment

Scholars and activists fundamentally opposed to prison-backed punishment have used the terminology of 'abolition' to describe their agenda. As Angela Davis puts it, 'I choose the word "abolitionist" deliberately. . . . Through the prison system, the vestiges of slavery have persisted. It thus makes sense to use a word that has this historical resonance'.[14] Drawing attention to the disproportionate impact of incarceration on people of colour, much recent scholarship has depicted the criminal justice system in the US as the latest stage in an evolving racial system. According to the sociologist Loïc Wacquant, a system based on sheer exploitation (chattel slavery) gave way to one propped up by legalised discrimination of the Jim Crow legislation, which was substituted by the 'ghetto' in 'the Northern Industrial metropolis'.[15] Genealogically traceable to the above forms of racial subordination, Wacquant argues, is the latest device of 'mass incarceration', which not only serves to physically segregate and marginalise huge numbers of young black Americans, but also 'induces the civic death of those it snares' through felon disenfranchisement and the denial of welfare and housing benefits to those with a criminal record.[16]

The antebellum slavery has cast a long shadow on the African-American experience of the criminal law. In a global perspective, it is fair to observe that punishments with more obvious slavish origins – branding, flogging, transportation, penal servitude – have long since fallen into disuse.[17] That said, imprisonment, the most commonly applied criminal penalty in the modern world, continues to bear certain unsettling parallels to slavery and other forms of 'servitude'.[18] These common features relate not only to the material relation of domination between prisoners and prison administrators. Rather, just as slaveholding societies appropriated the slave as 'the permanent enemy on the outside', someone who 'did not belong because he was the product of a hostile, alien culture', contemporary

14 Angela Davis, 'Incarcerated Women: Transformative Strategies' (1996) 1(1) *Black Renaissance/Renaissance Noir* 21, 26.

15 Loïc Wacquant, 'From Slavery to Mass Incarceration: Rethinking the Race Question in the US' (2002) 13 *New Left Review* 41, 41. See also Dorothy Roberts, 'Constructing a Criminal Justice System Free of Racial Bias: An Abolitionist Framework' (2007) *39 Columbia Human Rights Law Review* 261; Brian Jarvis, *Cruel and Unusual: A Cultural History of Punishment in America* (Pluto Press 2004) 78–125.

16 Wacquant (n 15) 57. See also Christopher Uggen and Jeff Manza, 'Lost Voices: The Civic and Political Views of Disenfranchised Felons' in Mary Pattillo, David Weiman and Bruce Western (eds), *Imprisoning America: The Social Effects of Mass Incarceration* (Russel Sage Foundation 2004) 165–204.

17 For the thesis that the modern state punishments are derived from slavery, see Thorsten Sellin, *Slavery and the Penal System* (Elsevier Scientific 1976).

18 Servitude is understood to be a broader category, which includes slavery, serfdom, indentured service, debt bondage, and penal servitude. See ML Bush, *Servitude in Modern Times* (Polity Press 2010) 3. See also Lori Gruen, 'Dignity, Captivity, and an Ethics of Sight' in Gruen (ed), *The Ethics of Captivity* (Oxford University Press 2014) 231–247.

societies have constructed the prisoner as the domestic enemy and the 'dangerous other' who must be quarantined and punished.[19] Classical penological justifications of both utilitarian and deontological varieties are implicated in the practice; just as crude forms of utilitarianism legitimise the othering of offenders in the name of public protection, retributive ideology reaches the same result with its focus on condemning and blaming. In terms of the parallels and interconnections between slavery and imprisonment, the most relevant issue for our purposes is what is variously described as convict labour, penal labour, or prisoners' work, with its tangled association with the aims of deterrence, retribution, and rehabilitation. It is, as we shall see, an enduring blind spot in international human rights law.

As mentioned in Chapter 1, it would be facile not to recognise the contribution of Enlightenment thinkers in the abolition of judicial torture and other irrational features of the criminal procedure, brutal penalties, such as breaking on the wheel, and the legal privileges which the nobility and the clergy had historically enjoyed. The classical liberal penology, however, did not represent unambiguous 'improvements'.[20] We have already seen the hold of Kantian and Hegelian theory on modern retributivism, with its lack of engagement with both the background conditions of crime and the consequences of punishment for the offenders, their families, and the society at large. Classical penal philosophy, more than any other field of inquiry perhaps, bears testimony to the fact that even the most sophisticated of Enlightenment thinkers 'suffered from a certain insularity of perspective; they thought they understood man and his limitations better than they did'.[21] Cesare Beccaria, the founder of classical criminology, could propose 'penal slavery' – a punishment dating back to the first century BC Roman society – as an alternative to the death penalty whilst condemning arbitrary punishments.[22] Jeremy Bentham, although opposed to capital punishment and infliction of unnecessary suffering on offenders, envisioned a regime of toil, drudgery, and surveillance that could scarcely be categorised as progress.

In George Orwell's insightful novel *Burmese Days* we find the native physician Veeraswami railing against Eastern ignorance and extoling the prison as a symbol of the rule of law and a mark of superior British civilisation. His fascination with the colonial 'penal reform' illustrates the internalisation by a non-European of the 'standard of civilization', which is also the inaugural normative framework of international law. To Veeraswami's assertion that he sees 'every British even the least inspired of them' as 'torchbearers upon the path of progress', the frustrated

19 Orlando Patterson, *Slavery and Social Death: A Comparative Study* (Harvard University Press 1982) 38–39; On the representation of prisoners as enemies of the public in the British context, see Deborah Drake, 'The "dangerous other" in Maximum-Security Prisons' (2011) 11(4) *Criminology and Criminal Justice* 367.

20 Roy Potter, *The Enlightenment* (2nd edn, Palgrave Macmillan 2001) 67.

21 Dante Germino, *Modern Western Political Thought: Machiavelli to Marx* (Rand McNally & Company 1972) 178.

22 Joan Burdon, 'Slavery as a Punishment in Roman Criminal Law' in Leonie Archer (ed), *Slavery and Other Forms of Unfree Labour* (Routledge 1988) 68.

settler, John Flory, probably modelled on Orwell himself, caustically replies, 'I see them as a kind of up-to-date, hygienic, self-satisfied louse. Creeping round the world building prisons. They build a prison and call it progress'.[23] In our immediate context, one indicator that belies the teleology of moral progress on the lines suggested, for example, by Steven Pinker in his bestseller *The Better Angels of Our Nature*, is the greater use of incarceration in modern times compared to the pre-Enlightenment era.[24] One may reasonably ask how and for whom this constitutes progress. The valorising historian also needs reminding that 'capital punishment as it is currently practiced in Africa' had no precedents in indigenous cultures and was 'very much a part of the legacy of colonialism'.[25] In India, capital punishment predated the colonial period. But the British made greater use of the penalty than their predecessors even as they replaced the pre-existing barbaric punishments by measures 'considered more consistent with reason and humanity'.[26] The practice of organising convicts to perform manual labour was also a distinctly colonial transplant.[27]

With the message of universal emancipation so deeply associated with the Enlightenment thought, it is all too easy to assume that there could have been no place for slavery, bondage, and imperialism in the worldview of the *philosophes* and other Enlightenment intellectuals. Historical evidence points to a far more ambiguous and variegated picture. As Roy Potter remarked in his reappraisal of the Enlightenment legacy, 'Thomas Jefferson, scion of Enlightenment, advocate of the rights of man, and third president of the United States, remained a slave-owner all his life'.[28] In stating that 'all men are created equal', Jefferson certainly did not intend those rousing words to cover black men.[29] J.S. Mill, an official of the East India Company, and one of the most influential liberal philosophers of the nineteenth century, observed in his much revered text, *On Liberty*, that

23 George Orwell, *The Burmese Days* (Penguin 2001) 41. See also Michael Mann, 'Torchbearers Upon the Path of Progress: Britain's Ideology of a Moral and Material Progress in India: An Introductory Essay' in Herald Fischer-Tine and Michael Mann (eds), *Colonialism as Civilizing Mission: Cultural Ideology in British India* (Wimbledon Publishing 2004) 1–26.

24 Steven Pinker, *The Better Angels of Our Nature: Why Violence Has Declined* (Penguin 2011). cf Jennifer Curtis, *Human Rights as War by Other Means: Peace Politics in Northern Ireland* (University of Pennsylvania Press 2014) 20.

25 William A. Schabas, 'African Perspectives on Abolition of the Death Penalty' in Schabas (ed), *The International Source Book on Capital Punishment* (Northeastern University Press 1997) 30–65, 31; Florence Bernault, 'The Shadow of Rule: Colonial Power and Modern Punishment in Africa' in Frank Dikotter and Ian Brown (eds), *Cultures of Confinement: A History of the Prison in Africa, Asia and Latin America* (Cornell University Press 2007) 55–94.

26 David Arnold, 'India: The Contested Prison' in Dikotter and Brown (n 25) 147–84, 150. See also Jorg Fisch, *Cheap Lives and Dear Limbs: The British Transformation of the Bengal Criminal Law, 1769–1817* (Franz Steiner Verlag 1983) 131–132.

27 Anand A. Yang, 'Indian Convict Workers in Southeast Asia in the Late Eighteenth and Early Nineteenth Centuries' (2003) 14(2) *Journal of World History* 179, 183.

28 Potter (n 20) 68. See also John Keane, *The Life and Death of Democracy* (Simon & Schuster 2009) 281.

29 Ned Sublette and Constance Sublette, *The American Slave Coast: A History of the Slave-Breeding Industry* (Lawrence Hill Books 2016) 264–265.

'despotism is a legitimate mode of government in dealing with barbarians' for their own good.[30] Earlier, John Locke, whose influence on classical human rights theory is well recognised,[31] had rationalised Britain's colonial ambitions in America in his 1689 *Treatise on Government*, deploying the Roman doctrine of *terra nullius* – the right to vacant or unclaimed territory:

> God gave the World to Men in Common; but since he gave it to them for their benefit, and the greatest Conveniences of Life they were capable to draw from it, it cannot be supposed he meant it should always remain common and uncultivated. He gave it to the use of the Industrious and Rational . . . not to the Fancy or Covetousness of the Quarrelsome and Contentious.[32]

Although John Locke famously denounced slavery in the first sentence of his *First Treatise*, his financial investments in a slave-trading company illustrate that slavery did not necessarily trouble his conscience.[33] The French scholar Louis Sala-Molins has scrutinised the works of Condorcet, Montesquieu, Rousseau, and Diderot to reveal how their humanist project 'stuttered' and 'vacillated' in the face of slave trade and slavery.[34] At the heart of the failure of the *philosophes* to come out unequivocally against slavery, argues Sala-Molins, is a particular construct of the human as defined by the rational capacity and accomplishments of the white man.[35] As Eliot Young has remarked in the context of the transportation of Chinese indentured labour from Macao to Peru during the mid-nineteenth century, a similar imagination was at play with European liberals embracing imperialism. On this seemingly paradoxical reasoning, imperialism was deemed necessary for extending natural rights to the 'uncivilized' parts of the world. A belief in universal rights thus fit in with 'the idea of European sovereignty'.[36]

This may all sound to some readers as mere historical nit-picking. Contemporary human rights law, after all, eschews all distinctions as to race, ethnicity, and other such arbitrary grounds. American historian Lynn Hunt has spoken of the 'inner logic' of human rights, embedded within the 'supposedly metaphysical nature of the Declaration of the Rights of Man and Citizen', which historically

30 John Stuart Mill, *On Liberty and Other Essays* (Oxford University Press 1991) 11. cf Jennifer Pitts, *A Turn to Empire: The Rise of Imperial Liberalism in Britain and France* (Princeton University Press 2005) 123–162.

31 Burn H. Weston, 'Human Rights' (1984) 6 *Human Rights Quarterly* 257, 259.

32 John Locke, *Two Treatises of Government* (Cambridge University Press 1988) 291.

33 Peter Gay, *The Enlightenment: The Science of Freedom* (W.W. Norton & Company Inc. 1969) 409–410.

34 Louis Sala-Molins, *Dark Side of the Light: Slavery and the French Enlightenment* (John Conte-Morgan tr, University of Minnesota Press 2006) 23. See also David Brion Davis, *The Problem of Slavery in Western Culture* (Oxford University Press 1966) 391–421.

35 Sala-Molins (n 34) 24.

36 Elliot Young, 'Chinese Coolies, "Universal Rights and the Limits of Liberalism in an Age of Empire"' (2015) 227 *Past and Present* 121, 124. See also Anthony Pagden, 'Human Rights, Natural Rights, and Europe's Imperial Legacy' (2003) 31(2) *Political Theory* 171.

led to the diffusion and extension of the concept to ever new claimants beyond the propertied white men.[37] Yet, despite an enormous expansion in its scope and outreach, the international human rights corpus carries a number of internal tensions. The express or implied exclusion of prisoners from the right to a minimum wage and freedom from forced labour is illustrative of the paradoxical nature of human rights law, its loyalty divided between emancipation and acceptable forms of exploitation. To go further back into history, the Thirteenth Amendment to the Constitution of the United States, when it finally abolished slavery in 1865, did so 'except as a punishment for crime whereof the party shall have been duly convicted'.[38] Hannah Arendt's notion of 'the right to have rights', which she had used to describe the situation of the stateless Jews on the eve of the Second World War, also speaks to the exclusionary tendency within human rights vis-à-vis offenders and prisoners.[39] To Arendt, the real test of human rights was whether it could protect individuals stripped of political status and reduced to being mere humans. She would find out, however, that 'the opposite is the case. It seems that a man who is nothing but a man has lost the very qualities which make it possible for other people to treat him as a fellow man'.[40]

Historians have called the eighteenth-century anti-slavery campaign the 'greatest of all human rights movements'[41] and 'the most successful episode ever in the history of international human rights law'.[42] Some critics have taken issue with this characterisation on the grounds that the eighteenth- and nineteenth-century abolitionists did not frame their demands in the language of human rights. Rights talk, when employed within the then prevalent natural rights paradigm, also had a double edge given the centrality of the right to property – including the right to own slaves – within that tradition.[43] Be that as it may, the issues the abolitionists were campaigning against will today easily be recognised as human rights concerns. What is less readily appreciated within the human rights canon is that 'the most important factor promoting the reaction against slavery was the deeply held conviction of religious men and women'.[44] The campaign which led to the formal abolition of slavery and slave trade was spearheaded by the evangelical Christians

37 Lynn Hunt, *Inventing Human Rights: A History* (W.W. Norton & Company 2008) 150.
38 'Neither slavery nor involuntary servitude, except as a punishment for crime whereof the party shall have been duly convicted, shall exist within the United States, or any place subject to their jurisdiction'. U.S. Const. amend. XIII, § 1.
39 Hannah Arendt, *The Origins of Totalitarianism* (7th edn, Harcourt Inc. 1976) 298.
40 Ibid 302.
41 Adam Hochschild, *Bury the Chains: Prophets and Rebels in the Fights to Free an Empire's Slaves* (Houghton Mifflin Company 2005) 102; Seymour Drescher, 'From Consensus to Consensus: Slavery in International Law' in Jean Allain (ed), *The Legal Understanding of Slavery* (Oxford University Press 2012) 85–102, 91.
42 Jenny S. Martinez, *The Slave Trade and the Origins of International Human Rights Law* (Oxford University Press 2012) 13.
43 Moyn, 'Human Rights and the Uses of History' (n 9) 58.
44 FSL Lyons, *Internationalism in Europe. 1815–1914* (A.W. Sythoff, Leyden 1963) 287; Erica Armstrong Dunbar, *A Fragile Freedom: African American Women and Emancipation in the Antebellum City* (Yale University Press 2008) 18.

and the Quakers, 'not by the liberal intelligentsia'.[45] And, it is these religious men – along with the much despised exponents of positivist criminology – who need to be credited with the internationalisation of penal reform during the first half of the twentieth century.

That said, it would be intellectually unfair to completely delink abolition from the powerful ideas about freedom and liberty generated by the Enlightenment. On one reading, in maintaining their witness against slaveholding, Quakers too advanced the Enlightenment ideals of freedom, democracy, and equality by calling on governments on both sides of the Atlantic to 'put the democratic rhetoric they frequently espoused into practice'.[46] However, Quakers' spiritually inflected prison work also transcended the classical penal doctrines in some significant ways. Taking a cue from Justin Roberts' painstaking study of plantation slavery in the eighteenth-century British Atlantic, we need to acknowledge, at the very least, that the Enlightenment project rested on a paradox. On the one hand, it 'gave rise to a new set of moral sensibilities that reduced some of the physical barbarity within slavery and ended the slave trade'.[47] Simultaneously, 'there was also a ruthless rationalism to the Enlightenment and a pragmatism and expediency', which besides nurturing industrialisation and factory discipline, led to 'more exhausting plantation work regimes in which planters strove to reduce the workers into the depersonalised and interchangeable units of production'.[48] Similar paradoxes inhere in international human rights law, for example, in the form of the prohibition of 'cruel and inhuman treatment or punishment' on the one hand, and the acceptance of prisoners' work as a lawful form of 'forced labour' on the other. The universalising tendencies of Enlightenment found their historic limits not only in imperialist expansion but also in convict labour and the question of prisoners' status as rights-bearers.

Legacy of the League of Nations

Having discussed the failure of the textbook narrative to engage critically with the Enlightenment thought, we can now move on to the second problematic feature running through some of its versions, namely the unreflective celebration of the founding of the United Nations as the 'big bang' moment in the history of human rights. Such accounts are hobbled, in the words of Mark Mazower, by the 'historical axiom' that 'the United Nations rose – like an Aphrodite – from the Second World War, pure and uncontaminated by any significant association

45 Potter (n 20) 68; Auguste Jorns, *The Quakers as Pioneers in Social Work* (Thomas Kite Brown tr, Kennikat Press, Inc. 1931) 197–233.

46 Sarah Crabtree, 'A Beautiful and Practical Lesson of Jurisprudence: The Transatlantic Quaker Ministry in an Age of Revolution' (2007) 99 *Radical History Review* 51, 64–65.

47 Justin Roberts, *Slavery and the Enlightenment in the British Atlantic, 1750–1807* (Cambridge University Press 2013) 6.

48 Ibid.

with that pre-war failure, the League of Nations'.[49] No doubt, in its scope and ambition, the UN system far exceeded all previous experiments in international co-operation and the international protection of human rights. However, to fully understand the substantive contents and the implementation machinery of the system, specifically in relation to penal policy and practice, we need to revisit the developments in the nineteenth and early twentieth century.

Michael Ignatieff begins an overview of human rights by stating that 'until 1945, international protection of individual human rights was confined to the treaties abolishing the slave trade, the laws of war, and minority rights treaties concluded after Versailles'.[50] To this catalogue, we must add the codification of international labour standards by the International Labour Organisation (a body affiliated to and funded by the League of Nations), and, more importantly for our purposes, the drafting of the Standard Minimum Rules for the Treatment of Prisoners by the Penitentiary Commission in the late 1920s and the adoption of the document by the League of Nations in 1934.[51] However, just as in the case of the anti-slavery movement, the term human rights 'did not appear in any official ILO document' until the closing days of the Second World War.[52] Until then, the standard-setting work of the ILO had intellectually been anchored to the concept of 'social justice'[53] and 'welfare', and not rights.[54] As we saw in Chapter 2, the terminology of rights was absent from the deliberations of the International Penitentiary Congresses held between 1875 and 1951. Similarly, it has been pointed out in respect of the protection of minorities under the League of Nations system that the older discourse was articulated in the language of 'guarantees' and not 'rights', the focus being on state obligations 'either voluntarily assumed as a gesture of good-will towards a particular group . . . or externally imposed upon new or weak states by the great powers in the interest of international peace and stability'.[55]

Taina Turi has offered a different reading of the legacy of the League of Nations. Based on archival research into the Minutes of the Mandates Commission during

49 Mark Mazower, *No Enchanted Palace: The End of Empire and the Ideological Origins of the United Nations* (Princeton University Press 2009) 14.

50 Michael Ignatieff, 'Human Rights' in Carla Hesse and Robert Post (ed), *Human Rights in Political Transitions: Gettysburg to Bosnia* (Zone Books 1999) 313–324, 313.

51 League of Nations OJ, Spec. Supp. 123, (1934). See also Paul Cornil, 'International Standards for the Treatment of Offenders' (1968) 26(3) *International Review of Criminal Policy* 3.

52 Daniel Roger Maul, 'The International Labour Organization and the Globalization of Human Rights, 1944–1970' in Stefan-Ludwig Hoffman (ed), *Human Rights in the Twentieth Century* (Cambridge University Press 2011) 301–320, 305.

53 Ibid 304. See also Virginia A. Leary, 'Lessons from the Experience of the International Labour Organisation' in Philip Alston (ed), *The United Nations and Human Rights: A Critical Appraisal* (Clarendon Press 1992) 580–619, 583.

54 Gerry Rodgers and others, *The International Labour Organization and the Quest for Social Justice, 1919–2009* (Cornell University Press 2009) 41.

55 Jennifer Jackson Preece, *Minority Rights: Between Diversity and Community* (Polity Press 2005). See also Mark Mazower, 'The Strange Triumph of Human Rights, 1933–1950' (2004) 47(2) *The Historical Journal* 379, 381.

the years 1921–1939 around the areas of land tenure, slavery, forced labour, and the position of women, she has argued that international lawyers were then engaged in creating 'proto-rights' language in discussing topics that are 'currently understood as rights issues'.[56] The emerging human rights discourse that Turi speaks of, however, was circumscribed within the limits imposed by the concept of a civilisational hierarchy that informed international law through the second half of the nineteenth century up until the end of the Second World War.[57] Thus, what Rudyard Kipling termed the 'white man's burden' found its way into Woodrow Wilson's famous 14 points and got enshrined into the Covenant of the League of Nations as 'the principle that the well-being and development' of 'peoples not yet able to stand by themselves under the strenuous conditions of the modern world' form 'a sacred trust of civilization'.[58] 'The best method of giving practical effect to this principle', the Covenant went on to state, apparently following the logic of John Locke and J.S. Mill,

> is that the tutelage of such peoples should be entrusted to advanced nations who by reason of their resources, their experience or their geographical position can best undertake this responsibility, and who are willing to accept it, and that this tutelage should be exercised by them as Mandatories on behalf of the League.[59]

The result was the formation of a Permanent Mandates Commission comprising of nine to ten members responsible for limited supervision of three classes of former German and Turkish-Ottoman colonies.[60] The Covenant further bound the members of the League to 'endeavour to secure and maintain fair and humane conditions of labour for men, women, and children, both in their own countries and in all countries to which their commercial and industrial relations extend', and to 'secure just treatment of the native inhabitants of territories under their control'.[61]

56 Taina Tuori, 'From League of Nations Mandates to Decolonization: A Brief History of Rights' in Pamela Slotte and Miia Halme-Tumisaari (eds), *Revisiting the Origins of Human Rights* (Cambridge University Press 2015) 267–292, 275. See also Kevin Grant, 'Human Rights and Sovereign Abolitions of Slavery, c. 1885–1956' in Grant and others (eds), *Beyond Sovereignty: Britain, Empire and Transnationalism, c. 1880–1950* (Palgrave Macmillan 2007) 80–99.

57 On the standard of civilization and the evolution of international law, see Gerrit W. Gong, *The Standard of "Civilization" in International Society* (Clarendon Press 1984) 54–93, 240; Martti Koskenniemi, *The Gentle Civilizer of Nations: The Rise and Fall of International Law 1870–1960* (Cambridge University Press 2001) 98–178; Antony Anghie, *Imperialism, Sovereignty and the Making of International Law* (Cambridge University Press 2004) 32–114.

58 Covenant of the League of Nations (adopted 28 June 1919, entered into force 10 January 1920) 1 League of Nations O. J. 3 (art 2).

59 Ibid.

60 Martti Koskenniemi, *The Gentle Civilizer of Nations: The Rise and Fall of International Law 1870–1960* (Cambridge University Press 2001) 171.

61 Art 23, paras (a) and (b).

There are some significant differences between the engagement of the League of Nations system with 'human rights concerns' and the international human rights discourse that emerged in the aftermath of the Second World War. However, it is possible to notice several continuities in the midst of change. The historical trajectory of the international protection of human rights – in the penal context, at least – is marked by jagged edges rather than clean breaks. What distinguishes the post-Second World War system from its predecessor is a much stronger and explicit normative focus on individual human rights as distinct from the older terminology of 'welfare', 'well-being', and 'social justice'. As Jennifer Prece has correctly suggested, contrasting the League of Nations' framework of the 'guarantees' of minority protection with contemporary 'human rights discourse', 'the power of the rights discourse originates in its normative content and moral authority'. At least in theory, if not always in practice, 'rights are comparatively more difficult to limit, repeal, annul or abolish and thus afford the possibility of greater protection'.[62] So far so good. However, an additional point that often escapes scholarly attention is whether anything is lost when human rights supplant other normative concepts, such as social justice. As we have seen, this issue has a significant bearing on the way 'crime' and 'criminal responsibility' are conceptualised in human rights discourse.

The second significant normative feature that marks the post-Second World War system out from the League of Nations is the principle of 'universality' as distinct from an overt discourse of civilisation and racial inequality embedded in the League Covenant. There is an interesting story to be told about how the time-worn notion of imperial tutelage and civilisational hierarchy staged a comeback during the formative era of the UN in the form of the 'Trusteeship Council', and a proposed 'colonial clause' meant to exclude the colonised from the full protection of international human rights. More to the point, it remains to be assessed whether in officially renouncing the dichotomy between civilised and non-civilised nations, the modern system of human rights protection has set up a new dichotomy, this time between citizens deserving of the full range of human rights and the convicted 'criminals' who fall beyond the pale. Further, even as the doctrine of civilisation no longer regulates the admission of new members into the international system, it appears that the liberal ideology of retributive justice and the 'rule of law' implicitly constitute the new criteria of what it means for a country to be civilised.

Overall, historical opinion has not been particularly kind to the legacy of the Mandates System. The same holds for the minority protection regime, which took the form of clauses guaranteeing the protection of minority groups included in specific treaties concluded with Greece Poland, Czechoslovakia, and other countries of the region with supervisory powers assigned to the Council of the League of Nations.[63] The system, many believe, provided little more than 'fig

62 Prece (n 55) 14.

63 For an overview, see C.A Macartney, 'League of Nations' Protection of Minority Rights' in Evan Luard (ed), *The International Protection of Human Rights* (Thames and Hudson 1967) 22–38.

leaves of respectability to the flowering of European imperialism' and preserving the territorial integrity of existing nation-states in Europe whilst paying lip service to the protection of minorities.[64] Necessarily a compromise between internationalism and 'the reality of Great Power hegemony' – perhaps a nervous response to the spectre of Bolshevism too – the League of Nations did, however, take the first tentative steps toward transcending nationalism and the war-time scramble for territory. And in so doing, it laid the preliminary groundwork for the recognition of human rights and state accountability.[65] Some scholars have rightly credited leading jurists such as René Cassin, then active with the ILO and later a key figure in the drafting of the Universal Declaration, for producing 'a far-reaching and fundamental critique of the concept of sovereignty', prompted in large part by the founding of the League of Nations in 1924.[66] Though it has received scant attention in historical or human rights scholarship, a sustained critique of sovereignty was also developed with particular reference to the rights of prisoners and the persecution of minorities through penal measures during the inter-war years by the Howard League for Penal Reform. More on this in the next chapter.

In another fine reassessment of the legacy of the League of Nations, Susan Pederson has argued that despite all its faults, racial prejudices and Euro-centrism, the League did serve as a 'vehicle of internationalization' of what would have previously been considered purely 'internal' matters for the states to sort out within their own territories and imperial possessions.[67] The point is not so much that the conditions of the inhabitants in the Mandates – or of European citizens for that matter – registered any significant material change as a result of the League taking up issues such as child welfare, trafficking, slavery, and forced labour. Rather, 'partly inadvertently and partly deliberately', the League of Nations opened up a forum for debate, lobbying, and publicity that gave impetus to 'the mobilization of new constituencies, the generation of new claims, the elaboration of new practices, and the articulation of new norms'.[68] The Permanent Mandates Commission, on Pederson's account, subjected the imperial rule to unprecedented scrutiny by regularly questioning and publishing its records, reports, and minutes

64 JM Roberts, *Penguin History of the World: The History of the World, 1901 to the Present* (Penguin 1999) 275.

65 Kevin Grant, Philippa Levine and Frank Trentmann, 'Introduction' in Grant, Levine and Trentmann (eds), *Beyond Sovereignty: Britain, Empire and Transnationalism, c. 1880–1950* (Palgrave Macmillan 2007) 1–15, 3. See also Amalia Ribi, '"The Breath of a New Life"? British Anti-Slavery Activism and the League of Nations' in Daniel Lacqua (ed), *Internationalism Reconfigured: Transnational Ideas and Movements Between the World Wars* (I.B. Taurus 2011) 93–113, 94.

66 Jay Winters and Antoine Prost, *Rene Cassin and Human Rights: From the Great War to the Universal Declaration* (Cambridge University Press 2013) 221–224.

67 Susan Pedersen, *The Guardians: The League of Nations and the Crisis of Empire* (Oxford University Press 2015) 4.

68 Ibid 405. For an earlier work that pursues a similar line of argument, see Jane K. Cowan, 'Justice and the League of Nations Minority Regime' in Kamari Maxine Clarke and Mark Goodale (eds), *Mirrors of Justice: Law and Power in the Post-Cold War Era* (Cambridge University Press, New York 2010) 270–290.

of meetings. Pederson highlights the forgotten role of the League Secretariat, the nerve-centre of what she calls 'the technical League', which under the chairmanship of its first Secretary General Eric Drummond, its staff of permanent officials chosen in their independent capacity, helped promote 'common norms about trusteeship' and the aspirations for self-determination.[69] The Secretariat under Drummond and 'the technical practices introduced by the League' formed the blueprint of an international civil service that would go on to inspire the structure of the United Nations.[70]

Pederson's thesis accords with the claims of Swiss academic and diplomat William E. Rappard, who served as the Director of the Mandates Section of the Secretariat between the years 1920 and 1924. Writing within a few months of the founding of the United Nations, Rappard recounted the partial success of the mandates system 'within the admittedly narrow boundaries of the international protection of certain human rights in backward countries'.[71] Crucially, in his article, Rappard also sought to temper over-enthusiasm about the prospects of the UN representing something fundamentally different from the League as he pointed out that Article 2 of the UN Charter debarred the newly formed body from intervening 'in matters which are essentially within the domestic jurisdiction of any state domestic matters'.[72] In relating the limited success of the Mandates System in terms of bringing 'human rights matters' up for discussion and scrutiny, Rappard admitted that the quality and extent of information about what actually went on in the Mandates varied according to the territories concerned and their administration. Nonetheless, he was confident that if the governments 'directly responsible for the administration of the mandates' failed to live up to the guarantees of the protection of the rights of the native populations, 'they would either have to withhold the facts from Geneva or withstand the criticism of the Permanent Mandates Commission, the Council, and the Assembly of the League, and especially of its own press and its own parliamentary opposition'.[73]

The channels of information-sharing and publicity opened up by the Mandates Commission played no insignificant role in the adoption of the 1926 Slavery Convention – remembered by some as 'the first, modern international treaty for the protection of human rights' – and subsequently, to the drafting of a Forced Labour Convention in 1930.[74] At the same time, it is also clear that in the absence of an enforcement machinery – other than voluntary reporting and questioning

69 Pedersen (n 67) 46–50.

70 Mark Mazower, 'The Guardians: The League of Nations and the Crisis of Empire by Susan Pederson Review – The Legacy of an Unlikely Hero', *The Guardian*, Friday 6 November 2015. See also Partha Chatterjee, *The Black Hole of Empire: History of a Global Practice of Power* (Princeton University Press 2012) 276.

71 William E. Rappard, 'Human Rights in Mandated Territories' (1946) 243 *Annals of the American Academy of Political and Social Science* 118.

72 Ibid 119.

73 Ibid 121.

74 Manfred Nowak, *U.N. Covenant on Civil and Political Rights: CCPR Commentary* (2nd edn, N.P. Engel 2005) 197.

by the Mandates Commission – the governments, in many cases, could cover up exploitative practices in their own countries and in the territories they held as 'a sacred trust of civilization'. As Seymour Drescher and Paul Finkelman have observed, the reports submitted 'to the League by the colonial powers in 1926 celebrated their own national histories of enlightened rule', lauding 'their imperial achievement in overcoming the hurdles of native ignorance, laziness and cultural backwardness'.[75] In what appears to be another carryover from the League of Nations system, the international human rights monitoring regime still relies heavily on self-reporting by the UN member states.

Slaves of the state? Convict labour and the development of international law

The prohibition of slavery and slave trade is today most certainly a part of customary international law. It has achieved the status of a peremptory norm, i.e. a norm from which no derogation is permitted, and an obligation *erga onmes*, a 'concern of all States', as the International Court of Justice put it in the *Barcelona Traction* case.[76] The Universal Declaration of Human Rights, itself believed to be a part of customary international law, prohibits 'slavery and slave trade in all its forms'.[77] The International Covenant on Civil and Political Rights, under Article 8(1), reproduces verbatim the relevant provision from the Universal Declaration: 'No one shall be held in slavery; slavery and the slave-trade in all their forms shall be prohibited'.[78] The same article provides that 'no one shall be held in servitude'.[79] More crucially, for the purposes of our discussion, the subsequent paragraph prohibits 'forced or compulsory labour' but goes on to state that the prohibition 'shall not be held to preclude, in countries where imprisonment with hard labour may be imposed as a punishment for a crime, the performance of hard labour in pursuance of a sentence to such punishment by a competent court'.[80] Subparagraph 3(c) contains specific exceptions to the prohibition of forced or compulsory labour, including any work or service 'normally required of a person who is under detention in consequence of a lawful order of a court, or of a person during conditional release from such detention'.[81] Employing more or less the same terminology, the European Convention on Human Rights and the

75 Seymour Drescher and Paul Finkelman, 'Slavery' in Bardo Fassbender and Anne Peteres (eds), *The Oxford Handbook of the History of International Law* (Oxford University Press 2012) 890–916, 912.
76 Barcelona Traction, Light and Power Company, Limited (Belgium v Spain) Second Phase [1970] ICJ Rep 3, at paras 33–34.
77 Art 4, Universal Declaration of Human Rights (adopted by the General Assembly Resolution 217A (III) 10 December 1948) UN Doc A/810.
78 International Covenant on Civil and Political Rights (adopted 16 December 1966, entered into force 23 March 1976) 999 UNTS 171.
79 Ibid Art 8 (2).
80 Ibid Art 8 (3) (b).
81 Ibid Art 8 (3) (c) (i–iv).

American Convention on Human Rights, both conceive of convict labour negatively as an exception to the prohibition of forced labour.[82] The African Charter of Human and People's Rights (also known as the Banjul Charter) is silent on the issue of forced labour or convict labour. In very broad terms, however, it prohibits 'all forms of exploitation and degradation of man particularly slavery, slave trade, torture, cruel, inhuman or degrading punishment and treatment'.[83]

As noted earlier, the exclusion of convict labour from the legal prohibition of forced labour and 'servitude' has a long pedigree, dating back to the Thirteenth Amendment to the US Constitution. In the wake of the First World War, slavery, slave-like practices, and forced labour were among the first issues addressed by the League of Nations. The growing attention toward the topic came about partly as a result of changing public opinion and partly due to geostrategic concerns. Although slavery had been abolished by an Act of Parliament in the British Empire in 1833, to allow other states to continue to benefit economically from slave trade and slavery would have posed a major strategic disadvantage to Britain's commercial interests.[84] Hence, Britain's leadership role in the abolition effort at the international level. Some historians miss out on this substantial connection between humanitarian concerns and the larger context of British imperial politics.[85]

The Slavery Convention of 1926 defined slavery as 'the status or condition of a person over whom any of all the powers attaching to the right of ownership are exercised' and obligated the signatories to combat slavery in all its form.[86] But this is to tell only half the story. Many European countries, including the Mandatory powers under the League system, had 'inward reservations' about the international abolition.[87] Many resisted the inclusion of forced labour within the scope of the 1926 Slavery Convention 'on grounds of infringement of national sovereignty'.[88] The matter was subsequently referred to the ILO.

The 1930 Convention against Forced Labour (also known as the ILO Convention 29) defined forced or compulsory labour as 'all work or service which is exacted from any person under the menace of any penalty and for which the said person has not offered himself voluntarily'.[89] In addition to compulsory military service, normal civic obligations, work or service exacted in cases of emergency,

82 Art 4 (3)(a), European Convention for the Protection of Human Rights and Fundamental Freedoms (adopted 1 November 1950, entered into force 3 September 1953) 213 UNTS 222; Art 6(2) and 6(3)(a) American Convention on Human Rights (adopted 21 November 1969, entered into force 18 July 1978) 1144 UNTS 143.

83 Art 5, African Charter on Human and Peoples' Rights ('Banjul Charter') (adopted 27 June 1981, entered into force 21 October 1986) 1520 UNTS 217.

84 Miers (n 12) 3.

85 See, for example, Rodgers and others (n 54) 41.

86 Art 1, Convention to Suppress the Slave Trade and Slavery (adopted 25 September 1926, entered into force 9 March 1927) 60 LNTS 253.

87 Pedersen (n 67) 243.

88 Drescher and Finkelman (n 75) 911.

89 Art 2(1), Forced Labour Convention, C29, International Labour Organisation (adopted 28 June 1930, entered into force 1 May 1932) 39 UNTS 55.

minor communal service, the 1930 Convention excluded from the prohibition of forced or compulsory labour, 'any work or service exacted from any person as a consequence of a conviction in a court of law'.[90] The drafting history suggests that 'none of the parties involved in the preparation of this convention ever questioned the legal basis for requiring obligatory work from sentenced prisoners', nor did the ILO office raise any objections in relation to 'the compulsory nature of prison labour'.[91] However, the exclusion of penal labour from the prohibition of forced labour came with 'a sting in the tale': It 'was not to be hired out for private use, as it was, for instance, in India, South Africa, and certain states in the United States'.[92] Concurrently, the continued permissibility of the use of convict labour for public works was crucial for the construction of irrigation canals, bridges, roads, military barracks, and other such colonial projects.[93] Thus, the British delegates in particular held strongly that the ILO Convention should not abolish compulsory labour within prisons, or 'compulsory labour imposed as a punishment in lieu of a fine or imprisonment, but that such labour should in all cases be employed on public works and that the practice of hiring out to private individuals should be forbidden'.[94]

The requirement that 'any work or service exacted from any person as a consequence of a conviction in a court of law' be 'carried out *under the supervision and control of a public authority*'[95] was dropped subsequently in the 1957 Abolition of Forced Labour Convention (ILO Convention 105) and the Covenant on Civil and Political Rights. The Covenant, in fact, formulated the exception of prison labour as a lawful form of forced labour more broadly than the 1930 Forced Labour Convention to cover compulsory labour performed during conditional release.[96] Up until the 1970s though, the management of prisons remained largely in state hands with the involvement of philanthropic groups in varying degrees across the world. The old debate as to whether the state alone could be entrusted with the administration of punishment and reformation, or whether private contractors would do a more 'efficient' job, resurfaced with the punitive turn in the 1980s and 1990s. Mediated by the ideology of 'new managerialism', privately run prisons are now a recognisable feature of the penal landscape, especially in the United States and Britain, and a swathe of services within public-sector prisons (catering, cleaning, rehabilitation programmes, and so on)

90 Art 2 (2).

91 Gerad De Jonge, 'Still "'Slaves of the State": Prison Labour and International Law' in Dirk van Zyl Smit and Frieder Dunkel (eds), *Prison Labour: Salvation or Slavery?* (Ashgate 1999) 313–334, 320, 323.

92 Miers (n 12) 146.

93 David Arnold, 'Labouring for the Raj: Convict Work Regimes in Colonial India, 1836–1939' in Christian De Vito and Lichtenstein (n 12) 119–221, 201.

94 Hynd (n 12) 262.

95 Art 2, para 2 (c), Forced Labour Convention, C29, International Labour Organisation (adopted 28 June 1930, entered into force 1 May 1932) 39 UNTS 55.

96 De Jonge (n 91) 323.

have been contracted out to private operators.[97] Whilst there is no evidence that privatisation has resulted in cost-efficiency, it certainly has given rise to a handful of companies dominating prison services.[98] In a landmark case that finds no parallel in the jurisprudence of international human rights courts, the Supreme Court of Israel in 2009 struck down a legislation providing for private prisons, holding that 'the very existence of a prison that operates on a profit making basis reflects a lack of respect for the status of [prisoners] as human beings'.[99]

To pick up on the developments in international law, the 1957 Abolition of Forced Labour Convention came into force against the backdrop of concerns about the treatment of political prisoners in the Chinese labour camps and Soviet gulags. It specifically extended the prohibition of forced or compulsory labour as a means of 'political coercion or education or as a punishment for holding or expressing political views or views ideologically opposed to the established political, social or economic system'; 'mobilising and using labour for purposes of economic development'; 'labour discipline'; 'punishment for having participated in strikes'; and 'racial, social, national or religious discrimination'.[100] Ordinary criminals convicted of 'non-political' crimes still fell beyond the pale of the prohibition of forced labour. The distinction is spurious in the sense that all convict labour is political as it is 'carried out at the behest of the state, according to rules that the state [has] devised, or for purpose of coercion, punishment, and reform that [conform] to the state's wider political agenda'.[101] Described by some as a 'Cold War relic', the 1957 Convention also carries a latent class-bias in that the so-called political prisoners typically come from the middle class whereas the 'non-political' prisoners predominantly belong to the working class stratum.[102] There are echoes here of an earlier period in Western history when distinctions along the lines of social class were made less surreptitiously. In late sixteenth- and early seventeenth-century Europe, the Houses of Correction – or the bridewells as the term went in England – emerged in the context of the early stages of capitalism, which in the words of Marx, involved the 'expropriation of the agricultural population from the land', turning dispossessed peasants into a mass of wage-labourers.[103] Subsequently, countries throughout Western Europe adopted

97 Susan Easton and Christine Piper, *Sentencing and Punishment: The Quest for Justice* (4th edn, Oxford University Press 2016) 269–273.

98 Ibid 272.

99 *Academic Centre of Law and Business v Minister of Finance* (November 19, 2009) HCJ 2605/05, Human Rights Division, para 36.

100 Art 1, Convention concerning the Abolition of Forced Labour, C105, International Labour Organisation (adopted 25 June 1957, entered into force 17 January 1959) 320 UNTS 291.

101 David Arnold, 'Labouring for the Raj' (n 93) 199–221.

102 Susan Kang, 'Forcing Prison Labor: International Labor Standards, Human Rights and the Privatization of Prison Labor in the Contemporary United States' (2009) 31(2) *New Political Science* 137, 144.

103 Karl Marx, *Capital: A Critique of Political Economy* (Volume 1, Penguin Classics 1990) 877. See also Joanna Innes, 'Prisons for the Poor: English Bridewells, 1555–1800' in Francis Snyder and Douglas Hay (eds), *Labour, Law and Crime: An Historical Perspective* (Tavistock Publications 1987) 42–122.

legislation criminalising the new class of paupers, petty thieves, prostitutes, vagabonds, beggars, and vagrants, sentencing them to 'a term of confinement at hard labour in the houses of correction'.[104] The obligation to perform labour was reserved for this class. The members of well-to-do families, when in rare cases confined in these establishments, were excluded.[105]

Along with 'political prisoners', there is another subset of prisoners who enjoy the protection of the forced labour prohibition under international law. The Geneva Convention Relative to the Treatment of Prisoners of War (1949) allows the 'Detaining Power' to 'utilize the labour of prisoners of war who are physically fit',[106] in specified fields,[107] but also provides that 'officers or persons of equivalent status . . . may in no circumstances be compelled to work'.[108] As we have begun to see, the principle of 'equality' stated in article 1 of the UDHR – 'all human beings are born free and equal in dignity and rights' – is easy to pronounce, but the devil is in the details. When it comes to the legal legitimacy of prisoners' work at least, some (humans) are more equal than others.

The continued exclusion of labour undertaken by the so-called non-political (civilian) prisoners from the prohibition of forced labour as well as the apparently regressive (tacit) approval of the privatisation of prisoners' work under the ICCPR provide plausible reasons to question the teleology of progress and modernisation. The absence of any sort of critical engagement with the topic in the mainstream human rights scholarship is astonishing, to say the least. Further, to narrate the success of the twentieth-century abolitionist movement without considering the historical deployment of convict labour as an ancillary to – and following the abolition – a 'functional substitute' to slavery, is to trade in half-truths.[109]

Without addressing the necessary implications for convict labour, Manfred Novak, in his commentary on the ICCPR, notes that 'the borders between slavery and servitude and other forms of forced or compulsory labour are not hard and fast'.[110] In fact, historical evidence gives us reasons to take the argument further and claim that the 'borders' practically dissipated in the context of convict leasing in the Southern states of America following the civil war, and the extensive use of convict labour in parts of the British Empire well into the twentieth century. Prior to the civil war, the institution of state punishment in the United

104 Randall S. Shelden, *Controlling the Dangerous Classes: A History of Criminal Justice in America* (2nd edn, Pearson 2008) 150–152.

105 Clive Emsley, *Crime, Police and Penal Policy: European Experiences 1750–1940* (Oxford University Press 2004) 36–37.

106 Art 49 (1) Geneva Convention Relative to the Treatment of Prisoners of War (adopted 12 August 1949, entered into force 21 October 1950) 75 UNTS 135.

107 Art 50.

108 Art 49 (3).

109 Brady Heiner, 'Excavating the Sedimentations of Slavery: The Unfinished Project of American Abolition' in Geoffrey Adelsberg, Lisa Guenther and Scott Zeman (eds), *Death and Other Penalties: Philosophy in a Time of Mass Incarceration* (Fordham University Press 2015) 13–42.

110 Nowak (n 74) 197.

States had been reserved for the white population. The blacks were punished on the plantation by their masters.[111] But even during the heydays of antebellum slavery – the late eighteenth century – there existed a private industry importing convicts from Britain who had 'received pardons for their crimes in exchange for indentures to labor in America'.[112] The convicts including those who were merely indebted – and in some cases as young as 16 – were made to work alongside the slaves, the only difference between the two being that the convict labourer 'was not bound for life, but the black slave was'.[113] After the war, faced with labour shortages and anxious to reassert racial supremacy, states such as Alabama, Georgia, Mississippi, and Virginia began to nab freed slaves on the slightest provocation. The convict leasing system, referred to by some as the 'American gulag', was introduced throughout the South.[114] The convicts would be leased to private contractors – and often subleased to middlemen – to work outside the jails on railroads, coalmines, and cotton farms with no protection against 'savage beatings, endless workdays, and murderous neglect'.[115] W.E.B. Du Bois, one of the earliest chroniclers of the continued subordination of blacks during the Reconstruction Era (whom we shall encounter again in our discussion of post-World War II codification of human rights), cited a white woman making the following observation about 'the horrible system of convict leasing' that had spread to every Southern state by 1876:

> In some states where convict labor is sold to the highest bidder the cruel treatment of the helpless human chattel in the hands of guards is such as no tongue can tell nor pen picture. Prison inspectors find convicts herded together, irrespective of age; confined at night in shackles; housed sometimes, as has been found, in old box cars; packed almost as closely as sardines in a box.[116]

In a book full of riveting details, David Oshinsky has documented the harrowing saga of the convict-lease system that grew out of the Parchman farm, Mississippi's state penitentiary situated in the cotton-rich Yazoo Delta. Following the passage of an act of the Legislature providing for leasing the convict labour of the state in 1876, 'a generation of black prisoners would suffer and die under condition far worse than anything they had experienced as slaves'.[117] Throughout the South, the system drew legal backing from the Thirteenth Amendment's

111 WEB Du Bois, *Black Reconstruction in America* (Russel & Russel 1935) 506.
112 Sublette and Sublette (n 29) 211.
113 Ibid.
114 David M Oshinsky, *"Worse Than Slavery": Parchman Farm and the Ordeal of Jim Crow Justice* (Free Press 1996) 29.
115 Ibid 44. See also James B. Jacobs, 'The United States of America: Prison Labour: A Tale of Two Penologies' in Yvonne Jewkes and Helen Johnston (eds), *Prison Readings: A Critical Introduction to Prisons and Imprisonment* (Routledge 2011) 268–275, 268.
116 Du Bois (n 111) 698.
117 Oshinsky (n 114) 34.

exception which had 're-inscribed slavery within the US penal system in ways which are still being felt today'.[118] In *Ruffin v Commonwealth of Virginia* (1871), a case concerning the appeal against the death sentence awarded to Woody Ruffian, a black convict, who had been leased to work without pay for Ohio Railroad Company, the Virginia Appellate Court held:

> A convicted felon, whom the law in its humanity punishes by confinement in the penitentiary instead of with death . . . is in a state of penal servitude to the State. He has, as a consequence of his crime, not only forfeited his liberty, but all his personal rights except those which the law in its humanity accords to him. He is, for the time being, the slave of the State.[119]

The convict-lease system was formally abolished in the late 1920s and replaced with private and state-operated convict labour within prisons. Though contemporary convict labour is nowhere as brutal as the lease system or the Southern plantation prisons, the United States today makes more widespread use of 'prison labor by private corporations as well as by federal or state-run prison employers' than any other country. The US, as it is known well, also leads the world in incarceration rates, with prison population heavily skewed in the former slave states, illustrating the enduring impact of antebellum slavery.[120] It was only in the 1960s and 1970s that the US Supreme Court and federal courts came to recognise that 'a prisoner is not wholly stripped of constitutional protections'.[121] This has had a profound effect on the treatment of prisoners. Yet the courts have refused to hold confinement with hard labour a violation of the Eighth Amendment prohibition of cruel and unusual punishment.[122] In the 1977 case *Jones v. North Carolina Prisoners' Labor Union*, the US Supreme Court upheld the refusal of a North Carolina warden to recognise a trade union.[123] The court has yet to revise its position on the subject. Barry Heiner of California State University has traced his office desk through commodity chain analysis back to California's Prison Industry Authority that employs prisoners at a rate of 30 to 95 cents per hour – no social security or health benefits provided – to produce a wide range of goods

118 Geoffrey Adelsberg, Lisa Guenther and Scott Zeman, 'Introduction' in Adelsberg, Guenther and Zeman (eds), *Death and Other Penalties: Philosophy in a Time of Mass Incarceration* (Fordham University Press 2015) 1–12, 2.

119 Ibid 3.

120 At over 650 per 100,000 people, the US incarceration rate remained highest in the world at the beginning of 2018. See Tapio Lappi-Seppälä, 'American Exceptionalism in Comparative Perspective: Explaining Trends and Variations in the Use of Incarceration' in Kevin R. Reitz (ed), *American Exceptionalism in Crime and Punishment* (Oxford University Press 2018) 195–271, 256.

121 See, for example, *Gideon v Wainwright* 372 US 335 (1963); *Wolff v McDonnell* 418 US 539 (1974).

122 *Gates v Collier* 501 F.2d 1291, 5th Cir (1974). The decision, nonetheless, outlawed certain forms of corporal punishment as violating the Eighth Amendment, including handcuffing inmates to the fence and to cells for long periods of time.

123 *Jones v North Carolina Prisoners' Labor Union* 433 US 119 (1977).

and services which public institutions are legislatively required to purchase.[124] On Heiner's account, 'There is a functional and semiotic continuity' between the current convict labour system and 'postbellum penality', which was, in turn, a replacement for chattel slavery.[125]

In a historical perspective, the overlaps between the dying institution of slavery and convict labour were not confined to the United States. The abolition of slave trade and slavery in the early nineteenth century created severe labour shortages in the British Empire.[126] At the same time as they claimed moral superiority over other European powers, the British authorities devised various substitutes to enslaved labour including indentured labour, convict labour both inside and outside prisons, and transportation to penal colonies. The economic imperatives were enmeshed with the project of reinforcing colonial authority and raising the 'natives' in the scale of civilisation. From the 1830s when slavery was formally abolished in the British Empire and roughly until the 1870s, thousands of Indian convicts and indentured workers (known locally as coolies) were 'despatched overseas to serve emerging colonial economies around the Indian Ocean region, from Mauritius to Singapore'.[127] Although embedded in South Asian folk memory, the story of these penal settlements is far less familiar in the West compared to the history of transportation from Ireland and England to Australia.[128] Convicts who stayed within British India were, until the mid-nineteenth century, employed on infrastructure projects outside prisons; existing jails, having been converted from forts and barracks, were ill-equipped to accommodate inmates in a disciplined environment.[129] The use of prisoners' labour ran in conjunction with the recruitment of indentured labour within the country to work on tea-estates. The slightest breach of discipline by a worker on an estate would result either in extra-legal measures such as flogging or a sentence of fine or imprisonment with hard labour.[130]

Throughout the nineteenth century, in India as well as in British Africa, the sentence most frequently handed down by courts was 'rigorous imprisonment' or 'confinement with hard labour'.[131] What that labour would constitute in practice was left to the discretion of prison authorities. The emerging influence of utilitarian thinking, combined with concerns about poor supervision and frequent escape attempts by prisoners assigned to work on extra-mural projects, led to a shift toward prison industries. Reflecting 'the whole Benthamite caste of mind', as Eric Stokes put it in his seminal study on the influence of utilitarianism on

124 Heiner (n 109) 13–42.
125 Ibid 32.
126 Yang (n 27) 183.
127 David Arnold, 'Labouring for the Raj' (n 93) 200; Clare Anderson, 'Convicts and Coolies: Rethinking Indentured Labour in the Nineteenth Century' (2009) 30(1) *Slavery and Abolition* 93, 95.
128 Richard Gott, *Britain's Empire: Resistance, Repression and Revolt* (Verso 2011) 194.
129 Ibid 207.
130 Ibid.
131 Hynd (n 12) 258; Arnold, 'Labouring for the Raj' (n 93) 202.

British India, the 1838 report of the Prison Discipline Committee called for the establishment of penitentiaries 'for all prisoners sentenced to more than one year's imprisonment', 'a better system of classification', greater use of solitary confinement, and the enforcement of 'monotonous, uninteresting labour within doors' upon all prisoners sentenced to rigorous imprisonment.[132] As prisons began to be built, 'some convicts were moved into temporary outdoor encampments in order to work on the construction of the new central jails they themselves were soon to occupy'.[133] In British Africa, penal reforms were late in the coming, gaining some impetus only during the inter-war period as a result of pressure exerted by the humanitarian lobbies in London, particularly the Howard League for Penal Reform.

On the eve of the Second World War, however, 'forced labour was reintroduced for military and agricultural purposes, and convict labour was switched to providing support for such endeavours, with the provision of military uniforms and supplies taking up the majority of man hours'.[134] Notwithstanding the emergence of welfarist rhetoric in the post-war period, the prison system continued to be plagued by violence and overcrowding in the African colonies. In the final decade of its rule in Kenya, the British administration shed all pretence of civilising the 'natives' as it launched a campaign of mass arrests, executions, confinement in camps, and forced labour against the Mau Mau rebels.[135] These episodes of exploitation and violent oppression stretching over two centuries seem to have been consigned to some unknown oubliette in the textbook history of human rights. They do not generally find a place in the standard list of what the Universal Declaration in its Preamble termed the 'barbarous acts which have outraged the conscience of mankind'.

At the conceptual level, the relationship between work and penological rationales is a complex one with deep historical linkages. Work has been used in a variety of penal contexts from the houses of correction to transportation to the penitentiary. In the colonial context, prisoners' labour was simultaneously a part of the civilising mission and an instrument of terror and subjugation. It has been considered a legitimate means of making prisons economically viable and profitable. In more explicit terms, convict labour has been justified as a means of retribution and deterrence, and since the birth of the penitentiary in the eighteenth century, simultaneously as a device for reforming offenders.[136]

In articulating the Voltarian maxim, 'Make men diligent and they will be honest', John Howard gave prison labour a central place in his reform agenda.[137]

132 'Legislative Dispatch to India, 30 October 1839, No. 19, at para 3. Cited in Eric Stokes, *The English Utilitarians and India* (Oxford University Press 1959) 217–218.

133 Arnold, 'Labouring for the Raj' (n 93) 204.

134 Hynd (n 12) 269.

135 Caroline Elkins, *Imperial Reckoning: The Untold Story of Britain's Gulag in Kenya* (Henry Holt and Company 2005).

136 Merry A Morash and Etta A Anderson, 'Liberal Thinking on Rehabilitation: A Work-Able Solution to Crime' (1978) 25(5) *Social Problems* 556.

137 Max Grunhut, *Penal Reform: A Comparative Study* (Clarendon Press 1948) 196.

Jeremy Bentham wanted convict labour to be dull, monotonous, and consisting of repetitive tasks to make a lasting impression on the offenders. Despite a shift in emphasis on reformation by the turn of the nineteenth century, positivist criminologists, who rebelled against the metaphysical notion of retribution, nonetheless continued to view compulsory labour as necessary to making the criminals fit for employment. Up until the early twentieth century, both the International Penitentiary Commission and the Howard League consistently championed productive work by prisoners. Such calls, in the period when prisoners were still assigned 'the dismal and unremmunerative [sic] occupation of picking oakum', were evidently intended to generate a better alternative.[138] These organisations also broke fresh ground by building a case for wages for prison labour, 'as scientific and reformative',[139] and addressing the issue of unfair competition with free labour.[140] As early as 1928, the Howard League was raising donations for a pilot scheme in Wakefield Prison to introduce a wage system for prisoners.[141] It seems fair to conclude though that humanitarian concerns melded together with anxieties about the working class and the shared religious and Enlightenment belief in industry as virtue and idleness as vice. Reformers, colonial administrators, and slaveholders seemed united in espousing this basic principle. Coerced labour was applied 'for their own good' to prisoners, convicts in penal colonies, 'natives' in general, and to former and current slaves. Thus, in 1925, before the Permanent Mandates Commission at the League of Nations, the Belgian representative could defend the recruitment of unpaid labour through local chiefs in the Congo as justified when 'imposed on the natives to remedy their lack of foresight'.[142]

If prison memoirs and personal accounts are any guide, prisoners themselves generally value opportunities for work and hands-on experience of a trade while incarcerated.[143] Few things are feared in prison as much as enforced idleness. Also, as argued previously, a system that at least makes some effort to help offenders turn their lives around is preferable to the one that imposes punishment for the sake of punishment. Yet the question remains whether prisoners' work can ever retain its rehabilitative character if it is forced and compulsory in nature. As a punitive measure imposed at the discretion of prison administrators, penal labour contravenes the liberal principle of the retention of rights. As Lord Wilberforce famously put it in a 1983 case, 'A prisoner retains all civil rights which are not taken away expressly or by necessary implication'.[144] It is reasonable to argue that

138 Enid Huws Jones, *Margery Fry: The Essential Amateur* (Oxford University Press 1966) 171.

139 Howard League for Penal Reforms, *For All Prisoners. Pamphlet Series* (Howard League 1937); Cicely M. Craven, *Punishment and Reform* (Oxford University Press 1951) 21.

140 Howard League, *Rehabilitating Work: What Are Prison Workshops for? Briefing Paper* (Howard League 2000) 18.

141 Howard League, *Annual Report (1928–9)* 7. See also Cicely M. Craven, *Punishment and Reform* (Oxford University Press 1951) 20–21.

142 Pedersen (n 69) 241.

143 See, for example, Erwin James, *A Life Inside: A Prisoner's Notebook* (Atlantic Books 2005) 180; Ahmed Othmani with Sophie Bessis, *Beyond Prison, the Fight to Reform Prison Systems around the World* (Marguerite Garling tr, Berghan 2008).

144 *Raymond v Honey* [1983] 1 AC 1 at p 10.

prisoners – just like ordinary citizens – ought to be obliged to eke out a living. The question remains, however, whether the state can justifiably deprive them of a minimum wage and labour protection guarantees afforded to everyone else. Does not such denial itself run counter to the professed ideal of rehabilitation? Extraction of unpaid or poorly remunerated work, after all, cannot be thought of as inculcating the right values for life in the community on release. Further, criminal justice clearly contributes to social injustice by denying convicts just and favourable conditions of work.

Although practice varies from one jurisdiction to another, prisoners are almost universally denied at least two of the four core labour rights enshrined in the 1998 *Declaration on Fundamental Principles and Rights at Work.*[145] The core labour rights include: freedom from forced labour; non-discrimination in the workplace; abolition of child labour; and freedom of association, including the rights to organise and engage in collective bargaining. Under international law – and domestic law in most countries – the prohibition of forced labour does not extend to prisoners' work.[146] Similarly, no country has granted prisoners the right to association and collective bargaining. The European Court of Human Rights, which otherwise sets high benchmarks, has repeatedly rejected claims by convict labourers. In *Stummers v Austria*, the Grand Chamber found no violation of the Article 4 prohibition of forced labour or the Article 14 guarantee of non-discrimination where the prisoner had been excluded from the old-age pension scheme.[147] Despite the stipulation in the European Prison Rules 2006 that 'as far as possible, prisoners who work shall be included in national social security systems', the majority cited a lack of consensus among the Council of Europe members on extending pensions-cover to working prisoners as the reason for rejecting the claim.[148] The Strasbourg court has similarly relied on the absence of a consensus among member states to hold that compulsory work carried out by a prisoner after retirement age does not necessarily breach the prohibition of forced labour.[149] Although elsewhere the court has insisted that there is no room in the European Convention for the notion of 'civic death',[150] it seems to have overlooked how this idea lies behind excluding prisoners from basic labour rights afforded to every individual otherwise.

145 ILO Declaration on Fundamental Principles and Rights at Work, (adopted 18 June 1998) ILC, 86th Session, Geneva, annex revised 15 June 2010.

146 The Constitution of the Republic of South Africa, 1996, is an exception in that it prohibits forced labour universally under art 13, chapter 2.

147 *Stummer v Austria* (App. 37452/02) ECHR [Grand Chamber] 7 July 2011.

148 Council of Europe, Committee of Ministers, *Recommendation Rec (2006)2 of the Committee of Ministers to Member States on the European Prison Rules*, 11 January 2006 (Appendix) para 26.17.

149 *Meier v Switzerland* (App 10109/14) 9 February 2016.

150 See *Hirst v United Kingdom* (No 2) (App. 74025/01) 6 October 2005 [Grand Chamber] (2006) 42 EHRR 849, ECHR 2005-IX (Joint Concurring opinion of judges Tulkens and Zagrebelsky).

5 The untold story of the Howard League's campaign for an international prisoners' convention

For us, there is only the trying. The rest is not our business.

T.S. Eliot[1]

Formed in London in 1921, following the merger of the Howard Association and the Penal Reform League, the Howard League for Penal Reform probably has a more extended history of prison and penal-reform work than any other existing non-governmental organisation. Although officially secular and non-denominational, the Howard League has historically drawn its leaders – and much of its membership – from the Quakers, a non-conforming Christian sect, popularly known as the Society of Friends. Whilst the Howard League's contributions to the British criminal justice system are well recognised, relatively little is known about the organisation's pioneering role as an international campaigner during the first half of the twentieth century.

Although the League enjoys consultative status with the UN, its impact on global policy agendas today is marginal compared to the likes of Amnesty International and Human Rights Watch. The relatively peripheral position that the Howard League occupies on the international scene is reflected – and reinforced – by a near-total silence in human rights discourse on the organisation's historical contributions in the penal context. To illustrate, *Human Rights Quarterly*, the foremost journal in the field, has not carried a single piece on the Howard League since its launch in 1979. The same holds for the equally prestigious *Columbia Human Rights Law Review*, *Harvard Human Rights Law Review*, and *Human Rights Law Review*. Books and journal articles on the history of human rights and prisoners' rights, which fail to mention the Howard League, are too numerous to list here.

The likely explanation for this omission is two-fold: One, although the Howard League was the first actor to explicitly frame international penal reform in the language of 'human rights' – as well as agitating against torture and capital punishment long before these issues acquired global recognition as human rights

1 T.S. Eliot, *Four Quartets* (A Harvest Book, Harcourt Inc. 1971) 31.

concerns – the organisation's ideological underpinnings were strongly coloured by the Quaker belief in spiritual equality, non-violence, and the possibility of redemption.[2] In the late nineteenth century, many Quakers in Britain became associated with the Christian socialist movement that embodied deep dissatisfaction with the conservative Anglican Church. Finding common moral ground between their faith and the political message of socialism, these Quakers came to believe that it was impossible to be a Christian without being a socialist.[3] This socially progressive and spiritually inflected ethos was fused with several key postulates of positivist criminology through the first half of the twentieth century. That resulted in a significant overlap between the agendas of the Howard League and the International Penal and Penitentiary Commission.

It is this dual-ideological heritage perhaps – Quaker faith on the one hand, and socialist and positivist ideas on the other – which accounts for the fact that even today the Howard League puts the stress squarely on rehabilitation of offenders, restorative justice, decarceration, and the interplay between social justice and criminal justice. This agenda affords sharp contrasts with the mainstream human rights organisations, which, echoing the classical tradition, represented by the German idealists and the *philosophes*, tend to be much more focused on securing punishment and making punishment fit the crime. Ironically, a prominent Quaker, Eric Baker, was one of the two individuals who joined the lawyer Peter Benenson in initiating the campaign 'Appeal for Amnesty, 1961' (later Amnesty International), aimed at securing the release of prisoners of conscience.[4] Despite a great deal of good the organisation has done globally, Amnesty's agenda today is a far cry from what could be characterised as a Quaker vision of justice.[5] More on this in Chapter 7.

The second possible reason why human rights discourse omits references to the Howard League arguably has to do with the 'big bang' school of historiography, which, as we have seen, tends to play down the historical antecedents of the contemporary human rights regime. Some fine historical works, such as the one written by Roger Normand and Sarah Zaidi as part of the UN Intellectual History Project, have not recognised the debt owed to the Howard League for effectively putting penal reform on the agenda of the League of Nations.[6] The contributions of the Howard League have been an odd omission in the more nuanced revisionist histories of the League of Nations as well as historical works tracing the origins of international humanitarianism.[7]

2 Mike Nellis and Maureen Waugh, 'Quakers and Penal Reform' in Stephen W Angell and Pink Dandellion (eds), *The Oxford Handbook of Quaker Studies* (Oxford University Press 2013) 377–391, 378.

3 Peter d'A. Jones, *The Christian Socialist Revival 1877–1914: Religion, Class, and Social Conscience in Late-Victorian England* (Princeton University Press 1968) 7.

4 Jonathan Power, *Like Water on Stone: The Story of Amnesty International* (Allen Lane 2001) 120.

5 cf Stephen Hopgood, *Keepers of the Flame: Understanding Amnesty International* (Cornell University Press 2006) 52–72.

6 Roger Normand and Sarah Zaidi, *Human Rights at the UN: The Political History of Universal Justice* (Indiana University Press 2008).

7 For example, none of the following works have a word on the Howard League's engagement with the League of Nations around penal issues: Susan Pedersen, *The Guardians: The*

Prior to making a modest attempt at setting the historical record straight, we need to sketch out the intellectual context of the Howard League's domestic and international efforts. Significant as the idea of an international convention was, it would be disingenuous to reduce the organisation's work to a campaign for 'prisoners' rights'. Human rights do not exhaust the whole domain of penal and justice reform that the Howard League has stood for at various points in history. This is not to suggest that the League – or the Quakers in general – have been immune from the sway of prevailing intellectual currents and political circumstances. To illustrate, during the 1970s retributive-turn, the American Friends Services Committee inadvertently played into the hands of the 'just deserts movement' by opposing indeterminate sentencing and rehabilitation schemes, only to see them replaced by tougher penalties and longer prison sentences.[8] Yet, there has been a radical undercurrent to the Quaker-inspired penal reform, providing distinct possibilities of transcending mainstream views and the conservative thinking of the men of Enlightenment – they were all men. The Howard League's unqualified opposition to capital punishment in early twentieth-century Britain was an idea well ahead of its time.[9] The same goes for the more recent work by many Quakers, who 'are now at the forefront of the movement to provide alternatives to imprisonment'.[10]

League of Nations and the Crisis of Empire (Oxford University Press 2015); Taina Tuori, 'From League of Nations Mandates to Decolonization: A Brief History of Rights' in Pamela Slotte and Miia Halme-Tumisaari (eds), *Revisiting the Origins of Human Rights* (Cambridge University Press 2015) 267–292; Mark Mazower, *Governing the World: The History of an Idea, 1815 to the Present* (Penguin 2012); Kevin Grant and others (eds), *Beyond Sovereignty: Britain, Empire and Transnationalism, c. 1880–1950* (Palgrave Macmillan 2007). Of the two notable recent histories of humanitarianism, Peter Stamatov's, *The Origins of Global Humanitarianism* deals at length with the role of the Quakers as pioneers of the anti-slavery campaign, but says nothing on their penal reform work. Michael Barnett's *Empires of Humanity* is silent altogether on the place of the Quakers and the Howard League in the history of humanitarianism. See Peter Stamatov, *The Origins of Global Humanitarianism: Religion, Empires, and Advocacy* (Cambridge University Press 2013) 7, 97–124; Michael Barnett, *Empire of Humanity: A History of Humanitarianism* (Cornell University Press 2013). The Howard League's international campaign for penal reform did not find a place in the earlier historical works on global humanitarianism either. See, for instance, FSL Lyons, *Internationalism in Europe. 1815–1914* (A.W. Sythoff 1963); Margaret E Keck and Kathryn Sikkink, *Activists beyond Borders: Advocacy Networks in International Politics* (Cornell University Press 1998).

8 Nellis and Waugh (n 2) 377–391, 386.

9 An Association for the Abolition of Capital Punishment, consisting principally of Quakers, was set up in England as far back as 1808. See Auguste Jorns, *The Quakers as Pioneers in Social Work* (Thomas Kite Brown tr, Kennikat Press Inc. 1931) 192; Ann Logan, *Feminism and Criminal Justice: A Historical Perspective* (Palgrave Macmillan 2008) 25–26.

10 Tim Newell, *Forgiving Justice: A Quaker Vision for Criminal Justice*- Swathmore Lecture 2000 (Quaker Home Service London 2000) 24; Quaker Home Service, *Six Quakers Look at Crime and Punishment: A Study Paper by a Group of Friends* (Quaker Social Responsibility and Education, Quaker Home Service 1979).

Intellectual and historical background

Since the publication in 1931 of Auguste Jorns' *The Quakers as Pioneers in Social Work*, several historians have described the Friends' interest in penal reform as deeply embedded in their experience as a persecuted sect during the seventeenth century, when many of them were imprisoned for preaching unorthodox beliefs and refusing to pay church tithes.[11] George Fox, credited as the founder of Quakerism, spent six years of his life in prison. Though modest compared to the ideology his followers would come to espouse, Fox's teachings sowed the seeds for the involvement of the Quakers in anti-slavery and penal-reform movements. In the mid-seventeenth century – when the Quakers in British colonies were themselves actively involved in slavery and slave trade – he pleaded with them to recognise 'the slaves' common humanity' and to treat them with mercy.[12] In what would subsequently form a keynote of the Friends' interventions in the penal system, Fox, in his 1658 address to 'the Protector and Parliament of England', emphasised the connections between crime, poverty, unemployment, and alcoholism.[13] On the other side of the Atlantic, William Penn (1644–1718), as part of his 'experiments' in Pennsylvania, abolished capital punishment for all crimes except murder in the 1680s and laid the foundations of the modern penitentiary.[14] These historical antecedents, and the first-hand experience of the corruption and brutality of the criminal justice system, would extend deep into the social consciousness of individual Quaker reformers, and the institutional fabric of the Howard Association and its successor, the Howard League for Penal Reform.

Britain's legendary prison reformer, John Howard (1726–1790), the inspiration for the original Howard Association, though a devout Christian, was not a Quaker himself. He is, however, known to have worked with the Quakers as part of his efforts to raise funds to ameliorate the conditions of the French prisoners of war.[15] Encouraged by the American Quaker Stephen Grellet, Elizabeth Fry (1780–1845) started working in London's overcrowded and squalid Newgate prison around 1813. She helped provide religious instruction and material support to women prisoners awaiting transportation to Australia, started a school for children inside Newgate, and set up a manufactory for women to produce quilts. The Association for the Improvement of Women Prisoners, which Fry set up in 1821, was perhaps the first charitable initiative of its kind anywhere in the world to arrange paid work for prisoners, the earnings set aside for their use upon release.[16] Fry also concerned herself with the 'causes of criminality' and 'juvenile delinquency', seeking in particular to address homelessness and lack of education

11 Jorns (n 9) 162–196. See also Pink Dandelion, *The Quakers: A Very Short Introduction* (Oxford University Press 2008) 12, 21–22; Nellis and Waugh (n 2) 378.

12 David Brion Davis, *The Problem of Slavery in Western Culture* (Oxford University Press 1966) 304–305.

13 Jorns (n 9) 163.

14 Newell (n 10) 20; Jorns (n 9) 172–173.

15 Jorns (n 9) 176.

16 Ibid 180. See also Dennis Bardens, *Elizabeth Fry: Britain's Second Lady on the Five-Pound Note* (Chanadon Publications 2004) 23–55.

by establishing various schools and shelters for children in London. Her initiatives were to have a notable impact on several aspects of the prison system in Britain, especially in terms of the separation of male prisoners from women and children, and the provision of 'purposeful activity of work or education' in the prison.[17]

The Howard Association itself was established as a secular body in 1866 at a 'Friends' Meeting' in Stoke Newington in north-west London.[18] Renamed the Howard League for Penal Reform upon its merger with Penal Reform League,[19] the organisation has consistently had Quakers as secretaries or chairpersons barring a few interludes. Interestingly, for much of its early existence, the organisation was led by women, resulting in some unique intersections between feminist concerns and penal reform agendas.[20]

William Tallack (1831–1908), a Quaker who served as the secretary of the Howard Association from its founding in 1866 until 1879, left behind a mixed legacy. He remained a staunch opponent of the death penalty, believed in the interconnections between poverty and crime, and advocated restitution as an alternative to punishment.[21] Simultaneously, in line with the conventional wisdom of the time, he held to the view that the prison ought to retain its deterrence function through austere conditions and a regime of hard work. That, he believed, was the only means for reformation in the case of certain 'incorrigible' individuals.[22] His successors at the Howard League would play down 'deterrence' and denounce 'punishment' as 'unscientific', endorsing the agenda of offender rehabilitation worked out within the emerging discipline of criminology.[23] Tallack himself represented the Howard Association at the inaugural International Prison Congress in London and went on to participate in the subsequent congresses.[24]

The inaugural issue of *The Howard Journal*, published in October 1921, described as its object – and that of the newly constituted Howard League –

> to effect an alteration in criminal jurisprudence that its basis and purpose shall be to 'improve the prisoner', not wholly, nor even chiefly, for the prisoner's

17 Dandelion (n 11) 21.
18 Nellis and Waugh (n 2) 377–391, 382.
19 The lesser known Penal Reform League existed between 1907 and 1921 and is believed to have been influenced by Thoreau, Tolstoy, and Edward Carpenter. Margery Fry, later honorary secretary of the Howard League for Penal Reform, served as secretary of the Penal Reform League between 1917 and 1921.
20 Logan (n 9) 150.
21 Nellis and Waugh (n 2) 382.
22 Ibid.
23 Repudiation of retributive punishment as unscientific and irrational is a recurrent theme in *The Howard Journal*, especially during the decades of 1940s and 1950s. See, for example, George Benson and Cicely Craven, 'The Purpose of Imprisonment' (1947–1948) VII(3) *Howard Journal* 162. See also Margery Fry, *Arms of the Law* (Victor Gollancz Ltd. 1951) 73–87; Wright M, *Making Good: Prisons, Punishment and Beyond* (Burnett Books 1982) 19–29.
24 Gordon Rose, *The Struggle for Penal Reform: The Howard League and Its Predecessors* (Stevens & Sons 1961) 315.

> sake, but because we hold that *no system of treating crime is a safe system unless it aims at protecting the community by reclaiming the offender.*[25]

Setting out the case for the Howard League, the journal noted with approval, the resolution adopted at the 1910 International Prison Congress that 'no person, whatever his age or past record should be assumed to be incapable of improvement'.[26] Despite some changes heralded by the 1895 Gladstone enquiry and the report, the Howard League's inaugural policy statement expressed dissatisfaction with the British criminal justice system for giving 'an entirely disproportionate place' to 'prisons and punishment', and according 'too great a value to the principle of retribution'.[27] Earlier in June 1921, Spencer Miller, former assistant warden at New York's famous Sing-Sing Prison, had delivered an address at the first annual general meeting of the Howard League held at Caxton Hall, Westminster, in what could be seen as an early clue to the international outlook of the newly reconstituted organisation. For the subsequent three decades, Margery Fry, a 'distant descendant of Elizabeth (Fry)', one of the first women to be appointed magistrates in England after the Sex Disqualification (Removal) Act came into force in 1919, and the first honorary secretary of the Howard League, would be at the forefront of the organisation's efforts to influence domestic penal policy and international collaboration on penal matters.[28] To retrieve the contributions of Margery Fry and her colleagues is an important intellectual task, not least because contrary to what Michel Foucault proposed, penal history is not simply a tale of authorities devising ingenious ways of extending social control; it is as much the story of the commitment and conviction, and the drive and dedication of some remarkable reformers.[29]

The Howard's League's forays into the international arena broadly involved lobbying for the improvement of penal administration in British colonies and mandated territories on the one hand, and the campaign for an international convention for prisoners, on the other. The Howard League also participated enthusiastically at the International Prison Congresses held in London in 1925 and in Prague in 1930. At the London congress, Margery Fry served on the committee making preliminary arrangements, and the Howard League hosted a reception for foreign delegates. At Prague, the Howard delegation (comprising 13 official delegates and 20 members participating in their private capacity)

25 'Our Case' (1921) 1(1) *Howard Journal* 1.
26 Ibid 1.
27 'The Howard League for Penal Reform: Statement of Policy' (1921) 1(1) *Howard Journal* 86.
28 Nellis and Waugh (n 2) 377–391, 384; Leon Radzinowicz, *Adventures in Criminology* (Routledge 1999) 132–133.
29 For critiques of Foucault along these lines, see WJ Forsythe, *Penal Discipline, Reformatory Projects and the English Prison Commission 1895–1939* (University of Exeter Press 1990) 5; Peter Spierenburg, 'Four Centuries of Prison History: Punishment, Suffering, the Body, and Power' in Norbert Finzsch and Robert Jutte (eds), *Institutions of Confinement: Hospitals, Asylums, and Prisons in Western Europe and North America, 1500–1950* (Cambridge University Press 1996) 17–35, 19–20.

formed the largest contingent from an individual organisation.[30] The relations between the Howard League and the Penitentiary Commission were strained on the eve of the 1935 Berlin Congress, which the Howard League refused to participate in. As will be discussed later, that was not a permanent fissure though; the collaboration resumed and continued in earnest until the outbreak of the Second World War.

At the same time, *The Howard Journal*, a publication which would 'stimulate a deep interest in progressive penal measures' among laypersons and public officials alike,[31] regularly published accounts of penal administration in other countries as well as emerging experiments in the 'scientific treatment' of crime and criminals, individualised sentencing, probation and parole, and sociological enquiries into the causes of crime.[32] The growing fascination of penal administrators and academics with the possibilities of reforming offenders found theological reinforcement in articles written from a Christian perspective.[33]

By the mid-1920s, the Howard Association already had affiliated societies in Australia, New Zealand, Hungary, Canada, Japan, and South Africa, and correspondents in several British colonies. In the mid-1930s, the international network had expanded with correspondents in as many as 22 countries, including Ceylon, India, Nigeria, Palestine, and Trinidad. In 1931, the Howard League set up an internal sub-committee to advise the organisation in regard to 'penal administration in Crown Colonies, Protectorates and Mandated Territories'.[34] At a time when many Europeans – penal reformers included – tended to view the world in a self-centred manner, insulated at home from the inconvenient details of colonial violence, the Howard League pressed 'for a court of criminal appeal in every colony, the right of legal representation for all inhabitants', and the development of progressive legislation for dealing with juveniles and adults in British colonies.[35] In the early 1930s, it added its voice to 'numerous allegations of cruelty made against Indian police and prison administration by Civil Disobedience prisoners',[36] and lodged a strong protest 'against the extension of

30 Howard League for Penal Reform, *Annual Report (1923–1924)* 4; *Annual Report (1924–1925)* 8–9; *Annual Report (1929–30)* 10. See also 'The International Prison Congress, August 1925' (1926) 2(1) *Howard Journal* 7; Rose (n 24) 315.

31 Negley K Teeters, *World Penal Systems: A Survey* (Pennsylvania Prison Society 1944) 27.

32 See, for example, 'Prison Reforms in Germany by Professor Liepmann Hamburg University' (1924) 1(3) *Howard Journal* 169; 'A Plea for Scientific Methods in The treatment of Criminals' (1926) II(1) *Howard Journal* 61; Arthur RL Gardner, 'Science Approaches the Lawbreaker' (1928) 2(3) *Howard Journal* 203; Cyril Burt, 'The Psychological Clinic' (1929) (II)(4) *Howard* Journal 290; R.D. Gillespie, 'The Service of Psychiatry in the Prevention and Treatment of Crime' (1930) III(1) *Howard Journal* 22; Yen Ching-Yueh, 'Crime and Economic Conditions in China' (1930) III(1) *Howard Journal* 28.

33 See, for example, A Herbert Gray, 'The Christian View of the Use of Punishment' (1929) II(4) *Howard Journal* 296; The Most Rev. William Temple, Archbishop of York, 'The Ethics of Punishment' (1930) III(1) *Howard Journal* 12.

34 Howard League, *Annual Report (1929–30)* 12.

35 Rose (n 24) 314.

36 Howard League, *Annual Report (1932–3)* 6.

the death penalty in Bengal to the offence of carrying arms with intent to commit terrorist crime'.[37] In 1934, the Howard League sponsored in *forma pauperis* an (unsuccessful) appeal to the Judicial Committee of the Privy Council against the death penalty awarded to a 17-year-old Palestinian boy convicted of murder.[38] It was largely as a result of the League's efforts that the colonial secretary appointed a Standing Advisory Committee on Penal Administration in 1937.[39]

The campaign for an international convention

Though there are conflicting accounts of how things unfolded, the origins of a campaign for an 'international convention' go back to the 1925 Prison Congress in London.[40] According to Gordon Rose, whose 1961 book remains the most comprehensive albeit dated history of the Howard League, the idea of some sort of minimum rules or standards for prison administration was first discussed on the side-lines of the London Congress.[41] On this account, the proposal for an international agreement on the treatment of prisoners had originally come from British delegates, Sir Walter Maurice Waller, Chairman Prison Commission of England and Wales (1922–8); Alexander Paterson, Her Majesty's Commissioner of Prisons (1922–47); and Lord Polwarth, Chairman of the Scottish Prison Commission (1909–1929).[42] Whilst agreeing in principle with the proposal, the Howard League maintained that it alone was in a position to take the lead on an 'international charter' for prisoners.

According to Margery Fry's biographer, Enid Huws Jones, 'In the eyes of the Howard League the [International Penal and Penitentiary] Commission suffered from the limitations of an official body'.[43] Along the same lines, Leon Radzinowicz noted in his memoirs that the Commission could not be entrusted with steering international collaboration on penal matters as 'it had become part of the establishment and officialdom'.[44] There is a grain of truth to this assertion, but it amounts to simplifying what was a dynamic and evolving relationship through the decades of 1920s and 1930s. As the subsequent turn of events showed, the Howard League's international campaign involved a delicate balancing act; the organisation sought to maintain its independent position whilst lobbying official delegates at the League of Nations, building on the spadework carried out by the Penitentiary Commission, and seeking common ground around penal issues with pacifists and feminists, represented by groups such as the International Council

37 Howard League, *Annual Report (1933–4)* 9.
38 Ibid.
39 *Annual Report (1936–7)* 5. See also Howard League, 'Crime in the Overseas Dependencies of Great Britain' (July 1931).
40 'The International Prison Congress, August 1925' (1926) 2(1) *Howard Journal* 7.
41 Rose (n 24) 315; VE Watkin, 'Penal Reform and the League of Nations' (1930) III(I) *Howard Journal* 80.
42 Mitchel P Roth, *Prisons and Prison Systems: A Global Encyclopedia* (Greenwood Press 2006) 203.
43 Enid Huws Jones, *Margery Fry: The Essential Amateur* (Oxford University Press) 168.
44 Radzinowicz (n 28) 376.

of Women, the Women's International League, and the International Federation of the League of Nations Societies.

To the Howard League, the conversations that had taken place on the margins of the London Congress immediately brought home the need for a 'more systematic collection of information' with regard to penal administration in different countries, and 'the gradual elaboration of a sort of charter of prisoners' rights which should be internationally adopted, and should serve to fix the *minimum* below which no country aspiring to be called civilised should dare to fall'.[45] The Howard League was quick to recognise the International Penitentiary Commission as an appropriate vehicle for the collection of information on penal matters; it would go on to make frequent use of the Commission's research to inform its own campaign for an international charter. However, by the 1920s, 'painful stories' had already reached the League from several countries regarding the mistreatment of prisoners, both 'political and criminal', underscoring the urgency of an international agreement on the matter.[46] With then secretary Margery Fry and vice-chair Gertrude Eaton (a suffragist, singer, musician, and Quaker humanitarian) taking a deep personal interest, and helped along by the executive body of the Society of Friends, the Howard League had come up with a ' "charter" for prisoners of all countries' by the end of 1926.[47]

The Howard League itself saw the charter as embodying a minimalist agenda, realising all too well that 'hardly any government in the world would yet accept, even in theory, what we should consider a soundly scientific and humane penal system'.[48] The 'charter' then was meant to 'state the *minimum* of human rights, of which no prisoner can be, to our thinking, deprived in any country laying claim to be regarded as civilised'.[49] Meagre as the proposed 'rights' were, their concession, according to the Howard League, 'would greatly ameliorate the conditions of thousands of prisoners in Europe and elsewhere'.[50] The use of the terminology of 'human rights' holds crucial theoretical and historical significance. For one, it provides a counterexample to Samuel Moyn's rather overstated argument that

> if rights (in modern history) had any internationalist pedigree flowing from the French Revolution, it was, alas, mainly to be found in Napoleon Bonaparte's claim to be spreading the flame of the rights of man as he engulfed the world in the conflation of his imperial designs.[51]

In the Howard League's charter, we have evidence that human rights were appropriated for uses other than rationalisation of imperialist expansion prior to World War II.

45 'The International Prison Congress, August 1925' (1926) 2(1) *Howard Journal* 7, 11.
46 Howard League, *Annual Report (1925–6)* 8.
47 Ibid.
48 Ibid.
49 Ibid.
50 Ibid.
51 Samuel Moyn, *Human Rights and the Uses of History* (Verso 2014) 14.

As previously noted, critical scholars have challenged historian Lynn Hunt's thesis that there was a 'long gap in the history of human rights, from their initial formulation in the American and French Revolutions to the United Nations' Universal Declaration'.[52] But the critics have yet to take note of the Howard League's campaign for an 'international charter for prisoners', which was, at least partly, framed in the language of human rights. That said, the appropriation of human rights by the Howard League was qualitatively different from the contemporary uses of the doctrine in that the organisation seemed to have no illusions as to its conceptual limits. Important as they were, 'human rights' were not the guiding ideal or a utopia; they merely outlined absolute minimum conditions that ought to attend the treatment of offenders and the accused universally. Seen from this angle, the history of the Howard League's international campaign bears out Samuel Moyn's more modest assertion that human rights were 'peripheral to most of the uplifting movements in modern history'.[53]

The 'charter' (referred to in subsequent Howard League publications also as the 'convention') was a succinct document containing seven articles altogether. The document first appeared in the Howard League's annual report for the year 1925–1926, and was published separately as a pamphlet, circa 1928.[54] The document reasserted classical liberal rights to fair trial and freedom from torture and outlined a '"Schedule of Conditions" to be observed as a minimum in all civilised countries, in the treatment of persons under arrest or in captivity on whatever charge'.[55] The Howard League struck a compromising note on capital punishment, calling for the prohibition of its application to juveniles. The text of the 'charter' is reproduced below:

1 Every prisoner should be entitled:

   i) To a public trial within six months of arrest.
   ii) To be defended by a lawyer if he so desires. If necessary this should be at the public expense in all cases where the penalty is death or prolonged imprisonment. The accused should have the right to private interviews with his lawyer before the trial and to call witnesses for the defence.

2 Prisons should have good light, warmth, and ventilation, and be kept in a sanitary state. Prisoners should be given food sufficient for health and an ample supply of water both for drinking and washing. They should have sufficient open-air exercise daily.

52 Lynn Hunt, *Inventing Human Rights: A History* (W.W. Norton & Company 2007) 176. cf. Jenny S. Martinez, *The Slave Trade and the Origins of International Human Rights Law* (Oxford University Press 2014) 148–175, 149.

53 Moyn (n 51) 137.

54 *Annual Report (1925–6)* 8–9; Howard League, 'An International Charter for Prisoners' *(c. 1928) 2–3. See also Gertrude Eaton, 'The Need for an International Charter for Prisoners' (1927) II(2) Howard Journal* 93.

55 Howard League, 'An International Charter for Prisoners' (c. 1928) 1.

Every prisoner should have facilities for the exercise of his religion and visits from an authorised chaplain.

Prisoners should be classified as far as possible. Children and young persons should be kept altogether apart from older criminals. Women prisoners should be attended by women warders and not by men.

3 Every prisoner should be allowed a visit from a relation or friend at least twice a year. Representatives of authorised societies working solely for the welfare of prisoners should be allowed to visit every prisoner in custody.

4 All forms of torture should be forbidden. No corporal punishment of a severity liable to result in permanent injury should be allowed. Corporal punishment should not be inflicted at the discretion of the police or prison officials, nor upon unconvicted prisoners, but only upon prisoners after conviction and sentence by a legal tribunal.

5 No child or young person should suffer the death penalty, nor should they be liable to imprisonment for a purely political offence not involving acts in their nature criminal.

6 The names of all prisoners sentenced to death, with particulars of the offence for which, and the tribunal by which, the sentence has been passed, should be officially published before sentence is carried out. Before the death sentence is carried out the condemned person should be allowed to see relations and friends. The fact that the sentence has been carried out, with the date, should also be officially published immediately.

7 The above conditions should not be varied in an adverse manner for any prisoner or class of prisoner whatever.[56]

With the proposed 'charter' as a prototype of an international agreement on prisoners' rights, the Howard League set out to lobby delegates in Geneva and elsewhere. For the matter to be taken up officially by the League of Nations, it had to be put up in the form of a resolution before the Assembly. A small office was set up in Geneva in 1927 as a base for canvassing official support for the idea. Earlier in 1926, Margery Fry had resigned as honorary secretary of the Howard League on her appointment as the principal of Somerville College, Oxford, but continued to serve on the executive committee. In 1927, Fry and Gertrude Eaton met the home secretary and officials at the British Foreign Office, urging them to bring a proposal before the League of Nations Assembly. The British government reacted hesitantly, 'sympathising' with the idea but refusing to sponsor an official resolution in Geneva.[57] The Howard League subsequently urged the Swedish foreign minister and the Canadian government through the Canadian Prisoners' Welfare Association to take the lead on the matter.[58]

56 Ibid. This draft was a slightly modified version of the one published in the Howard League's annual report for the year 1925–1926.

57 Rose (n 24) 316.

58 Howard League, *Annual Report (1927–8)* 6.

In the meantime, with a view to amplifying its voice, the Howard League had already approached the International Federation of League of Nations Societies. The Federation, at the Plenary Congress held in Berlin in May 1927, passed a resolution urging:

> [U]pon the Assembly of the League of Nations the necessity of instituting an enquiry at the earliest possible moment with a view to framing an international convention upon the conditions (including conditions of prison labour) to be observed in all civilised countries in the treatment of persons under arrest or in captivity, conditions which should be in reasonable relation to those generally existing in their various countries.[59]

In 1928, an appeal was circulated to the Assembly of the League of Nations, outlining the rationale for an 'international charter' for prisoners and collaboration on penal matters. Without naming names, the Howard League recounted several harrowing incidents of the mistreatment of prisoners and detainees that had come to its knowledge in recent years through 'the testimony of many witnesses, whose integrity and reliability cannot be challenged'.[60] International agreement on 'the irreducible minimum of decency and humanity', which the proposed 'charter' encapsulated, was to the Howard League necessary to stem the spread of crime across national borders. A penal system, the Howard League reasoned, which 'herds hardened criminals in prisons with first offenders and young delinquents breeds crime like a pestilence, and spreads from country to country, heedless of frontiers'.[61]

In what would become a recurring theme in the Howard League's international campaign, the appeal spoke of the mistreatment of foreign nationals in prisons as a potential source of friction among nations: 'For a Red Government which makes White Martyrs, or a White Government which makes Red Martyrs, thereby sows the seeds of a European conflict'.[62] Keenly aware of the reluctance of states to open up their penal systems to international scrutiny, the Howard League grounded its case on the 1926 Slavery Convention as a precedent. The adoption of a charter on prisoners, it was argued, would not entail any 'greater interference with the internal affairs of nations than the League of Nations abolition of slavery'.[63] In due course, the organisation would articulate a more thorough justification for international collaboration on penal matters, outlining a normative framework of universal validity in a seminal effort towards chipping away at the sacrosanct notion of sovereignty, the idea that the state had priority over the individual human being.

59 Howard League, 'An International Charter for Prisoners' (c. 1928) 4.
60 Ibid 1.
61 Ibid 3.
62 Ibid.
63 Rose (n 24) 316. See also G Lowes Dickinson, 'The League of Nations and an International Convention for Prisoners' (1928) II(3) *Howard Journal* 208.

Although there is no reference to it in official documents, Gordon Rose – admittedly with his inside knowledge of the association during the 1920s – referred to a letter from the International Prison Commission, which suggested 'that further action by the League might prejudice their attempts to bring the matter before the League of Nations'.[64] Following up on the proposal first mooted at the International Prison Congress in 1925, the Commission had apparently begun its work on a set of minimum rules for the treatment of prisoners sometime during 1927 or 1928. Through the second half of the 1920s and 1930s, the Howard League seemed to have a rather ambivalent stance toward the International Prison Commission. To those who saw the whole question of penal administration as 'one of domestic interest outside the sphere of international action', the League cited 'the existence of the International Prison Commission' as evidence that governments had already tacitly accepted the international nature of the problem.[65] Even as it solicited support among official delegates in Geneva around its own proposal for an international convention for prisoners, the Howard League approvingly took note of the fact that 'the International Prison Commission has been urging an agreement on the subject for many years'.[66]

A breakthrough came in early 1930, when the official delegate for Cuba, Ageriy Bethancourt, agreed to bring a motion before the Council of the League of Nations. Cuba at that time, as Leon Radzinowicz recalled in his memoirs, had been 'under the strong influence of the positivist school'.[67] Enrico Ferri, whose ideas had helped shape the Cuban Criminal Code of 1930, was himself 'strongly in favour of an extended role for the League of Nations in the penal sphere'.[68] In the first official albeit cautious recognition of the international nature of the question of penal administration, the Council of the League of Nations adopted the following resolution during its 58th session on 14 January 1930:

> In view of the fact that the improvement of penal administration is at present occupying the attention of many people of the world and that there are certain international aspects to the question, the Council requests the Assembly to place the question on its agenda with the object of deciding the best way in which the League of Nations can co-operate with the International Prison Commission and other interested organisations in their efforts to assist in the development of prisons in accord with modern economic, social and health standards.[69]

The Howard League was not specifically mentioned in the resolution. The Secretary General of the League of Nations Eric Drummond nonetheless requested the organisation in an appended letter to submit 'a memorandum indicating what

64 Ibid.
65 'The League of Nations and the State of the Prison' (1928) II (3) *Howard Journal* 184.
66 Howard League, 'International Co-operation in Penal Matters' (1930) 3–4.
67 Radzinowicz (n 28) 377.
68 Ibid.
69 Cited in Howard League, 'International Co-Operation in Penal Matters' (1930) 4.

in its opinion are the aspects of the question which could advantageously be dealt with internationally through the instrumentality of the League of Nations and on what evidence this opinion is based'.[70] That the Howard League was invited to advise the League of Nations on how best to proceed on international co-operation on penal matters testified to the organisation's success in making inroads into what was then the heart of global governance. A memorandum, probably drafted by Margery Fry (as her biographer suggests), was submitted to Drummond in May 1930, and copies circulated to official delegates and the press.[71] The memorandum repeated the testimonies of the Howard League's correspondents from various countries as to official brutalities and torture in detention. Rather naively – as it would seem in retrospect – the Howard League hoped that 'if such cases were reported to an international body set up by the League of Nations, the world publicity . . . would so instruct public opinion that the continuance of such barbarities would be rendered impossible'.[72]

The memorandum outlined 'direct' and 'indirect' aspects of the international nature of penal administration. In respect of the former, the Howard League raised the problem of the conviction, sentencing, and detention of the nationals of one country in another. The over-representation of foreign nationals in crime statistics had been noticed in several European countries since the end of World War I. The problem could be understood variably either as the 'reality of offending' by foreigners, or 'the result of suspicion leading to greater surveillance of the foreign-born, the result of the immigrant not finding the hoped-for work, or being the first to be laid off work in an economic downswing'.[73] Anticipating an issue that would exercise judicial imagination many decades later, the memorandum spoke of the morally fraught question of the extradition of 'fugitives' to face the death penalty in the countries of their nationality from jurisdictions which had abolished the death penalty – with Poland and Romania cited as examples. As to the situation of those deported following a term of imprisonment in a foreign country, the Howard League sketched the difficulties such individuals ran into upon release. In what was then a key theme in the Howard League's campaign – but rarely finds a place in the contemporary human rights discourse – the memorandum went on to suggest that

> an international organisation could provide for these persons, preventing their return to the crime centre in the big cities and securing for them through local and national agencies, the help which will rehabilitate them as useful citizens of their own countries.[74]

70 Howard League, 'Memorandum Submitted to the League of Nations by the Howard League for Penal Reform' (May 1930).

71 Jones (n 43) 168.

72 Ibid.

73 Clive Emsley, *Crime, Police, and Penal Policy: European Experiences 1750–1940* (Oxford University Press 2007) 245.

74 Howard League, 'Memorandum Submitted to the League of Nations' (n 70).

As regards the 'indirect' aspects of the international nature of penal administration, the memorandum spoke of the potential of the spread of disease and infection beyond the prison walls given the overcrowded and insanitary conditions of detention in many countries. Reference was made to goods produced by prisoners, which entered international commerce, 'thereby coming into competition with the products of the country to which they are transported'.[75] Since a number of countries had already banned the import of such products to protect domestic industry from 'unfair competition', the memorandum stressed the need for a global study to determine the 'basis for the fair and just regulation of international commerce of prison-made good'. As a further justification for bringing penal administration within the scope of international law, the memorandum cited the fact that 'children's welfare' already formed part of the League of Nations agenda. This existing mandate could be expanded to include comparative studies on 'institutional and other methods of treating juvenile delinquency . . . in the light of information gathered from all parts of the world by the League of Nations'.[76]

By the time the Howard League submitted its memorandum in May 1930, the International Prison Commission had already finalised a draft set of Standard Minimum Rules for the Treatment of Prisoners at its quinquennial congress held in Prague.[77] The Howard League was represented at the congress by Margery Fry, Gertrude Eaton, then Honorary Secretary Cecil Craven, and a total of 35 Howard League members participating in official and private capacity.[78] In its 1930 memorandum, the Howard League commended the Commission's work but suggested that 'no adequate reform can be secured without the assistance of unofficial as well as official opinion'. It was only the League of Nations, the memorandum suggested, which could 'collect data on a world-wide basis, and having stated the problem, can enable the world to co-operate in its solution'.[79] The line of reasoning is not entirely clear. Perhaps the underlying thinking was to mobilise resources and public opinion around an international convention on prisoners somewhat along the lines of the 1926 Slavery Convention, and to extricate the whole debate on penal administration from the technocratic world of the International Prison Commission.

Significantly, however, the Howard League seemed to concur with the substance of the draft Standard Rules, which were largely in accord with and far more exhaustive than the 'international charter' it had earlier proposed. Thus, the 1930 Howard League memorandum urged the League of Nations to 'set up a Commission of persons qualified, not only by official or legal expertise, but

75 Ibid.
76 Ibid.
77 According to one account, the Rules were drafted by Alexander Paterson and Sir Walter Maurice. See Roth (n 42) 203. W.J. Forsythe adds the name of Lord Polwarth to the list of drafters. See Forsyth (n 29) 83.
78 *Annual Report (1929–30)* 9.
79 Howard League, 'Memorandum Submitted to the League of Nations' (n 71).

also by active participation through their national societies in the work of penal reform'. The Commission, it was further suggested,

> should study existing methods of penal administration with a view to drafting a Convention which shall include, amongst other provisions, the International Prison Commission's "Set of Rules" and so establish an effective international standard for the treatment of persons in captivity.[80]

Pursuant to a resolution adopted unanimously by the League of Nations Assembly, the Secretary General communicated the 'Standard Minimum Rules for the Treatment of Prisoners Drawn up by the International Prison Commission' to the Council and the members of the League on October 15, 1930.[81] As discussed in Chapter 2, the Standard Minimum Rules, adopted at the First United Nations Congress on the Prevention of Crime and the Treatment of Offenders in 1955 (revised and renamed 'Mandela Rules' in 2015[82]), were essentially an updated and expanded version of this same document.[83] This historical connection remains unrecognised within human rights scholarship. The 1930 version began with a crucial preliminary statement to the effect that the Rules were not intended to describe a model system; rather, they served to 'indicate the minimum conditions that should be observed in the treatment of prisoners from the humanitarian and social points of view'.[84] The 55 Rules grouped under the broad categories of 'Location and Accommodation', 'Treatment', 'Discipline', and 'Assistance of Liberated Prisoners', were essentially a restatement of the 'progressive agenda' for penal administration that had evolved in the West since the late nineteenth century, carrying the imprint of both religious reformers and positivist criminologists. The language of the document oscillated between a soft, recommendatory tone, as in Rule 2 (providing that 'it is usually preferable that prisoners should sleep in separate cells'), to relatively strongly worded injunction in Rule 20 that the 'prison authorities must watch that prisoners, as well as their clothes . . . are thoroughly clean from the moment they are lodged in prison'.[85]

In April 1931 – around six months after the draft Rules had been officially circulated – the Howard League submitted a supplement to its 1930 memorandum

80 Ibid. See also Watkin (n 41).

81 League of Nations, 'Improvements in Penal Administration: Standard Minimum Rules for the Treatment of Prisoners Drawn Up by the International Prison Commission'. C.620.M.241.1930 IV, Geneva, October 15th, 1930.

82 United Nations Standard Minimum Rules for the Treatment of Prisoners (the Nelson Mandela Rules) (adopted 17 December 2015) UN Doc A/RES/70/175.

83 Adopted by the First United Nations Congress on the Prevention of Crime and the Treatment of Offenders, held at Geneva in 1955, and approved by the Economic and Social Council by its resolutions 663 C (XXIV) of 31 July 1957 and 2076 (LXII) of 13 May 1977. UN Doc A/CONF/611. See also, 'Standard Rules (Standard Minimum Rules for the Treatment of Prisoners)', Report by the Secretariat, 14 February 1955. UN Doc A/CONF.6/C/.1/L.1.

84 League of Nations, 'Improvements in Penal Administration' (n 81).

85 Ibid.

to the League of Nations. Whilst proposing certain additions and changes to the Standard Minimum Rules, the Howard League stated that 'the Rules prepared by the International Prison Commission and approved by the full Assembly of the International prison Congress at Prague in 1930, *should be accepted as the basis of the proposed Convention*'.[86] Any suggestions by historians to the effect that there was 'rivalry' between the Howard League and International Prison Commission must be tempered by the fact that once the Standard Minimum Rules had been officially circulated by the League of Nations, the Howard League had no major objection to the substance of the document.[87] As well as wanting to see the Rules embodied in a convention, the Howard League argued that the scope of the proposed document be extended 'to cover the treatment of accused persons in the custody of police authorities before trial or before sentence' rather than being limited to sentenced prisoners.[88] There might have been a general impression – based probably on the title of the document – that the proposed Rules applied only to prisoners *stricto sensu*. The criticism nonetheless seems unfair given that the Preamble to the draft Rules clearly stated that 'under the term "prisoners" are included all persons deprived of their liberty and shut up in prison for any reason whatever', and that the term 'prison' was being used 'in the widest sense of the word'.[89] More appropriately though, whereas the International Prison Commission had contemplated the acceptability of corporal punishment and solitary confinement under exceptional conditions in certain countries, the Howard League had 'grave misgivings' concerning the relevant provisions (Rules 36 and 37).

To the Howard League, 'corporal punishment and the dark cell' represented a 'form of torture', and it could not acquiesce 'in the proposal to allow such penalties a place among penal methods sanctioned by an International Convention designed to secure the humane treatment of prisoners'.[90] In its comments, the Howard League also urged the League of Nations 'to undertake a special study of the (penal) transportation system wherever it is still in operation' and to incorporate specific provision governing that system into the Standard Minimum Rules. In an observation which might have irked British officials – and had evidently escaped the Euro-centric imagination of the International Penitentiary Commission – the Howard League called attention to the 'evils' of penal settlements 'as revealed in the case of the Indian convict establishment in the Andaman Islands'.[91]

86 Howard League for Penal Reform, 'Supplement to Memorandum of May, 1930, on International Aspects of Penal Administration Submitted by the Howard League for Penal Reform to the Secretary-General of the League of Nations' (13 April 1931) (emphasis added).
87 Jones (n 43) 168.
88 Howard League, 'Supplement to Memorandum of May, 1930' (n 86). See also, *Annual Report (1932–1933)* 5–6.
89 League of Nations, 'Improvements in Penal Administration' (n 81).
90 Howard League, 'Supplement to Memorandum of May, 1930' (n 86).
91 Ibid. On the history of the Andaman Islands penal colony, see Satardu Sen, *Disciplining Punishment: Colonialism and Convict Society in the Andaman Islands* (Oxford University Press 2000).

In January 1934, the League of Nations Assembly, on the recommendation of the 5th (Humanitarian) Committee, passed a resolution endorsing the Rules with minor modifications and requesting governments – in pliant language that would be eerily echoed at the United Nations – to 'consider the possibility of adapting their penitentiary system to the Standard Minimum Rules if that system is below the minimum laid down in the said rules'.[92] The Howard League felt let down. Nonetheless, the organisation took comfort in the fact that even this tentatively worded resolution owed something to Gertrude Eaton's efforts in Geneva. Besides, it left room for continued lobbying for an international convention.[93]

The idea of a convention had apparently been met with some sympathy at the League of Nations, but it was opposed quite early during the campaign by the British delegate.[94] Crucially, there is no credible evidence that the International Penitentiary Commission had put up opposition to the Howard League's proposal. In recounting the League of Nations 1934 decision 'not to embody (the Rules) in a convention', Gordon Rose, in fact, noted – contradicting his comments elsewhere in the book – that this had come about despite 'the combined efforts of the International Prison Commission and the (Howard) League'.[95] Similarly, Margery Fry's biographer spoke of a commonality of purpose as he noted, 'The great hope shared by the Howard League and the International Prison Commission was that a substantial number of governments would bind themselves by a Convention to keep the Minimum Standard Rules'.[96] That vision was never fulfilled.

The year 1935 saw the holding of the International Penitentiary Congress in Berlin, an event that would later serve as a *casus belli* to discredit the Penitentiary Commission and breed a climate of prejudice against it that still lingers. After much deliberation, the Howard League decided not to participate in the Berlin congress. There was an apprehension that the organisation would not be welcomed in Germany since it had participated in a mock trial in 1933 concerning the burning of the *Reichstag*, allegedly set on fire by the Communist Party of Germany. With theoretical stamp readily supplied by Carl Schmitt, Hitler had exploited the event as a newly elected chancellor to issue an emergency decree dissolving the basic rights guaranteed by the Weimer Constitution.[97] The Howard League also feared that there 'would be no real freedom of discussion or reporting . . . that the Congress would be "packed" by Nazi delegates and the occasion used for propaganda purposes'.[98] The subsequent events did prove the

92 Howard League, *Annual Report (1933–1934)*. 8. See also Roger S. Clarke, *The United Nations Crime Prevention and Criminal Justice Program: Formulation of Standards and Efforts at Their Implementation* (University of Pennsylvania Press, Philadelphia 1994) 12.
93 *Annual Report (1933–1934)* 9; Rose (n 24) 318.
94 *Annual Report (1931–1932)* 5–6.
95 Rose (n 24) 318.
96 Jones (n 43) 180.
97 Forsythe (n 29) 234; Jones (n 43) 181. On the 'Reichstag Fire Decree', see Ingo Mueller, *Hitler's Justice: The Courts of the Third Reich* (Harvard University Press 1991) 29, 46–49.
98 Howard League, *Annual Report (1934–1935)* 10.

fear to be well founded. However, that is only half the story. On the eve of the 1935 Penitentiary Congress, Alexander Paterson had assured Margery Fry that as a British delegate he would 'not leave while there was a chance of hearing for penal affairs'.[99] At the Congress, Paterson and Lord Polwarth were among an unwavering group of European and American delegates who, vastly outnumbered by the Nazis, refused to endorse the 'retributive' function of imprisonment proposed by the latter.[100]

By the mid-1930s, an international convention was beginning to look like 'a forlorn hope and it was doubtful if it would have been ratified by sufficient countries'.[101] Margery Fry threw herself into collecting information on governments' compliance with the Standard Minimum Rules. Until the end of 1935 at least, Fry continued to believe though that 'a convention might (still) be in sight'.[102] On the eve of the Sixteenth Assembly of the League of Nations, the Howard League put together a pamphlet, 'Violations of the Standard Minimum Rules', which was circulated to the delegates with an appeal for effective observance of the Rules. Taking note of the communication of the Howard League, besides other relevant documents, the Sixteenth Assembly adopted a resolution in September 1935, instructing the Secretary General to request 'the Governments which accept the Standard Minimum Rules for the Treatment of Prisoner to give those Rules all possible publicity' and 'to inform the Governments that the attention of the Assembly has been drawn to the alleged existence in certain parts of the world of various reprehensible practices which are not only inconsistent with the Standard Minimum Rules, but are also contrary to the principles of rational treatment of prisoners'.[103] Commenting on the resolution, Margery Fry said she was not sure 'how far that will affect governments who rely on cruelty'. But she sent a letter of congratulations to Gertrude Eaton and told the Howard League's London Committee, 'All things considered penal affairs had gone

99 Jones (n 43) 181. See also Paul Knepper, *International Crime in the 20th Century: The League of Nations Era, 1919–1938* (Palgrave Macmillan 2011) 82–83.

100 Bureau of the International Penal and Penitentiary Commission, *Proceedings of the XITH International Penal and Penitentiary Congress held in Berlin. August 1935* (Staemfli & Cie. Printers 1937) 188–191, 229–233. Paterson's own views concerning the functions of the prison evolved considerably over time. In the early 1920s, he had little problem reconciling the punitive and rehabilitative aspects of imprisonment. By the end of his career though, Paterson appeared increasingly enthusiastic about finding alternatives to imprisonment. See S.K Ruck (ed), *Paterson on Prisons: Being the Collected Papers of Sir Alexander Paterson* (Frederick Muller Ltd. 1951) 157–158. For Paterson's early views on the subject, see Alexander Paterson, *A Report of Visits to Some German Prisons and Reformatories in August, 1922* (H.M.C Prison 1922); *Report on the Prevention of Crime and the Treatment of the Criminal in the Province of Burma* (Government Printing and Stationery 1927).

101 Rose (n 24) 317–318.

102 Jones (n 43) 182–183.

103 Howard League, *Annual Report (1934–1935)* 9–10; League of Nations. Sixteenth Ordinary Session of the Assembly September 28th, 1935. Home Office. Miscellaneous Circulars, Memoranda etc. 1935–1939.

better at Geneva than expected'.[104] The year 1936 brought another small victory with the imposition of an official ban on the use of standing handcuffs and fetters in parts of British India. The change happened after the Howard League had drawn attention of the India Office to the fact that such punishments constituted violations of Rule 39 of the Standard Minimum Rules.[105]

The Howard League followed up the resolution of the Sixteenth Assembly with two publications in 1936, which sought to build on the modest advances at the League of Nations as well as articulate broader arguments for minimal recourse to incarceration and the adoption of 'scientific' methods in penal administration. Many of the themes addressed in those texts remain thoroughly relevant in the contemporary world. Drawing on the work of the International Penitentiary Commission, the 1936 pamphlet, 'Prison Population of the World', offered statistics on numbers of prisoners per 100,000 people for several countries, including the European colonies and mandated territories. There were a number of countries for which data were missing, a gap which the Howard League used to urge members of the League of Nations to 'keep and publish accurate statistics regarding all persons deprived of their liberty by the State'.[106] The publication lamented the fact that there had 'perhaps never been, in all history, a time when so many men and women were shut away from liberty as in the last few years', with non-citizens deprived of 'any rights as nationals', and those belonging to minority groups making up disproportionate numbers of prisoners. In addition to pointing out continued violations of the 'Minimum Rules for the Treatment of Prisoners', the pamphlet suggested that 'the natural tendency of imprisonment is to unfit the prisoner for his functions as a responsible citizen'.[107]

The undercurrent of positivist criminology and a belief in the intersections of criminal justice and social justice found expression in the other pamphlet 'For All Prisoners'. Taking note of promising but uneven advances in many countries toward 'a truly preventive criminology', the Howard League submitted that:

> [T]he progress of our knowledge, medical and psychological, of human beings, in particular better understanding of the problems of adolescence, and the elaboration of statistical methods, bring hope that in the near future our present haphazard ways will be superseded by more scientific and methodical systems of guarding against crime and all the misery it brings.[108]

Whilst pointing out the need for greater international collaboration and consistency in the application of new penological experiments, the text also added that the Howard League did not 'overlook the fact that in many cases the "criminal" is more a victim than a villain, and society itself should stand in the

104 Jones (n 43) 181.
105 *Annual Report (1936–1937)* 7.
106 Howard League, 'Prison Population of the World' (1936).
107 Ibid.
108 Howard League, 'For All Prisoners' (1936).

dock'.[109] These occasional publications, as well as subsequent works by Margery Fry and Cecil Craven,[110] and articles appearing in *The Howard Journal* during the mid-twentieth century, can be seen as important contributions to the 'British criminological research in the years before the latter became institutionalised in the universities'.[111] Throughout, there was a distinctive emphasis on offender rehabilitation, 'aftercare' of prisoners, alternatives to incarceration, with the notion of 'punishment' occupying secondary importance, at best.[112]

During the second half of the 1930s, references to an 'international convention' became scarce in the Howard League's documents. The organisation did continue to use the Standard Minimum Rules as a benchmark as it called attention to frequent allegations of ill-treatment of prisoners in Palestine and India, for example, as part of its work with the Standing Advisory Committee on Penal Administration at the Colonial Office.[113] As late as 1941, while the Nazis were preparing plans of invading Britain and the Soviet Union, a conference was convened in London on 'Civil Liberties in the Colonial Empire', where delegates stressed 'the need for applying the Standard Minimum Rules for the Treatment of Prisoners, drawn up by the IPPC (International Penal and Penitentiary Commission)'.[114] To the Howard League's dismay, the outbreak of the war led to the abandonment by the British government of a far-reaching Criminal Justice Bill it had helped draft.[115] At the same time, the organisation feared with Alexander Paterson that 'the whole period of the war may, in itself, be a sort of black-out as far as the prisons and the treatment of prisoners is concerned'.[116]

Penal reform and the aftermath of World War II: turning point or false dawn?

As the League of Nations Secretariat was reduced to a skeleton staff and its international activities came to a halt, the Howard League put together an international committee, taking advantage of the presence of a significant number of prominent criminologists and penal experts in London who had fled the war.[117] The Committee held its first meeting in July 1941, with Cecil Craven and

109 Ibid.
110 See, for example, Fry, 'Arms of the Law' (n 23) 73–87; Benson and Craven (n 23).
111 Logan (n 9) 32.
112 Jorns (n 9) 187.
113 Howard League, *Annual Report (1937–1938)* 5.
114 *Annual Report (1940–1941)* 7. The conference was convened by the Nation Council for Civil Liberties.
115 Besides other measures, the Bill had strong provisions on rehabilitation and gave power to the home secretary to set up residential centres as an alternative to prisons. See Cicely M. Craven, *Punishment and Reform* (Oxford University Press 1951) 24–27.
116 Howard League for Penal Reform, *Annual Report (1940–1941)* 6–7.
117 See Roger Hood, 'Herman Mannheim (1889–1974) and Max Grünhut (1893–1964)' in Jack Beatson and Reinhard Zimmermann (eds), *Jurists Uprooted: German-Speaking Émigré Lawyers in Twentieth-century Britain* (Oxford University Press 2004).

M. Deliereneux (a Belgian penologist with a long association with the Penitentiary Commission) appointed as honorary secretaries. In 1942, the Committee had representatives from ten European countries in addition to Britain. On the eve of the Dumbarton Oak Conference, held between August and October 1944 (as the first concrete step by the Allies to set up the United Nations), the International Committee addressed a letter to various heads of states and the ambassadors of the United States and the Soviet Union in Britain, 'urging the governments of the United Nations during the reconstruction period to consider the importance of international co-operation in preventing crime and delinquency, the final expression of human waste'.[118]

With Leon Radzinowicz and Hermann Manheim, two of the most highly respected criminologists of the period among signatories, the letter recommended that future international collaboration on penal matters include 'the establishment of a Bureau of Penal Affairs as an integral part of any future international organisation'.[119] The committee urged the Allied powers to recognise 'the pressing importance of observing certain basic principles in relation to child offenders and adolescents', and 'the importance of co-coordination of the social services auxiliary to the courts, especially in relation to young offenders, so that the treatment might result in their return to good citizenship, and the community be safeguarded with the minimum restraint on person liberty'.[120] Summing up the contemporary consensus among progressive penologists against retributive philosophy, the International Committee called 'for all offenders the abandonment of punishment as an end in itself and of purely punitive measures such as capital and corporal punishment'.[121]

Although there is no acknowledgement of this in the UN documents or human rights scholarship, the Howard League was the first organisation to urge the future international body to concern itself with penal matters. In early 1945, a letter was sent to the Foreign Secretary urging that:

> [T]he subject [of penal reform] should be recognised as coming within the scope of the United Nations Organisation and that machinery should be provided in the original constitution of the Social and Economic Council for dealing with the matter and for utilising the great body of work done by the International Penal and Penitentiary Commission, especially in connection with the Standard Minimum Rules adopted by the League of Nations.[122]

With all the talk of a new and better world arising out of the ashes of the war, the Howard League once again saw it proper to speak of an 'international charter for prisoners'. Echoing an old line of argument, the Howard League said it believed

118 *Annual Report (1943–1944)* 10–11.
119 Ibid 11.
120 Ibid.
121 *Annual Report (1943–1944)* 11.
122 *Annual Report (1944–1945)* 18.

that 'ultimately the effectiveness of such Rules or of any *international Charter* for prisoners depends on public opinion in the various countries'.[123] Still unsure what the future would bring, Margery Fry, M.A Delierneux, and Alexander Paterson jointly addressed a press conference in July 1945, reiterating the appeal made to the Foreign Secretary.

The proposal for an international charter on prisoners' rights would recede into the background in the post-World War II codification of human rights. The idea was revived momentarily in a preparatory meeting for the Eleventh UN Congress on Crime Prevention and Criminal Justice held in Bangkok in 2005. In 2004, the African Regional Preparatory Meeting recommended that in 'view of the problems of poor prison conditions in most developing countries, including overcrowding and poor sanitary facilities and lack of health facilities' the Eleventh Congress consider endorsing a 'Charter on Fundamental Rights of Prisoners'.[124] The report of the meeting made no mention of the Howard League's proposal. It did contain a draft charter, outlining the right to inherent dignity; separation and classification; humane accommodation; decent food; health and medical care; legal consultation, fair trial, and equitable sentencing including non-custodial sanctions; independent inspections; and reintegration.[125] Nothing came of the proposal in the end. The Eleventh Congress on Crime Prevention did not follow through on the recommendation of the preparatory meeting.[126]

In a far-reaching philosophical enquiry, Margery Fry contributed an essay to a 1946 UNESCO symposium, bringing an anti-retributivist perspective to bear on the question of prisoners' rights. With occasionally pedantic but ambitious contributions by such luminaries as Mahatma Gandhi, Albert Einstein, Harold Laski, and Aldous Huxley, the publication itself did not go down well with the United Nations Commission on Human Rights. Members of the Commission were disquieted as they had not been consulted by UNESCO. Subsequently, as Roger Normand and Sarah Zaidi have remarked, they 'did their utmost to ignore and bury' the publication.[127]

'The object of punishment', Margery Fry wrote in her contribution to the UNESCO volume, 'should not be the infliction of pain but simply [to] deter',

123 Ibid (emphasis added).

124 UNGA, 'Report of the African Regional Preparatory Meeting for the Eleventh United Nations Congress on Crime Prevention and Criminal Justice' 16 March 2004, UN Doc A/CONF.203/RPM.3, at para 50.

125 Ibid 14–17.

126 Sara A. Rodriguez, '"The Impotence of Being Earnest": Status of the United Nations Standard Minimum Rules for the Treatment of Prisoners in Europe and the United States' (2007) 33 *New England Journal of Criminal & Civil Confinement* 61, 91.

127 Margery Fry, 'Human Rights and the Law Breaker' in UNESCO, *Human Rights: Comments and Interpretations – A Symposium Edited by UNESCO with an Introduction by Jacques Maritain* (Allan Wingle 1949) 246–249, 246. See also, Normand and Zaidi (n 6) 182–185, 183; Christopher N.J Roberts, *The Contentious History of the International Bill of Human Rights* (Cambridge University Press 2015) 126; Johannes Morsink, 'World War Two and the Universal Declaration' (1993) 15 *Human Rights Quarterly* 357, 397–398.

disclaiming a 'semi-theocratic duty laid upon the State to punish moral depravity as such'.[128] Fry invited attention to the question of the 'forfeiture' of rights by the 'law breaker', and the proper limits on a state's entitlement to strip an offender of their rights and freedoms. The observation that the question of certain 'guarantees is peculiarly difficult in the case of prisoners' as 'their voice, as against that of those in authority over them, cannot make itself heard through the prison walls', seems all the more poignant considering that prisoners have yet to be protected by a specific international convention. Recounting the Standard Minimum Rules as a 'step in the right direction', Fry noted that 'the absence of any system of international inspection and reporting' had allowed the regime to be, 'in many cases, a purely verbal one'.[129]

Finally, there is another little-known story from 1946 that bears mentioning here. The executive committee of the International Penitentiary Commission met for the first time after World War II in Berne, Switzerland, in April 1946. As previously noted, contrary to the misconceived impression about the Penitentiary Commission's association with the Nazis, the committee had unequivocally condemned war-time atrocities and supported the prosecution of war criminals. What is especially interesting for our purposes is that in a resolution proposed by Alexander Paterson, the executive committee called upon the Penitentiary Commission to move a step further from the Standard Minimum Rules and draw up rules for 'an ideal penal system'.[130] The Minimum Rules, the Resolution noted, had been 'intended to provide a somewhat negative basis essential to the super structure of a progressive penal system'.[131] Foreshadowing heady idealism that would animate 'penal welfarism' in parts of the world after the war, Paterson ventured to suggest in his Resolution that:

> The International [Penitentiary] Commission . . . engage in a more constructive and ambitious adventure, by adumbrating something that would be the ideal penal system. The medical and psychiatric scientists would contribute to such a compilation, not the bare minimum of medical supervision required in a modern prison, but the most complete scheme of medical and psychiatric care and examination of prisoners that the resources of modern science suggest.[132]

To what extent were the hopes, aspirations, and normative priorities articulated by the Howard League and the Penitentiary Commission taken on board by the post-World War II human rights project? Did the codification of human rights following the creation of the United Nations entail a continuation of the

128 Fry, 'Human Rights and the Law Break' (n 127) 247–248.
129 Ibid 249.
130 'Minutes of the Meeting of the Executive Committee of the International Penal and Penitentiary Commission', Berne, April 1946 (Staempfli & CIE 1946).
131 Ibid.
132 Ibid.

established trajectory of penal reform? Or did it represent a departure in some significant sense? What ideological currents, historical experiences, and political contestations underpin the emerging discourse of international human rights, specifically in relation to the idea of punishment? These are the questions we take up in the next two chapters.

6 The great force of history

Development of the global human rights regime

> For history, as nearly no one seems to know, is not merely something to be read. And it does not refer merely, or even principally, to the past. On the contrary, the great force of history comes from the fact that we carry it within us, are unconsciously controlled by it in many ways, and history is literally present in all that we do. It could scarcely be otherwise, since it is to history that we owe our frames of reference, our identities, and our aspirations.
>
> James Baldwin[1]

In one variant of the textbook narrative, as discussed in Chapter 4, the emergence of the international human rights regime is memorialised as a natural response to the horrors of the Holocaust, and an institutional embodiment of the sentiment, 'Never again!'[2] On this account, the rise of fascism and the atrocities of the Second World War had seriously undermined a belief in an all-embracing European civilisation. There was, then, a need to restate and renew the '"Enlightenment values" that had been betrayed by Nazism and fascism'.[3] Critical historians, most notably Samuel Moyn and Mark Mazower, have challenged this view, drawing attention to how realpolitik and state interests mediated the international system that the Allied powers negotiated into existence amidst the debris of the war.[4] The truth, it seems, lies somewhere in between.

1 James Baldwin, 'White Man's Guilt', *Ebony*, August 1965.

2 See, for example, William Korey, *NGOs and the Universal Declaration of Human Rights: "A Curious Grapevine"* (Palgrave Macmillan 1998) 1, 17; Lynda S. Bell and others, 'Introduction: Culture and Human Rights' in Bell and Others (eds), *Negotiating Culture and Human Rights* (Columbia University Press 2001) 3–20.

3 Francesca Klug, 'The Universal Declaration of Human Rights: 60 Years on' (2009) *Public Law* 205, 210.

4 Samuel Moyn, *The Last Utopia: Human Rights in History* (Harvard University Press 2010) 44–83; *Human Rights and the Uses of History* (Verso 2014) 69–97; Mark Mazower, *No Enchanted Palace: The End of Empire and the Ideological Origins of the United Nations* (Princeton University Press 2009); Mazower, 'The Strange Triumph of Human Rights, 1933–1950' (2004) 47(2) *The Historical Journal* 379. cf. G. Daniel Cohen, 'The Holocaust and the "Human Rights Revolution": A Reassessment' in Akira Iriye, Petra Goedde, and

Sure enough, sceptics have good reasons to question the 'uplifting backstories' of the modern human rights project.[5] The system that began to take shape in the late 1940s was indeed forged in the crucible of politics.[6] The fanfare with which Britain and the US had deployed the rhetoric of freedom and rights to sustain the war effort sat uncomfortably with their subsequent reluctance to allow an international supervisory mechanism to interfere with national sovereignty.[7] That said, it is stretching the argument to suggest that the experience of the Holocaust did not feed into the post-war human rights project.[8] The imprint of that experience shows up frequently in the *travaux préparatoires* and the text of a number of provisions of the Universal Declaration (UDHR) and the International Covenant on Civil and Political Rights (ICCPR), particularly those dealing with individual liberty and the administration of justice.[9] To illustrate, when the 'Draft International Covenant on Human Rights' came up for discussion before the Third Committee (Social, Humanitarian and Cultural Committee) of the General Assembly, the British representative Lord McDonald expressed his dissatisfaction with the 'vagueness' of the term, 'arbitrarily', in a proposed article concerning the deprivation of liberty. Prohibiting states from 'arbitrarily' depriving a person from their liberty, Lord McDonald thought, formed an inadequate safeguard because:

> When the Nazi and fascist governments before and during the war had consistently trampled on human rights, they had done so by means of laws which had been valid according to their national constitutions. If the final version of the covenant contained an article drafted in such terms, all that some future Hitler would require in order to avoid violating that article would be

---

William I. Hitchcock (eds), *The Human Rights Revolution: An International History* (Oxford University Press 2012) 53–72.

5 Moyn, 'The Last Utopia' (n 4) 5–6.

6 Mark Mazower, 'The Strange Triumph of Human Rights, 1933–1950' (2004) 47(2) *The Historical Journal* 379, 381; Peter Gowan, 'US: UN' (2003) (24) *New Left Review* 5. Tony Evans, *US Hegemony and the Project of Universal Human Rights* (Palgrave Macmillan 1996) 72–73.

7 Christopher NJ Roberts, *The Contentious History of the International Bill of Human Rights* (Cambridge University Press 2015) 72–112; Roger Normand and Sarah Zaidi, *Human Rights at the UN: The Political History of Universal Justice* (Indiana University Press 2008) 81–106; Mary Ann Glenden, *A World Made New: Eleanor Roosevelt and the Universal Declaration of Human Rights* (Random House 2002) xv–xvi; AW Brian Simpson, *Human Rights and the End of Empire: Britain and the Genesis of the European Convention* (Oxford University Press 2001) 158–172; Bonny Ibhawoh, *Imperialism and Human Rights: Colonial Discourses of Rights and Liberties in African History* (State University of New York Press 2007) 151–161.

8 Contra Moyn, see Burn H. Weston, 'Human Rights' (1984) *Human Rights Quarterly* 261.

9 Cohen (n 4) 53–71; David Weissbrodt and Mattias Hallendorff, '*Travaux préparatoires* of the Fair Trial Provisions – Articles 8 to 11 of the Universal Declaration of Human Rights' (1999) 21(4) *Human Rights Quarterly* 1061; J Morsink, 'WWII and the Universal Declaration' (1993) 15 *Human Rights Quarterly* 357.

to pass a law, making membership of a particular racial or religious group, for example, punishable by imprisonment.[10]

The foundational documents also represent a re-articulation of traditional Enlightenment values threatened by fascism and totalitarianism. René Cassin, the French representative on the Commission on Human Rights – who had lost family members in the Nazi occupation of France and had witnessed 'wholesale dismantling and humiliation of the French Republican tradition'[11] – hinted at this pedigree in a speech in Paris on 9 December 1948 as the UN General Assembly voted to adopt the UDHR. Speaking in the Palais de Chaillot, under the shadow of the Eiffel Tower, Cassin described the occasion as: 'An act which, 100 years after the revolution of 1848 and the abolition of slavery on all French territory, constitutes a step on the global level in the long battle for the *rights of man*'.[12]

Johannes Morsink has suggested that even economic and social rights in the UDHR were informed by the Holocaust experience.[13] In fact, the inclusion of the so-called second generation rights within the Declaration can more readily be understood against the backdrop of the mid-twentieth century crisis of liberal democracy and a concomitant left-ward shift in public opinion.[14] The American Declaration of the Rights of Man and Duties, adopted by the Ninth International Conference of American States in May 1948, contained at least six provisions concerning what are today categorised as economic, social, and cultural rights.[15] Elsewhere, on the eve of the Second World War, Franklin Roosevelt's Four Freedoms (freedom of speech, freedom of religion, freedom from want, and freedom

10 United Nations General Assembly Official Records (UNGAOR), Fifth Session, Third Committee, 288th Meeting (18 October 1950) UN Doc A/C.3/SR.288, para 15 (referring to Article 6 of the Draft International Covenant on Human Rights).

11 Jay Winter, *Dreams of Peace and Freedom: Utopian Moments in the Twentieth Century* (Yale University Press 2006) 100.

12 Cited in Winter (n 11) 116–117. A detailed account of René Cassin's contributions to international human rights law can be found in Jay Winter and Antoine Prost, *René Cassin and Human Rights: From the Great War to the Universal Declaration* (Cambridge University Press 2013). Cassin had also expressed this sentiment during the debate on the first article of the 'Draft International Declaration of Rights' at the Commission on Human Rights. See Commission on Human Rights, Drafting Committee, First Session, Summary Record of the Eighth Meeting, 20 June 1947. UN.Doc. E/CN.4/AC.1/SR.8, at p 2. For similar comments by the Egyptian representative to the Third Committee of the General Assembly, see UN General Assembly, Fifth Session, Official Records. Third Committee, 288th Meeting, 18 October 1950. UN Doc A/C.3/SR.288, para 23.

13 Johannes Morsink, *The Universal Declaration of Human Rights: Origins, Drafting, and Intent* (University of Pennsylvania Press 1999) 88–91. cf. Cohen (n 4) 53–71, 61.

14 Howard Zinn, *A People's History of the United States: 1942 – Present* (3rd edn, Pearson 2003) 428–429; Mark Mazower, *Dark Continent: Europe's Twentieth Century* (Allen Lane 1998) 1–39; Paul W. Drake, 'International Crises and Political Movements in Latin America: Chile and Peru from the Great Depression to the Cold War' in David Rock (ed), *Latin America in the 1940s: War and Postwar Transitions* (University of California Press 1994) 109–136.

15 The American Declaration on the Rights and Duties of Man adopted by the 9th International Conference of American States on 2 May 1948. See UN Doc E/CN.44/122.

from fear) sought to extend the New Deal as a blueprint for a global moral order.[16] In Britain, the influential Beveridge Report came out in 1942, preparing the ground for the universal extension of social security and health insurance. As the dust settled in Europe in 1945, the Western leaders could no longer overlook economic deprivations within their countries, if they were to provide a capitalist and democratic alternative to the Soviet model of centralised planning.

Yet, despite an emerging consensus around at least a minimal welfare programme, the question of the proper status and the enforcement of economic and social rights turned into a pitched battle between the opposing blocs at the UN. Ideological fault lines re-emerged as war-time allies turned into Cold War rivals. As a corrective to the textbook narrative, several scholars have historicised the contentious origins of two separate covenants.[17] But the scholarship remains silent about the implications on penal policy of the fragmentation of what was originally meant to be a single, legally binding document. It will be argued in this chapter that the division of human rights into distinct categories (civil and political rights on the one hand, and economic, social, and cultural rights on the other) mirrors as well as consolidates a conception of penal policy and penological aims, which does not adequately take social justice considerations into account.

Drafting of the UDHR and the two covenants

In February 1946, pursuant to Article 68 of the UN Charter, the Economic and Social Council established a nine-member Nuclear Commission on Human rights to recommend the structure and the scope of work for a full commission.[18] Meeting at New York's Hunter College between April and May that year, this provisional body, which included Eleanor Roosevelt and René Cassin as members,

16 William Hitchcock, '"Everywhere in the World": The Strange Career of the Four Freedoms since 1945' in Jeffery A. Engel (ed), *The Four Freedoms: Franklin D. Roosevelt and the Evolution of an American Idea* (Oxford University Press 2016) 193–220.

17 See, for example, Normand and Zaidi (n 7) 197–242; For earlier accounts, see Vrastislav Pechota, 'The Development of the Covenant on Civil and Political Rights' in Louis Henkin (ed), *The International Bill of Rights: The Covenant on Civil and Political Rights* (Columbia University Press 1981) 32–71, 41–43; Farrokh Jhabvala, 'On Human Rights and the Socio-Economic Context' in Fredrick E. Snyder and Surakiarat Sathirathai (eds), *Third World Attitudes Towards International Law: An Introduction* (Martin's Nijhoff 1987) *293–319. cf. Marco Odello and Francesco Seats, The UN Committee on Economic, Social and Cultural Rights: The Law, Process, and Practice* (Routledge 2013) 4–9; Jack Mahoney, *The Challenge of Human Rights: Origin, Development and Significance* (Blackwell Publishing 2007) 42–70; Julie A. Mertus, *The United Nations Human Rights Regime: A Guide for a New Era* (Routledge 2005) 54; Roger S. Clark, *A United Nations High Commissioner for Human Rights* (Martinus Nijhoff 1972) 18.

18 UN Economic and Social Council Res E/27 adopted on 22 February 1946. Article 68 of the Charter of the United Nations reads: 'The Economic and Social Council shall set up commissions in economic and social fields and for the promotion of human rights, and such other commissions as may be required for the performance of its functions'.

briefly discussed proposals submitted by Cuba and Panama.[19] However, it decided to recommend that the full Commission on Human Rights examine the documents in detail and draft 'an international bill of rights as soon as possible, and that this draft [be] circulated among United Nations members for comments'.[20] To lay the groundwork for the task, the Nuclear Commission asked the Secretariat to collect 'all available material on the subject'.[21]

The full Commission on Human Rights held its first session between 27 January and 8 February 1947 at Lake Success in New York.[22] At the first meeting, the Commission unanimously elected Eleanor Roosevelt as the chair, P.C. Chang of China as vice-chairman, and the Lebanese neo-Thomist, anti-Marxist philosopher Charles Malik as rapporteur. Malik would later go on to serve as president of the UN General Assembly.[23] Though Roosevelt herself lacked a background in law – a point some of her compatriots would use to question her competence to represent the United States on the Commission[24] – several other members happened to be academic lawyers with vast experience. Fernand Dehousse from Belgium, for example, had been a professor of international law at the University of Liege and the Academy of International Law at The Hague. He is also remembered as being one of the three main authors of the European Convention on Human Rights as it was drafted by the International Juridical Section of the European Movement in 1949.[25] Ricardo Joaquin Alfaro from Panama had a doctorate in law. René Cassin had been the National Commissioner for Justice and Public Instruction in Charles de Gaulle's government in exile during World War II. As a French delegate to the League of Nations between 1924 and 1928, Cassin had taken part in the development of the International Labour Organisation in its formative phase.[26]

19 UN Doc E/HR/1, and UN Doc E/HR/3.

20 United Nations Commission on Human Rights (UNCHR) 'Draft Report of the Commission on Human Rights to the Second Session of the Economic and Social Council' (15 May 1946) UN Doc E/HR/19, p 2.

21 'Draft Report of the Commission on Human Rights', UN Doc E/HR/19, at p 5.

22 The 18 members came from Australia, Belgium, Belorussian Soviet Socialist Republic, China, Egypt, India, Iran, Lebanon, Philippine Republic, United Kingdom, USA, USSR, and Uruguay.

23 UNHRC, First Session, Summary Record of the First Meeting (28 January 1947) UN Doc E/CN.4/SR.1, at p 4. For Malik's views on Marxist philosophy, see Charles Malik, 'The Individual in Modern Society: Keynote Address, May 18–20, 1961' in John Brooks (ed), *The One and the Many: The Individual in the Modern World. The Second Corning Conference* (Harper & Row 1962) 135–156. See also Alan John Hobbins (ed), *On the Edge of Greatness, Volume II: The Diaries of John Humphrey, First Director of the United Nations Division of Human Rights* (McGill University Libraries 1996) 285.

24 See, for example, Frank Holman, 'An "International Bill of Rights Bill of Rights": Proposals Have Dangerous Implications for U.S' (1948) 34 *American Bar Association Journal* 984.

25 The other two being David Maxwell Fyfe and Pierre-Henri Tietgen. See Ed Bates, *The Evolution of the European Convention on Human Rights: From Its Inception to the Creation of a Permanent Court of Human Rights* (Oxford University Press 2010) 51–52.

26 The International Labour Organisation was formed in 1919, as part of the Treaty of Versailles at the end of World War I.

In a UNESCO publication marking the 50th anniversary of the UDHR, Glen Johnson and Janusz Symonides commented, 'The range of backgrounds and interests among the Commission members, the staff and the NGOs working with them undoubtedly deepened and broadened the perspective which informed the deliberations leading to the declaration'.[27] This assessment is rather naïve. For one, competent as they were, none of the members had been actively associated with the tradition of progressive criminological thinking that had evolved since the mid-nineteenth century. Some of the ideas rooted in that tradition did surface during the drafting process but not in a sustained or comprehensive manner. As noted in the previous chapter, the Howard League was the first organisation to implore the world leaders on the eve of the founding of the United Nations to include penal reform within the mandate of the new organisation.[28] Though the League went on to acquire a 'special consultative status' with the Economic and Social Council in 1947, it did not participate in the drafting of the 'International Bill of Human Rights'. As far as the Howard League archives shed light on the matter, the organisation's major concern in the immediate post-war period was penal reform within Britain, which had come to a standstill during the war.[29]

Another organisation which had initially harboured high hopes in the United Nations but went missing through the drafting process was the National Association for the Advancement of Coloured People (NAACP), one of the oldest civil rights organisations in the United States. In April 1945, the NAACP had participated at the conference launching the UN Charter at San Francisco, alongside 'consultants' from several other NGOs. It was largely as a result of lobbying by smaller states and the NGO-delegates to the San Francisco Conference that the big powers agreed to include seven references to human rights in the UN Charter.[30] The NAACP was represented at San Francisco by one of the most outspoken anti-imperialists of the time, and a seminal figure in both American criminology and 'black criminology', W.E.B Du Bois.[31] Du Bois came out disappointed from the San Francisco conference because of the inclusion of a 'domestic jurisdiction clause' in the UN Charter and the failure to specifically recognise the human rights of the 750 million human beings who still lived under colonial

27 Glen Johnson and Janusz Symonides, *The Universal Declaration of Human Rights: A History of Its Creation and Implementation 1948–1998* (UNESCO 1998) 26.

28 Howard League for Penal Reform, *Annual Report (1944–1945)* 18.

29 On the interruption of the 'reform-rehabilitation' tradition in Britain by the Second World War, see Michael Adler and Brian Longhurst, *Discourse, Power and Justice: Towards a New Sociology of Imprisonment* (Routledge 1994) 36.

30 Charter of the United Nations adopted 26 June 1945, entered into force 24 October 1945) 1 UNTS XVI (Articles 1, 13(1), 55, 56, 62, 68, and 76). See John P. Humphrey 'International Protection of Human Rights' (1948) 225 *Annals of the American Academy of Political and Social Science* 15, 16; *Human Rights and the United Nations: A Great Adventure* (Transnational Publishers Inc. 1984) 12; Rowland Burcken, *A Most Uncertain Crusade: The United States, the United Nations, and Human Rights, 1941–1953* (NIU Press 2014) 250.

31 See Shuan L. Gabbidon, *W.E.B. Du Bois on Crime and Justice: Laying the Foundations of Sociological Criminology* (Ashgate 2007) 64–66.

subjugation.[32] The disenchantment was shared by Nnamdi Azikiwe, a leading figure in African and Nigerian nationalism, who would later serve as Nigeria's first president.[33]

On 23 October 1947, Du Bois submitted a petition to the UN on behalf of the NAACP, describing the history and current trajectory of social and legal discrimination against African Americans.[34] Titled 'An Appeal to the World', the petition opened with a blistering introduction by Du Bois and included contributions by prominent civil rights activists, describing the history and current trajectory of social and legal discrimination against African Americans. In his introduction, Du Bois, who had also witnessed the Paris Peace Congress at the end of the First World War, recalled how the victorious powers had, at the time, refused to recognise the equality of races and nations. The United States, Du Bois wrote, had objected to the compulsory protection of minorities under the League of Nations because it feared that the system would set a precedent for similar demands being made on behalf of African Americans. To Du Bois, the paradox of fighting for freedom and democracy abroad whilst sustaining a system of racial discrimination based on 'Jim Crow' laws at home, had emerged once more in the aftermath of World War II.[35] That led him to ask rhetorically:

> When will nations learn that their enemies are often within their own country as without? It is nor Russia that threatens the United States so much as Mississippi; not Stalin and Molotov but Bilbo and Rankin (notoriously racist southern legislators); internal injustice done to one's brothers is far more dangerous than the aggression of strangers from abroad.[36]

In his contribution, African American attorney Earl B. Dickenson sketched out 'four principal methods used in depriving African Negro citizens of the rights guaranteed' by the US Constitution. These methods, Dickenson explained,

32 Carol Anderson, *Eyes Off the Prize: The United Nations and the African American Struggle for Human Rights, 1944–1955* (Cambridge University Press 2003) 38. The 'domestic jurisdiction clause' enshrined in Article 2(7) of the Charter barred the UN from intervening in 'matters which are essentially within the domestic jurisdiction of any state'. Du Bois wanted a 'colonial commission' to ensure that human rights guarantees would extend to the European colonies. Instead, what emerged from the San Francisco conference was an imitation of the League of Nations Mandates System with some tinkering. The Trusteeship Council, the sixth principal organ of the UN, made up of the five permanent members of the Security Council, was tasked to oversee the 'Trust Territories', including former Mandates of the League of Nations and the territories taken from the Axes powers at the end of World War II.

33 Marika Sherwood, ' "There is no Deal for the Blackman in San Francisco": African Attempts to Influence the Finding Conference of the United Nations, April-July 1945' (1996) 29(1) *The International Journal of African Historical Studies* 71, 82.

34 NAACP, *An Appeal to the World!* (1947). See also Rowland Brucken, *A Most Uncertain Crusade: The United States, the United Nations, and Human Rights, 1941–1953* (NIU Press 2014) 114–115.

35 W.E.B Du Bois, 'Introduction by W.E. Burgharat Du Bois', in NAACP (n 34) 1–14, 11–12.

36 Ibid 12.

included statutory enactments such as prohibition on inter-racial marriages; 'acts and conspiracies' of private individuals, including 'the race covenant among white property owners', refusing accommodation to black citizens; the peculiar American institution of mob violence or 'lynching'; and finally, court decisions restricting the rights of African Americans.[37] In a related chapter, Milton R. Konvitz summarised the Supreme Court cases involving African Americans and came to the conclusion that the court had afforded to 'the Negroes' formal equality in terms of criminal procedure and due process, but had had failed to recognise their status as a historically disadvantaged group subjected to segregation.[38] Historian Rayford W. Logan made a spirited attempt to ground the NAACP petition within the human rights provisions of the UN Charter. Invoking the seven references to human rights, Logan suggested that the Economic and Social Council (the parent body of the Commission on Human Rights) had the authority and obligation to 'initiate studies and reports with respect to international economic, social, cultural, educational, health, and related matters', and to 'make recommendations for the purpose of promoting respect for, and observance of, human rights and fundamental freedoms for all'.[39] In a doomed attempt to overcome the difficulties presented by the domestic jurisdiction clause, Logan argued that the limitation on the UN not to intervene in domestic matters of a sovereign state needed to be interpreted liberally to 'avoid nullification' of the very concept of 'universal human rights'.[40]

In the event, the petition held little more than propaganda value. On 5 August 1947, two months before Du Bois presented the petition to John P. Humphrey, director of the UN's Human Rights Division, and Assistant Secretary-General Henri Laugier (in charge of the Division of Social Affairs), the Economic and Social Council had adopted a resolution, stating that the Commission on Human Rights did not have 'any power to take any action in regard to any complaints concerning human rights'.[41] Moreover, Du Bois angered Eleanor Roosevelt, then a member of the NAACP Board, who had threatened to resign from the US delegation to the United Nations 'if the petition was presented'.[42]

The NGOs, which were in attendance at the Human Rights Commission's initial sessions, namely the American Federation of Labour, the Inter-Parliamentary Union and the International Co-operative Alliance (in Category A with the 'general

37 Earl B. Dickenson, The Denial of Legal Rights of American Negroes from 1787 to 194', in NAACP (n 34) 16–34.

38 Milton R. Konvitz, 'The Legal Status of American Negro Descent Since World War I', in NAACP (n 34) 35–46.

39 Rayford W. Logan, 'The Charter of the United Nations and its Provisions for Human Rights and the Rights of Minorities and Decisions Already Taken Under this Charter', in NAACP (n 34) 85–94, 86.

40 Ibid 90.

41 UN ECOSOC Res 75 (V) (5 August 1947) UN Doc E/573.

42 Gerald Horne, *Black and Red: W.E.B. Du Bois and the Afro-American Response to the Cold War, 1944–1963* (State University of New York Press 1986) 101.

status'),[43] and the World Jewish Congress, International Council of Women, International Union of Catholic Women's League, International Committee of the Red Cross, the Consultative Council of Jewish Organisations, and other faith-based organisations (in Category B with 'special consultative status'),[44] did not, at any point, advocate alternatives to retributive justice and the prison system. That did not change as several other women's organisations, and Jewish and Catholic groups were added to Category B in the 1950s.[45] Setting aside the teleological version of history, it might help to engage in a little counterfactual thought experiment. Would the contents of the 'International Bill of Human Rights' have been any different if Margery Fry and Du Bois had been involved in its drafting? Having surveyed the history of the Howard League, it is not far-fetched to suggest that Fry would have championed rehabilitation of prisoners and alternatives to retributive punishment within the emerging human rights documents. Du Bois, as noted in Chapter 4, was the first scholar to document in painful detail how convict leasing had replaced antebellum slavery following the Thirteenth Amendment to the US Constitution.[46] He had undertaken pioneering sociological inquiries into crime and criminality as early as the 1890s, providing a searching analysis of the relationship between poverty, race, and justice.[47] With that perspective, he would perhaps have taken a stand against the exclusion of penal labour from the prohibition of forced labour, an abiding paradox in international law. As things turned out, this potentially subversive voice had been rendered inaudible before the ink was dry on the foundational text of the modern human rights movement.

To pick up the thread from the first session of the Human Rights Commission, the initial meetings were marked by a great deal of optimism about the possibility of adequate machinery for the protection of human rights being put in place. The point of departure was that the Commission would enumerate human rights

43 UN ECOSOC, 'Report of the Commission on Human Rights, Second Session, 2 December to 17 December 1947' (17 December 1947) UN Doc E/600, at p 3.

44 Ibid. Other organisations in Category B were: Catholic International Union for Social Service, Commission of the Churches on International Affairs, Co-ordinating Board of Jewish Organizations, International Abolitionist Federation, International Federation of Business and Professional Women, Women's International Democratic Federation, and World Federation of United Nations Associations.

45 By the summer of 1951, the World Federation of Trade Unions and the World Federation of United Nations Associations had found a place in Category A. Some new organisations in Category B included: Agudas Israel World Organization, All Pakistan Women's Association, Caritas Internationalis, Carnegie Endowment for International Peace, Friends World Committee for Consultation, International Federation of University Women, International Union for Child Welfare, and World's Young Women's Christian Association. For the full list, see UNCHR, 'Report to the Economic and Social Council on the seventh session of the Commission, held at the Palais des Nations, Geneva, from 16 April to 19 May 1951' UN Doc E/1992.

46 WEB Du Bois, *Black Reconstruction in America* (Russel & Russel 1935).

47 WEB Du Bois, *The Philadelphia Negro: A Social Study* (University of Pennsylvania Press 1996) 235–268. The study was first published in 1899.

in a single, legally enforceable document. Confusion crept in regarding the legal status and the nomenclature of the 'International Bill of Human Rights' as the US and the USSR began to voice opposition to a binding treaty. Britain, another of the three major powers on the winning side in the Second World War, was for a legally binding document (provided it included only a narrow list of traditional civil and political rights and did not extend to the colonies).[48] Anticipating the conservative backlash against a binding treaty at home, the US government formally set in motion the division of the Bill by proposing on 28 January 1947 'that the Commission should first prepare it in the form of a Declaration on Human Rights and Fundamental Freedoms to be adopted as a General Assembly Resolution'.[49]

At the 7th meeting of the first session held on 31 January 1947, Roosevelt drew the members' attention to the US proposal, expressing her preference for a 'Charter' that is 'kept flexible and general in order to meet new problems and situations'.[50] Representing the anti-communist government of Kuomintang (Chinese Nationalist Party), P.C. Chang endorsed the US position, observing that the Commission should proceed on the assumption that the bill would be drafted as a General Assembly resolution, 'and discuss the substance of the bill on that basis'.[51] Though the Commission would, in the subsequent sessions, get down to drafting a 'Declaration' and a 'Convention', the US proposal also anticipated the eventual bifurcation of the 'Convention' (or the 'Covenant', as it later came to be known). Even though it recognised 'social rights such as the right to employment and social security and the right to enjoy minimum standards/of economic, social and cultural well-being' as fit for consideration by the Commission, the US proposal suggested that the '[d]eclaration should make provision for the subsequent preparation by the Commission on Human Rights of *one or more* conventions on human rights and fundamental freedoms'.[52] Regarding the implementation of the Declaration, it was to be recommendatory in nature with the General Assembly proclaiming 'it as a standard to be observed by the Members'.[53] 'The conventions', it was suggested, 'might contain provisions for reporting by the signatories

48 Simpson (n 7). See also John P. Humphrey, 'The UN and the Universal Declaration of Human Rights' in Evan Luard (ed), *The International Protection of Human Rights* (Thames and Hudson 1967) 39–58, 50.

49 UN ECOSOC, 'Commission on Human Rights, United States Proposals Regarding an International Bill of Rights' (28 January 1947) UN Doc E/CN.4/4, at p 1.

50 UNCHR, First Session, Summary Record of the Seventh Meeting (31 January 1947) UN Doc E/CN.4/SR.7, at p 2.

51 UN Doc E/CN.4/SR. 7, at p 3. Though the Commission records indicate that Chang's suggestion was drawn from the US proposal, some chroniclers maintain that it was Chang who initiated the idea of the Declaration to be passed by the General Assembly. See, for example, David Weissbrodt and Mattias Hallendorff, 'Travaux Préparatoires of the Fair Trial Provisions – Articles 8 to 11 of the Universal Declaration of Human Rights' (1991) 21(4) *Human Rights Quarterly* 1061, 1063.

52 UNCHR, 'United States Proposals Regarding an International Bill of Rights' (28 January 1947) UN Doc E/CN.4/4, at p 1 (emphasis added).

53 Ibid 2.

on the application of the convention and on the position of their law and practice regarding the rights stipulated'.[54] As it turned out, these suggestions would all be implemented in due course, lending credence to the claim that the US moulded the UN human rights framework in its formative stage.[55]

On 3 February 1947, the Commission decided to form a Drafting Committee, comprising the Chair Eleanor Roosevelt, Vice-Chairman Chang, and the Rapporteur Charles Malik to work with the Secretariat to formulate 'a preliminary draft international bill of human rights'.[56] The committee was later enlarged to include representatives of Australia, Britain, Chile, France, and the USSR. When the Drafting Committee officially met on 9 June 1947, John P. Humphrey, and his staff at the Secretariat, had meticulously prepared for them a 'Draft Outline of an International Bill of Human Rights',[57] and a 'Documented Outline',[58] containing observations that the members had made at the first session of the Commission on Human Rights, and a comparison of the Secretariat outline with provisions in over 50 national constitutions as well as 'draft international declarations' put forward by Chile, Cuba, and Panama.[59] The Drafting Committee also had before it a 'Draft International Bill of Human Rights' presented by the UK government to the UN Secretary General a few days earlier, which essentially restated common-law freedoms and liberties. The UK Draft included, for example, prohibitions on arbitrary arrests and retrospective punishment; fair trial guarantees; and the freedom of religion, speech, and assembly.[60]

The more wide-ranging Secretariat outline echoed not just classical Enlightenment themes of freedom from arbitrary exercise of power, but more contemporary concerns engendered by the events of the Second World War as well. The latter were reflected in articles dealing with the 'right to a legal personality', 'equal opportunity of access to all vocations and professions', and the 'right to a nationality'.[61] In marked contrast to the UK Draft, the Secretariat's 'Draft

54 UNCHR, Drafting Committee, 'Text of Letter from Lord Dukeston, the United Kingdom representative on the Human Rights Commission, to the Secretary-General of the United Nations' (5 June 1947) UN Doc E/CN.4/AC.1/4.

55 Normand and Zaidi (n 7) 195; Gowan (n 6).

56 UNCHR, First Session, Summary Record of the Twelfth Meeting (3 February 1947) UN Doc E/CN.4/SR.12, at p 5.

57 UNCHR, Drafting Committee, 'Draft Outline of International Bill of Rights (prepared by the Division of Human Rights)' (4 June 1947) UN Doc E/CN.4/AC.1/3.

58 UNCHR, Drafting Committee, 'International Bill of Rights – Documented Outline' (11 June 1947) UN Doc E/CN.4/AC/1/3/Add.1.

59 On preparatory work done by Humphrey, see Clinton Timothy Curle, *Humanité: John Humphrey's Alternative Account of Human Rights* (University of Toronto 2007) *36–37; Eleanor Roosevelt, On My Own* (Harper 1958) 77.

60 UNCHR, Drafting Committee, 'Text of Letter from Lori Dukeston, the United Kingdom representative on the Human Rights Commission, to the Secretary-General of the United Nations' (5 June 1947) UN Doc E/CN.4/AC.1/4.

61 UNCHR, Drafting Committee, 'Draft Outline of International Bill of Rights (prepared by the Division of Human Rights)' (4 June 1947) UN Doc E/CN.4/AC.1/3 (art 12 'legal personality'; art 24 'access to all vocations'; art 32 'right to nationality').

International Bill of Human Rights' contained the rights to good working conditions, food, rest and leisure, and participation in cultural life.[62] In conventional accounts, John Humphrey's role in the drafting process has typically been eclipsed by that of Roosevelt and René Cassin. That seems to be changing with the publication of more nuanced histories of the UN human rights project.[63] However, seen from the perspective of penological questions, scholars of both varieties – those downplaying Humphrey's historical contribution as well as those attempting to salvage it – seem to have glossed over certain omissions in his 'Draft Bill of International Human Rights'. We will take up this topic again in Chapter 7.

A few days into the first session of the Drafting Committee, the division of the 'International Bill of Human Rights' into a 'Declaration' and a 'Convention' was a done deal. At its sixth meeting held on 16 June 1947, the Committee decided, following the suggestion of Professor Vladimir M Koretsky of the USSR, to form a working group comprising Roosevelt, René Cassin, Charles Malik, and Charles Wilson from the UK. The working group was charged to logically re-arrange and rephrase the Secretariat outline and to recommend the 'division of the substance of the articles between a Manifesto (another term for Declaration coined by Roosevelt) and a Convention'.[64] The working group, in turn, asked Cassin to write up 'a rough-draft Declaration'.[65] Cassin obliged quickly, producing and revising a draft, which, while giving the Secretariat outline greater clarity, retained almost two-thirds of the contents.[66] The revisions that the document went through within the Commission, the Economic and Social Council, and the Third Committee of the General Assembly over the next year and a half did not significantly alter its original shape.[67] The General Assembly adopted the UDHR on 10 December 1948.[68] In doing so, it requested 'the Economic and Social Council to ask the Commission on Human Rights to continue to give priority in its work to the preparation of a draft Covenant on Human Rights and Draft measures on implementation'.[69]

62 Ibid Arts 38, 42, 43, 44.

63 See Curle (n 59).

64 UNCHR, Drafting Committee, First Session, Summary Record of the Sixth Meeting (16 June 1947) UN Doc E/CN.4/AC.1/SR 6, at p 8.

65 UNCHR, Drafting Committee, First Session, Summary Record of the Seventh Meeting (17 June 1947) UN Doc E/CN.4/AC.1/SR.7, at p 2.

66 Allida Black (ed), *The Eleanor Roosevelt Papers, Volume 1, The Human Rights Years 1945–1948* (Thomas Gale 2007) 573. For Cassin's initial and revised drafts, see respectively UNDocE/CN.4/AC.l/W.2/Rev.1, 18 June 1947, and UN Doc. E/CN.4/AC.1/W.2/Rev.2, 20 June 1947. See also, 'Report of the Third Session of the Commission on Human Rights 24 May to 18 June 1948' (28 June 1948) UN Doc E/800.

67 In December 1947, the Working Group was reformulated to finalise the draft prepared by Cassin. The group included the United States of America, Union of Soviet Socialist Republics, Byelorussian U.S.S.R., Philippines, Panama, and China. See UNCHR, Second Session, Summary Record of the Thirtieth Meeting (5 December 1947) UN Doc E/CN.4/SR. 30.

68 Universal Declaration of Human Rights, UNGA Res 217A (III) UN Doc A/810.

69 UNGAOR, 3rd Session, 21 September – 12 December 1948, Part I (Resolutions), UN Doc A/810.

At its second session (2–17 December 1947), the Commission had already formed a separate 'Working Group on Convention' (also referred to as 'Working Party' in official records), which held nine meetings, debating a slightly revised version of the UK Draft and a US 'Proposal for a Human Rights Convention', which was circulated on 26 November 1947.[70] The latter document contained ten articles altogether – nine dealing with typical civil liberties and freedoms recognised within the American Bill of Rights tradition, and one which combined the right to work and a decent living, social security, health, education, and equal opportunities to participate in cultural life.[71] The 'Draft International Convention on Human Rights' produced by the Working Group in December 1947 omitted references to economic and social rights altogether. It further contained a 'federal clause', which spoke primarily to the concerns of the US government, providing that in the case of federal states the Convention would be applicable only to the federal government and not the constituent units.[72] The draft Convention also had a 'colonial clause' to the effect that the Convention shall apply in case of a colony or an overseas territory only when the state exercising a mandate or trusteeship has 'acceded on behalf and in respect of such Colony or territory'.[73]

The bifurcation of the International Covenant

With the UDHR already adopted, the Commission turned to the draft Covenant on Human Rights at its fifth session (1949) and the sixth session (1950), where members proposed new articles and clashed over the 'colonial clause' and the 'federal clause'. At the fifth session, Australia and the USSR separately put forward suggestions for economic and social rights, corresponding to those already enumerated in Article 32 through Article 37 of the UDHR as well as additional guarantees regarding trade union rights (USSR) and 'reasonable limitations on working hours' (Australia).[74] It was also at the Commission's fifth session that Cassin, as a French representative on the Commission, submitted what would later become, in its diluted version, article 10(3) of the Covenant on Civil and Political Rights, positing 'reformation of the offenders' as the *essential* 'purpose of the penitentiary' (See Chapter 7).[75] In a speech that resonated with several other members of the Commission, the UK representative stated that although she represented a 'democratic and socialist government', given the low level of economic development in parts of the world, the inclusion of economic and social

70 UN Doc E/CN.4/37.

71 UNCHR, Second Session, 'Proposal for a Declaration of Human Rights Submitted by the Representative of the United States' (26 November 1947) UN Doc E/CN.4/36.

72 UNCHR, Second Session, 'Report of the Working Party on An International Convention on Human Rights' (11 December 1947) UN Doc E/CN.4/56 (art 22).

73 UN Doc E/CN.4/5–6, Art 23.

74 UNCHR, Fifth Session, 'Recapitulation of Proposed Additional Articles for Part II of the Draft Covenant' (10 June 1949) UN Doc E/CN.4/313.

75 Emphasis added for reasons which will become apparent as we proceed through the chapter.

rights 'would make it impossible for many countries to adhere to the Covenant'.[76] These contentious issues were referred to the Third Committee of the General Assembly via the Economic and Social Council in 1950.

The composition of the General Assembly had, by then, begun to change with the arrival of several Asian and African nations, some of which joined forces with the communist bloc around self-determination and the state-led model of centralised economic development. The debate that took place at the fifth session of the 'politically uninhibited and procedurally unruly' Third Committee exposed the hardening ideological divisions.[77] Speaking for the UK government, Lord MacDonald said his delegation was satisfied with the scope of the Covenant as it stood. 'The catalogue of rights with which (the Covenant) dealt was obviously not exhaustive but it did comprise all those human rights which could properly be described as fundamental', Lord MacDonald stated, expressing doubts whether economic and social rights could 'properly be described as fundamental'.[78] At the next meeting, the Canadian delegate endorsed the UK position.[79] The statements made by the UK and Canada are indicative of the doubts harboured by some member states regarding the normative legitimacy of economic and social rights. And, as such, they weaken Daniel Whelan and Jack Donnelly's claim that the conflict over economic and social rights at the UN merely concerned their 'juridical character'.[80]

At the fifth session of the Third Committee held in the autumn of 1950, Poland, Ukraine, the Soviet Union, Yugoslavia, and several Latin American countries lamented the absence of economic and social rights in the draft Covenant in strongly worded statements.[81] The Belgian delegate mounted a defence of the 'colonial clause'.[82] Eleanor Roosevelt, keenly aware of the growing domestic opposition toward a legally binding treaty, especially one that would contain economic and social rights, defended the 'federal clause'.[83] In the event, the General

76 UNCHR, Fifth Session, Summary Record of One Hundred and Thirty-First Meeting (27 June 1949) UN Doc E/CN.4/SR.131, at p 5.

77 Humphrey, 'Human Rights and the United Nations' (n 30) 149.

78 UNGAOR, Fifth Session, Third Committee, 288th Meeting (18 October 1950) UN Doc A/C.3/SR 288, para 9.

79 UNGAOR, Fifth Session, Third Committee, 289th Meeting (19 October 1950) UN Doc A/C.3/SR 289, paras 15–16.

80 Daniel J. Whelan and Jack Donnelley, "The West, Economic and Social Rights, and the Global Human Rights Regime: Setting the Record Straight" (2007) 29(4) *Human Rights Quarterly* 908.

81 UNGAOR, Fifth Session, Third Committee, 290th Meeting (20 October 1950) UN Doc A/C.3/SR 290. See also Pechota (n 17) 41–42.

82 UNGAOR, Fifth Session, Third Committee, 290nd Meeting (25 October 1950) UN Doc A/C.3/SR 292.

83 Ibid, paras 10-14 In the US, the opposition to a binding human rights treaty, and to the inclusion of economic and social rights, was led initially by the president of the American Bar Association Frank Holman, and later by the Republican Senator John Bricker. Bricker introduced an amendment (known as the Bricker Amendment), which would have restricted the capacity of the president to sign international treaties without the approval of the Senate.

Assembly decided to instruct the Economic and Social Council to request the Commission on Human Rights to remove the 'colonial clause', to 'ensure the maximum extension of the Covenant to the constituent units of the federal States', and to incorporate 'in the draft Covenant a clear expression of economic, social, and cultural rights in a manner which relates them to the civic and political freedoms proclaimed by the Covenant'.[84] But that is not the end of the story.

At the seventh session of the Human Rights Commission (April–May 1951), despite clear instructions from the General Assembly to the contrary, several Western countries, as well as India, re-opened the question as to whether it was desirable to include economic, social, and cultural rights in the Covenant.[85] The delegates from these countries framed their misgivings in terms of difficulties that might be encountered in proposing implementation measures for the two categories of rights. In view of the discussions, the Economic and Social Council, by resolution 384 (XIII) of 29 August 1951 – sponsored by the United States, the UK, Belgium, and Uruguay – decided to 'invite the General Assembly to reconsider its decision in Resolution 421 E (V) to include in one covenant articles on economic, social, and cultural rights, together with articles on civil and political rights'.[86] As Roger Normand and Sarah Zaidi have explained, the resolution passed as a result 'of aggressive Anglo-American lobbying'.[87]

However, the ECOSOC resolution came up against stiff resistance in the Third Committee at the General Assembly's sixth session (November 1951–February 1952). Chile, Egypt, Pakistan, and Yugoslavia sponsored a resolution urging the General Assembly to reaffirm its earlier decision regarding a single covenant.[88] The resolution was approved by 29 votes in favour, 21 against, and six abstentions. At this stage, Charles Malik, then chair of the Third Committee – who himself harboured doubts about the desirability of a unified Covenant –[89] used his authority to allow the United States, Lebanon, India, and Belgium to

See Holman (n 24); Frank Holman, 'International Proposals Affecting So-Called Human Rights' (1949) 14 *Law and Contemporary Problems* 479; Elizabeth Borgwardt, *A New Deal for the World: America's Vision for Human Rights* (The Belkamp Press of Harvard University Press 2005) 267–268.

84 UNGA Res 421, 'Draft International Covenant on Human Rights and Measures of Implementation: Future Work of the Commission on Human Rights' (4 December 1950) UN Doc A/RES/421.

85 UNCHR, Seventh Session, Summary Records of 204th to 209th Meeting (25 April 1951 to 3 May 1951) UN Doc E/CN.4/SR. 204–209.

86 UN ECOSOC Res 384 (III), Official Records of the Thirteenth Session (30 July–21 September 1951) UN Doc E/2152.

87 Normand and Zaidi (n 7) 206.

88 UNGA, Sixth Session, 'Report of the Third Committee' (3 February 1952) UN Doc A/2112. 'Draft Resolution to Include Economic, Social and Cultural Rights in the International Covenant on Human Rights', UN Doc A/C.3/L.182.

89 Malik had voiced opposition to the inclusion of an extended list of economic and social rights in the Universal Declaration since, in his view, 'some of them would be true in a socialistic form of society, others would not'. See UNCHR, Drafting Committee, First Session, Summary Record of the Ninth Meeting (3 July 1947) UN Doc E/CN.4/AC.1/SR.9, at p 10.

introduce an amendment which essentially nullified the original resolution by proposing a change to 'the operative paragraph to the effect that the Economic and Social Council be requested to ask the Commission on Human Rights to draft two covenants on human rights'.[90] Transmitted to the General Assembly without a further vote, the resolution, as amended, called for two separate covenants to be prepared and opened for signatures simultaneously. Finally, on 5 February 1952, with the General Assembly split in the middle – 29 votes in favour and 25 against – a resolution was passed requesting the 'Economic and Social Council to ask the Commission on Human Rights to draft two Covenants on Human Rights'.[91]

The Commission on Human Rights completed the two draft covenants in 1954.[92] With the General Assembly embroiled in bigger Cold War issues, enthusiasm for human rights tapered off. Dag Hammarskjöld, Secretary General of the United Nations from 1953 to 1961, is said to have instructed John Humphrey in 1955 that, 'There is a flying speed below which an airplane will not remain in the air. I want you to keep the [human rights] program at that speed and no greater'.[93] In a cruel irony, Hammarskjöld met his end in a plane crash in 1961. It would take another 12 years before the Third Committee finalised the two covenants and submitted them, along with an Optional Protocol to the Covenant on Civil and Political Rights.[94] In separate votes, the General Assembly adopted the International Covenant on Economic, Social and Cultural Rights ('ICESCR'), the International Covenant on Civil and Political Rights ('ICCPR'), and its Optional Protocol on 16 December 1966.[95] The instruments entered into force only on 3 January 1976.

One indication of the priority accorded to civil and political rights is the divergent standards of implementation written into the two Covenants. The rights contained in the ICCPR are immediately binding upon state parties under article 2 (1) of the Covenant. On the other hand, the corresponding provision in the ICESCR provides that economic and social rights are to be implemented progressively.[96] Further, the Optional Protocol to the ICCPR would allow individuals to

90 UNGA, Sixth Session, 'Report of the Third Committee' (3 February 1952) UN Doc A/2112, at p. 23. 'Joint amendments by Belgium, India, Lebanon and the United States of America', UN Doc. A/C.3/L.185/Rev.1. See also, Normand and Zaidi (n 7) 206.

91 UNGA Res 543 (VI) 'Preparation of Two Draft Covenants on Human Rights'.

92 UNCHR, 'Report of the Tenth Session' (23 February–16 April 1954) UN Doc E/2573.

93 A.J. Hobbins, 'Human Rights Inside the United Nations: The Humphrey Diaries, 1948–1959' (1991) IV *Fontanus* 143, 164.

94 UNGA, Twenty-First Session, Report of the Third Committee, 'Draft International Covenants on Human Rights' (13 December 1966) UN Doc A/6564.

95 International Covenant on Civil and Political Rights (adopted 16 December 1966, entered into force 23 March 1976) 999 UNTS 171; Optional Protocol to the International Covenant on Civil and Political Rights (adopted 19 December 1966) 999 UNTS 171; International Covenant on Economic, Social and Cultural Rights (adopted 16 December 1966, entered into force 23 March 1976) 993 United UNTS 3.

96 Sarah Joseph and Melissa Castan, *The International Covenant on Civil and Political Rights: Cases, Materials, and Commentary* (3rd edn, Oxford University Press 2013) 7.

submit 'communications' regarding violations of their Covenant rights by states that ratified the Protocol. It was not until 2008 that the UN adopted a similar protocol to the ICESCR, which came into force only in 2013.[97]

According to Theo van Boven, 'The interdependence and indivisibility of human rights [has] become a leading axiom in the international human rights discourse'.[98] Critics have charged, not without justification, that in reality 'civil and political rights have dominated international agenda while economic, social and cultural rights have been accorded second-class status'.[99] More importantly, for the purposes of our discussion, the 'axiom' of indivisibility continues to have limited import as regards the institution of punishment. Matters related to punishment and the administration of justice are mediated primarily by traditional civil and political rights within international human rights jurisprudence. The Human Rights Committee (the body tasked with the enforcement of the ICCPR) does not seem particularly concerned about whether penal policy satisfies basic standards of social justice. There is little attention paid to the background conditions of criminality or the economic and social impact of imprisonment on prisoners' families. Similarly, the Committee on Economic, Social and Cultural Rights, whilst engaged in matters related to social policy, does not interrogate how individuals failed by certain social institutions – education, healthcare, welfare agencies – get trapped in the penal dragnet.

The same tendency is commonly reflected in human rights scholarship. Commentaries on civil and political rights, and the discussions of criminal justice from a human rights perspective, remain disassociated from problems of social injustice.[100] Conversely, discussions on economic and social rights rarely reflect on how punitive penal policies may drive some individuals into a cycle of social marginalisation and criminal activity.[101] The point of the argument is not that a

97 Optional Protocol to the International Covenant on Economic, Social and Cultural Rights (adopted 5 March 2009, entered into force 5 May 2013) UN Doc A/RES/63/117.

98 Theo van Boven, 'Categories of Rights' in Daniel Moeckli, Sangeeta Shah and Sandesh Sivakumaran (eds), *International Human Rights Law* (2nd edn, Oxford University Press 2014) 143–156, 147.

99 Philip Alston, 'Putting Economic, Social and Cultural Rights Back on the Agenda of the United States' in William F Schultz (ed), *The Future of Human Rights: U.S. Policy for a New Era* (University of Pennsylvania Press 2008) 120–138, 120.

100 See, for example, Dominic McGoldrick, *The Human Rights Committee: Its Role in the Development of the International Covenant on Civil and Political Rights* (2nd edn, Clarendon Press 1994); Walter Kälin and Jörg Künzli, *The Law of International Human Rights Protection* (Oxford University Press 2009) 440–465; Tom Bingham, *The Rule of Law* (Penguin 2010); Javaid Rehman, *International Human Rights Law* (2nd edn, Pearson 2010) 84–139; Yogesh Tyagi, *The UN Human Rights Committee: Practice and Procedure* (Cambridge University Press 2011); Ilias Bantekas and Lutz Oette, *International Human Rights Law and Practice* (Cambridge University Press 2013) 313–365.

101 See, for example, Mathew CR Craven, *The International Covenant on Economic, Social and Cultural Rights: A Perspective on Its Development* (Oxford University Press 1998); Mary Dowell-Jones, *Contextualising the International Covenant on Economic, Social and Cultural Rights. Assessing the Economic Deficit* (Martinus Nijhoff 2004); Kälin and Künzli (n 100) 420–439; Rehman, (n 100) 140–180; Marco Odello and Francesco Seatzu,

unified Covenant would necessarily have led to an expansive vision of justice. However, the division of human rights into separate categories squared with the split between criminal justice and social justice as the modern human rights movement took off the ground in the 1970s, coinciding with the resurgence of retributivist philosophy. Even if it is assumed, *arguendo*, that the fateful decision to draft separate covenants was driven by procedural considerations, the fact remains that the bifurcation was not particularly helpful in bridging the criminal justice-social justice divide. The split also adds to the legitimacy of retributivism; with criminal justice marooned from the wider social context, it is that much easier to 'locate the source of harm in wicked individuals' rather than in larger environmental influences, social structures, and public policies.[102]

The rise and rise of human rights

As mentioned in Chapter 4, the 'long seventies' provided an opening for the emergence of a human rights movement with the loss of faith in nationalist, post-colonial and socialist utopias, and the horrors of apartheid and the Vietnam war. Feminist, sexuality, and identity movements rose to prominence, articulating their demands in the language of human rights. Amnesty International, set up in 1961 to secure the release of prisoners of conscience, launched a campaign against torture in 1971 and won global recognition with the award of the Nobel Peace Prize in 1977.[103] Helsinki Watch, founded in 1978 to monitor the compliance of the 1975 Helsinki Accords in the Soviet Union and Eastern Europe, gave birth to other regional 'watch committees' in Africa, Asia, and the Middle East. In 1988, the committees merged to form Human Right Watch. Today, Amnesty International and Human Rights Watch are considered 'recognized authorities, if not uncontroversial ones, on the state of human rights protection in countries around the world'.[104]

Although human rights standards-setting within the UN would gather impetus only after the end of the Cold War, the long seventies saw the adoption of two core international human rights instruments: The Convention on the

---

The UN Committee on Economic, Social and Cultural Rights: The Law, Process, and Practice (Routledge 2013); Ben Saul, David Kinley, and Jaqueline Mowbray, *The International Covenant on Economic, Social and Cultural Rights: Commentary, Cases, and Material* (Oxford University Press 2014).

102 Dianne Otto, 'Decoding Crisis in International Law: A Queer Feminist Perspective' in Barbara Stark (ed), *International Law and Its Discontents: Confronting Crises* (Cambridge University Press 2015) 115–136, 121.

103 Aryeh Neier, *The International Human Rights Movement: A History* (Princeton University Press 2012) 186–203; Korey (n 2) 159–180.

104 Kerri Woods, *Human Rights* (Palgrave Macmillan 2014) 40. See also, Mahoney (n 17) 62–63. On the global reach and influence of Amnesty International and Human Rights Watch, see A. Trevor Thrall, Dominik Stecula, and Diana Sweet, 'May We Have Your Attention Please? Human-Rights NGOs and the Problem of Global Communication' (2014) 19(2) *The International Journal of Press/Politics* 135.

Elimination of All Forms of Discrimination against Women 1979, and the Convention against Torture and Other Cruel, Inhuman or Degrading Treatment or Punishment 1984. Whilst the seventies had registered the birth of the modern human rights movement, the 1990s saw its consolidation and globalisation. Fall of the Berlin Wall in 1989 and the break-up of the USSR in 1991 paved the way for the rise of human rights as the ideology 'after the end' and the 'defeat of ideologies'.[105] Ethnic tensions burst into open in the Balkans and Africa, catapulting the UN into the complicated business of peace-keeping and humanitarian interventions.[106] Concomitantly, there emerged a rule-of-law industry, bankrolled by bilateral donors and multilateral financial institutions, offering managerial solutions divorced from social change agenda, and exporting American-style criminal justice to the so-called transitional and post-conflict societies.[107]

In terms of the normative and institutional architecture of human rights, a watershed moment came in the mid-1990s. The UN Conference held in Vienna in June 1993 renewed the calls for international co-operation in the field of human rights. Representatives from 171 states adopted the Vienna Declaration and Platform for Action, famously reaffirming the 'indivisibility' and 'interdependence' of human rights.[108] In December that year, the General Assembly agreed to establish the Office of the High Commissioner for Human Rights, following up on the suggestion made in the Vienna Declaration. The year 1993 also saw the revival of the Nuremburg spirit with the setting up of an international tribunal to try those responsible for war crimes in the former Yugoslavia. That was followed a year later by the formation of the International Criminal Tribunal for Rwanda. With Amnesty International and Human Rights Watch campaigning energetically for a permanent tribunal, the Rome Statute of the International Criminal Court was adopted in 1998.[109] To Geoffrey Robertson, the rise of international criminal tribunals and humanitarian interventions in the late 1990s marked the third pivotal moment (after the Enlightenment and the Holocaust) in the history of human rights.[110] Just as the experience of the Second World War had left an imprint on the modern human rights project, subsequent historical and political circumstances impinged on its normative structure and priorities, as will be shown in the next chapter.

105 Costas Douzinas, 'The End(s) of Human Rights' (2002) 26 *Melbourne University Law Review* 445, 446.

106 See David Chandler, *From Kosovo to Kabul: Human Rights and International Intervention* (Pluto Press 2002).

107 Karen Engle, 'A Genealogy of the Criminal Turn in Human Rights' in Engle, Zinaida Miller and DM Davis (eds), *Anti-Impunity and the Human Rights Agenda* (Cambridge University Press 2016) 15–67, 47; Allegra M McLeod, 'Exporting U.S. Criminal Justice' (2010) 29 *Yale Law & Policy Review* 83.

108 UNGA, *Vienna Declaration and Programme of Action* (12 July 1993) UN Doc A/CONF.157/23.

109 Korey (n 2) 521–546.

110 Geoffrey Robertson QC, *Crimes Against Humanity: The Struggle for Global Justice* (4th edn, Penguin 2012) xii–xiii.

7 The evolution and interpretation of human rights norms and penal aims

A new standard of civilisation?

Civilization must, unfortunately, have its victims.

Lord Cromer[1]

As discussed at the beginning of this book, human rights scholars typically approach criminal punishment narrowly, focusing on the due process and fair trial guarantees, and the prohibition of ill-treatment in custody. The orthodox scholarship is not very helpful when it comes to telling us what states can justifiably punish, how much, and why. This chapter makes an attempt to cast fresh light on the idea of punishment as it features in the human rights credo. The analysis presented here draws on a cross-section of international human rights discourse, including the second cycle of the Universal Periodic Review (UPR):[2] the case law, General Comments, and concluding observations of the Human Rights Committee on periodic reports submitted by state parties:[3] the concluding observations of the Committee on Economic, Social and Cultural Rights ('CESCR Committee'):[4] and the pronouncements of Amnesty International and

1 Lord E.B. Cromer, 'The Government of Subject Races' in *Political and Literary Essays, 1908–1913* (Palgrave Macmillan 1913) 44.
2 The advantage in analysing the second cycle (2012–2017) is that the documentation frequently refers to recommendations given to and accepted by member states during the first cycle (2007–2012). That allows one to capture a relatively longer-term view of underlying normative proprieties and concerns.
3 The analysis is based on 376 concluding observations adopted by the Human Rights Committee in respect of 116 countries, covering the period 1987 to 2016. Some of the earlier concluding observations were omitted because they were based on a review of a limited number of Covenant rights. Additionally, I had to leave out the concluding observations which were either not available on the UN Treaty Monitoring database or were available in languages other than English.
4 The analysis captures a total of 285 concluding observations adopted by the CESCR Committee in respect of 138 countries covering the period 1993 to 2016. The CESCR Committee began considering periodic reports in 1987. The earlier documentation had to be omitted because it took the form of summary records or involved a dialogue with states around selected Covenant rights, making a comparison with later reports difficult.

Human Rights Watch, as embodied in their submissions to the UPR and their annual global human rights reports.[5]

The primary materials, although anchored in international human rights law, are diverse enough to allow comparative analysis between NGOs and independent human rights bodies on the one hand, and state delegates participating in the UPR on the other. Whereas the Human Rights Committee and the CESCR Committee are concerned about obligations arising out of each of the two covenants, the normative focus is broader with the UPR. Under the mechanism, the human rights record of each UN member state is reviewed in respect of the Charter of the United Nations, the UDHR, specific instruments to which the state is party, voluntary pledges and commitments made by the state, and international humanitarian law.[6] Moreover, whereas the treaty monitoring bodies can adopt concluding resolutions and consider 'individual communications' only in respect of the states that have ratified the Covenant and the Optional Protocol respectively, the UPR covers human rights situations in all of the 193 UN member states.

The UPR is based on a national report submitted by the state concerned, a compilation of relevant information from the UN mechanisms, and a summary of information provided by civil society, officially dubbed the 'Summary of Stakeholders' Submissions'. The UN information and the stakeholders' submissions are compiled and summarised by the Office of the High Commissioner on Human Rights. The interactive dialogue with each member state results in a 'Working Group Report', including recommendations made to the state party to improve the human rights situation on the ground. The state party will accept, reject, or 'note' (another word for reject in the UPR-speak) the recommendations.[7] The present analysis draws on the Working Groups Reports and Summaries of Stakeholders' Submissions for all 193 countries from the second cycle (2012–2017). Although the analysis does not encompass regional enforcement mechanisms, it does take into account some relevant case law of the European Court of Human Rights (ECtHR) since the court is known to be a trail-blazer in setting human rights benchmarks.[8]

To Michael Ignatieff, the diffusion of 'human rights instruments' counts as progress 'even if there remains an unconscionable gap between the instruments and the actual practices of states charged to comply with them'.[9] As we will find out, the problem is not merely of the 'enforcement gap' when it comes to the link between human rights and punishment. The normative structure of international

5 The analysis draws on the Summaries of Stakeholders' Submissions for all 193 UN member states from the UPR second cycle, and all annual reports published by Amnesty International (1961–2017), and by Human Rights Watch (1990–2017).

6 Human Rights Council, 'Institution-building of the United Nations Human Rights Council', resolution adopted on 18 June 2007. UN Doc A/HRC/RES/5/1.

7 For a more detailed summary of the process, see Bertrand G. Ramcharan, *The UN Human Rights Council* (Routledge 2011) 46–65.

8 On the European court's jurisprudence, see William Schabas, *The European Convention on Human Rights: A Commentary* (Oxford University Press 2015).

9 Michael Ignatieff, *Human Rights as Politics and Idolatry* (Princeton University Press 2001) 4.

instruments as well as ideological premises underpinning the interpretation of the instruments are equally important.

The remainder of the chapter proceeds as follows: In the first section below, I challenge the narrative of progressive humanisation from the perspective of social rehabilitation of offenders, describing how the only provision in the ICCPR on the topic got diluted during the drafting process and was later interpreted by the Human Rights Committee in an unduly restrictive manner. The next subhead shifts attention to the paradoxical role of the human rights as it seeks to simultaneously counter the punitive reach of the law in some areas and expand its application in others. The focus on criminalisation and tougher penalties, it is argued, is primarily indexed to violations of political freedoms and identity-based persecution, reflecting the privileged status of civil and political rights within international human rights discourse. Finally, we turn to the idea of rehabilitation as a sentencing aim and see how it could furnish additional grounds for challenging two of the most extreme manifestations of the coercive state power, namely the death penalty and whole-life sentences. The closing section also probes certain unanswered questions with respect to classical penological justifications and explains how human rights discourse is wedded to retributive justice and the fetish of the abstract individual.

The rehabilitative ideal and the tale of moral progress

Paulo Pinto de Albuquerque, the Portuguese judge at the ECtHR since 2011, is one of those individual voices who frequently enrich international jurisprudence by exposing ambiguities in majority judgments through well-thought-out dissenting notes and separate opinions.[10] Judge Pinto de Albuquerque was presented with one such opportunity to break with the majority position as the Grand Chamber handed down its judgment in the case of *Khamtokhu v Russia* on 24 January 2017.[11] At issue was the provision in the Russian Criminal Code which provided for life imprisonment for certain crimes whilst prohibiting the imposition of that punishment on women, persons below 18 years, and those over 65.[12] The complainants, who were both aged between 18 and 65 years and serving life sentences, claimed that in excluding them from the prohibition of life imprisonment, the Russian Criminal Code violated Article 14 of the European Convention (right not to be discriminated against) in conjunction with article 5 (right to liberty and security). The Russian government defended the differential treatment as reasonable and proportionate to certain legitimate aims. As regards juveniles and individuals aged 65 or over, the government argued that

10 William Schabas, 'Introduction' in Schabas (ed), *Research Handbook on International Courts and Tribunals* (Edward Elgar Publishing 2017) 1–38, 27.

11 *Khamtokhu and Aksenchik v Russia* (Apps 60367/08 and 961/11) ECHR [Grand Chamber] 24 January 2017.

12 Art 57, Criminal Code of the Russian Federation No. 63-FZ of June 13, 1996 (as amended up to Federal Law No. 120-FZ of June 7, 2017).

they constituted vulnerable social groups 'who had an underdeveloped or weakened capacity to understand the implications of their conduct'.[13] The exemption given to women from life imprisonment was defended in light of their 'special' role in society, particularly their 'reproductive function'.[14]

In assessing the merits of the application, the Grand Chamber reiterated its position on the compatibility of life sentences with the European Convention first articulated clearly in the 2012 case, *Vinter v the United Kingdom*.[15] In *Vinter*, the Grand Chamber had ruled that to comply with the European Convention's prohibition of cruel, inhuman, or degrading punishment or treatment (Article 3), a life sentence had to be reducible:

> [I]n the sense of a review which allows the domestic authorities to consider whether any changes in the life prisoner are so significant, and such progress towards rehabilitation has been made in the course of the sentence, as to mean that continued detention can no longer be justified on legitimate penological grounds.[16]

The implication of that ruling, the Grand Chamber reiterated in *Khamtokhu*, was that 'life imprisonment as a form of punishment for particularly serious offences remains compatible with the Convention' as long as it is *de facto* and *de jure* reducible.[17] In the instant case, that requirement was met since the Russian Criminal Code provided the complainants the prospect of release on parole after serving 25 years in prison. The imposition of life sentences had followed a consideration of specific facts of the complainants' cases by the Russian trial court and, thus, did not appear unreasonable considering the legitimate 'penological objectives of the protection of society and general and individual deterrence'.[18] In the absence of a consensus at the European and international level regarding life imprisonment, the Grand Chamber held that the Russian authorities had not overstepped their 'margin of appreciation'.[19] Regarding the prohibition of life imprisonment on certain groups, the majority had no difficulty accepting as legitimate the aim put forward by the government, namely the promotion of 'the principles of justice and humanity', taking into account the age and physiological characteristics of certain categories of offenders – juveniles, women, and those over 65 years of age. There had thus been no violation of Article 14 read together with Article 5.[20]

In his thoughtful dissent, Pinto de Albuquerque regretted the fact that the majority had not closely examined the discrimination issues raised by the case and

13 *Khamtokhu* (n 11) 24 January 2017, para 47.
14 Ibid.
15 *Vinter and Others v UK* (Apps 66069/09, 130/10, 3896/10) 9 July 2013, paras 119–122.
16 Ibid para 119. Reiterated in *Reid v United Kingdom* (App. 57592/08) 17 January 2017.
17 *Khamtokhu* (n 11) para 72.
18 Ibid para 75.
19 Ibid paras 78, 85, 86.
20 Ibid para 87.

had failed to 'seize the opportunity it was given to develop the protection offered by the Convention by making a further decisive step towards the abolition of life imprisonment'.[21] The dissent brought to light various ambiguities in the majority opinion as to the lines drawn between men and women on the one hand, and between young and elderly men on the other, for the purposes of imposing life imprisonment. The issue is relatively straightforward in legal terms when it comes to exempting children from that punishment. The Convention on the Rights of the Child, the most widely ratified of all human rights conventions, prohibits the death sentence and 'life imprisonment without the possibility of release' imposed on children.[22] Taking into account various 'soft law' instruments which guarantee special protection for women and the elderly, Pinto de Albuquerque correctly pointed out that there was no specific instrument which indicated the prohibition of life imprisonment on these groups.[23] Further, in his opinion, the acceptance by the majority of the claim that exempting women from life sentences was justified on the basis of their 'reproductive function' amounted to perpetuating a stereotypical image of women as victims in need of protection.[24]

The way out of the complexities engendered by the exclusion of certain groups from life sentences, on Pinto de Albuquerque's account, was to abolish it altogether. Given the absolute nature of the Article 3 prohibition of cruel, inhuman, or degrading punishment, he could not concur with the majority view that the provision of the life sentence in the Russian law was compatible with the Convention.[25] The majority position to the effect that life imprisonment as 'applied in Europe today offers the prospect of early release on parole', in his opinion, actually swung the balance in favour of abolition. In calling for a categorical rule against life imprisonment, Pinto de Albuquerque was not proposing something new. He had made this point forcefully as far back as 2005 in his partly dissenting opinion in the case of *Öcalan v Turkey (No 2)*, where the incarcerated Kurdish-separatist leader Abdullah Öcalan complained that the irreducible nature of life imprisonment imposed on him, and the conditions of his detention, violated Article 3 of the Convention.[26]

21 Ibid, Dissenting Opinion of Judge Pinto de Albuquerque, para 1.
22 Art 37(a) Convention on the Rights of the Child (adopted 20 November 1989, entered into force 2 September 1990) 1577 UNTS 3.
23 *Khamtokhu* (n 11) Dissenting Opinion of Judge Pinto de Albuquerque, paras 16–17.
24 Ibid paras 8, 11.
25 Ibid para 3.
26 *Öcalan v. Turkey* (application no. 46221/99) ECHR [Grand Chamber] 12 May 2005, Partly Dissenting Opinion of Judge Pinto de Albuquerque. Öcalan also complained of various other violations, including unlawful deprivation of liberty (art 5) and denial of a fair trial (art 6). Given the failure of the Turkish authorities to allow him to promptly challenge his detention before a court and to be tried by an independent tribunal, the majority found the state party to have violated Articles 5 and 6. Öcalan had initially been sentenced to death. The sentence was commuted to aggravated life imprisonment after the Turkish Parliament abolished the death penalty in peacetime in 2002. Given that the Turkish law allowed Öcalan no real prospect of a review or parole, the Grand Chamber found the life sentence imposed on him as incompatible with Article 3 prohibition of cruel and inhuman

In *Khamtokhu*, Pinto de Albuquerque recalled the Court's finding in *Vinter* that life imprisonment destroyed any prospect of 'social reintegration', thus excluding 'outright one of the fundamental purposes of criminal sentencing and retains only retribution and general prevention'.[27] Shifting the focus on the penological purpose of rehabilitation helps underscore the futility of making distinctions between men and women, and the young and old in the context of life imprisonment. If rehabilitation holds as a valid penal aim, it is not tenable to draw divisions on the grounds of gender and age. It would not be plausible to claim that female offenders deserve to be reintegrated into the society any more than their male counterparts. The same would apply to men in different age cohorts. The majority opinion in the present case, Pinto de Albuquerque took the view, ran counter to the Court's recognition in *Vinter* that 'there is also now clear support in European and international law for the principle that all prisoners, including those serving life sentences, be offered the possibility of rehabilitation and the prospect of release'.[28] Arguing that there was no evidence before the court that life imprisonment led to a reduction in serious crimes any more than prison terms, he saw no justification for retaining life imprisonment in the name of 'general prevention' either.[29] An 'evolutive and pro persona interpretation of the Convention', in his opinion required that:

> The Grand Chamber should have pursued the development set in motion in the case of Vinter, in which it acknowledged that 'whole life' sentences were incompatible with Article 3 of the Convention, and extended its reasoning to the very principle of life imprisonment. Such an interpretation of Article 3, in keeping with the international trend in favour of abolition of this type of punishment would have fully squared with the principles of an evolutive and pro persona interpretation of the Convention.[30]

It has to be said, with due respect, that there is scant evidence to back the claim that there is an 'international trend' in favour of the abolition of life imprisonment and towards offering the possibility of rehabilitation to all prisoners.[31] Despite Pinto de Albuquerque's frustrated hopes in *Khamtokhu*, Europe may indeed be on the brink of outlawing whole-life sentences in light of its evolving

---

punishment (see paras 193–207). The majority, however, reiterated that the imposition of a life sentence on an adult was not in itself prohibited by Article 3, the part of the ruling which Judge Pinto de Albuquerque dissented from.

27 *Khamtokhu* (n 11) para 27. See also *Vinter* (n 15) para 115.

28 *Khamtokhu* (n 11) *Dissenting Opinion of Judge Pinto de Albuquerque, para 32. See also Vinter* (n 15) para 114.

29 *Khamtokhu* (n 11), Dissenting Opinion of Judge Pinto de Albuquerque, para 29.

30 Ibid para 38. See also Öcalan (n 26), Partly Dissenting Opinion of Judge Pinto De Albuquerque, para 5.

31 *Khamtokhu* (n 11) Dissenting Opinion of Judge Pinto de Albuquerque, para 32; Öcalan (n 26) Partly Dissenting Opinion of Judge Pinto de Albuquerque, para 5. For a background, see Dirk van Zyl Smit, 'Outlawing Irreducible Life Sentences: Europe on the Brink?' (2010–2011) 23(1) *Federal Sentencing Reporter* 39.

jurisprudence on the subject. However, as we shall see, international human rights law, whilst disfavouring life imprisonment for children, remains ambiguous, at best, when it comes to imposing the penalty on adults. One reason for this, as I have already hinted, is the tendency within human rights discourse to associate cruelty with corporal punishment, whilst failing to fully appreciate the suffering that attends long years in custody.[32] More importantly, for the purposes of the present study, the idea of social reintegration remains subsumed to retribution, deterrence, incapacitation, and other unstated goals of criminal justice. That has implications for both life imprisonment without parole and the death penalty inasmuch as these forms of punishment negate the possibility of rehabilitation. In some contemporary case law, as well as academic commentaries and NGO materials, the rehabilitative ideal gets restricted to juveniles.[33] It is here that the tale of moral progress implicit in Judge Pinto de Albuquerque's dissenting note turns somewhat problematic. If anything, penal policy, from an international and comparative perspective, has registered a regression of the ideal of social reintegration rather than a steady evolution. To elaborate this, we need to return to the drafting of the 'International Bill of Human Rights'.

The Travaux Préparatoires of the ICCPR Article 10 (3)

On 7 June 1947, as the Drafting Committee of the Commission of Human Rights met for the first time, John Humphrey was quizzed by Colonel Hudgson, the Australian member on the Commission, 'regarding the principles adopted and the philosophy behind the draft outline submitted by the Secretariat'.[34] In response, Humphrey explained that the Documented Outline[35]:

> [C]ontained no statement about the philosophy on which the Secretariat document was based because this document had not been based on any philosophy. The Secretariat . . . had merely prepared an outline to serve as a basis for the discussion of the Drafting Committee. In doing so it had attempted to include *all of the rights* mentioned in various national Constitutions and in various suggestions for an International Bill of Human Rights.[36]

32 Talal Asad, 'On Torture, or Cruel, Inhuman and Degrading Treatment' in Richard A. Wilson (ed), *Human Rights, Culture & Context: Anthropological Perspectives* (Pluto Press 1997) 111–133.

33 See, for example, *Graham v Florida* 130 S Ct 2011, 2030 (2010), *and Miller v Alabama* 567 US 460, 132 S Ct 2455 (2012). See the commentary in Nadia Bernaz, 'Life Imprisonment and the Prohibition of Inhuman Punishments in International Human Rights Law: Moving the Agenda Forward' (2013) 35 *Human Rights Quarterly* 470. A seminal contribution to the topic is to be found in Dirk Van Zyl Smit, *Taking Life Imprisonment Seriously in National and International Law* (Kluwer Law International 2002).

34 UNCHR, Drafting Committee, First Session, Summary Record of the First Meeting (10 June 1947) UN Doc E/CN.4/AC.1/SR.1, at p 5.

35 UN Doc E/CN.4/AC.1/3/Add.1.

36 UN Doc E/CN.4/AC.1/SR.1, at p.5 (emphasis added).

Sure enough, the Secretariat had done a painstaking job of synthesising a range of fundamental rights guaranteed by national constitutions of over 50 countries representing diverse legal and political systems. However, there is no evidence that in preparing the 'Documented Outline', the Secretariat had consulted the Standard Minimum Rules for the Treatment of Prisoners as they stood then, having been drafted by the International Penal and Penitentiary Commission, and recommended to governments by the Assembly of the League of Nations in September 1934.[37] Nor was there any reference to the Howard League's 'International Charter for Prisoners' in the Secretariat outline. Of the national constitutions consulted by the Secretariat, at least three – all from Latin America, a region known to have been under the influence of nineteenth-century Italian positivist criminology – specifically mentioned offender rehabilitation or reintegration. The Constitution of Nicaragua declared that 'prisons are established for security and social defence', and that, 'the prevention of crime, the re-education of the convict, and his preparation for work outside will be undertaken in them'.[38] According to the Constitution of Panama, 'jails are places of security and regeneration' and 'all severity that is not necessary for express purposes is prohibited in them'.[39] The Constitution of Uruguay framed the principle more broadly, providing that, 'Penal institutions shall in no case be permitted to inflict humiliating punishments, but shall exist only for the security of the accused and condemned persons, pursuing their re-education, rehabilitation for work, and prevention of crime'.[40]

The provisions cited above are notable for a naïve and paternalistic belief in the potential of the prison. However, at the same time, the said provisions also disavow retributivist philosophy. The decision by the Secretariat not to include an article along these lines in the draft 'Bill of Human Rights' might well have been prompted by the need to focus on the lowest common denominator. In principle, there was nothing that stopped the Secretariat from incorporating an ideal that, at the time, featured widely in penal codes.[41] The Secretariat also chose not to include in its draft a prohibition of life imprisonment, which featured in the constitutions of El Salvador, Honduras, Nicaragua, and Portugal.[42] Further, the constitutions of at least five countries – Colombia, Ecuador, Honduras, Panama,

37 Standard Minimum Rules for the Treatment of Prisoners, League of Nations OJ, Spec. Supp. 123, (1934).

38 UN Doc E/CN.4/AC/1/3/Add.1, at p 22 (art 26, Constitution of Nicaragua).

39 Ibid, at p 23.

40 Ibid, at p 24.

41 Humphrey was probably not much of a fan of positivist criminology. A possible indication of this could be read into his decision in 1948 to turn down the suggestion that he take over the functions of the Social Defence Section as head of the United Nations Human Rights Division. See Roger S. Clark, *The United Nations Crime Prevention, and Criminal Justice Program: Formulations of Standards and Efforts at their Implementation* (University of Pennsylvania Press 1994) 13.

42 UN Doc E/CN.4/AC/1/3/Add.1, at pp. 21–23.

and Nicaragua – contained an absolute prohibition of the death penalty.[43] The Argentine Republic, the Dominican Republic, and El Salvador allowed the death penalty only as an exception in times of war.[44] Despite that, in the Secretariat's draft, the article dealing with the right to life adopted a fairly permissible attitude toward capital punishment, providing that the right to life 'can be denied only to persons who have been convicted under general law of some crime against society to which the death penalty is attached'.[45]

The Commission decided to drop a reference to the death penalty as an exception to the right to life in the UDHR.[46] But it did resurface in Article 6 of the ICCPR, albeit with safeguards and limitations: Sentence of death, according to Article 6 of the Covenant, may be imposed only for 'the most serious crimes'[47]; it may not be imposed on persons below 18 years of age, and may not be carried out on pregnant women[48]; and 'anyone sentenced to death shall have the right to seek pardon or commutation of the sentence'.[49] A proposal by Uruguay calling for the abolition of the death penalty was rejected.[50] However, as a compromise between the abolitionists and retentionists, para 6 provided that: 'Nothing in this article shall be invoked to delay or to prevent the abolition of capital punishment'.[51]

Since the late 1980s, many nations, mostly in Africa and the former USSR, have moved toward the abolition of capital punishment.[52] The Second Optional Protocol to the ICCPR adopted in 1989 obligates the ratifying states to abolish the death penalty within their jurisdictions.[53] The Council of Europe first adopted Optional Protocol 6 to the European Convention aimed at the abolition of the death penalty in peace time,[54] and then Protocol 13, concerning the abolition of the death penalty in all circumstances.[55] In a 2010 case, concerning the transfer to Iraqi authorities of two Iraqi nationals accused of killing British

43 UN Doc E/CN.4/AC/1/3/Add.1, at pp. 15–19.
44 Ibid.
45 UN Doc E/CN.4/AC/1/3/Add.1, at p 15 (rt 3).
46 William Schabas, *The Abolition of the Death Penalty in International Law* (3rd edn, Cambridge University Press 2002) 34–39.
47 International Covenant on Civil and Political Rights (adopted 16 December 1966, entered into force 23 March 1976) 999 UNTS 171 (art 6, para 2).
48 Art 6(5).
49 *International Covenant on Civil and Political Rights,* art 6, para. 4.
50 UNGAOR, Ninth Session, Third Committee, 573rd Meeting (3 November 1954) UN Doc A/C.3/SR.573, para 19.
51 Art 6, para 6. See also, Roger Hood and Carolyn Hoyle, *Death Penalty: A Worldwide Perspective* (5th edn, Oxford University Press 2015) 2015.
52 Between December 1988 and December 2014, the number of countries 'that were completely abolitionist had increased from 35 to 99'. Hood and Hoyle (n 51) 16.
53 UNGA, *Second Optional Protocol to the International Covenant on Civil and Political Rights, Aiming at the Abolition of the Death Penalty* (15 December 1989) UN Doc A/RES/44/128.
54 Council of Europe, *Protocol 6 to the European Convention for the Protection of Human Rights and Fundamental Freedoms concerning the Abolition of Death Penalty,* 28 April 1983, ETS 114.
55 Council of Europe, *Protocol 13 to the European Convention on Human Rights and Fundamental Freedoms on the Abolition of the Death Penalty in All Circumstances,* 3 May 2002, ETS 187.

soldiers, the court held that the death penalty now comprised a violation of the prohibition of 'inhuman or degrading treatment or punishment' in light of the emerging consensus against the penalty among the Council of Europe member states.[56] Advances made elsewhere in limiting the scope of the death penalty represent a crowning achievement of the human rights movement. However, some of the countries which continue to retain the death penalty *de facto* and *de jure* – for example, Bangladesh, Indonesia, China, India, Pakistan, and the United States – make up close to half the global population. To measure progress only in terms of the number of countries which have abolished the death penalty can thus be misleading. Although the number of executions within the shrinking pool of retentionist countries has also declined,[57] at least over 3 billion people in the world continue to live under the shadow of the ultimate punishment. Legal scholars and philosophers have engaged with capital punishment in great depth. It is not my intention to recapitulate the vast amount of excellent research that exists on the topic.[58] However, the relationship of the death penalty (and life imprisonment) with rehabilitation as a sentencing purpose has received little scholarly attention, so it will be examined more closely in the final section below.

For now, let us pick up on the drafting of foundational texts. On 10 June 1949, as the Commission on Human Rights held its fifth session (9 May – 10 June 1949), René Cassin proposed an additional article to be included in what was then the Draft International Covenant on Human Rights. The proposed article read as follows:

> All persons deprived of their liberty shall be treated with humanity,
> Accused persons shall be preserved from any corrupting influence.
> The penitentiary system shall comprise treatment directed to *the fullest possible extent* towards the reformation and social rehabilitation of prisoners.[59]

Over the next three years, the Commission debated and redrafted existing articles and wrestled with the question of whether to produce a single covenant or two separate ones. It returned to the article proposed by Cassin – and other additional articles – only during the ninth session (7 April – 30 May 1953) after

56 *Al-Saadoon and Mufdhi v the United Kingdom* (App no 61498/08) 2 March 2010.

57 Hood and Hoyle (n 51) 17.

58 See Tom Sorrel. *Moral Theory and Capital Punishment* (Basil Blackwell/Open University 1987); William Schabas, *The Death Penalty as Cruel Treatment and Torture: Capital Punishment Challenged in the World's Courts* (Northeastern University Press 1996); Peter Hodgkinson and William Schabas (eds), *Capital Punishment: Strategies for Abolition* (Cambridge University Press 2004); Schabas, '*The Abolition of the Death Penalty in International Law*' (n 46); *Andrew Hammel, Ending the Death Penalty: The European Experience in Global Perspective* (Palgrave Macmillan 2010); Roger Hood, 'Capital Punishment – A Global Perspective' (2011) 3(3) *Punishment and Society* 331.

59 UNCHR, Fifth Session, 'Draft International Covenant on Human Rights, Additional Article: France' (10 June 1949) UN Doc E/CN.4/309 (emphasis added).

the decision had been reached to bifurcate the Covenant. In proposing the article, Cassin might well have drawn inspiration from the provisions in the constitutions of Nicaragua, Panama, and Uruguay. Although there is no evidence that Cassin had engaged with the International Penitentiary Commission, the proposed article is reminiscent of the question put forward to the governments at the very first International Prison Congress held in London in 1872: '[Is] the reformation of the prisoners made the primary aim in the prisons of your country?'[60] When the proposed article came up for debate at the Commission on 4 May 1953, Cassin recalled that when he had submitted the draft article three years earlier, it had been 'favourably received by the International Group of Experts on the Prevention of Crime and Treatment of Offenders'.[61] Regarding the need for the penitentiary system to be directed towards the 'reformation and social rehabilitation of the offender', Cassin described it as a principle 'which was winning ever-increasing recognition among criminologists and jurists'.[62] Following an amendment proposed by the UK, Cassin suggested re-wording the first two paragraphs of the article for greater clarity.[63] No objections were raised to the paragraph dealing with 'reformation and social rehabilitation of offenders'.

One member of the Commission, Abdur Rahman from Pakistan, wanted Cassin to explain, 'How any sort of treatment could have the effect of reintegrating a prisoner in society'. 'Surely', Rahman observed, 'the decision on that point had to be taken by society itself'.[64] The question could have led to a debate around the responsibility of the state in providing assistance to 'liberated persons', a subject already addressed in the Standard Minimum Rules 1935.[65] Cassin's response was restrained though as he simply noted that 'the social rehabilitation of offenders posed some extremely complicated problems, in the solution of which a certain number of factors, such as the nature of the offence and the age of the offender, had to be taken into account'. He had, therefore, avoided putting in 'detailed measures of application in the article', confining it instead to 'a statement of principles'.[66] Several members then intervened with endorsements of the proposed article. The member from the USSR said that in 'his delegation's view the draft provision was wholly in accordance with the principles of penitentiary practice, which must always aim at restoring the individual to society'.[67] The Uruguayan

60 E.C. Wines, *Report on the International Penitentiary Congress of London, Held July 3–13, 1872* (Government Printing Office 1873) 14.

61 UNCHR, Ninth Session, Summary Record of the 371st Meeting (4 May 1953) UN Doc E/CN.4/SR.371, at p 8.

62 Ibid.

63 The revised version read as follows: 'All persons deprived of their liberty shall be treated with humanity'.

Accused persons shall be segregated from convicted persons and shall be subject to special treatment appropriate to their status as unconvicted persons'. UN Doc E/CN.4/SR.371, at p 9.

64 Ibid.

65 Standard Minimum Rules (n 37) Rules 54 and 55.

66 UN Doc E/CN.4/SR.371, at p 9.

67 Ibid at p 10.

member said he supported the proposed article, which was in keeping with Article 26 of the Uruguayan Constitution, 'especially inasmuch as it stressed the need for the social rehabilitation of prisoners'.[68] The article was adopted unanimously with no changes made to the part dealing with the purpose of the penitentiary.

Things took an interesting turn when Article 10 came up for discussion in the Third Committee of the General Assembly at its thirteenth session in 1958. In a memorandum, the Secretary General drew attention of the Committee to the Standard Minimum Rules as adopted by the First UN Congress on the Prevention of Crime and the Treatment of Offenders in August 1955, and approved by the Economic and Social Council in July 1957.[69] Since the Commission had finished its work on the Covenants by then, the Secretary General suggested that the Third Committee look into the relevance of the Rules to Article 10 in particular. Within the Third Committee, Greece argued that there was a need to refer specifically to the Minimum Rules in Article 10. However, the majority settled for including in the report of the Third Committee an indication of the discussion on the relationship between the provisions of Article 10 and the Rules. That decision was consistent with the policy of not inserting references to other instruments or treaties in the draft Covenants.[70] The rest of the Committee's discussion of Article 10 involved a great deal of hair-splitting over language. But the semantic issues were tied up with substantive matters.[71]

Ceylon and the Netherlands proposed amendments to para 2, which dealt with the separation of juveniles from adults, and the accused from the convicted.[72] Another amendment was put forward to rephrase para 3 as follows: 'The penitentiary system shall be *essentially* directed towards the reformation and social rehabilitation of prisons'.[73] The ensuing discussion suggests that the sponsors of the amendment did not mean to weaken the focus on 'reformation and social rehabilitation', and perhaps failed to anticipate the implications of replacing the phrase 'directed to the fullest possible extent' with 'essentially'. On second thought, the Tunisian delegate, Ms Farouk (one of the five sponsors of the amendment) said that in her view, the words 'to the fullest possible extent' in para 3 had a restrictive meaning. She wanted them to be replaced by the word 'increasingly',

68 Ibid.

69 UNGA Third Committee, Thirteenth Session, Agenda Item 32 (19 October 1958) UN Doc A/C.5/L.690; UN ECOSOC Res 663 CI (XX17) (31 July 1957).

70 UNGA, Thirteenth Session, 'Report of the Third Committee' (9 December 1958) UN Doc A/4045, at para 84. See also Sławomir Redo, 'United Nations Criminal Justice Norms and Standards and Customary Law' in M. Cherif Bassiouni (ed), *The Contributions of Specialised Institutes and Non-Governmental Organizations to the United Nations Criminal Justice Program* (Martinus Nijhoff 1995) 109–135, 111.

71 The Third Committee discussed Article 10 at its 867th to 869th and 880th and 883rd meetings.

72 See UN Doc A/C.3/L.691 and UN Doc A/C.3/L.69I/Rev.1.

73 The original amendment of Belgium, Cuba, France, Spain and Tunisia', UN Doc A/C.3/L.693.

which, while taking the realities of the situation into account, stressed the need for progress.[74]

At the next meeting, the representative of Spain – another sponsor of the amendment – suggested that the phrase 'to the fullest possible extent' was redundant, since in her country, 'The schools of thought according to which the purpose of detention was expiation or the protection of society were now obsolescent, and the only reason for detention was considered to be the rehabilitation of the offender'.[75] She also expressed dissatisfaction with the words 'to the fullest possible extent' as they had been rendered in French and Spanish ('*le plus possible*' and '*en todo lo posible*'). Similarly, the Cuban delegate expressed her dissatisfaction with the phrase '*en todo lo posible*' in the Spanish text, as it 'did not indicate that the primary aim of the treatment of convicted persons should be their reformation and social rehabilitation'.[76]

Mindful of the controversy generated by the proposed redrafting, Ms Farouk later explained that 'her objections to the words, '*le plus possible*', used in para 3, applied only to the French text'. The phrase, 'to the fullest possible extent', she said was 'obviously stronger and entirely satisfactory'.[77] Sir Samuel Hoare from the UK, whilst sympathetic to the idea of rehabilitation, disagreed with his Spanish counterpart, who in 'referring to the different theories which existed regarding punishment . . . had omitted the theory, which still had many defenders, that punishment should act as a deterrent'.[78] Sir Samuel, quite perceptively, noted an internal incoherence in the ICCPR directing attention to Article 8, 'under which hard labour was not be considered as forced or compulsory labour within the meaning of the article'.[79] The idea of deterrence, he took the view, 'was reflected in penal and penitentiary practice, and was countenanced by the draft Covenant'.[80] He did, however, favour retaining the phrase 'to the fullest possible extent', since 'it was intended to encourage penitentiary authorities to make the greatest effort possible to bring about the reformation and social rehabilitation of the prisoners under their care'.[81] The word 'essentially', Sir Samuel observed, was not at all satisfactory, and would affect the English text seriously.

It is also instructive to note that neither Sir Samuel nor any other delegate voiced support for the retributive function of the penitentiary. As the delegate

74 UNGAOR, Thirteenth Session, Third Committee, Summary Record of 861st Meeting (23 October 1958) UN Doc A/C.3/SR. 861, at para 23.

75 UNGAOR, Thirteenth Session, Third Committee, Summary Record of 868th Meeting (30 October 1958) UN Doc A/C.3/SR.868, at para 6. See also similar comments by Peru at para 25.

76 UNGAOR, Thirteenth Session, Third Committee, Summary Record of 869th Meeting (31 October 1958) UN Doc A/C.3/SR.869, at para 20.

77 Ibid at para 26.

78 UNGAOR, Thirteenth Session, Third Committee, Summary Record of 868th Meeting (30 October 1958) UN Doc A/C.3/SR.868, at para 21.

79 Ibid.

80 Ibid.

81 UN Doc A/C.3/SR.868, at para 22. See also UN Doc A/C.3/SR.881, at para 25.

from Greece saw it, 'People's attitude towards penitentiary treatment [had] evolved from the primitive *lex talionis*, through the doctrine of punishment as a deterrent, to the modern idea that the main object should be the reformation of prisoners'. At the 882nd meeting, Mr Thierry (who had by then replaced Cassin as the French representative on the Third Committee) moved a revised amendment to para 3, which read: 'The penitentiary system shall comprise treatment of prisoners the essential aim of which shall be their reformation and social rehabilitation'.[82] Elaborating the revised draft, Thierry explained that the 'purpose of the amendment was to ensure that the entire prison system, including buildings, discipline and the organization of work, should be directed towards the reformation and rehabilitation of the prisoner, not towards retribution'.[83] The delegate from Venezuela, whilst expressing his intention to vote for the amendment, remarked that 'he would have preferred the word ' "essential" to be omitted'.[84] The amendment was adopted by 48 votes to l, with 23 abstentions.

Summary records of the meetings clearly suggest that rephrasing of para 3 had been prompted by a linguistic confusion as it seemed difficult to render into French and Spanish the phrase 'to the fullest possible extent'. The Report of the Third Committee, however, seemed to cast the debate in more polarised terms as it observed that:

> The amendment did not go as far as to state that the sole purpose of the penitentiary system should be the reformation and social rehabilitation of prisoners, as some wished in keeping with what they described as the contemporary trend and the modern idea of the basic purpose of the detention of prisoners. Nor did it disregard the views of those who referred to the deterrent aspect attached to punishment and penitentiary systems.[85]

The chicken came home to roost as the Human Rights Committee issued its General Comment 21 on Article 10 in 1992. In the part dealing with para 3, which is often cited in human rights scholarship without critical comment,[86] the Committee observed, 'No penitentiary system can be only *retributory*; it should essentially seek the reformation and social rehabilitation of the prisoner'.[87] The

82 Revised amendment submitted by Belgium, Cuba, France, Spain and Tunisia. A/C.5/L.691/Rev.2; see also UNGAOR, Thirteenth Session, Third Committee, Summary Record of 882nd Meeting (14 November 1958) UN Doc A/C.3/SR.882, at para 1.

83 UN Doc A/C.3/SR.882, at para 1.

84 Ibid at para 28.

85 United Nations General Assembly, Thirteenth Session, 'Report of the Third Committee' (9 December 1958) UN Doc A/4045, at para 25.

86 See, for example, Alex Conte, Security of the Person in Alex Conte, Scott Davidson and Richard Burchill (eds), *Defining Civil and Political Rights: The Jurisprudence of the United Nations Human Rights Committee* (Ashgate 2004) 110.

87 UN Human Rights Committee, 'General Comment No. 21: Article 10 (Humane Treatment of Persons Deprived of Their Liberty)' (10 April 1992) UN Doc HRI/GEN/1/Rev.1, at para 10 (emphasis added).

idea that the penitentiary system can be retributory at all does not accord with the drafting intent behind the original version of the article proposed by Cassin, or the final version, which, as we have seen, was largely a product of linguistic confusion. At any rate, not a single delegate had argued that the penitentiary system ought to be retributory. Let us recall that the relevant part of Article 10 was rather restrictive to begin with in that it did not speak to social rehabilitation as a sentencing aim. By affirming that the penitentiary system could partly be retributory, the Human Rights Committee ended up diluting the practical import of what had already been a perilously watered-down provision. Coincidentally, the US ratified the Covenant the same year as the Committee issued General Comment 21. It did so with an 'understanding' that para 3 of Article 10 'does not diminish the goals of punishment, deterrence, and incapacitation as additional legitimate purposes for a penitentiary system'.[88]

Offender rehabilitation and the contemporary regime of international human rights

The jurisprudence of the Human Rights Committee under its individual communications mechanism in respect of Article 10(3) is rather underdeveloped. However, there have been some important cases where the compatibility of life imprisonment with the prohibition of cruel punishment and the requirement of rehabilitation has come under scrutiny. In *Blessington v Australia*, the authors of the communication were convicted of violent crimes they had committed as teenagers.[89] Both individuals had suffered abuse as children. Despite their young age, they were sentenced to life imprisonment in 1990. Subsequent changes in the domestic legislation meant that the authors would have to serve 30 years of their sentences before being permitted to apply for a review.[90]

Besides other claims, the authors in *Blessington* submitted that Australia was in breach of Article 10(3) as 'the imposition of a life sentence without the possibility of parole in respect of a juvenile offender was incompatible with the requirement that the essential aims of the penitentiary system be "reformation and social rehabilitation"'.[91] Given the lengthy period of detention before the authors would be eligible for parole, the restrictive eligibility criteria, and the fact that they were minors when they committed the crimes, the Committee held that the life sentences, 'as currently applied to the authors, do not meet the obligations of the State party under Article 7, read together with Articles 10, paragraph 3, and 24 of the Covenant'.[92] However, the Committee did not rule out the compatibility

88 International Covenant on Civil and Political Rights, 'Declarations and Reservations' (8 June 1992) 1057 UNTS 407.
89 *Blessington and Elliot v Australia*, Communication No. 1968/2010 (2014) UN Doc CCPR/C/112/D/1968/2010.
90 *Blessington* (n 89) para 2.8.
91 Ibid para 3.2.
92 Ibid para 7.12.

of life sentences with the said provisions – even when imposed on juveniles – as long as there was a possibility of review and a prospect of release. That did not mean, in the Committee's view, that release should necessarily be granted. Rather, the domestic authorities had an obligation to 'evaluate the concrete progress made by the authors towards rehabilitation and the justification for continued detention'.[93]

In *Teesdale v Trinidad and Tobago*, where the author of the communication had been denied a prompt trial and had spent seven years on death row before having his sentence commuted to '75 years' imprisonment with hard labour', the Committee found the government in violation of Article 7 (prohibition of cruel and inhuman punishment), Article 9 (freedom from arbitrary detention), and Article 14(3) (right to be tried without undue delay).[94] The author had not raised the issue of the compatibility of the sentence with Article 10. However, in an individual opinion, a member of the Committee, Rajsoomer Lallah, took up the issue, asking rhetorically if imprisonment for 75 years would meet the requirement set out in Article 10(1) that all persons deprived of their liberty be treated with humanity. In the context of Article 10(3), Lallah noted that 'both reformation and social rehabilitation assume that a prisoner will be released during his expected lifetime'.[95] Stating the obvious, Lallah expressed doubts as to 'whether a sentence of 75 years in prison could meet this requirement'.[96] The Committee's case law and concluding observations remain silent on the issue.

In *Jensen v Australia*, the Committee avoided tackling head-on the interplay between rehabilitation and other penological justifications.[97] The author, who was serving concurrent sentences on various counts of rape and indecent assault, argued that in prison he had followed intensive therapy and that the psychological reports showed that he was unlikely to reoffend. He argued that further imprisonment, 'after he was ready to be rehabilitated and reintegrated in society for offences that happened ten years ago, is detrimental to his rehabilitation'.[98] The Committee found the claim inadmissible observing that 'there were a variety of programmes and mechanisms in place in the State party's penitentiary system that were geared towards' his 'social rehabilitation and reformation'.[99] The author, in the Committee's view, had failed to substantiate that the government's

93 Ibid para 7.7. See also *Mikhail Pustovoit v Ukraine,* Communication No. 1405/2005 (2014) UN Doc CCPR/C/110/D/1405/2005 (holding that life imprisonment when imposed after an unfair trial, or when it involves inhuman treatment in custody, is contradictory to Articles 7, 14 and 10).

94 *Teesdale v Trinidad and Tobago,* Communication No. 677/1996 (2002) UN Doc CCPR/C/74/D/677/1996.

95 *Teesdale* (n 95) 'Individual Opinion by Committee Member Rajsoomer Lallah (concurring)'at p 9.

96 Ibid.

97 *Jensen v Australia,* Communication No. 762/1997 (2001) UN Doc CCPR/C/71/D/726/1997.

98 Ibid para 3.5.

99 Ibid para 6.4.

assessments of his 'reformative progress' raised issues of compliance with the requirements of Article 10.[100]

In *Yevdokimov v Russian Federation*, the authors alleged that the provision in the domestic constitution which restricted the right of persons deprived of liberty to vote contradicted Article 25 of the Covenant.[101] The Committee did not go as far as to hold the restriction on the right to vote imposed on top of a prison sentence incompatible with the Covenant. However, citing the principle set out by the European Court in *Hirst v United Kingdom*,[102] the Committee arrived at the conclusion that since the legislation in question provided 'a blanket deprivation of the right to vote to anyone sentenced to a term of imprisonment', there had been a violation of Article 25.[103] Although the authors had not raised a complaint under Article 10(3), the Committee went on to note that a blanket suspension of prisoners' right to vote did not accord with the 'essential aim' of reformation and social rehabilitation.[104]

Another issue that cuts to the heart of the idea of rehabilitation – and turns on the interconnections between criminal justice and social justice – is penal labour. In Chapter 4, we traced the long pedigree of the work performed by prisoners as an exception to the prohibition of forced labour provided in the Covenant's Article 8, para 3. Article 8 in the 'Draft International Covenant on Human Rights', as it stood at the end of the fifth session of the Commission on Human Rights, stated: 'No one shall be required to perform forced or compulsory labour except pursuant to a sentence to such punishment for a crime by a competent court'.[105] The subsequent paragraph excluded from the prohibition of forced labour, 'any work, not amounting to hard labour, required to be done in the ordinary course of prison routine by a person undergoing detention imposed by the lawful order of a court'.[106] When the Secretary General invited the governments to comment on the draft Covenant in July 1949, the Philippines made a couple of interesting interventions. The expression 'to such punishment', the Philippines said should be eliminated, as the 'idea of punishment for a crime has been abandoned by the most enlightened criminologists'.[107] It further proposed a proviso to Article 8: 'Every labour performed by prisoners shall be compensated at the rate, prevailing in the community, but the cost of their maintenance shall be deducted from

100 Ibid.

101 *Yevdokimov and Rezanov v Russian Federation*, Communication No. 1410/2005, UN Doc CCPR/C/101/D/1410/2005, para 3.1.

102 *Hirst v United Kingdom* (No 2) (App. 74025/01) 6 October 2005 [Grand Chamber] (2006) 42 EHRR 849, ECHR 2005-IX.

103 *Yevdokimov* (n 101) para 7.4.

104 Ibid.

105 UN ECOSOC, 'Compilation of the Comments of Governments on the Draft International Covenant on Human Rights and the Proposed Additional Articles – Memorandum by Secretary General' (20 March 1950) UN Doc E/CN.4/365.

106 Ibid (art 8, para 4a).

107 Ibid at p 28.

such compensation'.[108] Subsequently, the Commission decided to pass over the proposal and did not vote upon it.

The Human Rights Committee, in its Article 8 case law, seems to have sought the easy way out of the problem of the exclusion of prisoners from labour protection guarantees. In *Radosevic v Germany*, the author complained that the payment of lower wages to prisoners (compared to similar work performed by ordinary workers) amounted to a violation of the Article 26 guarantee of the equal protection of the law, read together with Article 8(1).[109] The Committee found the claim inadmissible as the author had failed to provide 'information on the type of work that he performed' and about 'the remuneration paid for comparable work in the labour market'.[110] In a passage that offers only lip service to the idea of rehabilitation, the Committee said that:

> Article 8, paragraph 3 (c) (i), read in conjunction with Article 10, paragraph 3, of the Covenant requires that work performed by prisoners primarily aims at their social rehabilitation, as indicated by the word 'normally' in Article 8, paragraph 3 (c) (i), but does not specify whether such measures would include adequate remuneration for work performed by prisoners. While reiterating that, rather than being only retributory, penitentiary systems should seek the reformation and social rehabilitation of prisoners, the Committee notes that States may themselves choose the modalities for ensuring that treatment of prisoners, including any work or service normally required of them, is essentially directed at these aims.[111]

In a popular commentary on the ICCPR, Sarah Joseph and Melissa Castan have observed that Article 10(3) 'seems a controversial inclusion in the ICCPR, as it purports to dictate the policy States should adopt regarding the treatment of offenders'.[112] The argument does not hold for the following reasons: First, as we have seen, the said provision enjoyed unanimous support when it was first proposed in 1949. The subsequent debate on the article did not evince a controversy over its inclusion in the Covenant as such. Second, in singling out Article 10(3) as a provision which allegedly seeks to dictate a policy for the states to follow, Joseph and Castan appear to overlook deeper normative issues at stake. One might equally contend, for example, that a penal system which simply warehouses individuals is ideologically wedded to neo-liberal political economy. How could such a system be morally preferable to the one that at least attempts to minimise

108 Ibid.

109 *Radosevic v Germany*, Communication No. (2005) UN Doc CCPR/C/84/D/1292/2004, para 3.1 and para 7.3.

110 Ibid para 7.2.

111 Ibid 7.3. See also *Singh v New Zealand*, Communication No. 791/97 (2001) UN Doc CCPR/C/ C/72/D/791/1997.

112 Sarah Joseph and Melissa Castan, *The International Covenant on Civil and Political Rights: Cases, Materials, and Commentary* (3rd edn, Oxford University Press 2013) 324.

the disadvantages that many individuals bring with them to the prison? However, Joseph and Castan are certainly correct in pointing out that:

> The rehabilitation' paradigm was more prevalent, at least in Western criminal justice systems, when the ICCPR was adopted in 1966. In more recent times in many States, there has been a trend towards harsher penalties and prison conditions, evincing a shift towards the 'retribution' model of criminal sociology. It is possible that the 'rehabilitation' aspect of Article 10(3) has been treated by States Parties as an anachronism.[113]

The question that follows from this pertinent observation is whether human rights lives up to the task of countering the tendency to treat 'rehabilitation' as an 'anachronism'. In light of the rather peripheral position that offender rehabilitation occupies in the discourse of human rights, the answer has to be in the negative. The reasons why the concept remains a marginal concern, and, at times, attracts deep suspicion, are both theoretical and historical. The revival of retributivism in the 1970s chimed in with human rights credo inasmuch as it drew on Kantian and Hegelian notions of punishment as a moral duty and as a right of (abstract) rational agents respectively. Second, in historical terms, the abuses associated with positivist criminology – a discipline which also lay at the heart of the rehabilitative ideal – deeply informed the discourse of human rights as it came into its own in the seventies. In many post-colonial and communist states, so-called re-education camps involved indoctrination, especially of political prisoners, which understandably resulted in anxieties about the idea of rehabilitation. Those suspicions suffuse, for example, the reports put out by Amnesty International during the period and linger on in human rights literature to this day.[114]

Of a total of 376 concluding observations adopted by the Human Rights Committee in respect of 116 countries covering the period 1987–2016 that I have looked at, the issue of offender rehabilitation and reintegration specifically comes up in 27 concluding observations in relation to 24 countries. Out of these, four concluding observations concerning as many countries include a recommendation for the state parties to strengthen social rehabilitation programmes for juvenile offenders only.[115] In one of the strongest pronouncements on the subject, the Human Rights Committee, following the review of the United States' combined second and third reports, criticised the practice of holding detainees in prolonged cellular confinement, lack of adequate out-of-cell recreation, and 'general

113 Ibid 324–325.

114 See, for example, Amnesty International, *Annual Report 1981* ('re-education' camps in Vietnam) 273; *Annual Report 1982* (Cameroon) 22–23; *Annual Report 1984* (re-education through labour in China) 216; *Annual Report 1986* (concerns about detention of suspected war criminals in re-education camps for prolonged periods in lieu of trials in Vietnam) 266; *Annual Report 1987* (Laos); *Annual Report 1988* (Angola) 21.

115 Albania, 22 August 2013, CCPR/C/ALB/CO/2, para 15; Cyprus, 30 April 2014, CCPR/C/CYP/CO/4, para 20; Georgia, 19 August 2014, CCPR/C/GEO/CO, para 16; Jamaica, 22 Nov 2016, CCPR/C/JAM/CO/4, para 44.

conditions of strict regimentation in a depersonalized environment'.[116] However, in the Committee's concluding observations, as in other material reviewed, the term 'rehabilitation' or 'reintegration' occurs mostly in the context of the victims of human trafficking, sexual abuse, torture, and war crimes, and by comparison, only rarely in relation to prisoners.

In respect of three countries – Iran, Kuwait, and Kyrgyzstan – the Committee called upon the states to release and rehabilitate incarcerated journalists.[117] Amnesty International's annual reports reveal an even more exclusive focus on the 'rehabilitation' of journalists and 'political' prisoners in the sense of financial help and other support upon release. In the mid-1960s, the organisation set up a 'Prisoner of Conscience Fund' 'used for the relief of prisoners and the relief and education of their families'.[118] The initiative fit into Amnesty International's original aim of securing the release of prisoners of conscience and the 'worldwide recognition of Articles 18 and 19 of the Universal Declaration of Human Rights'.[119] However, the relief programme did not extend to 'non-political' prisoners or their families even as the organisation's statute was revised in 1991, redefining its mandate as the promotion of and adherence to 'the Universal Declaration of Human Rights and other internationally recognised human rights instruments, the values enshrined in them, and the indivisibility and interdependence of all human rights and freedoms'.[120] The organisation's appeals to governments around rehabilitation remain confined to political prisoners and victims of torture.

Given that the concept of offender rehabilitation straddles both civil and political rights on the one hand, and economic and social rights on the other, one would have expected the CESCR Committee to prioritise that issue. Whilst the Committee has frequently highlighted poor prison conditions, recommendations concerning offender rehabilitation feature in only three out of 285 concluding observations, covering the period 1993–2016 and a total of 138 countries.[121] One likely reason for the scant attention given to the topic is the absence of a norm on the lines of ICCPR's Article 10(3) in the ICESCR. In General Comment No. 19 on Article 9 of the Covenant (the right to social security), the CESCR Committee urged state parties to 'give special attention to those individuals and groups

116 USA, 15 September 2006, CCPR/C/USA/CO/3, para 32.

117 Iran, 19 November 2011, CCPR/C/IRN/CO/3, para 27; Kuwait, 11 August 2016, CCPR/C/KWT/CO/3, para 41; Kyrgyzstan (Kyrgyz Republic), 24 July 2000, CCPR/CO/69/KGZ, para 20.

118 Amnesty International, *Annual Report 1968–69*. 18.

119 Amnesty International, *First Annual Report 1961–1962*. 1.

120 Amnesty International, 'Statute of Amnesty International as amended by the 20th International Council, meeting in Yokohama, Japan, 31 August to 7 September 1991', cited in *Annual Report 1992*. 293.

121 Dominican Republic, 12 December 1997, E/C.12/1/Add.16, E/C.12/1/Add.6, para 20; Yemen, E/C.12/1/Add.92 12 December 2003, para 37; and Moldova, E/C.12/MDA/CO/2, 12 July 2011, para 10.

who traditionally face difficulties in exercising this right', including prisoners.[122] However, the potential of this crucial intervention remains untapped within the human rights discourse. Neither the CESCR Committee nor the Human Rights Committee have referred to the General Comment in scrutinising rehabilitation programmes for prisoners, or penal policy more generally.

Both Committees have pressed state parties to reduce overcrowding in prisons and to improve health and hygiene standards, including with reference to the Standard Minimum Rules (Mandela Rules). Since the late 1990s, the concluding observations adopted by the Human Rights Committee in respect of a number of countries have either included a recommendation that the state under review make greater use of alternatives to incarceration or an appreciation of initiatives to that effect. However, a definitive and consistent position on the matter has yet to crystallise. Barring one exception, where the Committee expressly proposed non-custodial measures on account of their 'rehabilitative' potential, the underlying concern is overcrowding and high numbers of pre-trial detainees in prisons.[123] In some cases, the Committee has simultaneously approved the expansion of prisons and the increased use of non-custodial measures.[124] In respect of a number of countries, the Committee has raised concerns about overcrowding and poor prison conditions but stopped short of making a recommendation with regard to non-custodial or community-based alternatives.[125] In relation to at least some countries, the Committee seems to have acquiesced in prison expansion or renovation as a solution to overcrowding and associated problems.[126]

122 Committee on Economic, Social and Cultural Rights, 'General Comment No. 19: Article 9 (Right to Social Security)' (4 February 2008) UN Doc E/C.12/GC/19, at para 31.

123 Belgium, 19 November 1998, CCPR/C/79/Add.99, para 16.

124 For example, in relation to Colombia's fourth periodic report, the Committee stated the following: 'With particular regard to the problem of overcrowding, the Committee suggests that the adoption of alternative sentencing measures which would allow some convicted persons to serve their sentences in the community be considered and that greater resources be committed to enlarge the capacity and improve the conditions of the penitentiary system'. Colombia, 3 May 1997, CCPR/C/79/Add.76, para 39. For similar examples, see Croatia, 30 April 2015, CCPR/C/HRV/CO/3, para 19; Sri Lanka, 21 November 2014, CCPR/C/LKA/CO/5, para 18; Turkey, 13 November 2012, CCPR/C/TUR/CO/1, para 18.

125 See, for example, Chad, 11 August 2009, CCPR/C/TCD/CO/1, para 23; Chile, 13 August 2014, CCPR/C/CHL/CO/6, para 21; Czech Republic, 27 August 2001, CCPR/CO/72/CZE, para 19; Democratic Republic of Congo, 26 April 2006, CCPR/C/COD/CO/3, para 20; Equatorial Guinea, 13 August 2004, CCPR/CO/79/GNQ, para 6; Gabon, 10 November 2000, CCPR/CO/70/GAB, para 14; Honduras, 13 November 2006, CCPR/C/HND/CO/1, para 15; Iran, 29 November 2011, CCPR/C/IRN/CO/3, para 19; Madagascar 11 May 2007, CCPR/C/MDG/CO/3, para 22; Nicaragua, 12 December 2008, CCPR/C/NIC/CO/3, para 17; Syria, 9 August 2005, CCPR/CO/84/SYR, para 13.

126 See, for example, Ethiopia, 19 August 2011, CCPR/C/ETH/CO/1, para 23; India, 4 August 1997, CCPR/C/79/Add.81, para 26; Jamaica, 19 November 1997, CCPR/C/79/Add.83, para 9; Trinidad and Tobago 10 November 2000, CCPR/CO/70/TTO, para 17.

The Human Rights Committee has yet to take up rehabilitation as a sentencing aim and its relationship with other punishment goals in its concluding observations. The Committee has raised concerns specifically about life imprisonment in relation to a handful of countries. In none of these concluding observations did it refer to Article 10 of the ICCPR. In 2014, the Committee criticised the introduction of 'three-strike laws' in Hungary which provided for a mandatory life sentence.[127] The same year, in the concluding observations to the United States' fourth periodic report, it urged 'the State party to prohibit and abolish the sentence of life imprisonment without parole for juveniles, irrespective of the crime committed'.[128] Making some advance on its case law regarding whole-life sentences imposed on adults, the Committee further called upon the US to abolish mandatory and non-homicide-related sentence of life imprisonment without parole. In the concluding observations to Italy's fourth periodic report, the Committee commended the 'action taken to reduce the length of a nominal life sentence to a maximum finite sentence'.[129] At present, that is as far as the Committee seems willing to go on the subject.

The prohibition of life imprisonment on children under international law resonates positively in the UPR Working Group Reports and stakeholder submissions.[130] In its submission on Bulgaria, the Council of Europe-Committee for the Prevention of Torture expressed serious reservations 'about the very concept according to which life-sentenced prisoners were considered once and for all to be a permanent threat to the community and were deprived of any hope of being granted conditional release'. It urged Bulgaria to 'amend the legislation with a view to making conditional release (parole) available to all life-sentenced prisoners'.[131] States did not follow through on this strongly worded submission with a recommendation to Bulgaria – or indeed other countries – to abolish irreducible life sentences when imposed on adults. The only exception being a

127 Hungary, 16 November 2010, CCPR/C/HUN/CO/5, para 16.

128 USA, 23 April 2014, CCPR/ C/USA/CO/4, para 23.

129 Italy, 18 August 1998, CCPR/C/79/Add.94, para 4.

130 See, for example, Australia, A/HRC/31/14 (Recommendation 136.177 by Lithuania); the Netherlands, A/HRC/21/15, (Recommendation 98.20 by Belarus); United States of America, A/HRC/30/12, (Recommendation 176.51 by Fiji). In the Summaries of Stakeholder Submissions, the call for the abolition of life sentences on children comes mostly frequently by the London-based Child Rights Network (CRIN). See, for example, Human Rights Council, *Summary Prepared by the Office of the High Commissioner for Human Rights, in accordance with Paragraph 15(C) of the Annex to Human Rights Council Resolution 5/1:*Antigua and Barbados, A/HRC/WG.6/25/ATG/3, para 9; Botswana, A/HRC/WG.6/15/BWA/3, para 23; Guyana A/HRC/WG.6/21/GUY/3, para 29; Kiribati, A/HRC/WG.6/21/KIR/3, para 24; Maldives, A/HRC/WG.6/22/MDV/3, para 42; Tonga, A/HRC/WG.6/15/TON/3, para 17; and the United States of America, A/HRC/WG.6/22/USA/3, para 48.

131 Human Rights Council, *Summary Prepared by the Office of the United Nations High Commissioner for Human Rights: Bulgaria*. Twenty-Second Session, 9 February 2015, A/HRC/WG.6/22/BGR/3, para 22.

recommendation by Benin to the United States to 'abolish life imprisonment without the possibility of parole for nonviolent offenses'.[132]

As with Human Rights Committee's concluding observations, overcrowding in prisons is a recurring concern in the UPR Working Group Reports and Summaries of Stakeholders' Submissions.[133] States generally press the country under review to address the problem without specifying how they should go about it.[134] There are several examples from the second cycle where countries received recommendations to make greater use of non-custodial penalties to ease overcrowding.[135] In some cases, the call for non-custodial measures is made specifically in relation to children and/or women, with no explanation forthcoming as to why adult males should be left out.[136] It might be possible to give it all a positive spin, but the crucial point is that in the absence of an underlying commitment to prison abolitionism, social justice, or offender rehabilitation, prison expansion

132 Human Rights Council, *Report of the Working Group on the Universal Periodic Review: United States of America.* Thirtieth Session, 20 July 2015, A/HRC/30/12 (Recommendation 176.235).

133 See, for example, Human Rights Council, *Summary prepared by the Office of the United Nations High Commissioner for Human Rights: Albania.* Nineteenth Session, 24 January 2014, A/HRC/WG.6/19/ALB/3, para 11; Armenia, A/HRC/WG.6/21/ARM/3, para 42; Dominican Republic, A/HRC/WG.6/18/DOM/3, para 28; Ethiopia, A/HRC/WG.6/19/ETH/3, para 25; Finland, A/HRC/WG.6/13/FIN/3, para 20; France (A/HRC/WG.6/15/FRA/3, paras 37 and 48); Mexico, A/HRC/WG.6/17/MEX/3, para 8; Mozambique A/HRC/WG.6/24/MOZ/3, para 31; Nepal, A/HRC/WG.6/23/NPL/3, para 9; Nigeria, A/HRC/WG.6/17/NGA/3, para 56; Nicaragua, A/HRC/WG.6/19/NIC/3, para 28; Sri Lanka, A/HRC/WG.6/14/LKA/3, para 40; Thailand, A/HRC/WG.6/25/THA/3, para 21; Venezuela, A/HRC/WG.6/26/VEN/3, para 40; Yemen, A/HRC/WG.6/18/YEM/3, para 28; and Zambia, A/HRC/WG.6/14/ZMB/3, para 24.

134 For additional examples on this, see Human Rights Council, *Report of the Working Group on the Universal Periodic Review: Benin.* Twenty-Second Session, 11 December 2012, A/HRC/22/9 (Recommendation 108.37 by Iraq and 103.38 by the Netherlands); Costa Rica, A/HRC/27/12 (Recommendation 128.73 by the USA, 128.74 by Australia, and 128.75 by Switzerland); Czech Republic, A/HRC/22/3 (Recommendation 94.78 by Uzbekistan and 94.79 by Cuba); Italy, A/HRC/28/4 (Recommendation 145.101 by Hungary and 145.102 by Australia); Malawi, A/HRC/30/5 (Recommendation 110.80 by Angola and 110.82 Cape Verdi); Morocco, A/HRC/21/3 (Recommendation 129.52 by Austria); Namibia, A/HRC/32/4 (Recommendation 137.159 by Spain); Niger, A/HRC/32/5 (Recommendation 120.89 by USA and 190.90 by Ukraine); Nigeria, A/HRC/25/6 (Recommendation 131.106 by Germany); Rwanda, A/HRC/31/8 (Recommendation 132.26 by the Republic of Korea); and Zambia, A/HRC/22/13 (Recommendation 102.35 Slovakia, 102.36 Egypt, and 102.39 Iraq).

135 See, for example, Human Rights Council, *Report of the Working Group on the Universal Periodic Review: Haiti.* Thirty-fourth session, 20 December 2016. UN Doc. A/HRC/34/14 (Recommendation 115.81 by Switzerland); Lithuania, 27 December 2016, A/HRC/34/9 (Recommendation 100.129); Portugal, A/HRC/27/7 (Recommendation 127.31 by Norway).

136 See, for example, Human Rights Council, *Report of the Working Group on the Universal Periodic Review: Bolivia.* Thirty-fourth session, 17 December 2014, A/HRC/28/7 (Recommendation 113.15 by Austria).

could just as well be mooted as a solution to over-stretched prison services. That apprehension is borne out by recommendations made in some Working Group Reports. For example, the US recommended that Benin 'reduce overcrowding by building more prisons or reducing the length of pre-trial detention'.[137] Luxembourg received a recommendation – again by the US – that it 'increase available prison facilities to reduce overcrowding and ensure adequate capacity to enforce prison sentences'.[138]

Sure enough, governments may be tempted to look for alternatives to incarceration in a bid to reduce public expenditure on the prison system.[139] However, that justification again rests on shaky foundations; cost-cutting could also invite more convenient measures, such as prison privatisation or a race to bottom in terms of rehabilitation services. It has to be noted also that whilst both Amnesty International and Human Rights, as two of the most frequently cited NGOs in the summaries of stakeholder submissions, consistently raise concerns about overcrowding and ill-treatment of prisoners, it is usually lesser-known local NGOs, and accredited National Human Rights Institutions or Commissions, which put up a brief for non-custodial measures, including greater use of bail and parole.[140] The same pattern holds when it comes to concerns about the absence of rehabilitation services for prisoners.[141] The exception to this rule is Human Rights Watch's UPR submissions and entries in its World Reports on the US, which tend to be well-rounded, containing recommendations on non-custodial alternatives as well as rehabilitation.[142] The likely explanation for this is the location of the

137 Human Rights Council, *Report of the Working Group on the Universal Periodic Review: Benin*. Twenty-second session, 11 December 2012, A/HRC/22/9 (Recommendation 108.39).

138 Human Rights Council, *Report of the Working Group on the Universal Periodic Review: Luxembourg*. Twenty-third session, 25 March 2013, A/HRC/23/10 (Recommendation 118.37). See also Serbia, A/HRC/23/15 (Recommendation 132.73 by Spain); Antigua and Barbados, A/HRC/33/13 (Recommendation 77.61 by Germany); and Ecuador, A/HRC/21/4 (Recommendation 135.25 by Peru).

139 Susan Eaton and Christine Piper, *Sentencing and Punishment: The Quest for Justice* (OUP 2016) 299.

140 See, for example, *Summary Prepared by the Office of the United Nations High Commissioner for Human Rights: Burkina Faso*. Sixteenth Session, 28 January 2012, A/HRC/WG.6/16/BFA/3 (Joint Submission 1, para 16); Burundi, A/HRC/WG.6/15/BDI/3 (Joint Submission 6, para 45); Canada, A/HRC/WG.6/16/CAN/3, (Submission by the Assembly of First Nations, para 51); India, A/HRC/WG.6/13/IND/3 (Submission by the Commission of Human Rights India, para 68); Ireland, A/HRC/WG.6/25/IRL/3 (Joint Submission 3 and YRRN, para 46); Spain, A/HRC/WG.6/21/ESP/3 (Joint Submission 3, para 37).

141 See, for example, *Summary Prepared by the Office of the United Nations High Commissioner for Human Rights: Georgia*. Twenty-Third Session, 17 August 2015, A/HRC/WG.6/23/GEO/3 (Submission by the Public Defender, para 6, and JS7, para 39); Honduras, A/HRC/WG.6/22/HND/3 (Submission by the National Committee for the Prevention of Torture and Other Cruel, Inhuman or Degrading Treatment, para 24); United Kingdom, A/HRC/WG.6/13/GBR/3 (Submission by the Scottish Consortium for Learning Disability, para 70).

142 *Summary Prepared by the Office of the United Nations High Commissioner for Human Rights: United States of America*. Twenty-Second session, 16 February 2015, A/HRC/WG.6/22/USA/3, Submission by Human Rights Watch, para 41).

organisation's headquarters in Washington, glaring racial disparities in the country's criminal justice system, and the peculiarly American phenomenon of mass incarceration underlined by harsh conditions of detention.

With Working Group Reports serving as echo chambers for stakeholder submissions, the calls for rehabilitation and reintegration crop up most frequently in the UPR in connection with the victims of human trafficking, torture, violence against women, demobilised child soldiers, street children, and the disabled. It is to the modern human rights movement that the world owes a greater awareness of the abuses suffered by these groups. Paradoxically, however, rehabilitation of offenders is far less prominent in international debates today compared to the pre-World War II penal discourse. In the UPR documentation, the recommendations that speak specifically to the issue are few and far between. During the second cycle, Mexico urged Burkina Faso to 'provide access to legal aid from the moment of arrest and create programmes of rehabilitation, including for juvenile offenders'.[143] Sierra Leone recommended that the Congo 'take steps to improve prison conditions, including overcrowding and the lack of social rehabilitation measures'.[144] The member states which did not receive any recommendation in this area constitute a majority even if we count in more general recommendations, calling upon the country under review to incorporate the Standard Minimum Rules in prison administration.[145] The lack of a specific recommendation

143 Human Rights Council, *Report of the Working Group on the Universal Periodic Review: Burkina Faso*. Twenty-Fourth session, 8 July 2013, A/HRC/24/4 (Recommendation 135.69).

144 Human Rights Council, *Report of the Working Group on the Universal Periodic Review: Congo*. Twenty-Fifth session, 6 January 2014, A/HRC/25/16 (Recommendation 111.108). See also Ecuador, A/HRC/21/4 (Recommendation 135.31 by South Africa); France, A/HRC/23/3 (Recommendation 120.112 by Australia); El Salvador, A/HRC/28/5 (Recommendation 103.18 by Canada); Ethiopia, A/HRC/27/14 (Recommendation 155.71 by Bhutan); Guatemala, A/HRC/22/8 (Recommendation 99.51 by Spain); Trinidad and Tobago, A/HRC/33/15, (Recommendation 106.19 by Canada); Vanuatu, A/HRC/26/9 (Recommendation 99.67 by Mexico); Zambia, A/HRC/22/13 (Recommendation 102.40 by Italy).

145 Recommendations to implement the Standard Minimum Rules can be found in the Working Group Reports on the following member states: Antigua and Barbados, A/HRC/33/13, (Recommendation 77.63 by Canada); Argentina, A/HRC/22/4 (Recommendation 99.36 by Hungary and 99.45 by Austria); Bolivia, A/ HRC/28/7 (Recommendation 113.17 by United Kingdom); Central African Republic, A/HRC/25/11 (Recommendation 104.38 by Benin); Cuba, A/HRC/24/16 (Recommendation 170.140 by Canada); Egypt, A/HRC/28/16 (Recommendation 166.118 by Denmark); Hungary, A/HRC/33/9 (Recommendation 128.19 by Canada); Lithuania, A/HRC/34/9 (Recommendation 100.131 by Australia); Madagascar, A/HRC/28/13 (Recommendation 108.38 by Germany and 108.118 by Botswana); Mozambique, A/HRC/32/6 (Recommendation 128. 80 by Thailand); Nauru, A/HRC/31/7 (Recommendation 87.12 by Ghana); Panama, A/HRC/ 30/7 (Recommendation 90.17 by Germany); Peru, A/HRC/22/15 (Recommendation 116.67 by Thailand); Samoa, A/HRC/33/6 (Recommendation 95.71 Canada); Senegal, A/HRC/25/4 (Recommendation 124.34 by Austria); Sri Lanka, A/HRC/22/16 (Recommendation 127.74 by Thailand); Suriname, A/HRC/33/4 (Recommendation 135.34 by South Africa); Swaziland, A/HRC/33/14 (Recommendation 109.47 Canada); Thailand, A/HRC/33/16 (Recommendation 159.31 by United Kingdom); Togo, A/HRC/34/4 (Recommendation 128.75 by Switzerland and 128.78 by Canada); Venezuela,

in a Working Group Report cannot be taken lightly. Experience to date suggests that recommendations made in one UPR cycle are taken up by member countries as well as NGOs in the next cycle to remind the state under review of its commitments. Second, NGOs on the ground, which might want to use the UPR documentation as a social mobilisation tool, have little to draw on if a Working Group Report does not contain a recommendation on, say, reintegration of prisoners or the abolition of whole-life sentences.[146]

The human rights paradox: extending and curtailing the penal dragnet

The UPR has been described as a secular ritual that provides a space for consensus-building and 'reaffirming and legitimising' international community's core values.[147] Part of the UPR 'ritual' comprises exhortations on states under review to criminalise and punish certain practices and to de-criminalise others. Analysis of the second cycle reveals both expansionist and reductionist tendencies in relation to the criminal law. As was the case with the first cycle, the largest set of recommendations in the Working Group Reports from the second cycle involves urgings on the states to ratify or implement international treaties.[148] The instruments most frequently referred to in the stakeholder submissions and the Working Group recommendations, which implicitly carry a call to introduce a new criminal offence or to amend existing provisions in the domestic law, include the Convention against Torture; the Protocol to Prevent, Suppress and Punish Trafficking in Persons, especially Women and Children; and the International Convention for the Protection of All Persons from Enforced Disappearance. Another large chunk of recommendations called upon countries under review, in varying formulations, to ratify the Rome Statute of the International Criminal Court and the Agreement on the Privileges and Immunities of the International Criminal Court, align domestic legislation with international criminal law, and punish the perpetrators of genocide, war crimes and crimes against humanity. During the second cycle, Rwanda alone received 14 recommendations urging it to ratify the Rome Statute.[149]

A/HRC/34/6 (Recommendation 133.127 by New Zealand); Zambia, A/HRC/22/13 (Recommendation 102.41 by Japan).

146 On the role of NGOs in using UPR recommendations, see Heather Collister, 'Rituals and Implementation in the Universal Periodic Review and Human Rights Treaty Bodies' in Hilary Charlesworth and Emma Larking (eds), *Human Rights and the Universal Periodic Review: Rituals and Ritualism* (Cambridge University Press 2014) 109–125.

147 Walter Kalin, 'Rituals and Ritualism at the Universal Periodic Review: A Preliminary Appraisal' in Charlesworth and Larking (n 146) 25–41, 33.

148 Roland Chauville, 'The Universal Periodic Review's First Cycle: Successes and Failures' in Charlesworth and Larking (n 146) 87–108, 92.

149 Rwanda rejected the recommendations. See Human Rights Council, *Report of the Working Group on the Universal Periodic Review: Rwanda*. Thirty-first session, 18 December 2015, A/HRC/31/8 (Recommendations 135.2 to 135.15).

Following the 'interactive dialogue' with the country under review, states also call upon the country under review to criminalise a practice without always referring to a treaty source. Overlapping this category of recommendations are those that urge states to generally punish individuals responsible for human rights violations. The underlying assumption seems to be that the actions under question are already criminalised or ought to be criminalised. For example, in the second cycle, the United States recommended that Haiti 'vigorously investigate, prosecute, convict and sentence traffickers, including those responsible for domestic servitude and child sex trafficking'.[150] Sweden called upon Bosnia and Herzegovina to 'publicly and unequivocally condemn any attack, verbal or physical, against LGBTI groups and bring those responsible to justice'.[151]

Then, there are recommendations which specifically call for the introduction of criminal offences. For instance, Angola, and Antigua and Barbuda received recommendations to criminalise corporal punishment.[152] Spain and Uruguay called upon Cameroon to 'adopt a law on female genital mutilation and other harmful practices against women and girls by criminalising them specifically as offences'.[153] Leaving aside softer recommendations in this area (calling upon the country under review to 'prohibit', 'combat', or 'eliminate' the practice), several countries were specifically called upon to criminalise 'female genital mutilation'.[154] One of the largest sets of recommendations within the UPR second cycle that urges criminalisation and punishment concerns domestic and sexual violence against women. As examples of specifically formulated recommendations in this area, Norway and Iceland urged the Bahamas to criminalise marital rape, closely reflecting the submission by Amnesty International on the country under review.[155] Chile, Haiti, Kuwait, and Tonga were called upon to criminalise 'sexual

150 Human Rights Council, *Report of the Working Group on the Universal Periodic Review: Haiti*. Thirty-fourth session, 20 December 2016, A/HRC/34/14 (Recommendation 115.111). At least eight other countries made similar recommendations to Haiti.

151 Human Rights Council, *Report of the Working Group on the Universal Periodic Review: Bosnia and Herzegovina*. Twenty-eighth session, 4 December 2014, A/HRC/28/17 (Recommendation 107.53 by Sweden and 134.64 by Chile).

152 Human Rights Council, *Report of the Working Group on the Universal Periodic Review: Angola*. Twenty-eighth session, 5 December 2014, A/HRC/28/11 (Recommendation 134.95 by Portugal); Antigua and Barbuda, A/HRC/33/13 (Recommendation 77.69 by Honduras).

153 Human Rights Council, *Report of the Working Group on the Universal Periodic Review: Cameroon*. Twenty-fourth session, 5 July 2013, A/HRC/24/15 (Recommendation 131.41 by Spain and 131.44 by Uruguay).

154 Sierra Leone alone received at least 16 recommendations urging it to eliminate or address the practice of FGM. Human Rights Council, *Report of the Working Group on the Universal Periodic Review: Sierra Leone*. Thirty-second session, 14 April 2016, A/HRC/32/16 (Recommendations 111.106 to 111.125). See also Burkina Faso, A/HRC/24/4 (Recommendation 135.73 by Uruguay); Gambia, A/HRC/28/6 (Recommendation 109.113 by Italy); Togo, A/HRC/34/4 (Recommendation 128.79 the Russian Federation).

155 Human Rights Council, *Report of the Working Group on the Universal Periodic Review: Bahamas*. Twenty-third session, 22 March 2013, A/HRC/23/8 (Recommendations 92.35 and 92.36). Human Rights Council, *Summary prepared by the Office of the High Commissioner*

harassment' in addition to domestic violence.[156] Another related area where countries were urged to introduce new criminal offences included forced and early marriages.[157]

In some cases, where the country under review had already criminalised violence against women, it was urged either to enforce the law properly or enhance the severity of sanctions. For example, the US recommended that Afghanistan 'take measurable steps to fully implement the "Elimination of Violence Against Women law", and investigate thoroughly all suspected cases of gender-based violence and violence against defenders of women's rights and bring those responsible to justice'.[158] The recommendation echoed the submissions by Amnesty International and Human Rights Watch, both of which regretted that despite the introduction of 'tough new penalties', implementation had remained weak.[159] Likewise, Serbia called upon Bulgaria to amend its law on the protection against domestic violence to 'increase the punishment for repeated violations of violence against women'.[160] Parallel to strongly worded stakeholder submissions around the issue, several African, Asian, and former Soviet states received recommendations to prosecute and punish physical attacks and harassment directed against journalists and 'human rights defenders'.[161]

---

for Human Rights: Bahamas. A/HRC/WG.6/15/BHS/3 (Submission by Amnesty International at paras 13–14).

156 Human Rights Council, *Report of the Working Group on the Universal Periodic Review: Chile*. Twenty-sixth session, 2 April 2014, A/HRC/26/5 (Recommendation 121.92 by Italy and 121.93 by Republic of Moldova); Haiti, A/HRC/34/14 (Recommendation 115.86 by Australia and 115.91 by Ireland); Kuwait, A/HRC/29/17 (Recommendation 157.140 by Croatia); Tonga, A/HRC/23/4 (Recommendation 79.43 by Spain).

157 See, for example, Human Rights Council, *Report of the Working Group on the Universal Periodic Review: Cameroon*. Twenty-fourth session, 5 July 2013, A/HRC/24/15 (Recommendation 131.50 by Mexico); Myanmar, A/HRC/31/13 (Recommendation 131.50 by Paraguay); Somalia, A/HRC/32/12 (Recommendation 136.86 by Mexico).

158 Human Rights Council, *Report of the Working Group on the Universal Periodic Review: Afghanistan*. Twenty-sixth session, 4 April 2014, A/HRC/26/4 (Recommendation 136.136).

159 Human Rights Council, *Summary prepared by the Office of the High Commissioner for Human Rights: Afghanistan*. A/HRC/WG.6/12/AFG/3 (Submission by Amnesty International at para 15, and submission by Human Rights Watch at para 16).

160 Human Rights Council, *Report of the Working Group on the Universal Periodic Review: Bulgaria*. Thirtieth session, 8 July 2015, A/HRC/30/10 (Recommendation 123.94).

161 See, for example, Human Rights Council, *Report of the Working Group on the Universal Periodic Review: Kenya*. Twenty-ninth session, 26 March 2015, A/HRC/29/10 (Recommendation 142.123 by Slovakia); Kyrgyzstan, A/HRC/29/4 (recommendation 119.24 by Lithuania); Paraguay, A/HRC/32/9 (Recommendation 102.115 by Austria, 102.116 by Canada, and 102.119 by Italy); Russia, A/HRC/24/14 (Recommendation 140.192 by Spain); Rwanda, A/HRC/31/8 (Recommendation 134.56 by Austria); Serbia, A/HRC/23/15 (Recommendation 132.32 by Estonia); Sierra Leone, A/HRC/32/16 (Recommendation 111.148 by Canada); Somalia, A/HRC/32/12 (Recommendation 136.96 by Switzerland); Thailand, A/HRC/33/16 (Recommendation 158.121 by Botswana, 158.122 by Norway, and 158.123 by Romania). See also, Human Rights Council, *Summary prepared by the Office of the High Commissioner for Human Rights: Honduras*.

As regards criminalising and punishing violence against women and 'harmful traditional practices', the usual pattern within the UPR is the Western (and sometimes Latin American) countries making recommendations mostly to their African and Asian counterparts. The countries in the latter category have seized opportunities to reciprocate. For example, Burundi, Pakistan, Togo, and China all recommended that Canada specifically criminalise and punish violence based on race or religion. Sudan urged Canada to 'adopt a legislation concerning xenophobia, incitement to hatred and hatred to blacks and to criminalize racial violence'.[162] Sweden received a raft of similar recommendations, which it rejected.[163]

Although this is by no means an exhaustive list of all the relevant recommendations, it is safe to say that the emphasis within the UPR is on criminalising and punishing certain abusive practices by state officials; political persecution; and sexual, gender, and identity-based violence and ill-treatment. By contrast, business practices which devastate ecology and public health are passed over in silence. The pattern holds in annual human rights reporting by Amnesty International and Human Rights Watch. To illustrate, in its 2017 World Report, Human Rights Watch criticised Egyptian authorities for failing to 'protect Christian minorities from sometimes fatal attacks and imposed "reconciliation sessions" that allow Muslim perpetrators to escape prosecution and foster impunity'.[164] In relation to Gambia, the organisation said that although 'there were fewer reports of abuses against journalists in 2016 than in previous years, the culture of ***impunity*** that has permitted abuses against journalists to go unpunished under (the previous government) remained intact'.[165] About Kyrgyzstan, Human Rights Watch stated that LGBTI persons 'experience ill-treatment, extortion, and discrimination by both state and non-state actors', and that 'there is widespread ***impunity*** for these abuses'.[166] The entry on Brazil said that the 'perpetrators of human rights abuses during military rule from 1964 to 1985 continue to be shielded from justice by a 1979 amnesty law' and that 'their crimes remained unpunished'.[167] In its 2016–17 Annual Report, Amnesty regretted that 'the definition of rape in Finland's Criminal Code failed to incorporate a lack of consent' and that 'mediation continued to be used widely in cases of intimate partner violence'.[168] The organisation was

A/HRC/WG.6/22/HND/3 (Submission by Amnesty International at para 57); South Africa, A/HRC/WG.6/13/ZAF/3 (Submission by Amnesty International at para 54).

162 Human Rights Council, *Report of the Working Group on the Universal Periodic Review: Canada*. Twenty-fourth session, 28 June 2013, A/HRC/24/11 (Recommendation 128.19 by Sudan, and 128.17 by Burundi. 128.18 Pakistan, 128.20 Togo, 128.49 by China).

163 Human Rights Council, *Report of the Working Group on the Universal Periodic Review: Sweden*. Twenty-ninth session, 13 April 2015, A/HRC/29/13 (Recommendations 147.8 to 147.19).

164 Human Rights Watch, *World Report 2017 – Events of 2016* (HRW 2017) 237 (emphasis added).

165 Ibid 287.

166 Ibid 421 (emphasis added).

167 Ibid 145 (emphasis added).

168 Amnesty International, *Amnesty International Annual Report 2016–17: The State of the World's Human Rights* (London 2017) 159.

concerned that 'more than 90% of all killings and abuses against human rights defenders' in Honduras '*remained unpunished*'.[169]

Whether the calls for criminalisation are properly grounded in international law, and whether punishment is always an appropriate response to human rights violations under question, is something we shall turn to shortly. Before that, let me offer a summation of areas where the UPR proceedings lean towards decriminalisation.

In a testament to the ascendance of gay rights movement in recent decades, the largest numbers of recommendations in this category concern intimate relations between consenting adults of the same sex. Grenada alone received a dozen recommendations to repeal provisions in domestic law that criminalise same-sex relationships.[170] At least another 25 countries received similar recommendations.[171] Trailing closely behind is the issue of defamation and press-related offences. The Working Group Reports for at least 18 countries included multiple recommendations on decriminalisation of defamation.[172] Ireland and Pakistan were called upon to repeal blasphemy laws.[173] Some countries were urged to provide alternatives to military service to conscientious objectors, making sure that they were not imprisoned for their beliefs.[174] Belarus received recommendations to decriminalise the activities of 'non-registered NGOs', and Kyrgyzstan was urged to repeal the law 'stigmatizing' NGOs as 'foreign agents'.[175] Malta, Ireland, and some Latin American countries were called upon to decriminalise abortion either completely or at least in certain cases, such as an unwanted pregnancy

169 Ibid 180 (emphasis added).

170 Human Rights Council, *Report of the Working Group on the Universal Periodic Review: Grenada*. Twenty-ninth session, 9 April 2015, A/HRC/29/14 (Recommendations 72.64 to 72.76).

171 The countries were: Afghanistan, Antigua and Barbuda, Barbados, Belize, Bhutan, Botswana, Brunei Darus Salam, Cameroon, Comoros, Dominica, Gambia, Ghana, Grenada, India, Indonesia, Jamaica, Kenya, Mauritius, Nauru, Samoa, Solomon Islands, South Sudan, Saint Lucia, Saint Vincent and Lucia, and Tuvalu.

172 See, for example, Human Rights Council, *Report of the Working Group on the Universal Periodic Review: Jordan*. Twenty-fifth session, 6 January 2014, A/HRC/25/9 (Recommendations 118.75,120.32 and 120.33); Kazakhstan, A/HRC/28/10 (Recommendations 126.35 to 126.42); and Singapore, A/HRC/32/17 (Recommendations 166.200 to 166.206).

173 Human Rights Council, *Report of the Working Group on the Universal Periodic Review: Ireland*. Thirty-third session, 18 July 2016, A/HRC/33/17 (Recommendation 136.53 by France); Pakistan, A/HRC/22/12 (Recommendation 122.31 Belgium, 122.32 by Namibia, and 122.33 by the Holy See).

174 See, for example, Human Rights Council, *Report of the Working Group on the Universal Periodic Review: Republic of Korea*. Twenty-second session, 12 December 2012, A/HRC/22/10 (Recommendation 124.53);

Uzbekistan. Twenty-fourth session, A/HRC/24/7, 5 July 2013 (Recommendations 134.19 and 134.20).

175 Human Rights Council, *Report of the Working Group on the Universal Periodic Review: Belarus*. Thirtieth session, 13 July 2015, A/HRC/30/3 (Recommendation 129.71 to 129.74); Kyrgyzstan, A/HRC/29/4 (Recommendation 119.26 by Czech Republic).

as a result of rape or if the pregnancy poses a risk to the life of the woman.[176] Across all the areas which feature prominently in the UPR as candidates for decriminalisation – consensual same-sex relationships, abortion, defamation, and other offences related to speech and assembly – both Amnesty International and Human Rights Watch put in strong submissions, consistent with their annual reporting on human rights.

Decriminalisation and de-incarceration, howsoever limited in scope, are to be welcomed given the overwhelmingly negative impact of the punitive dragnet on offenders, their families, and the society at large. There is absolutely no quarrel either that consensual same-sex relations, women's right to abortion, and so on, should not invite criminal penalties. However, the question remains as to where does it leave us with laws that penalise poverty and vulnerability by categorising begging, drug possession, vagrancy, sex work, squatting in residential buildings, and other such activities as crimes punishable by prison terms? What about minor offences such as shop-lifting and petty theft? There are a few needles that can be found in a haystack of recommendations; for example, Ecuador urging the UK to 'adopt necessary measures to avoid criminalization of irregular migration', and Egypt calling upon the United States to amend laws that 'criminalize homelessness'.[177]

Whilst it is hard to detect much concern about the 'penalisation of poverty' in Amnesty International and Human Rights Watch's stakeholder submissions (as summarised by the Office on the High Commissioner for Human Rights), the organisations' annual reports do occasionally go beyond the UPR recommendations in terms of decriminalisation.[178] For example, Human Rights Watch, in its 2017 report, expressed concern that all states and the federal government in the USA criminalised 'possession of illicit drugs for personal use'.[179] One area where both the organisations have consistently sought to counter repressive laws is counter-terrorism. They have taken a stand against vaguely defined offences and the use of evidence obtained through torture. Similarly, the two organisations have made pointed criticisms of punitive responses as applied to refugees

176 Human Rights Council, *Report of the Working Group on the Universal Periodic Review: Malta*. Twenty-fifth session, 4 December 2013, A/HRC/25/17 (Recommendations 102.75 to 102.80); Ireland, A/HRC/33/17 (Recommendations 136.15 to 136.19). See also El Salvador, A/HRC/28/5 (Recommendations 104.49 to 104.60); Nicaragua, A/HRC/27/16 (Recommendations 117.19 to 117.31); and Paraguay, A/HRC/32/9 (Recommendations 105.3 to 105.6).

177 Human Rights Council, *Report of the Working Group on the Universal Periodic Review: United Kingdom*. Twenty-first session, 6 July 2012, A/HRC/21/9 (Recommendation 110.113); United States of America, A/HRC/30/12 (Recommendation 176.310; see also recommendation 176.252 by Sweden calling for a halt to detention of irregular migrants).

178 The term 'penalisation of poverty' is borrowed from Loïc Wacquant, who has situated new punitiveness within neoliberal modes of governing poverty and marginalisation. See, Loïc Wacquant, 'The penalisation of poverty and the rise of Neo-Liberalism' (2001) 9(4) *European Journal on Criminal Policy and Research* 401.

179 Human Rights Watch, *World Report 2017 – Events of 2016* (HRW 2017) 638.

and migrants.[180] Nevertheless, it has to be said, based on a review of all the annual reports produced by both Amnesty and Human Rights Watch, that human rights reporting stresses criminalisation and punishment more than decriminalisation. As regards decriminalisation, there is a sub-text that remains primarily concerned with laws which affect political expression and sexual freedoms or result in discrimination based on gender and ethnicity. The prominence of these issues within the human rights discourse both mirrors and consolidates identity politics that has, since the end of the Cold War, increasingly replaced class as the organising category of political and social life.

The Human Rights Committee's concluding observations along both axes – criminalisation and decriminalisation – largely accord with the UPR recommendations. However, it is not always possible to reconcile the concluding observations with the provisions of the ICCPR and the Committee's case law. To put this claim into perspective, it is necessary to note that the text of the ICCPR endorses criminal sanctions only with reference to the crime of genocide, and other international crimes of the type that were committed during the Second World War. Article 6, which sets limits on the applicability and execution of the death penalty, also provides, 'Nothing in this article shall authorize any State Party to the present Covenant to derogate in any way from any obligation assumed under the provisions of the Convention on the Prevention and Punishment of the Crime of Genocide'. The Genocide Convention, adopted by the UN General Assembly on 9 December 1948 – a day before the adoption of the UDHR – obligates state parties to enact legislation, making genocide, attempts, 'direct and indirect incitement', conspiracy to commit genocide, and complicity in genocide, punishable offences.[181] Article 15, which sets out the *nullum crimen* principle (no crime without law), excludes from its protective ambit 'the trial and punishment of any person for any act or omission which, at the time when it was committed, was criminal according to the general principles of law recognized by the community of nations'. The *travaux préparatoires* of Article 15 suggest that the provision was inserted to pre-empt the charge of ex-post facto application of the law against the backdrop of the Nuremburg and Tokyo tribunals.[182]

180 For instance, in its 2016–2017 report, Amnesty International reported with concern that in the Netherlands 'irregular migrants continued to be routinely deprived of their liberty and the government still did not adequately consider alternatives to detention'. Amnesty International, *Amnesty International Annual Report 2016–17: The State of the World's Human Rights* (AI 2017) 271.

181 Arts III, IV and V, Convention on the Prevention and Punishment of the Crime of Genocide (adopted 9 December 1948, entered into force 12 January 1951) 78 UNTS 277. For historical background and commentary, see William A. Schabas, *Genocide in International Law: The Crime of Crimes* (2nd edn, Cambridge University Press 2009).

182 See, for example, Commission on Human Rights (Sixth Session), Summary Record of the Hundred and Fifty-Ninth Meeting, UN.Doc. E/CN.4/SR. 159, 27 April 1950, paras 53–88. Article 7 of the European Convention reiterates the same exception, preferring to use the archaic term 'general principles of law recognized by civilized nations'. See Schabas, 'The European Convention on Human Rights' (n 8) 352; Tom Bingham, *The Rule of Law* (Penguin 2010) 73–74.

The ICCPR's Article 20 sets out an obligation to prohibit 'propaganda for war' and 'advocacy of national, racial or religious hatred that constitutes incitement to discrimination, hostility or violence shall be prohibited by law'. The 1965 Convention on the Elimination of Racial Discrimination goes a step further, obligating states to declare punishable by law 'all dissemination of ideas based on racial superiority or hatred, incitement to racial discrimination, as well as all acts of violence or incitement to such acts'.[183] It could be argued that the corresponding provision in the ICCPR leaves the states greater room to manoeuvre by stopping short of specifying whether the 'prohibition' of hate speech ought to be backed up by criminal or civil penalties or a combination of both. However, the Human Rights Committee appears to be following an increasingly punitive trajectory on the subject.

In *Vassilari v Greece*, the complainants claimed to the Human Rights Committee that Greek authorities had breached Article 20(2), read in conjunction with Article 2 (right to a remedy) of the Covenant by acquitting in criminal proceedings the authors of a letter published in a newspaper accusing the Roma community of being involved in crimes and calling for their eviction from a local settlement.[184] The domestic Anti-Racism Law, in the complainants' view, made conviction out of reach by imposing a high burden of proof and the requirement of intent as an element of the crime of hate speech.[185] The failure of authorities to punish perpetrators, they further claimed, constituted a violation of Article 26. The Committee found the claims based on Article 20 inadmissible as 'the authors had failed to substantiate their claims'.[186] With respect to the merits of the claim under Article 26, the Committee did not find a violation, observing that the Anti-Racism Law provided for sanctions in the event of a violation, and that there was 'no right under the Covenant to see another person prosecuted'.[187] The majority's decision not to consider the merits of the claim under Article 20 invited a dissenting note by a member of the Committee.[188] Without arriving at this conclusion in the instant case, the dissenting member, Abdelfattah Amor, noted that a domestic law without procedures for complaints and penalties would be ineffective and potentially fall foul of Article 20.[189] Indeed, the Committee itself had adopted a fairly stringent position on Article 20 a few years earlier, as it expressed concerns about anti-Semitic material published in Egyptian newspapers. In its concluding observations on Egypt's third periodic report, it remarked that 'the State party must take whatever action is necessary to punish such acts by ensuring respect for Article 20, paragraph 2, of the Covenant'.[190]

183 Art 4(a) International Convention on the Elimination of All Forms of Racial Discrimination (adopted 21 December 1965, entered into force 4 January 1969) 660 UNTS 195.
184 *Vassilari and others v Greece,* Communication No. 1570/2007 (2009) UN Doc CCPR/C/95/D/1570/2007.
185 Ibid para 3.1.
186 Ibid para 6.5.
187 Ibid para 7.2.
188 Ibid, Individual opinion of Committee member Mr. Abdelfattah Amor (dissenting), para 1.
189 Ibid.
190 Egypt, 28 November 2002, CCPR/CO/76/EGY, para 14.

Barely a month after it had adopted its views in *Vassilari*, the Committee's restrained position concerning legal responses to hate speech tilted back to a rather aggressive approach. In concluding observations on Sweden's sixth periodic report adopted in May 2009, the Committee expressed concerns about an increase in 'racially motivated crimes in recent years as well as the low number of prosecutions'.[191] It called upon Sweden to ensure that 'relevant criminal law provisions and policy directives are effectively implemented'.[192] By 2015, the Committee was on the front foot as it urged the UK to 'thoroughly investing[e] alleged cases of incitement to discrimination, hostility or violence, and alleged hate crimes, prosecuting the perpetrators and, if they are convicted, punishing them with appropriate sanctions, and providing victims with adequate remedies, including compensation'.[193] The comment can be construed to mean that compensation alone would not be adequate even when the offence was one of incitement to discrimination as distinct from a physical attack. In 2016, the Human Rights Committee recommended that Costa Rica adopt an act on the 'prevention and punishment of all forms of discrimination'.[194]

That domestic laws should prohibit hate speech and discrimination is not under question. Nor is the idea that those on the receiving end of such treatment should have access to a remedy. What is problematic is the Committee's suggestion that all forms of discrimination be brought under the scope of criminal penalties.[195] The purposive and evolutive approach to interpreting human rights instruments, then, is a double-edged sword. On the one hand, it enables courts and treaty monitoring bodies to extend the protective arm of human rights to shield disadvantaged groups against a broader range of ill-treatment than envisaged by the authors of those instruments. Simultaneously, it leads them to stretch the punitive scope of the law well beyond the original intent of the drafters.

In concluding observations on Togo's fourth periodic report, the Committee reiterated the position adopted in its case law that 'female genital mutilation' constituted cruel, inhuman, or degrading treatment within the terms of Article 7.[196] The Committee was concerned that 'the practice is not punished by the

191 Sweden, 7 May 2009, CCPR/C/SWE/CO/6, para 19.

192 Ibid.

193 United Kingdom, 17 August 2015, CCPR/C/GBR/CO/7, para 10. The Committee went on to make similar recommendations to Russia, South Africa, and Uzbekistan. See Russia, 28 April 2015, CCPR/C/RUS/CO/7, para 8; South Africa, CCPR/C/ZAF/CO/1, para 15; Uzbekistan, 17 August 2015, CCPR/C/UZB/CO/4, para 7. See also Namibia, 2016, CCPR/C/NAM/CO/2, para 10.

194 Costa Rica, 21 April 2016, CCPR/C/CRI/CO/6, para 33. See also Guatemala, 3 April 1996, CCPR/C/79/Add.63, para 33. See also Turkey, 13 November 2012 CCPR/C/TUR/CO/1, para 10.

195 See also, Malawi, 18 June 2012, CCPR/C/MWI/CO/1, para 7 (calling for the prosecution and punishment of those responsible for discrimination against individuals on the grounds of sexual orientation).

196 *Diene Kaba v Canada*, Communication No. 1465/2006 (2010) UN Doc CCPR/C/98/D/1465/2006, para 13.

Togolese criminal system'.[197] Drawing frequently on the Article 8 prohibition of slavery and forced labour, the Committee has urged state parties to effectively penalise and punish human trafficking.[198] Penal labour, by contrast, does not elicit the same level of censure in the Committee's jurisprudence. Further, the Committee's treatment of human trafficking exposes the flip side of rights talk. It can be argued that individualising the blame for this manifestly exploitative practice serves to depoliticise the issue and absolve states who directly fuel trafficking by closing off legal opportunities for migration.[199] Further, as Dianne Otto has suggested in her discussion of what she calls 'sexual panics about the cross-border trafficking of women and girls', it seems that 'human rights advocates' promote the rights of victims after they have been trafficked.[200] What gets filtered out of the debate is that some victims are trapped into trafficking because of 'aggressive criminal justice measures' towards sex work in their home countries.[201] The language adopted by the Committee to censure human trafficking is notable as it harkens back to Andrew von Hirsch's defence of retributivism. As the Committee put it across to the Republic of Moldova:

> The State party should strengthen its efforts to investigate, prosecute and, if convicted, punish individuals involved in trafficking in persons, including, where relevant, public officials, *with penalties commensurate with the gravity of the crime*, and provide victims with access to effective remedies, including rehabilitation.[202]

197 Togo, 18 April 2011, CCPR/C/TGO/CO/4, para 13. See also United Republic of Tanzania, 6 August 2009, CCPR/C/TZA/CO/4, para 11; and Burkina Faso, 17 October 2016, CCPR/C/BFA/CO/1.

198 See, for example, Angola, 29 April 2013, CCPR/C/AGO/CO/1, para 17; Armenia, 31 August 2012 CCPR/C/ARM/CO/2, para 16; Benin, 23 November 2015, CCPR/C/BEN/CO/2, para 15; Burundi, 21 November 2014, CCPR/C/BDI/CO/2, para 16; China Hong Kong, 29 April 2013, CCPR/C/CHN-HKG/CO/3, para 20; China Macau, 29 April 2013, CCPR/C/CHN-MAC/CO/1, para 13; Costa Rica, 16 November 2007 CCPR/C/CRI/CO/5.para 12; Croatia CCPR/CO/71/HRV, 30 April 2001, para 12; CCPR/C/SLV/CO/6, 18 November 2010, para 13; Germany, CCPR/C/DEU/CO/6, 12 November 2012, para 13; Greece, 3 December 2015, CCPR/C/GRC/CO/2, paras 21 and 22; Greece, 19 April 2012, CCPR/C/GTM/CO/3, para 19; Haiti, 21 November 2014, CCPR/C/HTI/CO/1, para 14; Iraq, 3 December 2015, CCPR/C/IRQ/CO/5, para 32; Israel, 18 August 1998, CCPR/C/79/Add.93, para 16; Kazakhstan, 19 August 2011, CCPR/C/KAZ/CO/1, para 17.

199 Dianne Otto, 'Decoding Crisis in International Law: A Queer Feminist Perspective' in Barbara Stark (ed), *International Law and Its Discontents: Confronting Crises* (Cambridge University Press 2015) 115–136. See also John Christman, 'Human Rights and Global Wrongs: The Role of Human Rights Discourse in Trafficking' in Diana Tietjens Meyers (ed), *Poverty, Agency, and Human Rights* (Oxford University Press 2014) 321–346.

200 Otto (n 199) 119.

201 Ibid 115–136, 121.

202 Republic of Moldova, 18 November 2016, CCPR/C/MDA/CO/3, para 20 (emphasis added).

The term 'commensurate' crops up in the Committee's concluding observations on numerous occasions in the context of torture, sexual violence, and harassment and attacks on human rights defenders, implying a desirability of longer prison sentences which 'fit' the crimes. In varying constructions, the Committee has repeatedly urged state parties to adopt legislation criminalising all forms of domestic violence, including spousal rape, and to step up prosecution and punishment.[203] In concluding observations on Japan's fifth periodic report, the Committee regretted that 'sentences for perpetrators of domestic violence are reportedly lenient and that violators of protection orders are only arrested in cases of repeated violations or when they ignore warnings'.[204] The tenor of the Committee's pronouncements on domestic and sexual violence exposes an undercurrent of robust retributivism. To illustrate, the Committee has urged Tajikistan to 'guarantee that cases of domestic violence are thoroughly investigated ex officio, regardless of the severity of the harm; that the perpetrators are brought to justice and, if convicted, punished with commensurate sanctions'.[205] In concluding observations to the Republic of Korea's fourth periodic report, the Committee stated with concern:

> [T]hat marital rape is not a specific punishable offence under the Criminal Code, and that perpetrators of domestic violence continue to be offered the chance to have the charges against them suspended in exchange for undergoing a period of education or counselling, which does not adequately protect victims or sufficiently convey the gravity of domestic violence. The State party should ensure that cases of domestic violence and marital rape are thoroughly investigated, that perpetrators are prosecuted and, if convicted, punished with appropriate sanctions, and that victims are adequately compensated. It should also revise its current procedures to ensure that victims are not channelled into alternative dispute resolution mechanisms.[206]

The Committee similarly took a stance against 'mediation' and 'conciliation' in domestic violence cases in respect of Greece.[207] Sure enough, imposing alternative dispute resolution on the survivors of domestic violence is not a morally

203 See, for example, Algeria, 12 December 2007, CCPR/C/DZA/CO/3, para 10; Armenia, 31 August 2012, CCPR/C/ARM/CO/2, para 8; Democratic Republic of Congo, 26 April 2006, CCPR/C/COD/CO/3, para 12; Denmark, 15 August 2016, CCPR/C/DNK/CO/6, para 20; El Salvador, 18 November 2010, CCPR/C/SLV/CO/6, para 9; Iraq, 3 December 2015, CCPR/C/IRQ/CO/5; India, 4 August 1997, CCPR/C/79/Add.81, para 16; Mali, 16 April 2003, CCPR/CO/77/MLI, para 12; The former Yugoslav Republic of Macedonia, 13 August 2015, CCPR/C/MKD/CO/3, para 10; Uzbekistan, 26 April 2001, CCPR/CO/71/UZB, para 19.

204 Japan, 18 December 2008, CCPR/C/JPN/CO/5, para 14. See also See, for example, Ghana, 9 August 2016, CCPR/C/GHA/CO, para 15; Namibia 21 April 2016, CCPR/C/NAM/CO/2, para 23. See also Indonesia, 21 August 2013, CCPR/C/IDN/CO/1, para 13.

205 Tajikistan, 22 August 201, 3CCPR/C/TJK/CO/2, para 7. See also Namibia, 21 April 2016, CCPR/C/NAM/CO/2, para 10.

206 Republic of Korea, 3 December 2015, CCPR/C/KOR/CO/4, paras 18 and 19.

207 Greece, 3 December 2015, CCPR/C/GRC/CO/2, para 20.

defensible proposition. To be meaningful, any act of reconciliation or forgiveness must be voluntary, well thought-out, and grounded in an honest recognition of the harm done.[208] However, imposing retribution as a universal model of justice, regardless of the circumstances of a case, is equally untenable. The retributive model rests on a truncated understanding of the human personality, being attuned to its vindictive side but blind to its transformative and transcendental capacities. The lack of reflexivity on this matter pervades contemporary human rights discourse, including the pronouncements of Amnesty International and Human Rights Watch.[209]

On the issue of domestic violence, the Human Rights Committee's unreservedly punitive stance finds resonance in the concluding observations of the CESCR Committee. The Committee has, quite creatively, read the requirement of criminalisation and punishment of domestic violence into Article 10(1) of ICESCR, which stipulates that 'the widest possible protection and assistance should be accorded to the family' and that 'marriage must be entered into with the free consent of the intending spouses'. Para 2 requires states to provide protection to women after childbirth and social security benefits to working mothers. Article 10(3) being the only provision in the ICESCR which sets out a requirement to criminalise and punish, does so with reference to child labour, specifying that states should 'set age limits below which the paid employment of child labour should be prohibited and punishable by law'. Whilst the Committee has taken up the issue of child labour on several occasions, the call for criminalisation and punishment occurs more frequently in relation to domestic violence either with reference to Article 10 of the ICESCR or without reference to any treaty provision.[210] The CESCR Committee has also recommended that state parties make

208 See Jeffrie G. Murphy, *Getting Even: Forgiveness and Its Limits* (OUP 2003) 33–38.

209 Since the 1990s, the tendency to equate justice with 'commensurate' punishment – and distaste toward alternative restorative approaches – has been particularly pronounced in relation to 'transitional societies' with a history of large-scale human rights abuses. See, for example, Amnesty International, *Report 1994*, p 208 (for criticism of national reconciliation process in Mauritania), p 225 (for disapproval of amnesty laws in El Salvador); Amnesty International, *Report 1998*, p 309 (criticism of amnesties granted by South Africa's Truth and Reconciliation Commission). Human Rights Watch's inaugural report regretted the lack of prosecution for past abuses in Argentina, Bulgaria, Chile, and Nicaragua. See Human Rights Watch, 'Quest for Justice' in *World Report 1990* (HRW 1990). In 1999, Human Rights Watch welcomed the release of South Africa's Truth and Reconciliation Commission's Report but put down a lack of prosecution of those responsible for past abuses to 'political constraints', misreading Nelson Mandela's principled position on reconciliation. See *Human Rights Watch, World Report 1999* (HRW 1999).

210 See for example, 16 July 2014, Armenia 2–3, E/C.12/ARM/CO/2–3, para 18; Democratic People's Republic of Korea, 12 December 2003, E/C.12/1/Add.95, para 19; Ethiopia, 31 May 2012, E/C.12/ETH/CO/1–3, para 14; Jordan, 1 September 2000, E/C.12/1/Add.46, para 31; Mongolia, 1 September 2000, E/C.12/1/Add.47, para 23; Mongolia, 7 July 2015, E/C.12/MNG/CO/4, para 21; Poland, 2 December2009, E/C.12/POL/CO/5, para 22; Sri Lanka, 9 December 2010, E/C.12/LKA/CO/2–4, para 25; Tanzania, 13 December 2012, E/C.12/TZA/CO/1–3, para 2.

sexual harassment at the workplace a punishable offence.[211] In relation to human trafficking in Latvia, the Committee expressed concern that although trafficking in persons carried a maximum penalty of 15 years' imprisonment under the Latvian Criminal Code, 'in most cases, the courts administer significantly lower prison sentences'.[212] Another area where the CESCR Committee has forcefully advocated punishment is the harassment of 'human rights defenders'.[213]

As regards the pronouncements on decriminalisation, both the Human Rights Committee and the CESCR Committee seem particularly concerned about religious, political, and gender-based persecution. Echoing the concerns expressed in the UPR, the Human Rights Committee has urged a number of countries to provide alternatives to military service in case of conscientious objection with reference to Article 18 (freedom of religion) and Article 26 (equality before law) of the Covenant.[214] It has also called upon state parties to provide for alternative service, 'the duration of which is without punitive effect'.[215] The two Committees have joined forces to urge several countries to decriminalise relations between consenting adults of the same sex.[216] Another area where the Committees converge

211 See, for example, Argentina, 14 December 2011, E/C.12/ARG/CO/3, para 16; Chile, 1 December 2004, E/C.12/1/Add.105, paras 21 and 45; China Hong Kong, 13 May 2005, E/C.12/1/Add.107, para 120; Croatia, 5 December 2001, E/C.12/1/Add.73, para 25; Kuwait, 19 December 2013, E/C.12/KWT/CO/2, para 20; Mongolia, 1 September 2000, E/C.12/1/Add.47, para 23; Morocco, 22 October 2015, E/C.12/MAR/CO/4, para 32; Russia, 12 December 2003, E/C.12/1/Add.94, para 48.

212 Latvia, 7 January 2008, E/C.12/LVA/CO/1, para 22.

213 See, for example, Angola, 15 July 2016, E/C.12/AGO/CO/4–5, para 18. See also Congo, 16 December 2009, E/C.12/COD/CO/4, para 12; Equatorial Guinea, 13 December 2012, E/C.12/GNQ/CO/1, para 14; Indonesia, 19 June 2014, E/C.12/IDN/CO/1, para 28; Sri Lanka, 9 December 2010, E/C.12/LKA/CO/2–4, para 10.

214 Armenia, 31 August 2012, CCPR/C/ARM/CO/2, para 16; and 19 November 1998, CCPR/C/79/Add.100, para 3. See also Azerbaijan, 12 November 2001, CCPR/CO/73/AZE, para 21; Belarus, 19 November 1997, CCPR/C/79/Add.86, para 16; Cyprus, 6 April 1998, CCPR/C/79/Add.88, para 17 and 1 August 1994, CCPR/C/79/Add.39, para 10; Israel, 21 November 2014, CCPR/C/ISR/CO/4, para 23; Serbia, 12 August 2004, CCPR/CO/81/SEMO, para 21; Uzbekistan, 7 April 2010, CCPR/C/UZB/CO/3, para 26.

215 Estonia, 15 April 2003, CCPR/CO/77/EST, para 15. See also Georgia, 19 April 2002, CCPR/CO/74/GEO, para 18; France, 4 August 1997, CCPR/C/79/Add.80, para 19.

216 For Human Rights Committee see Chile, 13 August 2014, CCPR/C/CHL/CO/6, para 14; Iran, 29 November 2011, CCPR/C/IRN/CO/3, para 10; Jamaica, 17 November 2011, CCPR/C/JAM/CO/3, para 8; Kenya, 29 April 2005, CCPR/CO/83/KEN, para 27; Togo, 18 April 2011, CCPR/C/TGO/CO/4, para 14; Turkmenistan, 19 April 2012, CCPR/C/TKM/CO/1, para 21. Examples from the concluding observations of the CESCR Committee can be found in: Kenya 2–5, 6 April 2016, E/C.12/KEN/CO/2–5, para 21; Tanzania 1–3, 13 December 2012, E/C.12/TZA/CO/1–3, p 1; Uganda 1, 8 July 2015, E/C.12/UGA/CO/1, para 16; Kenya 2–5, 6 April 2016, E/C.12/KEN/CO/2–5, para 21; Tanzania 1–3, 13 December 2012, E/C.12/TZA/CO/1–3, page 1.

on the need for decriminalisation is abortion.[217] The Human Rights Committee, in light of a large number of recommendations it has directed at East European and former Soviet republics – across a fairly limited range of subjects – appears to be keenly aware of the legacies of communism. The Human Rights Committee has urged Croatia, the Czech Republic, Kazakhstan, Poland, and Russia (besides some countries from other parts of the world) to decriminalise defamation, libel, and other press-related offences.[218] As the Committee put it in the concluding observations to Russia's seventh periodic report, restating the position adopted in its General Comment 34[219] on Article 19 (freedom of expression), 'The State party should consider decriminalising defamation, and, in any case, it should countenance the application of criminal law only in the most serious of cases, bearing in mind that imprisonment is never an appropriate penalty for defamation'.[220]

The concern about punitive responses to drug-users features in only two out of 375 concluding observations by the Human Rights Committee reviewed as part of this study.[221] The CESCR Committee has taken a stronger stance on the issue, drawing authority from Article 12 of the ICESCR (right to mental and physical health). In respect of the Dominican Republic, the Committee expressed concern 'that the State party imposes disproportionate punishments on users of illicit drugs and persons who traffic in small quantities of such drugs'.[222] It went on to recommend that 'the State party adopt a health and rights based approach to drug abuse problems, reconsider its penalization of drug use and take steps to ensure adequate living conditions in prisons'.[223] The Committee advised Mauritius and Poland respectively to consider decriminalising 'drug-use'[224] and 'possession of

217 For Human Rights Committee, see, for example, Cameroon, November 1999, CCPR/C/79/Add.116, para 13; Côte d'Ivoire, 28 April 2015, CCPR/C/CIV/CO/1, para 15; El Salvador, 18 November 2010, CCPR/C/SLV/CO/6, para 10; Guatemala, 19 April 2012, CCPR/C/GTM/CO/3, para 20 and 27 August 2001, CCPR/CO/72/GTM, para 19; United Republic of Tanzania, CCPR/C/79/Add.97, 18 August 1998, para 15. For examples from the CESCR concluding observations calling for decriminalization of abortion, see Ecuador, 13 December 2010, E/C.12/ECU/CO/3, para 29; Kenya, 6 April 2016, E/C.12/KEN/CO/2–5, para 22; Nepal, 24 September 2001, E/C.12/1/Add.66, para 23; United Kingdom, 14 July 2016, E/C.12/GBR/CO/6, para 61.

218 Croatia, 30 April 2015, CCPR/C/HRV/CO/3, para 23; Czech Republic, 22 Aug 2013, CCPR/C/CZE/CO/3, para 21; Kazakhstan, 19 Aug 2011, CCPR/C/KAZ/CO/1, para 25; Poland, 23 November 2016, CCPR/C/POL/CO/7, para 38; and Russia, 28 April 2015, CCPR/C/RUS/CO/7, para 19.

219 Human Rights Committee, General Comment No. 34, Article 19: Freedoms of Opinion and Expression. 12 September 2011, CCPR/C/GC/34, para 47.

220 Russia, 28 April 2015, CCPR/C/RUS/CO/7, para 19.

221 Cambodia, 27 April 2015, CCPR/C/KHM/CO/2, para 16; Georgia, CCPR/C/GEO/CO 19 August 2014, para 15.

222 Dominican Republic, 21 Oct 2016, E/C.12/DOM/CO/4, para 62; see also Canada, 23 March 2016, E/C.12/CAN/CO/6, para 50.

223 Ibid para 63.

224 Mauritius, 8 June 2010, E/C.12/MUS/CO/4, para 27.

small amounts of drugs'.[225] In relation to a couple of countries at least, the Committee has also addressed the laws that criminalise homelessness. It has questioned the use of criminal law provisions in the Philippines for the conviction of squatters, and 'criminalization of rough sleeping' in the UK, referring to Article 11 of the Covenant (right to housing and an adequate standard of living).[226]

The Human Rights Committee has trained its sights on penalisation of poverty and homelessness sparingly. It took issue with Ireland's 2002 Housing Act, which criminalised trespassing on land, disproportionately affecting Travellers.[227] In concluding observations to the UK's sixth periodic report, the Committee was concerned about the anti-social behaviour orders (ABSOs), particularly the fact that they were being imposed on children, some as young as 10, and that their breach constituted a criminal offence.[228] Beyond these interventions, the silence in the Committee's reports on laws which disproportionately target the poor and the homeless is quite conspicuous. In fact, it is very rare for the Committee to use terms such as 'poverty', 'inequality', or 'unemployment' in its concluding observations. Clearly, 'class', as an analytical category, does not have traction within the Committee's deliberations in quite the same way as gender, ethnicity, or sexual orientation. Further, considering the scant attention given to drug use and homelessness, compared to, say, defamation and gay sex, it is fair to conclude that the Committee's emphasis in terms of decriminalisation remains elsewhere.

Justifications for criminal punishment: questioning the self-evident?

This closing section is aimed at teasing out the theoretical and ideological premises that inform the contemporary human rights discourse vis-à-vis the all-important and much-evaded question, 'Why punish?' An attempt will be made to show how rehabilitation as a sentencing aim could be used to challenge the validity of capital punishment as well as life imprisonment and excessively long fixed sentences. The discussion then broadens out to consider how global human rights regime relates with consequentialist justifications for punishment, namely individual and general deterrence, and incapacitation based on the notion of predictive dangerousness. In wrapping up the discussion, we will turn once again to the implicit and explicit endorsement of retributivism within the discourse of human rights.

225 Poland, 26 October 2016, E/C.12/POL/CO/6, paras 53 and 54. In some cases, the Committee has also noted with alarm a high incidence of injecting drug use and HIV/AIDS in prisons and lack of adequate drug substitution programmes. See, for example, Lithuania, E/C.12/LTU/CO/2, 24 June 2014, para 21; Sweden, 14 July 2016, E/C.12/SWE/CO/6, para 41; Ukraine, 4 January 2008, E/C.12/UKR/CO/5, paras 26 and 51; Uruguay, 1 December 2010, E/C.12/URY/CO/3–4, para 27.

226 Philippines, 7 June 1995, E/C.12/1995/7, para 15; United Kingdom, 14 July 2016, E/C.12/GBR/CO/6, para 51.

227 Ireland, 30 July 2008, CCPR/C/IRL/CO/3, para 23.

228 United Kingdom, 30 July 2008, CCPR/C/GBR/CO/6, paras 20–23.

Sentencing aims and the death penalty debate

In 1995, the Constitutional Court of South Africa declared the death penalty to be inconsistent with Section 11(2) of the country's Interim Constitution, which prohibited 'torture of any kind, whether physical, mental', and 'cruel, inhuman or degrading treatment or punishment'.[229] In the leading judgment, President of the Court Arthur Chaskalson held that 'retribution could not be accorded the same weight as the rights to life and dignity', which were 'the most important of all the rights in our Constitution'.[230] Before arriving at the conclusion, President Chaskalson was careful to emphasise that the ruling did not involve 'contrasting the death penalty with no punishment at all', but the death sentence with 'severe punishment of a long term of imprisonment which, in an appropriate case, could be a sentence of life imprisonment'.[231]

The arguments in favour of retaining the death sentence, President Chaskalson held, had failed to show that it would 'be materially more effective to deter or prevent murder than the alternative sentence of life imprisonment would be'.[232] Arbitrariness and 'the possibility of error in enforcing the death penalty', in his view, further weakened the case for retaining the 'death sentence as a penalty for murder'.[233] In separate concurring opinions, three judges put forward additional reasons as to why they would declare the death penalty unconstitutional. In an eloquent passage that prefigured the reasoning of Judge Paulo Pinto de Albuquerque in *Öcalan* (No 2) and *Khamtokhu* with regards to life imprisonment, Justice Ismail Mohamed observed:

> The death sentence must, in some measure, manifest a philosophy of indefensible despair in its execution, accepting as it must do, that the offender it seeks to punish is so beyond the pale of humanity as to permit of no rehabilitation, no reform, no repentance, no inherent spectre of hope or spirituality; nor the slightest possibility that he might one day, successfully and deservedly be able to pursue and to enjoy the great rights of dignity and security and the fundamental freedoms. . . . The finality of the death penalty allows for none of these redeeming possibilities.[234]

In the same vein, Justice Tholakele Madala enquired if the 'rejection of rehabilitation as a possibility accorded with *ubuntu*' and found it did not.[235] In the opinion

229 *S v Makwanyane* 1995 (3) SA 391 (1995) 16. See also 'Constitution of the Republic of South Africa', Act 200 of 1993, Chapter III.

230 Ibid para 146. Section 9 of the Interim Constitution, 1993 provided that 'every person shall have the right to life'. According to Section 10: 'Every person shall have the right to respect for and protection of his or her dignity'.

231 *Makwanyane* (n 229) para 123.

232 Ibid para 146.

233 *Makwanyane* (n 229) para 146.

234 Ibid para 271.

235 Ibid para 241. *Ubuntu* being an African ethical concept that speaks to the inter-connectedness of all humanity and the affirmation of a person's humanity though that of another person.

of Justice Yvonne Mokogoro, the death penalty was unacceptable as it could not serve the rehabilitative function of punishment even as it might deter some potential criminals.[236] Although the separate opinions focused on the question at hand, namely the constitutional validity of the death penalty, the line of reasoning could easily be extended to build a case against life imprisonment and long prison terms, which render any meaningful social reintegration very difficult, if not impossible. One unhappy consequence of the demise of the rehabilitative ideal has been that its potential to counter extreme forms of punishment remains underutilised: The abolitionists, as a standard practice, do not tend to argue that the death penalty nullifies the possibility of rehabilitation. As exceptions to the rule, there are two pertinent references to the 'goal of rehabilitation' in Amnesty International's steadfast campaign against the death penalty as documented in its annual reports since 1961.[237] In academic writings, charting the interface between religious lobbies and the abolitionist movement in the US, James J. Megivern cited a 1958 statement by the Methodist Church calling for the abolition of capital punishment on the grounds that the focus in 'penology should be upon the process of creative, redemptive rehabilitation'.[238] That line of argument needs to be explored further. This is because in some jurisdictions the prohibition of cruel and inhuman punishment has led the courts to narrow down the scope of the death penalty but not to invalidate it altogether.

To illustrate, the Supreme Court of India, in *Bachan Singh v State of Punjab*, held that the death penalty was to be applied in the rarest of rare cases and life imprisonment had to be the norm for the offence of murder.[239] The Court's reasoning in *Bachan Singh* was eerily reminiscent of the majority opinion in the US Supreme Court case of *Gregg v Georgia*, in which the court ended the moratorium on the death penalty.[240] Legislative will and public opinion, the Indian

236 Ibid paras 315–316.

237 In the 1984 Annual Report, the organisation said that 'the increased use of the death penalty contradicted the aim of rehabilitation acknowledged in Chinese law'. See *Amnesty International Report 1984* (AI 1984) 217. In 1999, an overview essay restated the standard position that there was a 'consistent lack of scientific evidence' that the death penalty acted 'as a deterrent more effectively than other punishments' and went on to add that 'the death penalty negates the internationally accepted goal of rehabilitating offenders'. See Amnesty International, 'The death penalty: an affront to our humanity', in *Amnesty International Report* 1999 (AI 1999) 1–20, 19.

238 James J. Megivern, 'Religion and the death penalty in the United States of America: Past and Present' in Hodgkinson and Schabas (n 58) 116–142, 120.

239 *Bachan Singh v State of Punjab* AIR 1980 SC 898, para 165 (a).

240 *Gregg v Georgia* 428 US 153 (1976). Four years earlier, in *Furman v Georgia*, the US Supreme Court had held that the death penalty under Georgia and other state statutes constituted cruel and unusual punishment insofar as these laws gave the juries untrammelled discretion to impose or withhold the penalty. The US Congress and 35 state legislatures, including Georgia's, enacted new statutes retaining the death penalty but providing safeguards to curtail discretion in imposing sentences. See *Furman v Georgia* (1972) 408 US 238, 33 L Ed 2d 346. In *Gregg*, the Supreme Court ruled that new statutes provided adequate guidance to sentencing authorities, and that in enacting new statutes, the American public had, through their elected legislatures, expressed approval of capital punishment as an appropriate and necessary criminal sanction.

Supreme Court reasoned, were on the side of the retentionist position and capital punishment was not devoid of public interest.[241] With regard to the retributive function of the penalty, the Court held that

> Punishment is the way in which society expresses its denunciation of wrong-doing; and in order to maintain respect for law, it is essential that the punishment inflicted for grave crimes should adequately reflect the revulsion felt by the great majority of citizens for them.[242]

In response to the petitioners' argument that capital punishment nullifies the rehabilitative purpose of punishment, the court conveniently cited an excerpt from Justice Brennan's opinion in *Trop v Dulles*: 'Rehabilitation is but one of the several purposes of the penal law. Among other purposes are deterrence of the wrongful act by the threat of punishment and insulation of society from dangerous individuals by imprisonment or execution'.[243] The significant point overlooked in the academic literature – and brushed aside by the Supreme Court of India – is this: Rehabilitation may be only one of the stated penological aims, but there is no reason why it should not be taken into account consistently alongside other justifications. Even if it is accepted that certain crimes warrant retribution, it is facile not to provide any arguments as to why the possibility of rehabilitation is being discounted. The decision to exclude rehabilitation as a sentencing aim in capital cases is quite arbitrary since the possibility of reform and rehabilitation depends on the needs and capacities of the offender – as well as the effectiveness of rehabilitative programmes – rather than the nature of the crime itself.

Besides President Chaskalson in *Makwanyane*, the death penalty abolitionists have frequently pointed out that capital punishment does not uniquely serve the criminal justice functions of deterrence and incapacitation.[244] An undesirable implication that follows from this well-intentioned argument is that life imprisonment – or long prison sentences – may fit the bill. However, if the evidence is weak regarding the deterrent function of the death penalty, it is not particularly convincing in relation to imprisonment either. It has to be recognised, at the very least that 'there is a great asymmetry between what is expected of the legal system through deterrence and what the system delivers'.[245] Few offenders pause to think about the prospect of spending time in prison before committing a crime. For those who are socialised into crime early in life, acting in conformity

241 *Bachan Singh* (n 239) paras 67–70.

242 Ibid para 102.

243 *Trop v Dulles* 356 U.S. 86 (1958). *Cited in Bachan Singh* (n 239) at para 84.

244 See, for example, International Bar Association, *The Death Penalty under International Law: A Background Paper to the IBAHRI Resolution on the Abolition of the Death Penalty* (IBA 2008) 13–14; Amnesty International, 'Death Penalty: No Solution to Crime', in *Amnesty International 1997 Report* (AI 1997) 36–42.

245 Raymond Paternoster, 'How much do we really know about criminal deterrence?' (2010) 100(3) *The Journal of Criminal Law and Criminology* 765. See also, Mirko Bagaric and Theo Alexander, '(Marginal) general deterrence doesn't work – and what it means for sentencing' (2011) 35 *Criminal Law Journal* 269.

with the demands of the sub-culture is a bigger constraint on the choices they make compared to avoidance of 'pain' associated with the prison.[246] As for incapacitation, short of executing an individual, or locking them away for the rest of their lives, the idea is an illusion inasmuch as prisons are known to be universities of crime. In many cases, offenders return to society 'further criminalized and/or deeply marginalized, socially and economically'.[247]

A full recognition of these shortcomings in the conventional penal model requires a sociologically grounded perspective on justice as distinct from the liberal model based on the idea of the atomised individual. In the material reviewed, one does not find leading NGOs or human rights bodies challenging deterrence on empirical grounds beyond the question of the death penalty.[248] The second issue is whether the consequentialist goal of punishing an individual to deter would-be offenders can be reconciled with the human rights doctrine in the first place. In a text widely relied upon by activists and academics, Roger Hood and Carolyn Hoyle have argued that even if the death penalty was shown to have a deterrent effect, it would be incompatible with the human rights framework.[249] We need not restrict the argument to the death penalty though. If human dignity is inviolable and if individuals are not to be toyed with – as Kantian philosophers would have us believe – why lock away individuals as a means to the end of preventing crime? Another reason why deterrence ought to be taken with extreme caution from a human rights perspective is that it could easily lead authorities to introduce longer sentences and more repressive prison regimes in the vain hope of deterring further offending.[250]

Deterrence, impunity, and predictive dangerousness

Whilst the predominant idea within the global human rights regime is punishment for the sake of punishment, deterrence also makes an appearance every now and then. For example, in the UPR Working Group Reports, the UK called

246 Donald Black, *The Behavior of Law* (Academic Press 1976) 79. See also Allegra M. McLeod, 'Prison Abolition and Grounded Justice' (2015) 62 *UCLA Law Review* 1156.

247 Baz Dreisinger, *Incarceration Nations: A Journey to Justice in Prisons around the World* (Other Press 2016) 17–18. See also John Bryant and others, 'Life Behind Bars' in Lori Gruen (ed), *The Ethics of Captivity* (Oxford University Press 2014) 102–112; William Higham, 'Punishment and Social Justice' in Ben Shimshon (ed), *Social Justice: Criminal Justice* (Smith Institute 2006) 164–172, 170.

248 See, for example, Summary of Stakeholder Submissions – Bahamas (UPR Second Cycle), A/HRC/WG.6/15/BHS/3, 29 October 2012. Submission by Amnesty International noting with regret at para 10 that 'elected officials in the Bahamas continue to present the retention of the death penalty as a measure to deter crime, despite evidence from around the world indicating that the death penalty has no uniquely deterrent effect'. See also Amnesty International's submission on Saint Kitts and Navis. 17 Aug 2015, A/HRC/WG.6/23/KNA/3, at para 16.

249 Hood and Hoyle (n 51) 23.

250 Andrew Ashworth, 'Criminal Justice Act 2003: The Sentencing Provisions' (2005) 68(5) *Modern Law Review* 822, 826.

upon Madagascar and Mauritius to strengthen efforts to tackle gender-based violence through improved reporting of the crime and 'increased investigations, prosecutions, convictions and sentences to *deter* offenders'.[251] Malaysia, in turn, advised the UK to 'take more effective measures to ensure that the perpetrators of acts of discrimination, hate crimes and xenophobia are adequately *deterred* and sanctioned'.[252] Unless we are willing to suspend the empirical lens, these pronouncements warrant some substantiating evidence. Do we know if stricter penalties have led to a decrease in re-offending, for instance?

Admittedly, government delegates at the UPR could not be expected to get into complex criminological debates. However, the more specialised and independent treaty monitoring bodies fare no better. In concluding observations to Iraq's fourth periodic report, the CESCR Committee recommended that the 'State party step up its efforts to combat and deter all acts of violence' against women and girls.[253] More specifically, further down in the document, the Committee urged Iraq to provide for 'deterrent punishments for forced marriages'.[254] The Committee also urged Uganda to 'investigate, deter and prevent acts of discrimination against [LGBTI] people, bring perpetrators to justice and provide compensation to victims'.[255] The Human Rights Committee uses the term 'deterrence' sparingly in its concluding observations. In regard to France, the Committee said the state party 'must establish adequate systems for monitoring and deterring abuses' by law enforcement officials.[256] The Dominican Republic was advised to introduce 'much more severe sanctions' to 'effectively *discourage* torture and other abuses by prison and law enforcement officials'.[257]

One of the most frequently used terms within the material under review is 'impunity' (from Latin *impunis*, unpunished). It is also a key normative locus of the modern human rights movement. The term comes charged with dual meaning: as a rhetorical shorthand for the moral problem of certain individuals going unpunished or being punished leniently (retributivism), and as a signifier of a culture where offenders do not fear punishment (lack of deterrence). For example, the Human Rights Committee noted 'with concern that numerous serious human rights violations have been and continue to be committed with total *impunity* in the Central African Republic' and that 'any sanctions tend to be administrative and military in nature, rather than judicial'.[258] In respect of

251 Human Rights Council, *Report of the Working Group on the Universal Periodic Review: Madagascar*, 23 December 2014, A/HRC/28/13 (Recommendation 108.94); Mauritius, 26 December 2013, A/HRC/25/8 (Recommendation 128.75).

252 Human Rights Council, *Report of the Working Group on the Universal Periodic Review: United Kingdom*, 6 July 2012, A/HRC/21/9 (Recommendation 110.90) (emphasis added). See also Croatia A/HRC/30/14 (Recommendation 99.49 by Timor-Leste).

253 Iraq, 27 October 2015, E/C.12/IRQ/CO/4, para 39.

254 Ibid para 42.

255 Uganda, 8 July 2015, E/C.12/UGA/CO/1, para 16.

256 France, 31 July 2008, CCPR/C/FRA/CO/4, para 19.

257 Dominican Republic, 26 April 2001, CCPR/CO/71/DOM, para 10 (emphasis added).

258 Central African Republic, 27 July 2006, CCPR/C/CAF/CO/2, para 7 (emphasis added).

Peru, the Committee recommended that the state party 'review and repeal the 1995 amnesty laws, which help create an atmosphere of *impunity*'.[259] In the UPR documentation, the template of the Summary of Stakeholder Submissions even carries a heading, 'Administration of justice, including impunity and the rule of law', perhaps phrased so to accommodate the vast amount of NGO submissions dealing with the subject of 'impunity'.

What is worth noting at this stage is that there is no engagement on the part of the treaty monitoring bodies with the question of whether the prison actually works as a deterrent and helps prevent crime. For instance, one does not come across a concluding observation by either of the two Committees where they ask the state party to provide information on recidivism rates as a proxy indicator of individual deterrence. The omission is puzzling because, as mentioned earlier, the Committees do frequently call upon states to produce detailed statistics on certain subjects, such as the number of prosecutions and convictions for crimes based on ethnicity[260] or gender.[261] A lack of corresponding interest in, say, re-offending rates, or evaluations of penal policy in terms of a general deterrence effect, indicates a preference for intuitive reasoning over empirical evidence.

We will turn to the other dimension of 'impunity' (the imperative of punishment) shortly. Let us first tackle the penal aims of incapacitation and deterrence as they play out in the context of preventive detention and indeterminate sentences based on the risk of future offending. Detention of individuals without or beyond charge, and sentences imposed on the basis that a person is likely to reoffend, raise legal issues around guarantees of freedom from arbitrary arrest (UDHR Article 3, ICCPR Article 9), right to a fair trial, including the prohibition of double jeopardy (UDHR Article 6, ICCPR Article 14), and the *nullum crimen* principle (UDHR Article 11, ICCPR Article 15). Since the onset of the post-9/11 'war on terror', countries around the globe have taken recourse to internment and other forms of security detention not only in light of past offending, but with a view to pre-empting offending altogether.[262] Whilst human rights bodies have frequently challenged sentencing and detention practices based on such criteria, the discourse is marked by some unsettling ambiguities.

In concluding observations to New Zealand's third periodic report, the Human Rights Committee called for amendments to provisions in the domestic law, which provided for a 'sentence of indeterminate detention for offenders convicted of serious crimes who are likely to repeat such crimes'.[263] The imposition of punishment in respect of possible future offence, the Committee stated, was

259 Peru, 15 November 2000, CCPR/CO/70/PER, para 9 (emphasis added).

260 See, for example, Finland, 16 January 2008, E/C.12/FIN/CO/5, para 22.

261 See, for example, Ireland, 30 July 2008, CCPR/C/IRL/CO/3, para 9.

262 The latter phenomenon is peculiarly defined in criminological literature as 'pre-crime'. See Jude McCulloch and Dean Wilson, *Pre-crime: Pre-emption, Precaution, and the Future* (Routledge 2016).

263 New Zealand, Report of the Human Right Committee, 1995. A/50/40, para 186.

inconsistent with Article 9 and Article 14 of the Covenant.[264] The Committee called upon France, consecutively in 2008 and 2015, to review the practice of seeking to reduce 'the risk of criminal recidivism' by placing individuals in detention owning to their 'dangerousness' after they had served their prison sentences.[265] In regard to the UK's Prevention of Terrorism Act 2005, the Committee expressed concern about the control order regime, 'which involves the imposition of a wide range of restrictions, including curfews of up to 16 hours, on individuals suspected of [terrorist activity], but who have not been charged with any criminal offence'.[266] Although the House of Lords in *R (McCann & others) v Crown Court at Manchester* had categorised 'control orders' as civil orders, the Committee was worried that they could give rise to criminal liability if breached.[267] But the Committee did not recommend a repeal of the relevant statutory provisions. It merely suggested that the 'State party ensure that those subjected to control orders are promptly charged with a criminal offence'.[268]

The Committee has had to grapple with the notion of 'predictive dangerousness' in the context of sentences imposed at the time of conviction as well as post-sentence preventive detention and parole decisions in a number of individual communications. In *Rameka v New Zealand*, authors of the communication had received sentences which included a preventive component based on pre-sentencing reports suggesting a propensity to commit sexual offences. The first author, Rameka, was convicted and sentenced to preventive detention (indefinite detention until release by the Parole Board) under section 75 of New Zealand's Criminal Justice Act 1985, on one count of rape, and concurrently to 14 years' imprisonment in respect of the second charge of rape, two years' imprisonment for aggravated burglary, and another two years for the assault with intent to commit rape.[269] The second author, Harris, was originally sentenced by the trial court to six years on two counts of unlawful sexual connection, and to four years to be served concurrently on charges of indecent assault. The Court of Appeal substituted a sentence of preventive detention on each count, holding that whilst offences in question warranted a finite sentence of no less than seven-and-a-half years, 'no appropriate finite sentence would adequately protect the public', and that preventive detention with continuing supervision after release was the appropriate sentence.[270] The third author, Tawari, was sentenced to preventive detention for sexual violation charges based on 'the psychiatric assessment of a

264 Ibid para 186–188. See also Portugal Macau, 5 May 1997, CCPR/C/79/Add.77, para 8.
265 Such post-sentence preventive detention orders, in the Committee's view, were problematic under articles 9, 14, and 15 of the Covenant. France, 31 July 2008, CCPR/C/FRA/CO/4, para 16; France, 17 August 2015, CCPR/C/FRA/CO/5, para 11; see also Uzbekistan, 17 August 2015, CCPR/C/UZB/CO/4, para 17.
266 United Kingdom, 30 July 2008, UN doc CCPR/C/GBR/CO/6, para 17.
267 [2002] UKHL 39 [2003] 1 AC 787, [2002] 4 All ER 593.
268 Ibid para 17.
269 *Rameka and others v New Zealand*, Communication No. 1090/2002 (2003) UN Doc CCPR/C/79/D/1090/2002, para 2.2.
270 *Rameka and others v New Zeeland*, para 2.5.

imprisonment could be divided into a punitive detention part consisting of fixed (non-parole period) and a flexible preventive detention component rested on an artificial division. The dissenting members had no problem accepting that sentences of preventive detention designed solely to protect the community against future dangerous conduct were compatible with the Covenant, and that Article 9(4) could not 'be construed so as to give a right to judicial review of a sentence on an unlimited number of occasions'.[277]

Two subsequent cases – *Fardon v Australia* and *Tilman v Australia* – where the Committee did find preventive detention to be incompatible with the Covenant differed from *Rameka* primarily because in these cases, unlike in *Rameka*, the courts had not contemplated preventive detention at the time of conviction.[278] Rather, continued detention for preventive purposes was added on to completed sentences following civil proceedings. In *Fardon*, the author served a 14-year sentence for sexual offences. After his sentence expired, he continued to be detained pursuant to Queensland's Dangerous Prisoners (Sexual Offences) Act 2003 (DPSOA). The Act provided that 'a prisoner who is proven to be a serious danger to the community may be detained in custody for an indefinite term for control, care or treatment'.[279] In finding a violation of Article 9, the Committee explained that Fardon's detention 'amounted, in substance, to a fresh term of imprisonment which, unlike detention proper, is not permissible in the absence of a conviction for which imprisonment is a sentence prescribed by law'.[280] The Committee further stated that imprisonment being penal in character could only 'be imposed on conviction for an offence in the same proceedings in which the offence is tried', and not 'in respect of predicted future criminal conduct which had its basis in the very offence for which [the author] had already served his sentence'.[281] In a passage that raises more questions than it answers, the Committee went on to declare that:

> The concept of feared or predicted dangerousness to the community applicable in the case of past offenders is inherently problematic. It is essentially based on opinion as distinct from factual evidence, even if that evidence consists in the opinion of psychiatric experts. But psychiatry is not an exact science. The DPSOA, on the one hand, requires the Court to have regard to the opinion of psychiatric experts on future dangerousness but, on the other hand, requires the Court to make a finding of fact of dangerousness. While Courts are free to accept or reject expert opinion and are required to

277 Ibid, Individual Opinion of Committee members Mr. Shearer and Mr. Roman Wyszynski, in which Committee member Mr. Netsuke Ando joins (dissenting in part), p 24.

278 *Fardon v Australia,* Communication No. 1629/2007 (2010) UN Doc CCPR/C/98/D/1629/2007; *Tillman v Australia,* Communication No. 1635/2007 (2010) UN Doc CCPR/C/98/D/1635/2007.

279 Ibid para 2.2.

280 Ibid para 7.4, sub-para 1.

281 Ibid para 7.4, sub-para 2. The Committee arrived at a similar conclusion in a communication from Australia where the author had been subjected to a new term of imprisonment without a conviction. See *Tillman* (n 278).

> consider all other available relevant evidence, the reality is that the Courts must make a finding of fact on the suspected future behaviour of a past offender which may or may not materialise.[282]

Here lies the rub: If the concept of 'predictive dangerousness' is 'inherently problematic', why allow it as part of sentences imposed at the time of conviction? The assessment of risk, whether upon conviction or at a later stage, is based on the same 'inexact' science of psychiatry.[283] Let us recall that in *Rameka* the majority had no problem accepting the 'preventive' component of the original sentences imposed on the complainants based on the risk of re-offending. In *Fardon*, the Court would have been on safer grounds restricting its ruling on a violation of Article 15 since the DPSOA had been retroactively applied to the author. A further question that arises from the Committee's suspicion of psychiatric evidence relates to the deterrent function of criminal sentencing. As argued earlier, the very notion that a term in prison would deter the convicted individual – or potential offenders – rests on certain psychological assumptions. It could be said in favour of the kind of preventive detention regimes discussed above that they at least draw on some form of 'scientific' assessments of risk. Sentencing courts, on the other hand, enjoy freedom to contemplate individual and general deterrence in determining sentences without even having to cite expert opinion.

In 2014, the Human Rights Committee issued General Comment 35 on Article 9, which, at least in part, reads like a rationalisation of its case law on preventive detention.[284] The Committee's explanations muddied the waters even further. The Covenant, the Committee claimed, was 'consistent with a variety of schemes for sentencing in criminal cases'.[285] It did not pause to unpack this far-reaching assertion. Did the Committee mean to imply that a sentencing scheme based purely on deterrence would comply with the Covenant? Does this broad-church approach to sentencing have any limits? After restating its position that 'consideration for parole or other forms of early release must be in accordance with the law' and 'must not be denied on grounds that are arbitrary within the meaning of Article 9',[286] the Committee again exposed ambivalence towards 'predicted dangerousness' by stating that 'prediction of the prisoner's future behaviour may

282 *Fardon* (n 278) para 7.4, sub-para 4.

283 This point has been uniformly overlooked in commentaries discussing preventive detention in the context of the Human Rights Committee's jurisprudence. See, for example, Manfred Nowak, *UN Covenant on Civil and Political Rights: CCPR Commentary* (2nd edn, N.P. Engel 2005) 210–240; Ronli Sifirs, 'An international Human Rights Perspective on Detention without Charge or Trial: Article 9 of the International Covenant on Civil and Political Rights' in Bernadette McSherry and Patrick Keyze (eds), *Dangerous People: Policy, Prediction, and Practice* (Routledge 2011) 13–24; Joseph and Castan (n 112) 358–362.

284 Human Rights Committee, General Comment No.35, Article 9 (Liberty and security of person) (16 December 2014) UN Doc CCPR/C/GC/35.

285 Ibid para 20.

286 Ibid. See also, *De Léon Castro v Spain,* Communication No. 1318/2005 (2009) UN Doc CCPR/C/95/D/1388/2005.

be a relevant factor in deciding whether to grant early release'.[287] The subsequent paragraph could be seen as a serious attempt at clarifying the issue, except that it throws up a moral minefield:

> When a criminal sentence includes a punitive period followed by a non-punitive period intended to protect the safety of other individuals, then once the punitive term of imprisonment has been served, to avoid arbitrariness, the additional detention must be justified by compelling reasons arising from the gravity of the crimes committed and the likelihood of the detainee's committing similar crimes in the future. States should only use such detention as a last resort and regular periodic reviews by an independent body must be assured to decide whether continued detention is justified. State parties must exercise caution and provide appropriate guarantees in evaluating future dangers. The conditions in such detention must be distinct from the conditions for convicted prisoners serving a punitive sentence and must be aimed at the detainee's rehabilitation and reintegration into society. If a prisoner has fully served the sentence imposed at the time of conviction, Articles 9 and 15 prohibit a retroactive increase in sentence and a State party may not circumvent that prohibition by imposing a detention that is equivalent to penal imprisonment under the label of civil detention.[288]

It is not clear at all why in the opinion of the Committee additional detention ought to be justified with reference to the 'gravity of crimes committed'. If the distinction between the punitive and preventive components of a sentence is valid, why should the latter element be based on the gravity of crimes? Presumably, that is something already taken care of by the punitive part of the sentence. Is it the case, then, that the Committee is unwittingly encouraging a sentencing practice which would punish an offender twice in relation to 'the gravity of crimes committed' – first in the name of a punitive sentence, and then for the sake of preventing the public?[289] The Committee's observations regarding the conditions of detention, implicitly referring to Article 10(3) of the ICCPR, are equally problematic. The said provision (even in its watered-down version) posits 'reformation and social rehabilitation' as the 'essential aim' of the 'treatment' of all prisoners and not just those in preventive detention or nearing release. To suggest that 'convicted prisoners serving a punitive sentence' are somehow less

287 Human Rights Committee, General Comment No. 35 (16 December 2014) UN Doc CCPR/C/GC/35, para 20.

288 Ibid para 21.

289 A similar confusion is discernible in the European Court's jurisprudence on offenders' disenfranchisement. Whilst invalidating blanket bans, the Court has imported a retributive rationale through the backdoor by giving a nod to voting restrictions based on the 'gravity of offence', in addition to the express aims of public protection and promotion of democratic values. See *Scopola v Italy* (No. 3) *(App 126/05) 22 May 2012 [Grand Chamber] 56 EHRR 19, para 96; Hirst v United Kingdom* (n 102) para 86.

deserving of a regime aimed at social rehabilitation might be the straw that breaks the camel's back.

Punishment for the sake of punishment

Let us now shift attention once more to the 'retributive' element itself, the article of faith with the human rights community, and the *cause celebre* of the keepers of the (Kantian) flame – Amnesty International and Human Rights Watch.[290] In General Comment 35, the Committee interpreted the notion of arbitrariness within the terms of Article 9 broadly to 'include elements of inappropriateness, injustice, lack of predictability and due process of law as well as elements of reasonableness, necessity, and proportionality'.[291] By implication, the punitive or retributive element of a prison sentence must have certain safeguards. The Committee is mostly vigilant about the due-process requirements even where it calls upon a state party to punish the perpetrators of human rights violation 'commensurate' with the gravity of crimes.[292] Similarly, Amnesty International in its submissions to the UPR is careful to specify that it wants governments to prosecute and punish people but in 'fair trials and without resorting to the death penalty'.[293] The protective role of human rights comes unstuck in relation to 'proportionate' punishment for the following reasons: First, as previously suggested, the demands for proportionate or commensurate penalties (in the material under review) are framed more frequently in the sense of punishment adequately fitting the crime rather than in the defensive sense of the prohibition of excessive punishment. Second, where human rights bodies and leading NGOs criticise disproportionate or severe penalties, the animating concern is the exercise of traditional civil and political rights or political persecution. In other words, when punishment is deemed disproportionate, the underlying context is more likely to be 'political crimes' rather than so-called non-political crimes.

To furnish some examples from the Human Rights Committee's jurisprudence, in *Fernando v Sri Lanka*, the Committee held that a sentence of one year in prison with hard labour for contempt of court was too severe and 'draconian', constituting a violation of the prohibition of arbitrary detention 'in the absence of adequate explanation and without independent procedural safeguards'.[294] In *Dissanayake v Sri Lanka*, the author, a prominent politician, was sentenced to

290 The term 'keepers of the flame' is gratefully adapted here from the title of Stephen Hopgood's ethnography of Amnesty International. See Stephen Hopgood, *Keepers of the Flame: Understanding Amnesty International* (Cornell University Press 2006).

291 Human Rights Committee, General Comment No. 35 (16 December 2014) UN Doc CCPR/C/GC/35, para 12.

292 Ibid para 26. See also Iran, 29 November 2011, CCPR/C/IRN/CO/3.

293 See Summaries of Stakeholder Submissions (UPR Cycle 2): Saudi Arabia, A/HRC/WG.6/17/SAU/3, 24 July 2013, para 18; Libya, 23 Feb 2015, A/HRC/WG.6/22/LBY/3, para 52; Sri Lanka, 30 July 2012, A/HRC/WG.6/14/LKA/3, para 23.

294 *Fernando v Sri Lanka,* Communication No. 1189/2003 (2005) UN Doc CCPR/C/83/D/1189/2003, para 9.2.

two years of rigorous imprisonment for saying in a speech that he 'would not accept any shameful decision the Court gives', in a reference to pending proceedings on the dissolution of the Parliament by the Sri Lankan president.[295] After committal to prison, pursuant to a constitutional provision, the author was also disqualified from voting or running as a candidate for a period of seven years. The state party submitted that the author had previously been charged with contempt but not convicted and that the Supreme Court had passed the sentence of two years rigorous imprisonment as a deterrent punishment as its earlier leniency had had no impact on the author's behaviour.[296] The Committee disagreed, holding that 'it would thus appear that the severity of the author's sentence was based on two contempt charges, of one of which he had not been convicted'.[297] That makes a contrast with the Committee's case law dealing with sexual offences where it has not questioned state parties for imposing deterrent penalties based on past offending. In *Dissanayake*, the Committee held the sentence imposed on the author had been arbitrary, in violation of Article 9(1). It further found a violation of the Article 19 guarantee of freedom of expression, as the sentence imposed upon the author was disproportionate to any legitimate aim under Article 19(3).[298]

The Committee has also held prolonged detention of asylum-seekers, pending the processing of their refugee status applications, as a form of disproportionate punishment incompatible with the Article 9 prohibition of arbitrary detention.[299] In its concluding observations on Uzbekistan's fourth periodic report, the Committee was concerned 'about the alleged practice of arbitrarily extending the soon-to-be-completed prison sentences of human rights defenders, government critics and persons convicted of religious extremism'.[300] It urged Uzbekistan to ensure that 'due process rights are fully respected and the proportionality principle is strictly observed in all sentencing decisions'.[301] Elsewhere, in the Committee's concluding observations, the proportionality principle is invoked to recommend tougher penalties illustrated by several examples cited earlier. As for the CESCR Committee, it expressed concern in regard to the Dominican Republic that 'the State party imposes disproportionate punishments on users of illicit drugs and persons who traffic in small quantities of such drugs'.[302] Other examples from the Committee's concluding observations (from 1993 to 2016)

295 *Dissanayake v Sri Lanka,* Communication No. 1373/2005 (2008) UN Doc CCPR/C/93/D/1373/2005, paras 2.2 and 2.3.
296 Ibid para 4.1.
297 Ibid para 8.3.
298 Ibid para 8.4.
299 *A v Australia,* Communication No. 560/1993 (1997) UN Doc CCPR/C/59/D/560/1993. See also the following concluding observations: Czech Republic, 22 August 2013, CCPR/C/CZE/CO/3, para 17; Denmark, 15 August 2016, CCPR/C/DNK/CO/6, para 32; Greece, 3 December 2015, CCPR/C/GRC/CO/2, para 28.
300 Uzbekistan, 17 August 2015, CCPR/C/UZB/CO/4, para 17.
301 Ibid para 17.
302 Dominican Republic, 21 October 2016, E/C.12/DOM/CO/4, para 62.

employ the term 'commensurate' or 'proportionate' in terms of tougher punishment required in the context of trafficking, domestic violence, sexual harassment, violations of migrant workers' rights, and the violations of the right to participate in cultural life.[303]

Moving on to the proportionality of punishment to crime as it features in the UPR second cycle, Belgium recommended that Thailand remove from its criminal law 'prison terms for offences stemming from the legitimate exercise of the right to freedom of opinion and expression' and ensure that 'sanctions are proportionate to the act committed'.[304] Similarly, France urged Jordan to 'ensure in law and judicial practice, the proportionality of sentences for defamation or expression offences'.[305] In its stakeholder submission on Hungary, the Council of Europe urged that penalties for defamation ought to be 'strictly proportionate to the actual harm caused'.[306] As an exceptional intervention turning on the defensive role of proportionality, International Prison Watch expressed concern about systematic handing down of 'more severe penalties for repeat offenders' in France between 2005 and 2011.[307] Other examples from the UPR all speak to the offensive role of the proportionality principle, such as the US urging Croatia and Barbados to ensure that trafficking offenders 'are punished with sentences commensurate with the gravity of the crime',[308] and Amnesty International, in its submission on Montenegro, drawing attention to the high number of acquittals of those accused of international crimes 'on procedural grounds' and the handing down of 'sentences incommensurate with the gravity of the crimes'.[309]

303 See, for example, Azerbaijan, 5 June 2013, E/C.12/AZE/CO/3, para 20 (trafficking); Bulgaria, 11 December 2012, E/C.12/BGR/CO/4–5, para 16 (trafficking); Philippines, 26 October 2016, E/C.12/PHL/CO/5–6, para 40 (domestic violence); Morocco, E/C.12/MAR/CO/4, 22 Oct 2015, para 32 (sexual harassment); Slovenia, 15 December 2014, E/C.12/SVN/CO/2, para 17 (migrants' labour rights); Thailand, 19 June 2015, E/C.12/THA/CO/1–2, para 35 (violations of right to participate in cultural life).

304 Human Rights Council, *Report of the Working Group on the Universal Periodic Review: Thailand*. Thirty-third session, 15 July 2016, A/HRC/33/16 (Recommendation 159.52).

305 Human Rights Council, *Report of the Working Group on the Universal Periodic Review: Jordan*. Twenty-fifth session, 6 January 2014, A/HRC/25/9 (Recommendation 118.75).

306 Human Rights Council, *Summary prepared by the Office of the United Nations High Commissioner for Human Rights: Hungary*. Twenty-fifth session, 23 February 2016, A/HRC/WG.6/25/ATG/3, para 9. See also Antigua and Barbuda, A/HRC/WG.6/25/ATG/3, para 9 (Submission by Child Rights Network, arguing that that life imprisonment and lengthy sentences of children are grossly disproportionate and amount to a form of cruel and inhuman punishment').

307 Human Rights Council, *Summary prepared by the Office of the United Nations High Commissioner for Human Rights: France*. Fifteenth session, 8 November 2012, A/HRC/WG.6/15/FRA/3, para 33.

308 Human Rights Council, *Report of the Working Group on the Universal Periodic Review: Croatia*. Thirtieth session, 20 July 2015, A/HRC/30/14 (Recommendation 99.91); Barbados, 12 March 2013, A/HRC/23/11 (Recommendation 102.89).

309 Human Rights Council, *Summary prepared by the Office of the United Nations High Commissioner for Human Rights: Montenegro*. Fifteenth session, 8 November 2012, A/HRC/WG.6/15/MNE/3, para 29.

One last point that needs to be made in respect of 'proportionate' punishment concerns the 'fetish of the abstract individual' discussed in the previous chapters.[310] In Chapter 2, we reviewed contemporary literature that provides at least partial backing to the once-dominant positivist belief in the primacy of psychological, neurobiological, and situational factors in shaping criminal behaviour. The point was not that those committing violent offences have no control over their behaviour; rather, the plea was that a single-minded focus on individual free will in liberal theory has a paralysing effect on addressing the underlying causes of crime. The construction of the legal subject as an abstract individual directly manifests – as well as helps sustain – the retributive model of justice divorced from social justice considerations. To try to understand what drives certain individuals to commit horrible acts of violence is not to condone those acts. What are we to make of the fact, for example, that according to the Prison Reform Trust, '72% of male and 70% of female sentenced prisoners in [England and Wales] suffer from two or more mental disorders'?[311] Similarly, it has been said about the US that 'more people with mental and emotional disorders' find themselves 'in jails and prisons than in medical institutions'.[312] Does that inspire confidence in the retributive model of justice? We have already taken stock of sociological and ethnographic accounts which speak to the hidden costs of punishment in the form of difficulties encountered by ex-convicts in finding employment, and the social and economic implications of incarceration on the families of the convict. Does the contemporary discourse of human rights address these concerns as it builds a case for retributive punishment?

With regards to persons with mental illness who come into conflict with the law, the global human rights regime appears to play a minimalist role. The interventions by human rights bodies rarely go to the heart of the matter. They do not question the criminal liability of mentally ill defendants or the validity of retributive justice as applied to such individuals.[313] In the UPR Working Group Reports from the second cycle, there is just one recommendation – out of thousands – that addresses the matter squarely, with France urging Australia to 'ensure that people with severe mental disorders and/or in poor health, especially those whose

310 Bob Fine, *Democracy and the Rule of Law: Liberal Ideals and Marxist Critiques* (Pluto Press 1984).

311 House of Lords – House of Commons Joint Committee on Human Rights, *The Implications for Access to Justice of the Government's Proposals to Reform Legal Aid. Seventh Report of Session 2013–2014.* 56.

312 Angela Y. Davis, *Are Prisons Obsolete?* (Seven Stories Press 2003) 108. See also, Allegra M. McLeod, 'Confronting Criminal Law's Violence: The Possibilities of Unfinished Alternatives' (2012–13) 8 *Unbound* 109.

313 An exception to the rule is the imposition of death sentences or execution of a person suffering from a mental disorder, which is believed to be prohibited under customary international law. See UN ECOSOC, Implementation of the Safeguards Guaranteeing Protection of the Rights of those Facing the Death Penalty, ECOSOC Res. 1996/15, UN.Doc. E/CN.15/1996/15, July 23, 1996). See William A. Schabas, 'International Norms on Execution of the Insane and the Mentally Retarded' (1993) 4 *Criminal Law Forum* 95.

state of health is at risk of further deterioration due to their incarceration, are not imprisoned'.[314] There are a few other recommendations that basically concern mental healthcare in detention. For example, New Zealand called upon Mexico to 'ensure effective implementation of the rights of persons with disabilities in detention facilities, including persons with mental disabilities'.[315] France urged the US to ensure that 'no person with a mental disability is executed'.[316] Amnesty International reiterated this call in its submissions on Pakistan and Singapore.[317] Interventions by Human Rights Watch on the subject of mental illness as captured in the Summaries of Stakeholder Submissions invariably refer to the abuses and coercive methods used in psychiatric and drug-abuse treatment centres.[318] This concern, in addition to the commitment of political dissidents in mental institutions, also reverberates in the organisation's global state of human rights reports.[319]

The Human Rights Committee, in its concluding observations, has urged a number of countries to improve mental healthcare in prisons.[320] It has also called upon state parties to put an end to solitary confinement in view of its detrimental psychological effects and incompatibility with ICCPR's Article 7.[321] Curiously

314 Human Rights Council, *Report of the Working Group on the Universal Periodic Review: Australia*. Thirty-first session, 13 January 2016, A/HRC/31/14 (Recommendation 141.61).

315 Human Rights Council, *Report of the Working Group on the Universal Periodic Review: Mexico*. Twenty-fifth session, 11 December 2013, A/HRC/25/7 (Recommendation 148.164).

316 Human Rights Council, *Report of the Working Group on the Universal Periodic Review: United States of America*. Thirtieth Session, 20 July 2015, A/HRC/30/12 (Recommendation 176.197).

317 Human Rights Council, *Summary prepared by the Office of the United Nations High Commissioner for Human Rights: Pakistan*. Fourteenth session, 26 July 2012, A/HRC/WG.6/14/PAK/3, para 72; Singapore, 6 November 2015, A/HRC/WG.6/24/SGP/3, para 12. See also, Amnesty International, *Annual Report 1987* (London 1987) 205; *Annual Report 1991* (London 1991) 240; *Annual Report 1998* (London 1998) 8–10: *Annual Report 2001* (London 2001) 15: *Annual Report 2003* (London 2003) 267).

318 See, for example, Human Rights Council, *Summary prepared by the Office of the United Nations High Commissioner for Human Rights: Ghana*. Fourteenth session, 20 July 2012, A/HRC/WG.6/14/GHA/3, paras 57–8; Lao, A/HRC/WG.6/21/LAO/3, para 18.

319 See, for example, Human Rights Watch, *World Report 2011: Events of 2000* (HRW 2011) 367, 388 (expressing concerns about drug treatment centres in Singapore and Vietnam); *World Report 2010: Events of 2009* (HRW 2010) 49 (on political dissidents committed to rehabilitation institutions in China). Human Rights Watch has also documented mental health problems induced by solitary confinement in the American prisons, and the detention of immigrants with mental problems who cannot afford legal representation. See, for example, Human Rights Watch, *World Report 2013: Events of 2012* (HRW 2013) 642; *World Report 2012: Events of 2011* (HRW 2012) 53.

320 See, for example, Austria, 3 December 2015, CCPR/C/AUT/CO/5, para 23; Bosnia-Herzegovina, 22 November 2006, CCPR/C/BIH/CO/1, para 19; Ireland, 30 July 2008, CCPR/C/IRL/CO/3, para 15.

321 Japan, 18 December 2008, CCPR/C/JPN/CO/5, para 21; USA, 15 September 2006, CCPR/C/USA/CO/3, para 20. The Committee has also taken up the issue of the high incidence of suicides in prisons in some countries. See, for example, Canada, 13 August 2015, CCPR/C/CAN/CO/6, para 14; United Kingdom, 17 August 2015, CCPR/C/GBR/CO/7, para 16.

though, the Committee has not quizzed state parties as to why individuals with mental illness get sentenced in the first place. Nor has it emphasised the more modest idea of mental disorders or learning disability as a factor reflecting personal mitigation in sentencing. That stands in sharp contrast with the Committee's consistent stand that imprisonment is never an appropriate penalty for political offences, such as defamation. The only occasion where the Committee called upon a state to furnish 'reasons for the courts' findings of mitigating circumstances' concerned the imposition of the death penalty in Botswana.[322] The Committee's concluding observations are also silent on the need for leniency in punishment for property and street crimes, which have been shown, in varied contexts, to have correlations with various dimensions of disadvantage, including income inequality, family disruption, low education levels, and joblessness.[323] The same holds for the CESCR Committee, except that in relation to at least a couple of countries, it has expressed a concern that that 'individuals who should be receiving mental health care have been held criminally responsible, convicted and imprisoned'.[324]

In the UPR second cycle, Organisation Mondiale pour l'Éducation Préscolaire (OMEP), an NGO based in New Zealand, put in a submission stating, 'Children with a parent in prison were one of the most marginalized groups and invisible in social policy'.[325] Another lesser-known organisation, International Presentation Association, referred to 'levels of offending and victimisation having significant inter-generational impact' in New Zealand.[326] In respect of Côte d'Ivoire, a local association of women jurists (AFJCI) suggested, '[T]he authorities computerize the records of detainees, by entering factual information such as marital status and physical address, in order to allow the competent services to take care of the children of detainees'.[327] These submissions resonate powerfully with

322 Botswana, 24 April 2008, CCPR/C/BWA/CO/1, para 13.

323 See, for example, Morgan Kelly, 'Inequality and Crime' (2016) 82(4) Review of Economics and Statistics 530; Siu Kwong Wong, 'Reciprocal Effects of Family Disruption and Crime: A Panel Study of Canadian Municipalities' (2011) 12(1) *Western Criminology Review* 43; G. Demombynes and B. Özler, 'Crime and Local Inequality in South Africa' (2005) 76(2) Journal of Development Economics 265; William C. Heffernan and John Kleinig, 'Introduction' in Hefferman and Kleinig (eds), *From Social Justice to Criminal Justice: Poverty and the Administration of Criminal Law* (OUP 2000) 1–24. *E.B. Patterson, 'Poverty, Income Inequality, and Community Crime Rates' (1991) 29(4) Criminology* 755; Stephen Cernkovich and Peggy Giordano, 'Family Relationships and Delinquency' (1987) 25 *Criminology* 295; Judith Blau and Peter Blau, 'The Cost of Inequality' (1982) 47 *American Sociological Review* 121.

324 Cambodia, 12 June 2009, E/C.12/KHM/CO/1, para 33. See also Norway, 13 December 2013, E/C.12/NOR/CO/5, para 18.

325 Human Rights Council, *Summary prepared by the Office of the United Nations High Commissioner for Human Rights: New Zealand*. Eighteenth session, 4 November 2013, A/HRC/WG.6/18/NZL/3, para 37.

326 Ibid para 37.

327 Human Rights Council, *Summary prepared by the Office of the United Nations High Commissioner for Human Rights: Côte d'Ivoire*. Nineteenth session, 6 February 2014, A/HRC/WG.6/19/CIV/3, para 27.

the critique of the 'justice model' that I presented earlier in the book. What is remarkable is that none of these submissions were followed through in the form of a recommendation in any of the 193 Working Group Reports adopted during the second cycle.

In its concluding observations, the Human Rights Committee routinely takes up matters related to juvenile justice as well as the rights of vulnerable subgroups, such as street children, with reference to Article 24 (rights of the child) of the ICCPR. However, in none of the concluding observations reviewed as part of this study did it raise concerns about the situation of prisoners' children, employment prospects of released prisoners, or problems such as inter-generational patterns of criminal behaviour. Despite the rhetoric of 'indivisibility' and 'interdependence', the implications of criminal sentencing on economic and social rights fall through the cracks. Whilst the CESCR Committee has stepped in to partially bridge the criminal justice-social justice divide by, for example, calling for decriminalisation of drug offences, it too remains silent about the impact of incarceration on the prisoner's dependants. Leaving aside the broader collateral consequences of 'commensurate' penalties, one would have expected the two Committees to recognise punishment that is tacked on to a prison term in the form of 'criminal records'. However, the CESCR Committee has not specifically addressed the problem in any of the 285 concluding observations that I have reviewed. Of the 376 concluding observations adopted by the Human Rights Committee that I have analysed, the issue has come up in just one, and that too rather restrictively, concerning the practice of Ecuadorian authorities asking immigrants and refugees to submit criminal records for the determination of their applications.[328]

In view of the fault lines running through the traditional penal model, human rights discourse could perhaps pay a modest level of attention to alternative restorative or reconciliatory approaches to justice. My suspicion that it is theoretically ill-equipped and historically ill-prepared to do so is borne out by the analysis of the primary material. In the UPR Working Group Reports, I could find five recommendations in respect of as many countries regarding the need for greater reliance on restorative justice. All five recommendations came from a single country, Indonesia, and each one of them talked about the incorporation of 'restorative justice principles' only in juvenile justice systems.[329] Summaries of Stakeholders' Submissions include suggestions by local NGOs in respect of a few countries regarding restorative justice, again mostly in the context of juvenile justice. For instance, the Assembly of First Nations recommended 'that Canada

328 Ecuador, CCPR/C/ECU/CO/5, at para 18.

329 Human Rights Council, *Report of the Working Group on the Universal Periodic Review: Albania*. Twenty-seventh session, 7 July 2014, A/HRC/27/4 (Recommendation 104.79); Iraq, A/HRC/28/14 (Recommendation 127.160); Mexico, A/HRC/25/7 (Recommendation 148.110); Nicaragua, A/HRC/27/16 (recommendation 114.67); Spain, A/HRC/29/8 (Recommendation 131.96).

move towards a restorative and rehabilitative model of youth justice'.[330] In regard to El Salvador, a joint submission by local NGOs recommended that the state 'adopt a restorative justice approach for young people rather than a merely punitive one'.[331]

The Human Rights Committee, as previously noted, has opposed alternative dispute resolution in relation to domestic violence. Further, it has opposed 'amnesty laws' in several countries, including Bolivia, Colombia, El Salvador, Lebanon, Niger, Peru, Sierra Leone, Spain, Sudan, Republic of Macedonia, and Uruguay.[332] The Committee did welcome the introduction of a law on the juvenile justice system in China Macau 'which introduced restorative justice principles'.[333] In 1999, it appreciated Costa Rica's initiative to promote 're-education and conciliation between offenders and victims'.[334] These interventions, however, pale into insignificance when compared to scores of recommendations calling for more vigorous prosecution and punishment. My attempts at finding references to restorative justice or restitution in the CESCR Committee's concluding observations have been fruitless.

The analysis in this chapter is susceptible to criticism on the grounds of being insensitive to the suffering of the victims of human rights violations. Critics might argue, for example, that not all individuals who commit crimes and cause harm to others suffer from mental disorders or come from disadvantaged backgrounds. Detractors could also contend that calls for punishment in the human rights discourse are normally directed against those who commit war crimes and torture, or those who prey on vulnerable groups in society, such as children, women, gays, and political dissidents. It could be argued that social justice considerations warrant that those who take advantage of historical vulnerabilities of these groups are brought to justice.

The response to such criticism could be three-fold. First, the problem with the human rights discourse is that it subscribes to a particularly strong form of retributivism, which posits punishment not just as a permissible option but a moral obligation à la Kant. Punishment as a 'categorical imperative' could be valid for an ideal world. In the complex world that we live in, the demands of

330 Human Rights Council, *Summary prepared by the Office of the United Nations High Commissioner for Human Rights: Canada*. Sixteenth session, 29 January 2013, A/HRC/WG.6/16/CAN/3, para 51.

331 Human Right Council, *Summary prepared by the Office of the High Commissioner for Human Rights: El Salvador*. Twentieth session, 21 July 2014, A/HRC/WG.6/20/SLV/3, para 44.

332 Bolivia, 6 December 2013, CCPR/C/BOL/CO/3, para 19; Colombia, August 2010, CCPR/C/COL/CO/6, para 9; El Salvador, 18 April 1994, CCPR/C/79/Add.34, para 7; Lebanon, 5 May 1997, CCPR/C/79/Add.78, para 12; Niger, 29 April 1993, CCPR/C/79/Add.17, para 7; Peru, 15 November 2000, CCPR/CO/70/PER, para 9; Sierra Leone, 17 April 2014, CCPR/C/SLE/CO/1, para 17; Spain, 14 August 2015, CCPR/C/ESP/CO/6, para; 29; Sudan, 29 August 2007, CCPR/C/SDN/CO/3, para 9; The former Yugoslav Republic of Macedonia, 17 April 2008; CCPR/C/MKD/CO/2, para 12; Uruguay, 2 December 2013, CCPR/C/URY/CO/5, para 19.

333 China Macau, 29 April 2013, CCPR/C/CHN-MAC/CO/1, para 4.

334 Costa Rica, 8 April 1999, CCPR/C/79/Add.107, para 8.

Kantian ethics are not only difficult to fulfil,[335] they could give rise to additional ethical problems, for example, in the form of the deterioration of an offender's pre-existing mental conditions whilst in prison and social marginalisation of her children. Second, the notion of punishment as a moral duty serves as a conversation-stopper, preventing wider debates on the causes of crime as well as the social impact of criminal penalties.[336] And, third, moral indignation about violence and human rights violations need not translate into a call for retributive justice. Human beings are capable of responding to 'unimaginable atrocities' with equally unimaginable feats of sympathy and generosity.[337]

In the human rights narrative, the demand for punishment is commonly framed as one based on principles, whereas suggestions implying an acceptability of restorative justice or reconciliation are deemed pragmatic compromises at best and moral sell-outs at worst.[338] To punish and prosecute is the new standard of civilisation. To seek to mend fences, a mark of civilisational backwardness. What prosecution enthusiasts fail to notice is that whilst the decision not to punish could be pragmatic, at times, it is informed by a deep moral sensitivity that seeks to reaffirm humanity in all its traits. To categorise alternatives to retributive justice as pragmatic 'compromises' manifests an ignorance of the moral depth underlying the kind of 'amnesty' that resulted from 'a gentleman's agreement between Mandela and de Klerk',[339] later reiterated in South Africa's interim Constitution that sought to forge a new beginning on the basis 'that there is a need for understanding but not for vengeance, a need for reparation but not for retaliation, a need for *ubuntu* but not for victimization'.[340]

335 Martti Koskenniemi, 'The Police in the Temple Order, Justice and the UN: A Dialectical View' (1995) 6 *European Journal of International Law* 325.

336 Barbara A. Hudson, *Penal Policy, and Social Justice* (Macmillan 1993) 178–180.

337 cf. Preamble to the Rome Statute: 'Mindful that during this century millions of children, women and men have been victims of unimaginable atrocities that deeply shock the conscience of humanity . . .'

338 See for example, Tristan Garcia, 'Amnesties, and the Rome Statute – A Legitimate Bar to Prosecution?' (2006) 13 *Australian International Law Journal* 187; Andreas O' Shea, *Amnesty for Crime in International Law and Practice* (Kluwer Law International 2004); Ben Chigara, *Amnesty in International Law: The Legality Under International Law of National Amnesty Laws* (Longman 2002).

339 William Schabas, *Unimaginable Atrocities: Justice, Politics, and Rights at the War Crimes Tribunals* (OUP 2012) 180.

340 See Lyn S. Graybill, *Truth and Reconciliation in South Africa: Miracle or Model?* (Boulder 2002) 32–35.

Conclusion

> 'Would you tell me, please, which way I ought to go from here?'
> 'That depends a good deal on where you want to get to . . .'
>
> Lewis Carrol[1]

Inverting a famous Marxist dictum, the British historian Eric Hobsbawm once told an audience at Cambridge University that sometimes the point 'really is not so much to change the world as to understand it'.[2] That would be sound advice for anyone engaged in academic research lest political goals should distort one's understanding of reality. Yet, as we have seen in this book, academic debates do not take place in a political vacuum. They are enmeshed in specific historical circumstances. Scholarly works, in turn, impinge on the practical world of politics and policy. From the 'scientific' theories of Social Darwinism to the pronouncements of 'Nothing Works' in rehabilitating offenders[3] to the revival of Kant's retributive theory of punishment, the links between intellectual projects on the one hand, and shifting political landscapes on the other, are hard to dismiss. As this study approaches its end, it is worth holding on to Hobsbawm's lesson in dispassionate analysis as well as the fundamental insight of critical scholarship that theory cannot be detached from practice.

Let us now, in a set of concluding remarks, return to the questions with which this inquiry began: *How does the discourse of international human rights relate to the justifications of criminal punishment? What are the causes and consequences of that relationship?* In retrospect, the methodological approach of interdisciplinary discourse analysis has served to address a three-fold deficit in orthodox human rights and legal scholarship. First, scholarly works, which appear neutral with

1 Lewis Carrol, *Alice in Wonderland* (2nd edn, W.W. Norton 1992) 49.

2 Reference being Karl Marx's 11th thesis on Feuerbach. Tony Judt with Timothy Synder, *Thinking the Twentieth Century* (Penguin 2013) *79. See also Karl Marx, Early Writings* (Greger Benton tr, Penguin 1992) 423.

3 The slogan used by the American press to sum up Robert Martinson's famous study. See Robert Martinson, 'What Works? – Questions and Answers about Prison Reform' (1974) 35 *The Public Interest* 22.

respect to penological purposes, carry certain tacit ideological assumptions. The intellectual move to frame the discussion on criminal punishment around the principles of legality, the due process, and proportionality, without questioning the theoretical bases of, say, retribution or deterrence, is to acquiesce in the moral validity of those classical justifications. Second, the mainstream scholarship is marked by an absence of broader social science perspectives and empirical inquiries into the social reality of crime and punishment. This can partly be attributed to the division of intellectual labour between academic lawyers and scholars working in other social science disciplines. Nonetheless, the pursuit of abstract analysis serves to legitimate the conventional justifications of punishment. And third, the orthodox scholarship subscribes to the teleological version of history, with politics and discontent written out of it.

As acknowledged at the outset, classical penal theory certainly marked an advance on the penal practices of the *ancien regime*, such as extraction of evidence through torture, and arbitrary penalties which corresponded more to the social status of the offender rather than the gravity of the crime. In line with the Enlightenment spirit, the classical thinkers stood against religious dogma, hereditary aristocracy, and absolutism in government. However, the Enlightenment thought preserved the Judeo-Christian ideal of individual responsibility connected with sin and salvation. There was little attention paid to the context and causes of crime in both the deontological accounts of criminal punishment proffered by Kant and Hegel, and consequentialist theories formulated by Beccaria and Bentham. Underpinning the classical penal thinking was a particular image of the legal subject defined by his or her rational capacity and subtracted from concrete social circumstances. Beholden to a vision of a consensual society inaugurated by the social contract theory, classical thinkers also stopped short of analysing the socially constructed nature of 'crime' and 'criminals'.

It is a well-trodden theme in philosophical literature that modern human rights theory falls back on Enlightenment thinking, particularly the philosophy of Immanuel Kant. This study has argued that Kant's paradoxical commitment to human autonomy and dignity on the one hand, and the notion of punishment as a categorical imperative on the other, also animates the contemporary discourse of human rights where justice is equated with retributive punishment. However, the 'common sense' idea that a wrongdoer must be made to suffer is not beyond questioning. In the actual world we inhabit, the principle of punishment as an absolute duty can result in more ethical problems than it solves. That is precisely the case, for example, when a prisoner returns to the society with additional economic and social disadvantages. To feel moral outrage at violent and harmful behaviour is, indeed, a mark of empathy and self-respect. A Kantian retributivist, I have argued, conflates a psychological necessity with a moral obligation in suggesting that the penal law ought to follow the retributive impulse. There is no denying that the ideology of human rights has helped moderate *lex talionis*, or the 'Law of Retaliation', as it featured in Kantian theory, by ruling out torture and barbaric forms of punishment. However, it does not go as far as to challenge the basic premises of retributivism.

A key norm that human rights law has borrowed from the Kantian theory is the principle of proportionality in sentencing, a modern re-working of *lex talionis*. The principle went through a revival in the 1970s, finding one of its most erudite defenders in the liberal theorist Andrew von Hirsch. On his influential account, the quantum of punishment ought to be determined through a fixed sentencing scheme on the basis of 'proportionality' – or commensurate deserts, to use von Hirsch's preferred term – with the seriousness of an offence rather than the instrumental concerns of reforming offenders or preventing crime. There is no questioning the importance of the proportionality principle in its defensive role as prohibiting excessive penalties. But extending the arguments of non-retributivist philosophers and critical criminologists and sociologists, this study has attempted to unmask the limits of proportionality in the context of penal policy and practice.[4] It was argued that the principle, typical of liberal theory, rests on the image of the abstract individual, failing to recognise the full impact of a term in prison on the offender and her family. A neat approximation between the gravity of crimes and a sentence of imprisonment is illusory. T.S. Eliot's 'The Hollow Men' resonates profoundly: Between the idea and the reality falls the shadow.[5]

G.W.F Hegel, the other leading figure of German idealism, has also cast a shadow on human rights discourse, especially in terms of the notion that criminal punishment vindicates victims' rights. This justification rests on a specific model of victims' behaviour. It ignores wider possibilities of human understanding and human sympathy. Hegel's insistence that punishment is a right of a criminal as a rational agent, and that it upholds the recognitive basis of rights in a society, is also problematic. The state could just as well honour the moral agency of the wrongdoer by focusing on restitution and rehabilitation, instead. Further, a more expansive interpretation of Hegel's notion of 'the recognition of rights' leads one to conclude that just as a criminal violates rights on multiple fronts, so does the state in failing to prevent the conditions which pave the way for criminal actions. The narrow focus on rights, in fact, deflects attention from social justice considerations and insulates penal policy from social policy.

The history of human rights and penal philosophy, this book has shown, is marked by jagged edges rather than clean breaks. There has been progress as well as inertia. Advances in some areas can be contrasted with regression to earlier periods in others. Critical historians have already shed light on unexplained 'temporal leaps' and untenable 'backstories' that characterise the orthodox human

4 Nigel Walker, *Why Punish? Theories of Punishment Reassessed* (Oxford University Press 1991); 'Nozick's Revenge' (1995) 70 (274) *Philosophy* 581; 'Desert: Some Doubts' in Andrew von Hirsch and Andrew Ashworth (eds), *Principled Sentencing: Readings on Theory and Policy* (2nd edn, Hart Publishing 1998) 156–160; Marc Mauer and Meda Chesney-Lind (eds), *Invisible Punishment: The Collateral Consequences of Mass Imprisonment* (Free Press 2002); Megan Comfort, *Doing Time Together: Love and Family in the Shadow of the Prison* (University of Chicago Press 2008); Joyce A. Arditti, *Parental Incarceration and the Family: Psychological and Social Effects of Imprisonment on Children, Parents, and Caregivers* (New York University Press 2012).

5 T.S Eliot, *Complete Poems and Plays* (Faber & Faber 1968) 85.

rights history.[6] Applying this sceptical lens to the relationship between human rights and the idea of punishment, I have called attention to several gaps in the conventional history.

The textbook narrative duly recognises the advances represented by the Enlightenment. However, it is hard to find critical comment on how the universalising tendencies of Enlightenment met their historic limits in imperialist expansion and convict labour. The fact that slavery, after its formal abolition, was replaced in the United States and Europe's imperial outposts with various forms of forced labour, particularly involving criminal offenders, is well-documented.[7] However, that historical reality does not fit into the narrative of progressive humanisation. It thus gets dropped out of the textbook version of human rights history. Similarly, there is complete silence on the legacy of positivist and Marxist criminology. This claim is not made lightly. It is backed up by a review of dozens of key texts in human rights and international law. The reasons for this omission, it has been argued, are both historical and conceptual, having to do with the association of the positivist school with eugenics and fascism, and the theoretical kinship between human rights and classical retributivist philosophy.

I hope to have shown that there is more to the legacy of positivist criminology than the idea of the 'born criminal' and its cynical appropriation by the Nazis.[8] Recall that positivist thinkers broke fresh ground by turning to the aetiology of crime. Although the pioneers in criminology are today often dismissed swiftly, contemporary evidence bears out the relevance of psychological, biological, and situational influences to harmful and violent behaviour.[9] The impact of positivist criminology was also reflected in the founding of international bodies, most notably the International Penal and Penitentiary Commission. This study has made an addition to the scant literature on the topic by attempting to refute the

6 Jan Herman Burges, 'The Road to San Francisco: The Revival of the Human Rights Idea in the Twentieth Century' (1992) 14 *Human Rights Quarterly* 447; Samuel Moyn, *The Last Utopia: Human Rights in History* (Harvard University Press 2010) 5–6; Miia Halme-Tuomisaari and Pamela Slotte, 'Revisiting the Origins of Human Rights: An Introduction' in Slotte and Halme-Tumisaari (eds), *Revisiting the Origins of Human Rights* (Cambridge University Press 2015) 1–36.

7 David M. Oshinsky, *"Worse than Slavery": Parchman Farm and the Ordeal of Jim Crow Justice* (Free Press 1996); Caroline Elkins, *Imperial Reckoning: The Untold Story of Britain's Gulag in Kenya* (Henry Holt and Company 2005); Justin Roberts, *Slavery and the Enlightenment in the British Atlantic, 1750–1807* (Cambridge University Press 2013); David Arnold, 'Labouring for the Raj: Convict Work Regimes in Colonial India, 1836–1939' in Christian Giuseppe De Vito and Alex Lichtenstein (eds), *Global Convict Labour* (Brill 2015).

8 Nicole Rafter, 'Criminology's Darkest Hour: Biocriminology in Nazi Germany' (2008) 41(2) *The Australian and New Zealand Journal of Criminology* 287.

9 Cathy S. Widom, 'Does Violence Beget Violence? A Critical Examination of the Literature' (1989) 106(1) *Psychological Bulletin* 3; Adrian Raine, *The Psychopathology of Crime: Criminal Behavior as a Clinical Disorder* (Academic Press 1993); Philip Zimbardo, *The Lucifer Effect: How Good People Turn Evil* (Rider 2007); Adrian Raine, *The Anatomy of Violence: The Biological Roots of Crime* (Allen Lane 2013); Siddhartha Mukherjee, *The Gene: An Intimate History* (Allen Lane 2016).

allegation that the Commission was 'Nazified' during the 1930s.[10] Instead, it has been our argument that history owes an unacknowledged debt of gratitude to some key figures in the Penitentiary Commission for fighting a rear guard action at the 1935 Penitentiary Congress in Berlin against Nazi ideologues who insisted on strict prison discipline and the retributive function of criminal penalties.

Human rights scholarship has yet to recognise the pioneering work in international collaboration around criminal justice carried out by the Howard League for Penal Reform during the first half of the twentieth century under the influence of Quaker teachings and positivist criminology. Revisionist histories of the League of Nations (which the Howard League was engaged with in the 1920s and 1930s), and historical works tracing the trajectory of international humanitarianism, have also remained silent on the subject.[11] I have argued that the peripheral position that the organisation today occupies on the international scene is both reflected and reinforced by a near-total silence in literature on the organisation's historical contributions, particularly its efforts to codify prisoners' rights into an international convention.

The purpose of revisiting the history of the Penitentiary Commission and the Howard League was not to present some romanticised version of the past. To be sure, the Commission reproduced gender and racial biases of its times. It was not fully tuned into to the potential of abuse inherent in indeterminate sentencing schemes either. Likewise, the early Quaker reformers exhibited a naïve faith in the potential of the penitentiary to reform offenders. One reason why the concept of human rights needs to be cherished is precisely that it can provide the basis for a critique of some of the paternalistic and pseudo-scientific ideas which early criminologists and penal reformers had bought into. At the same time, the dismissal of the legacy of positivist criminology, the Penitentiary Commission, and the Howard League has several repercussions for how the idea of punishment is framed within the discourse of human rights: First, the tradition of empirical investigations into the causes of crime is further marginalised. That invariably entails a split between criminal justice and social justice, since it is the individual who is to blame and not the social and political arrangements which often form the underlying context of criminal behaviour. And second, retribution is implicitly accepted as beyond questioning and takes precedence over the relatively less repressive idea of offender rehabilitation and resocialisation. Further, alternatives to conventional justifications for punishment, such as restitution and reconciliation, as advocated by the Howard League, are ignored.

10 United Nations, *The United Nations and Crime Prevention* (UN 1996) 5; *Bureau of the International Penal and Penitentiary Commission, Proceedings of the XITH International Penal and Penitentiary Congress held in Berlin. August 1935* (Staemfli & Cie. Printers 1937).

11 Michael Barnett's *Empires of Humanity* (Cornell University Press 2013); Peter Stamatov, *The Origins of Global Humanitarianism: Religion, Empires, and Advocacy* (Cambridge University Press 2013); Susan Pedersen, *The Guardians. The League of Nations and the Crisis of Empire* (OUP 2015); Taina Tuori, 'From League of Nations Mandates to Decolonization: A Brief History of Rights' in Pamela Slotte and Miia Halme-Tumisaari (eds), *Revisiting the Origins of Human Rights* (Cambridge University Press 2015) 267–292.

The analysis of contemporary materials, including the documentation produced under the Universal Periodic Review, the concluding observations and the case law of treaty monitoring bodies, and the reporting of Amnesty International and Human Rights Watch, provides some vital clues about the normative relationship between the contemporary human rights discourse and penological justifications. We can frame that relationship in terms of a series of paradoxes, indexing them to three inter-linked questions: What to punish? How to punish? And why punish?

Regarding the first question, the analysis has revealed both expansionist and reductionist tendencies. Human rights bodies and NGOs simultaneously seek to counter the punitive reach of the law in some areas and call for its expansion in others. There is a strong emphasis on criminalising and prosecuting certain abusive practices by state officials, such as torture and ill-treatment of detainees; war crimes and genocide; various forms of political persecution; and gender, sexual, and identity-based violence and discrimination. The calls for criminalisation and prosecution reflect old roots as well as more recent influences. The traditional emphasis in liberal theory on individual criminal responsibility endures. By contrast, 'crimes of globalisation', such as the devastating effects of the Structural Adjustment Programmes on the economies of the global South, receive little mention. Similarly, the problem of human trafficking is understood primarily in terms of the exploitation of victims by 'evil' individuals rather than as a function of an unjust global economic order. The emphasis on the criminalisation of the harassment of journalists and human rights defenders can be read as a sign of the traditional primacy of civil and political rights. At the same time, it can also be seen as indicative of the growing influence of NGOs and media organisations in the globalised post-Cold War world.

The pattern holds when we analyse the other side of the equation, namely decriminalisation. Where human rights bodies and NGOs demand that states repeal or amend penal laws, the underlying context most frequently is the exercise of personal and political freedoms, for instance, consensual same-sex relationships and freedom of expression. This is far less the case when it comes to the laws that disproportionately affect the poor, such as those that criminalise squatting in residential buildings, petty theft, and commercial sex work.

Within the criminalisation-decriminalisation dynamic, this book has also identified the paradoxical nature of the purposive approach to legal interpretation. By way of illustration, it allows judges and treaty monitoring bodies to interpret domestic laws prohibiting same-sex relations or abortion as contradictory to human rights to equality and privacy. At the same time, the purposive approach is used to extend the punitive arm of the law beyond the original intent of the drafters. A case in point is the view adopted by both the Human Rights Committee and the Committee on Economic, Social and Cultural Rights that state parties have a positive obligation to criminalise and punish all forms of discrimination. This is an idea that does not find backing in either the text or the drafting history of the two covenants. There is no questioning, of course, that the law should prohibit discrimination. The problem lies in the insistence that the correct response to discriminatory actions is criminal prosecution and punishment.

In terms of the permissible mode of punishment (how to punish?), this study has looked, in some detail, at the death penalty and prison sentences, including irreducible life sentences. The most significant paradox that confronts us in this area is that the prohibition of cruel, inhuman, and degrading punishment – as interpreted by international human rights bodies – holds corporal punishment as unacceptable in the penal field or other settings. By contrast, long prison terms and irreducible life sentences are tolerated. We must credit the modern human rights movement for helping reduce the use of the death penalty across the world. However, mounting an effective challenge to capital punishment, long prison sentences, and life without parole requires a normative commitment to offender rehabilitation and reintegration.

The comforting notion that the modern human rights project represents steady progress in moral sensibilities needs to be reassessed. As we have seen, the pre-World War II experiments in international collaboration on penal matters, in fact, put a far greater focus on rehabilitation of offenders than is the case with the contemporary human rights discourse. It is also significant to note that the exclusion of penal labour from the prohibition of forced and compulsory labour, which was inscribed into the Forced Labour Convention in 1930, survives to this day. To be sure, human rights treaty monitoring bodies and NGOs are aware of the worldwide persistent crisis of the prison system; they routinely express concerns about overcrowding and poor health and hygiene standards. However, a clear international legal norm has yet to crystalise in favour of non-custodial sentences as the standard criminal penalty and imprisonment as ultima ratio – a measure of last resort.

The engagement of scholars and NGOs, especially Amnesty International, with the question of the death penalty reveals another paradox, which turns on the broader relationship between human rights and penological justifications. The abolitionists have consistently challenged capital punishment on the grounds that it does not deter crimes any more than long terms in prison. This well-meaning argument has a flip side: It presumes that long prison sentences serve the purpose of individual or general deterrence. As we have seen, there is no convincing evidence to back that claim. Yet, human rights advocates stop short of challenging deterrence as a penological justification in contexts other than the death penalty. In an indication of a tacit approval of deterrence, the Human Rights Committee has yet to ask state parties to furnish information on recidivism rates. The legal fiction that the prison protects the public goes unchallenged.

Having reviewed legal scholarship as well as other primary material, we are driven to conclude that those who question the prison's presumed role in protecting the public and reducing crime do not come from the mainstream human rights community. Rather, they belong to different intellectual traditions of restorative justice and prison abolitionism. They articulate their demands in the language of social justice, forgiveness, and reconciliation, rather than human rights.

This study has shown that the primary justification for punishment that is expressed implicitly or explicitly within the UN and the NGO campaigns is the backward-looking Kantian notion of retribution or just deserts. In temporal terms, retributivism has gained added currency within human rights circles since the post-Cold War diffusion of neoliberal ideology and the renaissance of international criminal justice in the 1990s. In the formative years of the modern human rights project, positivist criminology – what was then referred to as the progressive school in penal thinking – still had some advocates within the UN system. To them, the word 'punishment' rang outmoded and ill-informed. That contrasts markedly with the intellectual posture struck in the UN documents and submissions by Amnesty International and Human Rights Watch today. Some of the terms which crop up most frequently in these venerated materials are 'impunity', 'punish', 'prosecute', and 'bring to justice'. From its modest beginnings in the aftermath of World War II, the human rights regime has expanded to create a large edifice of treaties, conventions, and declarations, covering an impressive range of subjects and vulnerable groups. Paradoxically, the rise of human rights has gone hand in hand with modern punitiveness.

One problematic feature of the contemporary human rights discourse that this study has identified is the prevalence of a particularly strong form of retributivism. In calling upon states to prosecute and punish individuals, major human rights actors do not posit punishment simply as a moral option but an absolute obligation. The Human Rights Committee, for example, has repeatedly opposed amnesty laws in post-conflict contexts. Echoing the position of leading human rights NGOs, the Committee has also stood against the use of mediation and alternative dispute resolution in cases involving domestic violence. The paradox that emerges here is that the doctrine of universal human rights does not embrace moral plurality when it comes to responding to conflict and harmful behaviour. No doubt, imposing reconciliation on victims is morally untenable. I have argued that the same principle applies to retributive justice, which operates with a particular construct of human nature wedded to classical liberal theory and a moral outlook inherited from Hegelian and Kantian philosophy.

The treaty monitoring bodies associated with the two covenants have both borrowed modern retributivist language in urging states to impose 'commensurate' penalties, especially in the context of war crimes, torture, domestic violence, spousal rape, hate speech, and discrimination based on gender, ethnicity, or sexual orientation. The principle of proportionality of punishment to crime, as employed in human rights literature, turns on the abstract individual of classical penal theory, and the split between criminal justice and social justice. This study has taken stock of the collateral consequences of criminal punishment in terms of the social and psychological impact of imprisonment on prisoners' families, and the difficulties ex-offenders face in finding employment and reintegrating into society. Yet, these are marginal concerns, at best, within human rights discourse.

The contentious history of the bifurcation of the 'International Bill of Human Rights' into two separate covenants was retold because it has specific implications on the relationship between human rights and the idea of punishment. It was argued that despite the rhetoric of 'indivisibility and interdependence', the separation of human rights into distinct categories of civil and political rights on the one hand, and economic, social, and cultural rights on the other, helps formalise and legitimate retributive justice. In the context of penological justifications, criminal justice is abstracted from the wider social context. At the same time, debates on economic and social rights do not question how punishment contributes to the violation of those rights by leaving offenders and their families economically and socially marginalised.

The concept of human rights is still worth defending since it provides minimum moral benchmarks beneath which no one is allowed to sink. That is all the more necessary considering the upsurge of xenophobic and isolationist nationalism and religious fanaticism across the world in recent years. However, we need a stronger transformative vision than the one offered by human rights to imagine a world in which criminal punishment and the prison are used sparingly, if at all. Even as we cherish human rights, we would do well to remain alert to its pitfall: the fact that it can just as well be deployed to expand criminal law and to ratchet up punishment. We must continue to probe the way human rights discourse constructs and reproduces various forms of subjectivity, including the victim, who, modelled on the Hegelian logic, is expected to demand his pound of flesh. We need to hedge human rights round with other values, such as caring, compassion, generosity, hospitality, and solidarity. The rhetoric of rights must not be allowed to shut down conversation on the context of crime and punishment and wider social change agendas.

Given the conceptual loopholes in classical penological justifications and the well-known dehumanising effects of the prison system, the burden of proof ought to be on the proponents of the traditional penal model and not on those who seek alternatives. As we have seen, international human rights discourse frames criminal punishment within the conceptual parameters inherited from classical liberal penology, particularly Kantian retributivism. It focuses on punishment at the expense of rehabilitating offenders. Whether and to what extent can we reconfigure human rights to make room for projects such as restorative justice and penal abolitionism is a question that requires more in-depth, cross-disciplinary work.[12] Research in this area could take the form of empirical studies of how human rights advocates comprehend the normative underpinnings of these projects, for example, forgiveness and a commitment to restoring broken relationships. Similarly, sociological and ethnographic research into how prison abolitionist groups relate to the framework of international human rights may yield insights into the possible roadmaps to a better world. In this connection, a

12 Some helpful philosophical clues can be found in Andrew von Hirsch and others (eds) *Restorative Justice and Criminal Justice: Competing or Reconcilable Paradigms* (Hart Publishing 2003); Gerry Johnstone and Daniel W. Van Ness, *Handbook of Restorative Justice* (Willan Publishing 2007). On innovative rehabilitative and restorative justice projects, see Baz Dreisinger, *Incarceration Nations: A Journey to Justice in Prisons around the World* (Other Press 2016).

sequel to Gordon Rose's 1961 history of the Howard League is long overdue.[13] There is an urgent need to extend the empirical base of research into the collateral consequences of imprisonment beyond the United States.

I hope that this study will contribute to breaking the stalemate that has characterised the study of criminal punishment in human rights and legal scholarship. However, as the philosopher Theodor W. Adorno once said, 'The finished work is, in our times and climate of anguish, a lie'.[14] So I end this book not with any claims to finality or completeness, but with an invitation to fresh thinking, robust criticism, and a reinvigorated dialogue.

13 Gordon Rose, *The Struggle for Penal Reform: The Howard League and its Predecessors* (Stevens & Sons 1961).

14 Cited in George Steiner, 'A Man of Many Parts', *The Observer,* 3 June 2001.

Bibliography

Books

Aas KF and Bosworth M, *The Borders of Punishment: Migration, Citizenship, and Social Exclusion* (Oxford University Press 2013)

Adler M and Longhurst B, *Discourse, Power and Justice: Towards a New Sociology of Imprisonment* (Routledge 1994)

Adorno TW and Horkheimer M, *Dialectic of Enlightenment* (Verso 1997)

Ahmad A, *In Theory: Classes, Nations, Literatures* (Verso 1992)

Amos M, *Human Rights Law* (2nd edn, Oxford University Press 2014)

Anderson C, *Eyes Off the Prize: The United Nations and the African American Struggle for Human Rights, 1944–1955* (Cambridge University Press 2003)

Anderson C, *Legible Bodies: Race, Criminality and Colonialism in South Asia* (Berg 2004)

Anghie A, *Imperialism, Sovereignty and the Making of International Law* (Cambridge University Press 2004)

Arditti JA, *Parental Incarceration and the Family: Psychological and Social Effects of Imprisonment on Children, Parents, and Caregivers* (New York University Press 2012)

Arendt H, *The Origins of Totalitarianism* (7th edn, Harcourt Brace Jovanovich Inc. 1976)

Ashworth A and Redmayne M, *The Criminal Process* (4th edn, Oxford University Press 2010)

Bair J, *The International Covenant on Civil and Political Rights and Its (First) Optional Protocol: A Short Commentary Based on Views, General Comments and Concluding Observations by the Human Rights Committee* (Peter Lang 2005)

Bantekas I and Oette L, *International Human Rights Law and Practice* (Cambridge University Press 2013)

Bardens D, *Elizabeth Fry: Britain's Second Lady on the Five-Pound Note* (Chanadon Publications 2004)

Barnes HE and Teeters NK, *New Horizons in Criminology: The American Crime Problem* (Prentice-Hall Inc. 1945)

Barnett M, *Empire of Humanity: A History of Humanitarianism* (Cornell University Press 2013)

Bartelson J, *A Genealogy of Sovereignty* (Cambridge University Press 1995)

Bates E, *The Evolution of the European Convention on Human Rights: From Its Inception to the Creation of a Permanent Court of Human Rights* (Oxford University Press 2010)

Bates S, *Prisons and Beyond* (Palgrave Macmillan 1937)
Beccaria C, *On Crimes and Punishment* (GR Newman and P Marongiu tr, 5th edn, Transaction Publishers 2009)
Beckett A, *When the Lights Went Out: Britain in the Seventies* (Faber and Faber 2009)
Bell LS and others (eds), *Negotiating Culture and Human Rights* (Columbia University Press 2001)
Bentham J, *The Works of Jeremy Bentham, Vol 1& 2* (W. Tait 1843)
———, *An Introduction to the Principles of Morals* (Dover Publications 2007)
———, *The Theory of Legislation* (Forgotten Books 2012)
Best S and Kellner D, *Postmodern Theory: Critical Interrogations* (Palgrave Macmillan 1991)
Bingham T, *The Rule of Law* (Penguin 2010)
Black A (ed), *The Eleanor Roosevelt Papers, Volume 1, The Human Rights Years 1945–1948* (Thomas Gale 2007)
Black D, *The Behavior of Law* (Academic Press 1976)
Blackburn S, *The Oxford Dictionary of Philosophy* (Oxford University Press 2005)
Blustein J, *The Moral Demands of Memory* (Cambridge University Press 2008)
Bonger WA, *Criminality and Economic Conditions* (Little, Brown, and Company 1916)
Borgwardt B, *A New Deal for the World: America's Vision for Human Rights* (Belknap Press of Harvard University Press 2005)
Braithwaite J, *Crime, Shame and Reintegration* (Cambridge University Press 1989)
Braithwaite J and Petit P, *Not Just Deserts: A Republican Theory of Criminal Justice* (Clarendon Press 1998)
Bruinius H, *Better for All the World: The Secret History of Forced Sterilization and America's Quest for Racial Purity* (Vintage Books 2007)
Buchanan AE, *Marx and Justice: The Radical Critique of Liberalism* (Rowman & Littlefield 1984)
Burcken R, *A Most Uncertain Crusade: The United States, the United Nations, and Human Rights, 1941–1953* (Northern Illinois University Press 2014)
Burkhead MD, *The Search for the Causes of Crime* (McFarland & Company 2006)
Bush ML, *Servitude in Modern Times* (Polity Press 2010)
Carey J, *Intellectuals and the Masses: Pride and Prejudice Among the Literary Intelligentsia, 1880–1939* (Faber and Faber 1992)
Carrol L, *Alice in Wonderland* (2nd edn, W.W. Norton & Company Inc. 1992)
Chandler D, *From Kosovo to Kabul: Human Rights and International Intervention* (Pluto Press 2002)
Charlesworth H and Larking E (eds), *Human Rights and the Universal Periodic Review: Rituals and Ritualism* (Cambridge University Press 2014)
Chatterjee P, *The Black Hole of Empire: History of a Global Practice of Power* (Princeton University Press 2012)
Childs D, *Modernism and Eugenics: Woolf, Eliot, Yeats and the Culture of Degeneration* (Cambridge University Press 2001)
Chigara B, *Amnesty in International Law: The Legality Under International Law of National Amnesty Laws* (Longmans Green and Co 2002)
Christie N, *Crime Control as Industry* (Routledge 1983)
———, *Limits to Pain: The Role of Punishment in Penal Policy* (Wipf & Stock 2007)
Clark RS, *A United Nations High Commissioner for Human Rights* (Martinus Nijhoff 1972)

———, *The United Nations Crime Prevention and Criminal Justice Program: Formulation of Standards and Efforts at Their Implementation* (University of Pennsylvania Press 1994)

Clear TR and Frost NA, *The Punishment Imperative: The Rise and Failure of Mass Incarceration in America* (New York University Press 2014)

Cohen S, *Visions of Social Control: Crime Punishment and Classification* (Polity Press 1985)

Comfort M, *Doing Time Together: Love and Family in the Shadow of the Prison* (University of Chicago Press 2008)

Comte A, *Introduction to Positive Philosophy* (Frederick Ferre tr, Bobbs-Merril Company Inc. 1970)

Conrad J, *The Heart of Darkness* (Penguin Classics 2007)

Conte A and Burchill R (ed), *Defining Civil and Political Rights: The Jurisprudence of the United Nations Human Rights Committee* (Ashgate 2009)

Coser LA, *Masters of Sociological Thought: Ideas in Historical and Social Context* (2nd edn, Harcourt Brace Jovanovich Inc. 1977)

Craven CM, *Punishment and Reform* (Oxford University Press 1951)

Craven MCR, *The International Covenant on Economic, Social and Cultural Rights: A Perspective on Its Development* (Oxford University Press 1998)

Cromer EB, *Political and Literary Essays, 1908–1913* (Palgrave Macmillan 1913)

Cryer R, *Prosecuting International Crimes: Selectivity and the International Criminal Law Regime* (Oxford University Press 2005)

Cryer R and others, *An Introduction to International Criminal Law and Procedure* (3rd edn, Cambridge University Press 2014)

Cullen FT and Gilbert KE, *Reaffirming Rehabilitation* (Anderson Publishing 1982)

Curle TC, *Humanité: John Humphrey's Alternative Account of Human Rights* (University of Toronto Press 2007)

Curtis J, *Human Rights as War by Other Means: Peace Politics in Northern Ireland* (University of Pennsylvania Press 2014)

Dandelion P, *The Quakers: A Very Short Introduction* (Oxford University Press 2008)

Daube D, *Studies in Biblical Law* (2nd edn, Ktav 1969)

Davis AY, *Are Prisons Obsolete?* (Seven Stories Press 2003)

Davis DB, *The Problem of Slavery in Western Culture* (Oxford University Press 1966)

Dembour M, *Who Believes in Human Rights? Reflections on the European Convention* (Cambridge University Press 2006)

Douzinas C, *The End of Human Rights: Critical Legal Thought at the Turn of the Century* (Hart Publishing 2000)

———, *Human Rights and Empire: The Political Philosophy of Cosmopolitanism* (Routledge, Cavendish 2007)

Dowell-Jones M, *Contextualising the International Covenant on Economic, Social and Cultural Rights. Assessing the Economic Deficit* (Martinus Nijhoff 2004)

Drake DH, *Prisons, Punishment and the Pursuit of Security* (Palgrave Macmillan 2012)

Drake DH, Muncie J and Westmarland L, *Criminal Justice: Local and Global* (Sage 2010)

Dreisinger B, *Incarceration Nations: A Journey to Justice in Prisons Around the World* (Other Press 2016)

Drumbl MA, *Atrocity, Punishment, and International Law* (Cambridge University Press 2007)

Du Bois WEB, *Black Reconstruction in America* (Russel & Russel 1935)

———, *The Philadelphia Negro: A Social Study* (University of Pennsylvania Press 1996)
Duff A, *Punishment, Communication, and Community* (Oxford University Press 2001)
Dunbar EA, *A Fragile Freedom: African American Women and Emancipation in the Antebellum City* (Yale University Press 2008)
Dworkin R, *Taking Rights Seriously* (Harvard University Press 1978)
Easton S and Piper C, *Sentencing and Punishment: The Quest for Justice* (4th edn, Oxford University Press 2016)
Elias N, *The Civilizing Process* (6th edn, Blackwell 2000)
Eliot TS, *Four Quartets* (A Harvest Book/Harcourt Inc. 1971) 31
Elkins C, *Imperial Reckoning: The Untold Story of Britain's Gulag in Kenya* (Henry Holt and Company 2005)
Emmerson B, Andrew Ashworth and Alison MacDonald, *Human Rights and Criminal Justice* (Sweet & Maxwell 2007)
Emsley C, *Crime, Police and Penal Policy: European Experiences 1750–1940* (Oxford University Press 2004)
Engels F, *The Conditions of the Working Classes of England* (Penguin 2009)
Evans RJ, *The Third Reich in History and Memory* (Little Brown 2015)
Evans T, *US Hegemony and the Project of Universal Human Rights* (Palgrave Macmillan 1996)
Farrah EA, *Criminology: Past, Present and Future* (Palgrave Macmillan 1997)
Feinberg J, *Doing & Deserving: Essays in the Theory of Responsibility* (Princeton University Press 1970)
Ferri E, *Criminal Sociology* (Fisher Unwin 1895)
Fine B, *Democracy and the Rule of Law: Liberal Ideals and Marxist Critiques* (Pluto Press 1984)
Fisch J, *Cheap Lives and Dear Limbs: The British Transformation of the Bengal Criminal Law, 1769–1817* (Franz Steiner Verlag 1983)
Fiss O, *The Law as It Could Be* (New York University Press 2003)
Fitzpatrick P and Hunt A (eds), *Critical Legal Studies* (Blackwell 1987)
Forsythe WJ, *Penal Discipline, Reformatory Projects and the English Prison Commission 1895–1939* (University of Exeter Press 1990)
Foucault M, *Discipline and Punish: The Birth of the Prison* (Penguin 1977)
———, *Power/Knowledge* (Harvester 1980)
———, *Archaeology of Knowledge* (A.M. Sheriden Smith tr, Routledge 1989)
France A, *The Red Lily* (IndyPublish.com 2002)
Freedman R, *The United Nations Human Rights Council: An Early Assessment* (Routledge 2013)
Fry M, *Arms of the Law* (Victor Gollancz Ltd. 1951)
Gabaldon SL, *W.E.B Du Bois on Crime and Justice: Laying the Foundations of Sociological Criminology* (Ashgate 2007)
Gallant KS, *The Principle of Legality in International and Comparative Criminal Law* (Cambridge University Press 2009)
Galston WA, *Kant and the Problem of History* (University of Chicago Press 1975)
Garland D, *Punishment and Welfare* (Gower Publishing 1985)
———, *The Culture of Control: Crime and Social Order in Contemporary Society* (Oxford University Press 2001)

Gay P, *The Enlightenment: The Science of Freedom* (W.W. Norton & Company Inc. 1969)
Gearty C, *On Fantasy Island: Britain, Europe and Human Rights* (Oxford University Press 2016)
Germino D, *Modern Western Political Thought: Machiavelli to Marx* (Rand McNally & Company 1972)
Glenden MA, *A World Made New: Eleanor Roosevelt and the Universal Declaration of Human Rights* (Random House 2002)
Goffman E, *Asylums: Essays on the Social Situation of Mental Patients and Other Inmates* (Penguin 1961)
Gong GW, *The Standard of 'Civilization' in International Society* (Clarendon 1984)
Gott R, *Britain's Empire: Resistance, Repression and Revolt* (Verso 2011)
Gramsci A, *Selections from the Prison Notebooks* (Lawrence and Wishart 1971)
Graybill LS, *Truth and Reconciliation in South Africa: Miracle or Model?* (Boulder 2002)
Green TA, *Freedom and Criminal Responsibility in American Legal Thought* (Cambridge University Press 2014)
Greenfield K, *The Myth of Choice: Personal Responsibility in a World of Limits* (Biteback Publishing 2011)
Griffin R, *Modernism and Fascism: The Sense of Beginning Under Mussolini and Hitler* (Palgrave Macmillan 2007)
Grunhut M, *Penal Reform: A Comparative Study* (Clarendon Press 1948)
Hammel A, *Ending the Death Penalty: The European Experience in Global Perspective* (Palgrave Macmillan 2010)
Harris S, *The Moral Landscape: How Science Can Determine Human Values* (Black Swan 2010)
Hart HLA, *Punishment and Responsibility: Essays in the Philosophy of Law* (Oxford University Press 1968)
Hawkins M, *Social Darwinism in European and American Thought, 1860–1945: Nature as Model and Nature as Threat* (Cambridge University Press 1997)
Hayek F, *The Road to Serfdom* (George Routledge & Sons Ltd. 1944)
Hayner PB, *Unspeakable Truths: Transitional Justice and the Challenge of Truth Commissions* (Taylor & Francis 2010)
Heffernan WC and Kleinig J (eds), *From Social Justice to Criminal Justice: Poverty & the Administration of Criminal Law* (Oxford University Press 2000)
Hegel GWF, *Elements of the Philosophy of Right* (H.B. Nisbet tr, Cambridge University Press 1991)
Henderson CR, *Correction and Prevention: Four Volumes Prepared for the Eighth International Prison Congress* (Russell Sage Foundation, Charities Publication Committee 1910)
Henham R, *Punishment and Process in International Criminal Trials* (Ashgate 2005)
Herivel T and Wrights P (eds), *Prison Profiteers: Who Makes Money from Mass Incarceration* (New Press 2007)
Hinkle WG and Hartley WJ, *The Decisive Decade in the History of the Elmira Reformatory 1867–1877* (The Edwin Mellen Press 2012)
Hirsch AV, *Doing Justice: The Choice of Punishments. Report of the Committee for the Study of Incarceration* (Hill and Wang 1976)
———, *Censure and Sanctions* (Clarendon Press 1993)

Hirsch AV and Ashworth A, *Proportionate Sentencing: Exploring the Principles* (Oxford University Press 2005)
Hobbins AJ (ed), *On the Edge of Greatness: The Diaries of John Humphrey, First Director of the United Nations Division of Human Rights*, Vol. 1, 1948–9 (McGill University 1994)
———, *On the Edge of Greatness, Volume II: The Diaries of John Humphrey, First Director of the United Nations Division of Human Rights* (McGill University Libraries 1996)
Hobsbawm E, *The Age of Revolution: 1789–1848* (Abacus 1962)
Hochschild A, *Bury the Chains: Prophets and Rebels in the Fights to Free an Empire's Slaves* (Houghton Mifflin Company 2005)
Hood R and Hoyle C, *Death Penalty: A Worldwide Perspective* (5th edn, Oxford University Press 2015)
Hopgood S, *Keepers of the Flame: Understanding Amnesty International* (Cornell University Press 2006)
Horne G, *Black and Red: W.E.B. Du Bois and the Afro-American Response to the Cold War, 1944–1963* (State University of New York Press 1986)
Howard J, *The State of the Prisons* (J. M. Dent & Sons 1929)
Hudson BA, *Justice Through Punishment: A Critique of the 'Justice' Model of Corrections* (Palgrave Macmillan 1987)
———, *Penal Policy and Social Justice* (University of Toronto Press 1993)
———, *Understanding Justice: An Introduction to Ideas, Perspectives and Controversies in Modern Penal Theory* (Open University Press 1996)
Hughes R, *The Fatal Shore* (Collins Harvill 1987)
Hugo V, *Les Misérables, Vol. I & II* (Isabel F. H. Hapgood tr, First World Library 2007)
Humphrey J, *Human Rights and the United Nations: A Great Adventure* (Transnational Publishers Inc. 1984)
Hunt L, *Inventing Human Rights: A History* (W.W. Norton & Company Inc. 2008)
Ibhawoh B, *Imperialism and Human Rights: Colonial Discourses of Rights and Liberties in African History* (State University of New York Press 2007)
Ignatieff M, *A Just Measure of Pain: Penitentiary in the Industrial Revolution 1750–1850* (Columbia University Press 1978)
———, *Human Rights as Politics and Idolatry* (Princeton University Press 2001)
Ishay MR, *The History of Human Rights: From Ancient Times to the Globalization Era* (University of California Press 2008)
Jacobson J, Herd C and Fair H, *Prison: Evidence of its Use and Overuse from Around the World* (Institute for Criminal Policy Research 2017)
James E, *A Life Inside: A Prisoner's Notebook* (Atlantic Books 2005)
Jarvis B, *Cruel and Unusual: A Cultural History of Punishment in America* (Pluto Press 2004)
Jennings F, *The Invasion of America: Indians, Colonialism, and the Cant of Conquest* (W.W. Norton & Company Inc. 1975)
Jewkes Y and Johnston H (eds), *Prison Readings: A Critical Introduction to Prisons and Imprisonment* (Routledge 2011)
Johnson MG and Symonides J, *The Universal Declaration of Human Rights: A History of its Creation and Implementation 1948–1998* (UNESCO Publishing 1998)
Jones EH, *Margery Fry: The Essential Amateur* (Oxford University Press 1966)
Jones PD, *The Christian Socialist Revival 1877–1914: Religion, Class, and Social Conscience in Late-Victorian England* (Princeton University Press 1968)

———, *Rights* (Palgrave Macmillan 1994)
Jones T and Newburn T, *Policy Transfer and Criminal Justice: Exploring US Influence over British Crime Control Policy* (Open University Press 2007)
Jorns A, *The Quakers as Pioneers in Social Work* (Thomas Kite Brown tr, Kennikat Press, Inc. 1931)
Joseph S and Castan M, *International Covenant on Civil and Political Rights: Cases Material and Commentary* (3rd edn, Oxford University Press 2013)
Judt T, *Thinking the Twentieth Century* (Penguin 2013)
Kälin W and Künzli J, *The Law of International Human Rights Protection* (Oxford University Press 2009)
Kant I, *Foundations of the Metaphysics of Morals* (Lewis White Beck tr, Bobbs-Merrill Company Inc., New York 1959)
———, *The Metaphysical Elements of Justice: Part I of the Metaphysics of Morals* (John Ladd tr, Bobbs-Merril Company Inc. 1965)
Keane J, *The Life and Death of Democracy* (Simon & Schuster 2009)
Keck ME and Sikkink K, *Activists Beyond Borders: Advocacy Networks in International Politics* (Cornell University Press 1998)
Kennedy D, *The Dark Sides of Virtue: Reassessing International Humanitarianism* (Princeton University Press 2004)
King ML Jr., *A Testament of Hope: Essential Writings of Martin Luther King* (James Washington ed, Harper & Row 1986)
———, *The Measure of a Man* (Fortress Press 1988)
Kleinig J, *Punishment and Desert* (Martinus Nijhoff 1973)
Knepper P, *International Crime in the 20th Century: The League of Nations Era, 1919–1938* (Palgrave Macmillan 2011)
Korey W, *NGOs and the Universal Declaration of Human Rights: "A Curious Grapevine"* (Palgrave Macmillan 1998)
Koskenniemi M, *The Gentle Civilizer of Nations: The Rise and Fall of International Law 1870–1960* (Cambridge University Press 2001)
Lacey N, *State Punishment: Political Principles and Community Values* (Routledge 1988)
———, *The Prisoners' Dilemma: Political Economy and Punishment in Contemporary Democracies* (Cambridge University Press 2008)
Lauren PG, *The Evolution of International Human Rights: Visions Seen* (University of Pennsylvania Press 1998)
Lewy G, *The Nazi Persecution of the Gypsies* (Oxford University Press 2000)
Little D, *Essays on Religion and Human Rights: Ground to Stand on* (Cambridge University Press 2015)
Locke J, *Two Treatises of Government* (Cambridge University Press 1988)
Logan A, *Feminism and Criminal Justice: A Historical Perspective* (Palgrave Macmillan 2008)
Lombroso C, *Crime: Its Causes and Remedies* (William Heinemann 1911)
Lyons FSL, *Internationalism in Europe 1815–1914* (A.W. Sythoff 1963)
Macpherson CB, *The Life and Times of Liberal Democracy* (Oxford University Press 1977)
Mahoney J, *The Challenge of Human Rights: Origin, Development and Significance* (Blackwell Publishing 2007)
Mallinder L, *Amnesty, Human Rights and Political Transitions: Bridging the Peace and Justice Divide* (Hart Publishing 2008)

Marks S and Clapham A, *International Human Rights Lexicon* (Oxford University Press 2005)
Martinez JS, *The Slave Trade and the Origins of International Human Rights Law* (Oxford University Press 2012)
Marx K, *Capital: A Critique of Political Economy, Vol. 1* (Penguin 1990)
———, *Early Writings* (Greger Benton tr, Penguin 1992)
———, *Dispatches for the New York Tribune: Selected Journalism of Karl Marx* (Penguin 2007)
Mathiessen T, *Prison on Trial* (Sage 1990)
———, *Prison on Trial* (3rd edn, Waterside Press 2006)
Matthews R, *Doing Time: An Introduction to the Sociology of Imprisonment* (2nd edn, Palgrave Macmillan 2009)
Mayhew H and Binny J, *The Criminal Prison of London and Scenes of Prison Life* (Charles Griffin and Company 1862)
Mazower M, *Dark Continent: Europe's Twentieth Century* (Allen Lane 1998)
———, *No Enchanted Palace: The End of Empire and the Ideological Origins of the United Nations* (Princeton University Press 2009)
McCulloch J and Wilson D, *Pre-Crime: Pre-Emption, Precaution and the Future* (Routledge 2016)
McGoldrick D, *The Human Rights Committee: Its Role in the Development of the International Covenant on Civil and Political Rights* (2nd edn, Clarendon Press 1994)
Mertus JA, *The United Nations Human Rights Regime: A Guide for a New Era* (Routledge 2005)
Miers S, *Slavery in the Twentieth Century: The Evolution of a Global Problem* (Altamira Press 2003)
Mill JS, *On Liberty and Other Essays* (Oxford University Press 1991)
Morsink J, *The Universal Declaration of Human Rights: Origins, Intent, Drafting* (University of Pennsylvania Press 1999)
Mowbray A, *The Development of Positive Obligations Under the European Convention on Human Rights by the European Court of Human Rights* (Hart Publishing 2004)
———, *Cases, Materials, and Commentary on the European Convention on Human Rights* (3rd edn, Oxford University Press 2012)
Moyn S, *The Last Utopia: Human Rights in History* (Harvard University Press 2010)
———, *Human Rights and the Uses of History* (Verso 2014)
Mukherjee S, *The Gene: An Intimate History* (Allen Lane 2016)
Muller I, *Hitler's Justice: The Courts of the Third Reich* (Deborah Lucas Schneider tr, I.B. Tauris & Co Ltd. 1991)
Murphy JG, *Retribution, Justice and Therapy* (D. Reidel Publishing Company 1979)
———, *Getting Even: Forgiveness and Its Limits* (Oxford University Press 2003)
———, *Punishment and the Moral Emotions: Essays in Law, Morality and Religion* (Oxford University Press 2012)
Mutua M, *Human Rights: A Political and Cultural Critique* (University of Pennsylvania Press 2002)
Naffine N, *Law & the Sexes: Explorations in Feminist Jurisprudence* (Allen & Unwin 1992)
———, *Feminism & Criminology* (Temple University Press 1996)
Neier A, *The International Human Rights Movement: A History* (Princeton University Press 2012)

Newell T, *Forgiving Justice: A Quaker Vision for Criminal Justice. Swathmore Lecture 2000* (Quaker Home Service 2000)
Nietzsche F, *Thus Spoke Zarathustra* (R. J. Hollingdale tr, Penguin 1961)
———, *Beyond Good and Evil* (Walter Kaufman tr, Vintage 1989)
———, *On the Genealogy of Morals* (Douglas Smith tr, Oxford University Press 1996)
Normand R and Zaidi S, *Human Rights at the UN: The Political History of Universal Justice* (Indiana University Press 2008)
Norrie A, *Crime, Reason and History: A Critical Introduction to Criminal Law* (3rd edn, Cambridge University Press 2014)
Nowak M, *U.N. Covenant on Civil and Political Rights: CCPR Commentary* (2nd edn, N.P. Engel 2005)
Nozick R, *Anarchy, State and Utopia* (Basic Books Inc. 1974)
———, *Philosophical Explanations* (Belknap, Harvard 1981)
Oberleitner G, *Global Human Rights Institutions: Between Remedy and Ritual* (Polity Press 2007)
O'Brien P, *The Promise of Punishment: Prisons in Nineteenth-Century France* (Princeton University Press 1982)
Odello M and Seats F, *The UN Committee on Economic, Social and Cultural Rights: The Law, Process, and Practice* (Routledge 2013)
O'Shea A, *Amnesty for Crime in International Law and Practice* (Kluwer Law International 2004)
Oshinsky DM, *"Worse than Slavery": Parchman Farm and the Ordeal of Jim Crow Justice* (Free Press 1996)
Othmani A with Bessis S, *Beyond Prison: The Fight to Reform Prison Systems Around the World* (Marguerite Garling tr, Berghan 2008)
Orwell G, *Nineteen Eighty-Four* (Penguin 2003)
———, *Burmese Days* (Penguin 2009)
Pahuja S, *Decolonising International Law: Development, Economic Growth and the Politics of Universality* (Cambridge University Press 2011)
Parenti C, *Lockdown America: Police and Prisons in the Age of Crisis* (2nd edn, Verso 2008)
Parkin F, *Max Weber* (Routledge 1982)
Patterson O, *Slavery and Social Death: A Comparative Study* (Harvard University Press 1982)
Pattillo M, Weiman D and Western B (eds), *Imprisoning America: The Social Effects of Mass Incarceration* (Russel Sage Foundation 2004)
Pedersen S, *The Guardians: The League of Nations and the Crisis of Empire* (Oxford University Press 2015)
Peffer RG, *Marxism, Morality and Social Justice* (Princeton University Press 1990)
Pettit B, *Invisible Men: Mass Incarceration and the Myth of Black Progress* (Russell Sage Foundation 2012)
Pick D, *Faces of Degeneration: A European Disorder, c. 1848 – c. 1918* (Cambridge University Press 1989)
Pinker S, *The Better Angels of Our Nature: Why Violence Has Declined* (Penguin 2011)
Pitts J, *A Turn to Empire: The Rise of Imperial Liberalism in Britain and France* (Princeton University Press 2005)
Plato, *The Republic* (Desmond Lee tr, 2nd edn, Penguin 2003)
Playfair G, *The Punitive Obsession: An Unvarnished History of the English Prison System* (Gollancz 1971)

Porter R, *The Enlightenment* (2nd edn, Palgrave Macmillan 2001)

Power J, *Like Water on Stone: The Story of Amnesty International* (Allen Lane 2001)

Pratt J and others (eds), *The New Punitiveness: Trends, Theories and Perspectives* (Willian Publishing 2005)

Prece JJ, *Minority Rights: Between Diversity and Community* (Polity Press 2005)

Priemel KC, *The Betrayal: The Nuremberg Trials and German Divergence* (Oxford University Press 2016)

Radzinowicz L, *Ideology and Crime: A Study of Crime in Social and Historical Context* (Heinemann Educational Books 1966)

———, *The Roots of the International Association of Criminal Law and Their Significance: A Tribute and a Re-Assessment on the Centenary of the IKV* (Eigenverlag Max-Plank-Institut 1991)

———, *Adventures in Criminology* (Routledge 1999)

Raine A, *The Psychopathology of Crime: Criminal Behavior as a Clinical Disorder* (Academic Press 1993)

———, *The Anatomy of Violence: The Biological Roots of Crime* (Allen Lane 2013)

Ramacharan BG, *The UN Human Rights Council* (Routledge 2011)

Rehman J, *International Human Rights Law* (2nd edn, Pearson 2010)

Richardson JE, *Analysing Newspapers: An Approach from Critical Discourse Analysis* (Palgrave Macmillan 2006)

Roberts CNJ, *Slavery and the Enlightenment in the British Atlantic, 1750–1807* (Cambridge University Press 2013)

———, *The Contentious History of the International Bill of Human Rights* (Cambridge University Press 2014)

Roberts JM, *Penguin History of the World: The History of the World, 1901 to the Present* (Penguin 1999)

Robertson G, *Crimes Against Humanity: The Struggle for Global Justice* (4th edn, Penguin 2012)

Robinson LN, *Should Prisoners Work? A Study of the Prison Labour Problem in the United States* (John C. Winston Company 1930)

Rodgers G and others, *The International Labour Organization and the Quest for Social Justice, 1919–2009* (Cornell University Press 2009)

Rodley N and Pollard M, *The Treatment of Prisoners Under International Law* (3rd edn, Oxford University Press 2009)

Roosevelt E, *On My Own* (Harper & Row 1958)

Rose G, *The Struggle for Penal Reform: The Howard League and Its Predecessors* (Stevens & Sons 1961)

Rosen M, *Dignity: Its History and Meaning* (Harvard University Press 2012)

Roth MP, *Prisons and Prison Systems: A Global Encyclopaedia* (Greenwood Press 2006)

Rothe D and Friedrichs DO, *Crimes of Globalization* (Routledge 2015)

Rothman DJ, *The Discovery of the Asylum: Social Order and Disorder in the New Republic* (2nd edn, Little Brown and Company 1990)

———, *Conscience and Convenience: The Asylum and Its Alternatives in Progressive America* (2nd edn, Aldine de Gruyter 2002)

Rotman E, *Beyond Punishment: A New View on the Rehabilitation of Criminal Offenders* (Greenwood Press 1990)

Royce E, *Classical Social Theory and Modern Society: Marx, Durkheim, Weber* (Rowman & Littlefield 2015)

Ruck SK (ed), *Paterson on Prisons: Being the Collected Papers of Sir Alexander Paterson* (Frederick Muller Ltd. 1951)
Ruggiero V, *Penal Abolitionism* (Oxford University Press 2010)
Ruggles-Brise E, *Prison Reform at Home and Abroad* (Palgrave Macmillan 1925)
Rusche G and Kirchheimer O, *Punishment and Social Structure* (Columbia University Press 1939)
Russell B, *History of Western Philosophy* (Routledge 2004)
Said E, *Orientalism* (Vintage 1978)
Sala-Molins L, *Dark Side of the Light: Slavery and the French Enlightenment* (John Coneth-Morgan tr, University of Minnesota Press 2006)
Saleilles R, *The Individualization of Punishment* (Little Brown and Company 1911)
Sandel M, *Justice: What's the Right Thing to Do?* (Penguin 2009)
Sanford B, *Prisons and Beyond* (Palgrave Macmillan 1937)
Sanford L, *Strong at the Broken Places: Overcoming the Trauma of Childhood Abuse* (Virago Press 1991)
Sasson D, *One Hundred Years of Socialism* (3rd edn, I.B. Tauris 2014)
Saul B, Kinley D and Mowbray J, *The International Covenant on Economic, Social and Cultural Rights: Commentary, Cases, and Material* (Oxford University Press 2014)
Scarre G, *After Evil: Responding to Wrongdoing* (Ashgate 2004)
Schabas WA, *The Death Penalty as Cruel Treatment and Torture: Capital Punishment Challenged in the World's Courts* (Northeastern University Press 1996)
———, *The Abolition of the Death Penalty in International Law* (3rd edn, Cambridge University Press 2002)
———, *Genocide in International Law: The Crime of Crimes* (2nd edn, Cambridge University Press 2009)
———, *Unimaginable Atrocities: Justice, Politics and Rights at the War Crimes Tribunals* (Oxford University Press 2012)
———, *The European Convention on Human Rights: A Commentary* (Oxford University Press 2015)
Schlicke P, *The Oxford Companion to Charles Dickens* (Oxford University Press 2011)
Seidler VJ, *The Moral Limits of Modernity: Love, Inequality and Oppression* (Palgrave Macmillan 1991)
Sellars K, *The Rise and Rise of Human Rights* (Sutton Publishing 2002)
Sellin JT, *Slavery and the Penal System* (Elsevier Scientific 1976)
Sen A, *The Idea of Justice* (Penguin 2010)
Sen S, *Disciplining Punishment: Colonialism and Convict Society in the Andaman Islands* (Oxford University Press 2000)
Shah S, Mockeli D and Sivakumaran S (eds), *International Human Rights Law* (2nd edn, Oxford University Press 2014)
Shapiro I, *The Evolution of Rights in Liberal Theory* (Cambridge University Press 1986)
Shea A, *Amnesty for Crime in International Law and Practice* (Kluwer Law International 2004)
Shelden RS, *Controlling the Dangerous Classes: A History of Criminal Justice in America* (2nd edn, Pearson 2008)
Shelton D, *Regional Protection of Human Rights* (Oxford University Press 2008)
Sim J, *Punishment and Prison: Power and the Carceral State* (Sage 2009)
Simon R, *Gramsci's Political Thought* (Lawrence and Wishart 1982)

Simpson AWB, *Human Rights and the End of Empire: Britain and the Genesis of the European Convention* (Oxford University Press 2001)
Smit DVZ, *Prison Labour: Salvation or Slavery?* (Ashgate 1999)
———, *Taking Life Imprisonment Seriously in National and International Law* (Kluwer Law International 2002)
Smith J and Fried W, *The Uses of American Prison* (Lexington Books 1974)
Smith R, *The Fontana History of Human Sciences* (Fontana Press 1997)
Smith RKM, *Textbook on International Human Rights* (5th edn, Oxford University Press 2011)
Sorrel T, *Moral Theory and Capital Punishment* (Basil Blackwell, Open University 1987)
Southwood M, *John Howard: Prison Reformer. An Account of His Life and Travels* (Independent Press 1958)
Stamatov P, *The Origins of Global Humanitarianism: Religion, Empires, and Advocacy* (Cambridge University Press 2013)
Stern A, *Eugenic Nation: Faults and Frontiers of Better Breeding in Modern America* (University of California Press 2005)
Stokes E, *The English Utilitarians and India* (Oxford University Press 1959)
Sublette N and Sublette C, *The American Slave Coast: A History of the Slave-Breeding Industry* (Lawrence Hill Books 2016)
Tarnas R, *The Passion of the Western Mind: Understanding the Ideas that Have Shaped Our World View* (Pimlico 1991)
Teeters NK, *World Penal Systems: A Survey* (Pennsylvania Prison Society 1944)
Thompson EP, *Whigs and Hunters: The Origin of the Black Act* (Pantheon Books 1975)
Todd S, *The People: The Rise and Fall of the Working Class* (John Murray 2014)
Turner BS, *Vulnerability and Human Rights* (Pennsylvania State University Press 2006)
Tyagi Y, *The UN Human Rights Committee: Practice and Procedure* (Cambridge University Press 2011)
United Nations, *The United Nations and Crime Prevention* (United Nations 1996)
Vito CGD and Lichtenstein A (eds), *Global Convict Labour* (Brill 2015)
Waldron J, *Liberal Rights: Collected Papers 1981–1991* (Cambridge University Press 1993)
Walker N, *Why Punish? Theories of Punishment Reassessed* (Oxford University Press 1991)
Wells C, *Corporations and Criminal Responsibility* (2nd edn, Oxford University Press 2001)
Whitman JQ, *Harsh Justice: Criminal Punishment and the Widening Divide Between America and Europe* (Oxford University Press 2003)
Whitman W, *The Complete Poems* (Penguin 2005)
Wilson AN, *Hitler: A Short Biography* (Harper & Row 2012)
Wilson M, *The Crime of Punishment* (Jonathon Cape 1931)
Winter J, *Dreams of Peace and Freedom: Utopian Moments in the Twentieth Century* (Yale University Press 2006)
Winter J and Prost A, *Rene Cassin and Human Rights: From the Great War to the Universal Declaration* (Cambridge University Press 2013)
Wood LA and Kroger RO, *Doing Discourse Analysis: Methods for Studying Action in Talk and Text* (Sage 2000)

Woods K, *Human Rights* (Palgrave Macmillan 2014)
Wright M, *Making Good: Prisons, Punishment and Beyond* (Burnett Books 1982)
Zedner L, *Women, Crime and Custody in Victorian England* (Clarendon Press 1991)
Zimbardo P, *The Lucifer Effect: How Good People Turn Evil* (Rider 2007)
Zinn H, *A People's History of the United States: 1942-Present* (3rd edn, Pearson 2003)
Zinoman P, *The Colonial Bastille: A History of Imprisonment in Vietnam*, 1862–1940 (University of California Press 2001)

Contributions to edited books

Alston P, 'Putting Economic, Social and Cultural Rights Back on the Agenda of the United States' in Schultz WF (ed), *The Future of Human Rights: U.S. Policy for a New Era* (University of Pennsylvania Press 2008) 120–138
Arnold D, 'The Colonial Prison: Power, Knowledge and Penology in Nineteenth-Century India' in Arnold D and Hardman D (eds), *Subaltern Studies VIII: Essays in Honour of Ranjit Guha* (Oxford University Press 1994) 148–187
———, 'Labouring for the Raj: Convict Work Regimes in Colonial India, 1836–1939' in Vito CGD and Lichtenstein A (eds), *Global Convict Labour* (Brill 2015) 119–221
Asad T, 'On Torture, or Cruel, Inhuman and Degrading Treatment' in Wilson RA (ed), *Human Rights, Culture & Context: Anthropological Perspectives* (Pluto Press 1997) 111–133
Beyleveld D, 'Deterrence Research and Deterrence Policies' in Hirsch AV and Ashworth A (eds), *Principled Sentencing: Readings on Theory and Policy* (2nd edn, Hart Publishing) 66–85
Boven TV, 'Categories of Rights' in Mockeli D, Shah S and Sivakumaran S (eds), *International Human Rights Law* (Oxford University Press 2010) 143–156
Bryant J and others, 'Life Behind Bars' in Gruen L (ed), *The Ethics of Captivity* (Oxford University Press 2014) 102–112
Burdon J, 'Slavery as a Punishment in Roman Criminal Law' in Leonie Archer (ed), *Slavery and Other Forms of Unfree Labour* (Routledge 1988) 68–85
Cain M, 'Gramsci, the State and the Place of Law' in Sugarman D (ed), *Legality, Ideology and the State* (Academic Press 1983) 95–117
Carlen P, 'Against Rehabilitation; For Reparative Justice' in Carrington K and others (eds), *Crime, Justice and Social Democracy* (Palgrave Macmillan 2013) 89–10
Carrabine E, 'Punishment, Rights and Justice' in Morris L (ed), *Rights: Sociological Perspectives* (Routledge 2006) 191–208
Christman J, 'Human Rights and Global Wrongs: The Role of Human Rights Discourse in Trafficking' in Meyers DJ (ed), *Poverty, Agency and Human Rights* (Oxford University Press 2014) 321–346
Cohen GD, 'The Holocaust and the "Human Rights Revolution": A Reassessment' in Iriye A, Goedde P and Hitchcock WI (eds), *The Human Rights Revolution: An International History* (Oxford University Press 2012) 53–72
Cowan JK, 'Justice and the League of Nations Minority Regime' in Clarke KM and Goodale M (eds), *Mirrors of Justice: Law and Power in the Post-Cold War Era* (Cambridge University Press, New York 2010) 270–290
Cullen FT, 'Rehabilitation: Beyond Nothing Works' in Tonry M (ed), *Crime and Justice in America, 1975–2025. Crime and Justice: A Review of Research* (Volume 42, University of Chicago Press 2013) 299–376

Drake PW, 'International Crises and Political Movements in Latin America: Chile and Peru from the Great Depression to the Cold War' in Rock D (ed), *Latin America in the 1940s: War and Postwar Transitions* (University of California Press 1994) 109–136

Drescher S, 'From Consensus to Consensus: Slavery in International Law' in Allain J (ed), *The Legal Understanding of Slavery* (Oxford University Press 2012) 85–102

Dünkel F and Smit D, 'Conclusion' in Smit and Dünkel (eds), *Imprisonment Today and Tomorrow: International Perspectives on Prisoners' Rights and Prison Conditions* (2nd edn, Kluwer Law International 2001) 796–859

Dworkin R, 'Rights as Trumps' in Waldron J (ed), *Theories of Rights* (Oxford University Press 1984) 153–167

Foucault M, 'Prison Talk' in Gordon C (ed), *Power/Knowledge: Selected Interviews and Other Writings, 1972–1977* (Pantheon Books 1980) 37–54

———, 'Politics and the Study of Discourse' in Burchell G, Gordon C and Miller P (eds), *The Foucault Effects: Studies in Governmentality. With Two Lectures and an Interview with Michel Foucault* (Harvester Wheatsheaf 1991) 53–57

Fry M, 'Human Rights and the Law Breaker' in UNESCO (ed), *Human Rights: Comments and Interpretations – A Symposium Edited by UNESCO with an Introduction by Jacques Maritain* (Allan Wingle 1949) 246–249

Garland D, 'Of Crimes and Criminals: The Development of Criminology in Britain' in Maguire M and Morgan R (eds), *Oxford Handbook of Criminology* (3rd edn, Oxford University Press 2002) 7–50

Grant K, 'Human Rights and Sovereign Abolitions of Slavery, c. 1885–1956' in Grant and others (eds), *Beyond Sovereignty: Britain, Empire and Transnationalism, c. 1880–1950* (Palgrave Macmillan 2007) 80–99

Grubb F, 'Penal Slavery' in Drescher S and Engerman SL (eds), *A Historical Guide to World Slavery* (Oxford University Press 1998) 312–314

Gruen L, 'Dignity, Captivity, and an Ethics of Sight' in Gruen L (ed), *The Ethics of Captivity* (Oxford University Press 2014) 231–247

Hagan J and Dinovitzer R, 'Collateral Consequences of Imprisonment for Children, Communities, and Prisoners' in Tonry M and Petersilla J (eds), *Prisons, Vol. 26 of Crime and Justice: A Review of Research* (1999) 121–126

Hall S, 'The State in Question' in McLennan G, Held D and Hall S (eds), *The Idea of the Modern State* (Open University Press 1984) 1–28

———, 'Foucault: Power, Knowledge and Discourse' in Wetherell M and others (eds), *Discourse Theory and Practice: A Reader* (Sage 2001) 72–78

Halme-Tuomisaari M and Slotte P, 'Revisiting the Origins of Human Rights: An Introduction' in Slotte and Halme-Tumisaari (eds), *Revisiting the Origins of Human Rights* (Cambridge University Press 2015) 1–36

Haney C, 'The Contextual Revolution in Psychology and the Question of Prison Effect' in Liebling A and Maruna S (eds), *The Effects of Imprisonment* (Willan Publishing 2005) 66–93

———, 'Foreword' in David Jones (ed), *Humane Prisons* (Radcliff Publishing 2006) vi–x

Hawkins DJB, 'Retribution' in Grupp SE (ed), *Theories of Punishment* (Indiana University Press 1972)

Heffernan E, 'Irish (or Crofton) System' in Bosworth M (ed), *Encyclopedia of Prisons and Correctional Facilities* (Volume 1, Sage Publications 1995) 482–485

Heiner B, 'Excavating the Sedimentations of Slavery: The Unfinished Project of American Abolition' in Adelsberg G, Guenther L and Zeman S (eds), *Death and*

Other Penalties: Philosophy in a Time of Mass Incarceration (Fordham University Press 2015) 13–42

Higham W, 'Punishment and Social Justice' in Shimshon B (ed), *Social Justice: Criminal Justice* (The Smith Institute 2006) 164–170

Hinkkanen V and Lappi-Seppälä T, 'Sentencing Theory, Policy, and Research' in Tonry M and Lappi-Seppälä T (eds), *Crime and Justice in Scandinavia: Crime and Justice – A Review of Research* (Volume 40, University of Chicago Press 2011) 349–404

Hirsch AV, 'Penal Theories' in Tonry M (ed), *The Handbook of Crime and Punishment* (Oxford University Press 1998) 659–682

Hitchcock W, '"Everywhere in the World": The Strange Career of the Four Freedoms Since 1945' in Engel JA (ed), *The Four Freedoms: Franklin D. Roosevelt and the Evolution of an American Idea* (Oxford University Press 2016) 193–220

Hofer HV, 'Punishment and Crime in Scandinavia, 1750–2008' in Tonry M and Lappi-Seppälä T (eds), *Crime and Justice in Scandinavia: Crime and Justice – A Review of Research* (Volume 40, University of Chicago Press 2011) 33–108

Hoffman S, 'Genealogies of Human Rights' in Hoffman (ed), *Human Rights in the Twentieth Century* (Cambridge University Press 2011) 1–28

Hood R, 'Herman Mannheim (1889–1974) and Max Grünhut (1893–1964)' in Beatson J and Zimmermann R (eds), *Jurists Uprooted: German-speaking Émigré Lawyers in Twentieth-Century Britain* (Oxford University Press 2004) 709–738

Hudson B, 'Punishing the Poor: Dilemmas of Justice and Difference' in Heffernan WC and Kleinig J (eds), *From Social Justice to Criminal Justice: Poverty and the Administration of the Criminal Law* (Oxford University Press 2000) 189–216

Hulsman L, 'Critical Criminology and the Concept of Crime' in Bianchi H and Swaaningen RV (eds), Abolitionism*: Towards a Non-Repressive Approach to Crime. Proceedings of the Second International Conference on Prison Abolition, Amsterdam, 1985* (Free University Press 1986) 25–40

Humphrey JP, 'The UN and the Universal Declaration of Human Rights' in Luard E (ed), *The International Protection of Human Rights* (Thames and Hudson 1967) 39–58

Ignatieff M, 'Human Rights' in Hesse C and Post R (eds), *Human Rights in Political Transitions: Gettysburg to Bosnia* (Zone Books 1999) 313–324

Innes J, 'Prisons for the Poor: English Bridewells, 1555–1800' in Snyder F and Hay D (eds), *Labour, Law and Crime: An Historical Perspective* (Tavistock Publications 1987) 42–122

Jhabvala F, 'On Human Rights and the Socio-Economic Context' in Snyder FE and Sathirathai S (eds), *Third World Attitudes Towards International Law: An Introduction* (Martinus Nijhoff 1987) 293–319

Johnson J, 'Hegel on Punishment: A More Sophisticated Retributivism' in White MD (ed), *Retributivism: Essays on Theory and Policy* (Oxford University Press 2011) 146–169

Kant I, 'On the Common Saying: "This May be True in Theory but it Does Not Apply in Practice"' in Reiss H (ed), *Kant: Political Writings Political Writings* (H.B. Nisbet tr, Cambridge University Press 1991) 61–92

Kennedy D, 'Legal Education as Training for Hierarchy' in Kairys D (ed), *The Politics of Law. A Progressive Critique* (3rd edn, Basic Books 1998) 54–75

Kleinig J, 'What Does Wrongdoing Deserve?' in Tonry M (ed), *Retributivism Has a Past? Has It a Future?* (Oxford University Press 2011) 46–62

Krever T, 'Ending Impunity? Eliding Political Economy in International Criminal Law?' in Mattei U and Haskell JD (eds), *Research Handbook on Political Economy and Law* (Edward Elgar 2015) 298–314

Lappi-Seppälä T, 'American Exceptionalism in Comparative Perspective: Explaining Trends and Variations in the Use of Incarceration' in Reitz KR (ed), *American Exceptionalism in Crime and Punishment* (Oxford University Press 2018) 195–271

Leary VA, 'Lessons from the Experience of the International Labour Organisation' in Alston P (ed), *The United Nations and Human Rights: A Critical Appraisal* (Clarendon Press 1992) 580–619

Lopez-Rey M, 'United Nations Social Defence Policy and the Problem of Crime' in Hood R (ed), *Crime, Criminology and Public Policy: Essays in Honour of Sir Leon Radzinowicz* (Heinmann 1974) 489–508

Macartney CA, 'League of Nations' Protection of Minority Rights' in Luard E (ed), *The International Protection of Human Rights* (Thames and Hudson 1967) 22–38

Macpherson CB, 'Natural Rights in Hobbes and Locke' in Macpherson (ed), *Political Theory and the Rights of Man* (Palgrave Macmillan 1967) 1–26

Malik C, 'The Individual in Modern Society: Keynote Address, May 18–20, 1961' in Brooks J (ed), *The One and the Many: The Individual in the Modern World. The Second Corning Conference* (Harper & Row 1962) 135–156

Mann M, 'Torchbearers Upon the Path of Progress: Britain's Ideology of a Moral and Material Progress in India. An Introductory Essay' in Fischer-Tine H and Mann M (eds), *Colonialism as Civilizing Mission: Cultural Ideology in British India* (Wimbledon Publishing 2004) 1–26

Mauer M and Chesney-Lind M (eds), *Invisible Punishment: The Collateral Consequences of Mass Imprisonment* (Free Press 2002)

Maul DR, 'The International Labour Organization and the Globalization of Human Rights, 1944–1970' in Hoffman S-L (ed), *Human Rights in the Twentieth Century* (Cambridge University Press 2011) 301–320

Megivern JJ, 'Religion and the Death Penalty in the United States of America: Past and Present' in Hodgkinson P and Schabas WA (eds), *Capital Punishment: Strategies for Abolition* (Cambridge University Press 2004) 116–142

Neisah V, 'Doing History with Impunity' in Engle K, Miller Z and Davis DM (eds), *Anti-Impunity and the Human Rights Agenda* (Cambridge University Press 2016) 95–122

Nellis M and Waugh M, 'Quakers and Penal Reform' in Angell SW and Dandellion P (eds), *The Oxford Handbook of Quaker Studies* (Oxford University Press 2013) 377–379

Nickel JW, 'Personal Deserts and Human Rights' in Cruft R, Matthew Liao S and Renzo M (eds), *Philosophical Foundations of Human Rights* (Oxford University Press 2015) 153–165

Orentichler DF, 'Settling Accounts: The Duty to Prosecute Human Rights Violations of a Prior Regime' in Kritz NJ (ed), *Transitional Justice: How Emerging Democracies Reckon with Former Regimes* (Volume 1, United States Institute of Peace 1995) 375–416

Otto D, 'Decoding Crisis in International Law: A Queer Feminist Perspective' in Stark B (ed), *International Law and Its Discontents: Confronting Crises* (Cambridge University Press 2015) 115–136

Parekh B, 'Finding a Proper Place for Human Rights' in Tunstall KE (ed), *Displacement, Asylum, Migration: The Oxford Amnesty Lectures* 2004 (Oxford University Press 2006) 17–43

Peay J, 'Mental Health, Mental Disabilities, and Crime' in Liebling A, Maruna S and McAra L (eds), *The Oxford Handbook of Criminology* (6th edn, Oxford University Press 2017) 639–662

Pechota V, 'The Development of the Covenant on Civil and Political Rights' in Henkin L (ed), *The International Bill of Rights: The Covenant on Civil and Political Rights* (Columbia University Press 1981) 32–71

Redo S, 'United Nations Criminal Justice Norms and Standards and Customary Law' in Bassiouni MC (ed), *The Contributions of Specialised Institutes and Non-Governmental Organizations to the United Nations Criminal Justice Program* (Martinus Nijhoff 1995) 109–135

Renzo M, 'Human Needs, Human Rights' in Cruft R, Matthew Liao S and Renzo M (eds), *Philosophical Foundations of Human Rights* (Oxford University Press 2015) 570–587

Ribi A, '"The Breath of a New Life"? British Anti-Slavery Activism and the League of Nations' in Lacqua D (ed), *Internationalism Reconfigured: Transnational Ideas and Movements Between the World Wars* (I.B. Taurus 2011) 93–113

Rorty R, 'Human Rights, Rationality and Sentimentality' in Shute S and Hurley S (eds), *On Human Rights: The Oxford Amnesty Lectures, 1993* (Basic Books, New York 1993) 111–134

Santamaria RA, 'Citizen Insecurity and Human Rights: Toward the Deconstruction of the Security Discourse and a New Criminal Law' in Rodriguez-Garavito C (ed), *Law and Society in Latin America: A New Map* (Routledge 2015) 251–278

Schabas WA, 'African Perspectives on Abolition of the Death Penalty' in Schabas (ed), *The International Source Book on Capital Punishment* (Northeastern University Press 1997) 30–65

———, 'Introduction' in Schabas (ed), *Research Handbook on International Courts and Tribunals* (Edward Elgar Publishing 2017) 1–38

Shah S, 'Detention and Trial' in Moeckli S, Shah S and Sivakumaran S (eds), *International Human Rights Law* (2nd edn, Oxford University Press 2014) 259–285

Sifirs R, 'An international Human Rights Perspective on Detention without Charge or Trial: Article 9 of the International Covenant on Civil and Political Rights' in McSherry B and Keyze P (eds), *Dangerous People: Policy, Prediction, and Practice* (Routledge 2011) 13–24

Simpson GJ and Charlesworth H, 'Objecting to Objectivity: The Radical Challenge to Legal Liberalism' in Hunter R, Ingleby R and Johnstone R (eds), *Thinking About Law: Perspectives on the History, Philosophy and Sociology of Law* (Allen & Unwin 1995) 86–132

Smit DVZ, 'Punishment and Human Rights' in Simon J and Sparks R (eds), *The Sage Handbook of Punishment and Society* (Sage 2013) 395–415

Spencer MG, 'Introduction' in Marx K (ed), *Capital* (Wordsworth Editions 2013) xi–xxi

Spierenburg P, 'Four Centuries of Prison History: Punishment, Suffering, the Body, and Power' in Finzsch N and Jutte R (eds), *Institutions of Confinement: Hospitals, Asylums, and Prisons in Western Europe and North America, 1500–1950* (Cambridge University Press 1996) 17–35

Summers C, 'Criminology Through the Looking Glass' in Amatrudo A and Rauxloh R (eds), *Law in Popular Belief: Myth and Reality* (Manchester University Press 2017) 15–29

Tasioulas J, 'On the Foundations of Human Rights' in Cruft R, Matthew Liao S and Renzo M (eds), *Philosophical Foundations of Human Rights* (Oxford University Press 2015) 45–70

Tonry M, 'Punishment and Human Dignity: Sentencing Principles for Twenty-First Century America' in Tonry (ed), *Crime and Justice: A Review of Research* (Volume 47, University of Chicago Press 2018) 119–158
Tulkens F and Kerchove MV, 'Criminal Law and Human Rights: A Paradoxical Relationship' in Bady-Gendrot S and others (eds), *The Routledge Handbook of European Criminology* (Routledge 2014) 91–108
Tuori T, 'From League of Nations Mandates to Decolonization: A Brief History of Rights' in Slotte P and Halme-Tumisaari M (eds), *Revisiting the Origins of Human Rights* (Cambridge University Press 2015) 267–292
Walker N, 'Desert: Some Doubts' in Hirsch AV and Ashworth A (eds), *Principled Sentencing. Readings on Theory and Policy* (2nd edn, Hart Publishing 1998) 156–160
Wetzell RF, 'The Medicalization of Criminal Law Reform in Imperial Germany' in Finzsch N and Jutte R (eds), *Institutions of Confinement: Hospitals, Asylums, and Prisons in Western Europe and North America, 1500–1950* (Cambridge University Press 1996) 275–283
Williams WW, 'The Equality Crisis: Some Reflections on Culture, Courts, and Feminism' in Nicholson L (ed), *The Second Wave: A Reader in Feminist Theory* (Routledge 1997) 71–91
Wilson RA, 'Representing Human Rights Violations' in Wilson (ed), *Human Rights, Culture, and Context: Anthropological Perspectives* (Pluto Press 1997) 134–160
Woltring H, 'The Evolution of United Nations Policy Approaches to Crime Prevention and Criminal Justice: From the Committee on Crime Prevention and Control to the Commission on Crime Prevention and Criminal Justice' in Bassiouni MC (ed), *The Contributions of Specialized Institutes and Non-Governmental Organizations to the United Nations Criminal Justice Program. In Honor of Adolfo Beria di Argentine* (Martinus Nijhoff 1995) 65–82

Journal articles

———, 'Our Case' (1921) 1(1) *Howard Journal* 1
———, 'The Howard League for Penal Reform: Statement of Policy' (1921) 1(1) *Howard Journal* 86
———, 'The International Prison Congress, August 1925' (1926) 2(1) *Howard Journal* 7
———, 'A Plea for Scientific Methods in the Treatment of Criminals' (1926) II(1) *Howard Journal* 61
———, 'Current Notes: International Penal and Penitentiary Commission' (1934) 25(3) *Journal of Criminal Law and Criminology* 481
———, 'Current Notes: Relations to Be Developed Between the International Penal and Penitentiary Commission and the United Nations Organization (U. N. O.)' (1946) 37(3) *Journal of Criminal Law and Criminology* 242
———, 'International Penal and Penitentiary Commission' (1946) *Proceedings of the Annual Congress of Correction of the American Prison Association* 243
———, 'United Nations Activities in the Field of Social Defence' (1968) 26 *International Review of Criminal Policy* 101
Alston P, 'Ships Passing in the Night: The Current Status of Human Rights and Development Debate Seen Through the Lens of the Millennium Development Goals' (2005) 27(3) *Human Rights Quarterly* 755
Anderson C, 'Convicts and Coolies: Rethinking Indentured Labour in the Nineteenth Century' (2009) 30(1) *Slavery and Abolition* 93

Ashworth A, 'Criminal Justice Act 2003: The Sentencing Provisions' (2005) 68(5) *Modern Law Review* 822

———, 'Prisons, Proportionality and Recent Penal History' (2017) 80(3) *Modern Law Review* 473

Bagaric M and Alexander T, '(Marginal) General Deterrence Doesn't Work – And What It Means for Sentencing' (2011) 35 *Criminal Law Journal* 269

Bagaric M and Morss J, 'International Sentencing Law: In Search of a Justification and a Coherent Framework' (2006) 6 *International Criminal Law Review* 191

Bates S, 'One World in Penology' (1948) 38(6) *Journal of Criminal Law and Criminology* 565

Bazelon DL, 'The Morality of the Criminal Law' (1975–76) 49 *Southern California Law Review* 385

Bedau HA, 'Retribution and the Theory of Punishment' 1978 LXXV(11) *Journal of Philosophy* 601

Benson G and Craven C, 'The Purpose of Imprisonment' (1947–1948) VII(3) *Howard Journal* 162

Bernaz N, 'Life Imprisonment and the Prohibition of Inhuman Punishments in International Human Rights Law: Moving the Agenda Forward' (2013) 35 *Human Rights Quarterly* 470

Blau J and Blau P, 'The Cost of Inequality' (1982) 47 *American Sociological Review* 121

Buergenthal T, 'The Evolving International Human Rights System' (2006) 100(4) *American Journal of International Law* 783

Burges JH, 'The Road to San Francisco: The Revival of the Human Rights Idea in the Twentieth Century' (1992) 14 *Human Rights Quarterly* 447

Burt C, 'The Psychological Clinic' (1929) II(4) *Howard Journal* 290

Cernkovich S and Giordano P, 'Family Relationships and Delinquency' (1987) 25 *Criminology* 295

Ching-Yueh Y, 'Crime and Economic Conditions in China' (1930) III(1) *Howard Journal* 2

Choudhry S, 'Towards a Transformative Conceptualization of Violence Against Women – A Critical Frame Analysis of Council of Europe Discourse on Violence Against Women' (2016) 79(3) *Modern Law Review* 406

Christie N, 'Conflicts as Property' (1977) 17(1) *British Journal of Criminology* 1

Connell R and Dados N, 'Where in the World Does Neo-Liberalism Come from? The Market Agenda in Southern Perspective' (2014) 43(2) *Theory and Society* 117

Cook KJ and Powell C, 'Christianity and Punitive Mentalities' (2003) 39 *Crime, Law & Social Change* 69

Cornil P, 'International Standards for the Treatment of Offenders' (1968) 26(3) *International Review of Criminal Policy* 3

Crabtree S, 'A Beautiful and Practical Lesson of Jurisprudence: The Transatlantic Quaker Ministry in an Age of Revolution' (2007) 99 *Radical History Review* 51

Cullen FT, Fischer BS and Applegate BK, 'Public Opinion About Punishment and Corrections' (2000) 27 *Crime and Justice* 1

Dana S, 'The Limits of Judicial Idealism: Should the International Criminal Court Engage with Consequentialist Aspirations?' (2014) 3(1) *Penn State Journal of Law & International Affairs* 30

Davis AY, 'Incarcerated Women: Transformative Strategies' (1996) 1(1) *Black Renaissance/Renaissance Noir* 21

Delierneux A, 'The United Nations in the Field of Prevention of Crime and Treatment of Offenders' (1949) *United Nations Year Book* 248

Demombynes G and Özler B, 'Crime and Local Inequality in South Africa' (2005) 76(2) *Journal of Development Economics* 265

Dickinson GL, 'The League of Nations and an International Convention for Prisoners' (1928) II(3) *Howard Journal* 208

Douzinas C, 'The End(s) of Human Rights' (2002) 26 *Melbourne University Law Review* 445

Drake DH, 'The "dangerous other" in Maximum-Security Prisons' (2011) 11(4) *Criminology and Criminal Justice* 367

Eaton G, 'The Need for an International Charter for Prisoners' (1927) II(2) *Howard Journal* 93

Edelstein D, 'Enlightenment Rights Talk' (2014) 86(3) *Journal of Modern History* 530

Evans T, 'International Human Rights Law as Power/Knowledge' (2005) 27(3) *Human Rights Quarterly* 1046

Fish MJ, 'An Eye for an Eye: Proportionality as a Moral Principle of Punishment' (2008) 28(1) *Oxford Journal of Legal* Studies 57

Flew A, 'The Justification of Punishment' (1954) XXIX(III) *Philosophy* 291

Freedman R, 'The United Nations Human Rights Council: More of the Same?' (2013) 31(2) *Wisconsin International Law Journal* 208

Galton F, 'Eugenics, Its Definition, Scope, and Aims' (1904) 10(1) *American Journal of Sociology* 1

Garcia T, 'Amnesties and the Rome Statute – A Legitimate Bar to Prosecution?' (2006) 13 *Australian International Law Journal* 187

Gardner ARL, 'Science Approaches the Lawbreaker' (1928) 2(3) *Howard Journal* 203

Gardner M, 'The Renaissance of Retribution: An Examination of "Doing Justice"' (1976) *Wisconsin Law Review* 781

Garland D, 'Criminal and His Science: A Critical Account of the Formation of Criminology at the End of the Nineteenth Century' (1985) 25(2) *British Journal of Criminology* 109

———, 'What Is a "history of the present"? On Foucault's Genealogies and Their Critical Preconditions' (2014) 16(4) *Punishment & Society* 365

Gavron J, 'Amnesties in the Light of Developments in International Law and the Establishment of the International Criminal Court' (2002) 51 *International and Comparative Law Quarterly* 91

Gay P, 'The Enlightenment in the History of Political Theory' (1954) 69 *Political Science Quarterly* 374

Gillespie RD, 'The Service of Psychiatry in the Prevention and Treatment of Crime' (1930) III(1) *Howard Journal* 22

Gordon R and Jon S, 'Deconstructing Development' (2004) 22 *Wisconsin International Law Journal* 1

Gowan P, 'US: UN' (2003) 24 *New Left Review* 5

Gray AH, 'The Christian View of the Use of Punishment' (1929) II(4) *Howard Journal* 296

Heiner B, 'Developing Contextualized Rationales for Sentencing in International Criminal Trials' (2007) 5 *International Criminal Justice* 757

Hobbins AJ, 'Human Rights inside the United Nations: The Humphrey Diaries, 1948–1959' (1991) IV *Fontanus* 143

Hola B, Smuelers A and Bijleveld C, 'International Sentencing Facts and Figures: Sentencing Practice at the ICTY and ICTR' (2011) *Journal of International Criminal Justice* 9

Holman F, 'An "International Bill of Rights Bill of Rights": Proposals have Dangerous Implications for U.S' (1948) 34 *American Bar Association Journal* 984

———, 'International Proposals Affecting So-called Human Rights' (1949) 14 *Law and Contemporary Problems* 479

Hood R, 'Capital Punishment – A Global Perspective' (2011) 3(3) *Punishment & Society* 331

Humphrey JP, 'International Protection of Human Rights' (1948) 225 *Annals of the American Academy of Political and Social Science* 15

Hunt A, 'Rights and Social Movements: Counter-Hegemonic Strategies' (1990) 17(3) *Journal of Law and Society* 309

———, 'Getting Marx and Foucault into Bed Together' (2004) 31(4) *Journal of Law and Society* 592

John LB, 'The New International Law: Protection of the Rights of Individuals Rather Than States' (1982) 32 *American University Law Review* 1

Jones A, 'Insights into an Emerging Relationship: Use of Human Rights Jurisprudence at the International Criminal Court' (2016) 16(4) *Human Rights Law Review* 701

Kang S, 'Forcing Prison Labor: International Labor Standards, Human Rights and the Privatization of Prison Labor in the Contemporary United States' (2009) 31(2) *New Political Science* 137

Keller AN, 'Punishment for Violation of International Criminal Law: An Analysis of Sentencing at the ICTY and ICTR' (2001–2002) 12 *International and Comparative Law Review* 53

Kelly M, 'Inequality and Crime' (2016) 82(4) *Review of Economics and Statistics* 530

Khosla M, 'Proportionality: An Assault on Human Rights? A Reply (2010) 8(2) *International Journal of Constitutional Law* 298

King RD and McDermott K, 'British Prisons: The Ever-Deepening Crisis' (1989) 29 *British Journal of Criminology* 107

Klatt M and Meister M, 'Proportionality – A Benefit to Human Rights? Remarks on the I.CON Controversy' (2012) 10(3) *International Journal of Constitutional Law* 689

Klug F, 'The Universal Declaration of Human Rights: 60 Years on' (2009) *Public Law* 205

Koskenniemi M, 'The Police in the Temple Order, Justice and the UN: A Dialectical View' (1995) 6 *European Journal of International Law* 325

Lacey N and Pickard H, 'The Chimera of Proportionality: Institutionalising Limits on Punishment in Contemporary Social and Political Systems' (2015) 78(2) *Modern Law Review* 216

Logan CH and Gaes GG, 'Mata-Analysis and the Rehabilitation of Punishment' (1993) 10 *Justice Quarterly* 245

Lopez-Rey M, 'The Quinquennial United Nations Congresses on the Prevention of Crime and the Treatment of Offenders' (1978) 34 *International Review of Criminal Policy* 3

Lyons W, 'Deterrent Theory and Punishment of the Innocent' (1974) 4(4) *Ethics* 346

Martin G, 'The Renaissance of Retribution: An Examination of "Doing Justice"' (1976) *Wisconsin Law Review* 781

Martinson R, 'What Works? – Questions and Answers About Prison Reform' (1974) 35 *Public Interest* 22

———, 'New Findings, New Views: A Note of Caution Regarding Sentencing Reform' (1979) 7(2) *Hofstra Law Review* 24

Mazower M, 'The Strange Triumph of Human Rights, 1933–1950' (2004) 47(2) *Historical Journal* 379
McLeod AM, 'Exporting U.S. Criminal Justice' (2010) 29 *Yale Law & Policy Review* 83
———, 'Confronting Criminal Law's Violence: The Possibilities of Unfinished Alternatives' (2012–13) 8 *Unbound* 109
———, 'Prison Abolition and Grounded Justice' (2015) 62 *UCLA Law Review* 1156
McTaggart JE, 'Hegel's Theory of Punishment' (1986) 6(4) *International Journal of Ethics* 479
Mohney S, 'The Great Power Origins of Human Rights' (2013–2014) 35 *Michigan Journal of International Law* 827
Moran RF, 'What Counts as Knowledge? A Reflection on Race, Social Science and the Law' (2002) 44(3/4) *Law & Society Review* 515
Morash MA and Anderson EA, 'Liberal Thinking on Rehabilitation: A Work-Able Solution to Crime' (1978) 25(5) *Social Problems* 556
Morris H, 'Persons and Punishment' (1968) 52 *Monist* 475
Morris N, 'Psychiatry and the Dangerous Criminal' (1968) 41 *Southern California Review* 514
Morse SJ, 'The Twilight of Welfare Criminology: A Reply to Judge Bazelon' (1975–76) 49 *Southern California Law Review* 1247
Morsink J, 'The Philosophy of Universal Declaration' (1984) 6 *Human Rights Quarterly* 309
———, 'World War Two and the Universal Declaration' (1993) 15 *Human Rights Quarterly* 357
Müller M, 'The Rise of the Penal State in Latin America' (2012) 15(1) *Contemporary Justice Review* 57
Murphy JG, 'Marxism and Retribution' (1973) 2(3) *Philosophy & Public Affairs* 217
Mutua M, 'Savages, Victims and Saviours: The Metaphor of Human Rights' (2001) 42(1) *Harvard International Law Journal* 201
Nelken D, 'Critical Criminal Law' (1987) 14 *Journal of Law and Society* 105
Newburn T, '"Tough on Crime": Penal Policy in England and Wales' (2007) 36(1) *Crime and Justice* 425
O'Brien P, 'Crime and Punishment as Historical Problem' (1978) 11(4) *Journal of Social History* 508
Pagden A, 'Human Rights, Natural Rights, and Europe's Imperial Legacy' (2003) 31(2) *Political Theory* 171
Pagels E, 'Human Rights: Legitimizing a Recent Concept' (1979) 442 *Annals of the American Academy of Political and Social Science* 58
Palmer T, 'Martinson Revisited' (1975) 12 *Journal of Research in Crime and Delinquency*
Paternoster R, 'How Much Do We Really Know About Criminal Deterrence?' (2010) 100(3) *Journal of Criminal Law and Criminology* 765
Patterson EB, 'Poverty, Income Inequality, and Community Crime Rates' (1991) 29(4) *Criminology* 755
Pauley WCD, 'Beccaria and Punishment' (1925) 35(4) *International Journal of Ethics* 404
Pijoan EL, 'Criminal Record Disclosure and the Right to Privacy' (2015) 10 *Criminal Law Review* 723
Pilon R, 'Criminal Remedies: Restitution, Punishment, or Both?' (1978) 88(4) *Ethics* 348
Pratt J, '"This is not a prison": Foucault, the Panopticon and Pentonville' (1993) 2(4) *Social and Legal Studies* 373

———, 'Scandinavian Exceptionalism in an Era of Penal Excess: Part I: The Nature and Roots of Scandinavian Exceptionalism' (2007) 48 *British Journal of Criminology* 119

Psciotta AW, 'Scientific Reform: The "New Penology" at Elmira' (1983) 29 *Crime and Delinquency* 620

Quirk J, 'The Anti-Slavery Project: Linking the Historical and the Contemporary' (2006) 28 *Human Rights Quarterly* 565

Radzinowicz L, 'Lombroso and His Place in Modern Criminology' (1936) V(1) *Sociological Review* xxviii

———, 'International Collaboration in Criminal Science' (1941 1942) 4 *University of Toronto Law Journal* 307

Rafter N, 'Criminology's Darkest Hour: Biocriminology in Nazi Germany' (2008) 41(2) *Australian and New Zealand Journal of Criminology* 287

Rappard WE, 'Human Rights in Mandated Territories' (1946) 243 *Annals of the American Academy of Political and Social Science* 118

Roberts D, 'Constructing a Criminal Justice System Free of Racial Bias: An Abolitionist Framework' (2007) 39 *Columbia Human Rights Law Review* 261

Rodriguez SA, '"The Impotence of Being Earnest": Status of the United Nations Standard Minimum Rules for the Treatment of Prisoners in Europe and the United States' (2007) 33 *New England Journal of Criminal & Civil Confinement* 61

Sadurski W, 'Social Justice and Legal Justice' (1984) 3 *Law and Philosophy* 329

Sartorius R, 'Utilitarianism, Rights and Duties to Self' (1985) 22(3) *American Philosophical Quarterly* 241

Schabas WA, 'International Norms on Execution of the Insane and the Mentally Retarded' (1993) 4 *Criminal Law Forum* 95

———, 'Sentencing by International Tribunals: A Human Rights Approach' (1997) 7 *Duke Journal of Comparative and International Law* 461

Shestack JJ, 'The Philosophic Foundations of Human Rights' (1998) 20 *Human Rights Quarterly* 201

Sherman LW, 'The Use and Usefulness of Criminology, 1751–2005: Enlightened Justice and Its Failures' (2005) 600 *Annals of the American Academy of Political and Social Science* 115

Sherwood M, '"There is no Deal for the Blackman in San Francisco": African Attempts to Influence the Finding Conference of the United Nations, April – July 1945' (1996) 29(1) *International Journal of African Historical Studies* 71

Smit DVZ, 'Punishment and Human Rights in International Criminal Justice' (2002) 2(1) *Human Rights Law Review* 10

———, 'Regulation of Prison Conditions' (2010) 39(1) *Crime and Justice* 503

———, 'Outlawing Irreducible Life Sentences: Europe on the Brink?' (2010–2011) 23(1) *Federal Sentencing Reporter* 39

Smit DVZ and Ashworth A, 'Disproportionate Sentences as Human Rights Violations' (2004) 541 *Modern Law Review* 67

Smith R, '"To see Themselves as Others see Them": The Five Permanent Members of the Security Council and the Human Rights Council's Universal Periodic Review' (2013) 1(35) *Human Rights Quarterly* 1

Swaaningen RV, 'Public Safety and the Management of Fear' (2005) 9(3) *Theoretical Criminology* 289

Teeters NK, 'The International Penal and Penitentiary Congress 1910 and the Indeterminate Sentence' (1949) 39(5) *Journal of Criminal Law and Criminology* 618

Teitel R, 'Human Rights Genealogy' (1997–1998) 67 *Fordham Law Review* 301

Temple W, 'The Ethics of Punishment' (1930) III (1) *Howard Journal* 12

Thrall AT, Stecula D and Sweet D, 'May We Have Your Attention Please? Human-Rights NGOs and the Problem of Global Communication' (2014) 19(2) *International Journal of Press/Politics* 135

Tsakyrakis S, 'Proportionality: An Assault on Human Rights?' (2009) 7(3) *International Journal of Constitutional Law* 466

———, 'Proportionality: An Assault on Human Rights? A Rejoinder to Madhav Khosla' (2010) 8(2) *International Journal of Constitutional Law* 307

Tushnet M, 'Critical Legal Studies: A Political History' (1991) 100 *Yale Law Journal* 1515

Unger R, 'The Critical Legal Studies Movement' (1983) 96 *Harvard Law Review* 561

Wacquant L, 'The Penalisation of Poverty and the Rise of Neo-Liberalism' (2001) 9(4) *European Journal on Criminal Policy and Research* 401

———, 'From Slavery to Mass Incarceration: Rethinking the Race Question in the US' (2002) 13 *New Left Review* 41

Walker N, 'Nozick's Revenge' (1995) 70(274) *Philosophy* 581

Watkin VE, 'Penal Reform and the League of Nations' (1930) III(I) *Howard Journal* 80

Weisburd D, Lum CM and Yang S, 'When Can We Conclude that Treatments or Programs Don't Work?' (2003) 31(32) *Annals of the American Academy of Political and Social Science* 587

Weisburd D, Lum CM, Yang S and Hallendorff M, 'Travaux Préparatoires of the Fair Trial Provisions-Articles 8 to 11 of the Universal Declaration of Human Rights' (1999) 21(4) *Human Rights Quarterly* 1061

Weston BH, 'Human Rights' (1984) 6 *Human Rights Quarterly* 257

Whelan DJ and Donnelley J, 'The West, Economic and Social Rights, and the Global Human Rights Regime: Setting the Record Straight' (2007) 29(4) *Human Rights Quarterly* 908

Widom CS, 'Does Violence Beget Violence? A Critical Examination of the Literature' (1989) 106(1) *Psychological Bulletin* 3

Wong SK, 'Reciprocal Effects of Family Disruption and Crime: A Panel Study of Canadian Municipalities' (2011) 12(1) *Western Criminology Review* 43

Wright JP and others, 'Lombroso's Legacy: The Miseducation of Criminologists' (2008) 19(3) *Journal of Criminal Justice Education* 32

Yang AA, 'The Agrarian Origins of Crime: A Study of Riots in Saran District, India, 1886–1920' (1979) 13(2) *Journal of Social History* 289

Young E, 'Chinese Coolies, 'Universal Rights and the Limits of Liberalism in an Age of Empire'' (2015) 227 *Past and Present* 121

Zaibert L, 'Punishment and Revenge' (2006) 25 *Law and Philosophy* 81

Conference proceedings, pamphlets, and reports

IPPC (International Penal and Penitentiary Commission), *Minutes of the Meeting of the Executive Committee of the International Penal and Penitentiary Commission. Berne, April 1946* (Staempfli & CIE 1946)

Amnesty International, *Annual Report[s]: The State of World's Human Rights* (1961–2017)

Bureau of the International Penal and Penitentiary Commission, *Proceedings of the XITH International Penal and Penitentiary Congress held in Berlin. August 1935* (Staemfli & Cie. Printers 1937)

———, *Twelfth International Penal and Penitentiary Congress, The Hague 14–19 August 1950. Proceeding Volume II. The Record of the Meetings* (IPPC 1951)

House of Lords – House of Commons Joint Committee on Human Rights, *The Implications for Access to Justice of the Government's Proposals to Reform Legal Aid: Seventh Report of Session 2013–2014* (2014)
Howard Association, *The Prison Congress of London* (July 1872)
Howard League for Penal Reforms, *Annual Report[s]* (1923–1945)
———, *An International Charter for Prisoners* (c. 1928)
———, *International Co-Operation in Penal Matters* (1930)
———, *Memorandum Submitted to the League of Nations by the Howard League for Penal Reform* (May 1930)
———, *Crime in the Overseas Dependencies of Great Britain* (July 1931)
———, *Supplement to Memorandum of May 1930, on International Aspects of Penal Administration Submitted by the Howard League for Penal Reform to the Secretary-General of the League of Nations* (13 April 1931)
———, *Prison Population of the World* (1936)
———, *For All Prisoners.* Pamphlet Series (1937)
———, *Rehabilitating Work: What Are Prison Workshops for? Briefing Paper* (2000)
Human Rights Watch, *World Report [s]* (1990–2017)
International Bar Association, *Paper to the IBAHRI Resolution on the Abolition of the Death Penalty* (IBA 2008)
National Association for the Advancement of Coloured People, *An Appeal to the World!* (NAACP 1947)
Paterson A, *A Report of Visits to Some German Prisons and Reformatories in August, 1922* (H.M.C Prison 1922)
———, *Report on the Prevention of Crime and the Treatment of the Criminal in the Province of Burma* (Government Printing and Stationery 1927)
Pears E (ed), *Prisons and Reformatories at Home and Abroad Being the Transactions of the International Penitentiary Congress Held in London July 3–13, 1872* (Longmans Green and Co 1872)
Penal Reform International, *Global Prison Trends* (2017)
Prison Reform Trust, Prison, *The Facts: Bromley Briefings* (Summer 2014)
United Nations, *In Larger Freedom: Towards Development, Security and Human Rights for All: Report of the Secretary-General* (21 March 2005)
Wines EC, *International Congress on the Prevention and Repression of Crime, Including Penal and Reformatory Treatment. Preliminary Report of the Commissioner Appointed by the President to Represent the United States in the Congress in Compliance with a Joint Resolution of March 7, 1871* (Government Printing Office 1872)
———, *Report on the International Penitentiary Congress of London, Held July 3–13, 1872* (Government Printing Office 1873)

PhD theses

Flynn CJ, *Sentencing at the International Criminal Court: A Practice in Search of a Rationale* (PhD thesis, University of Leicester 2017)
Scott DG, *Ghosts Beyond Our Realm: A Neo-Abolitionist Analysis of Prisoner Human Rights and Prison Officer Occupational Culture* (PhD thesis, University of Central Lancashire 2006)

Index

For Product Safety Concerns and Information please contact our EU representative GPSR@taylorandfrancis.com Taylor & Francis Verlag GmbH, Kaufingerstraße 24, 80331 München, Germany